An empire of many cultures

Manchester University Press

STUDIES IN IMPERIALISM

When the 'Studies in Imperialism' series was founded by Professor John M. MacKenzie more than thirty years ago, emphasis was laid upon the conviction that 'imperialism as a cultural phenomenon had as significant an effect on the dominant as on the subordinate societies'. With well over a hundred titles now published, this remains the prime concern of the series. Cross-disciplinary work has indeed appeared covering the full spectrum of cultural phenomena, as well as examining aspects of gender and sex, frontiers and law, science and the environment, language and literature, migration and patriotic societies, and much else. Moreover, the series has always wished to present comparative work on European and American imperialism, and particularly welcomes the submission of books in these areas. The fascination with imperialism, in all its aspects, shows no sign of abating, and this series will continue to lead the way in encouraging the widest possible range of studies in the field. 'Studies in Imperialism' is fully organic in its development, always seeking to be at the cutting edge, responding to the latest interests of scholars and the needs of this ever-expanding area of scholarship.

General editors:
Andrew Thompson, Professor of Global and Imperial History at Nuffield College, Oxford
Alan Lester, Professor of Historical Geography at University of Sussex and LaTrobe University

Founding editor: Emeritus Professor John MacKenzie

Editorial board:
Robert Bickers, University of Bristol
Christopher L. Brown, Columbia University
Pratik Chakrabarti, University of Houston
Elizabeth Elbourne, McGill University
Bronwen Everill, University of Cambridge
Kate Fullagar, Australian Catholic University
Chandrika Kaul, University of St Andrews
Dane Kennedy, George Washington University
Shino Konishi, Australian Catholic University
Philippa Levine, University of Texas at Austin
Kirsten McKenzie, University of Sydney
Tinashe Nyamunda, University of Pretoria
Dexnell Peters, University of the West Indies
Sujit Sivasundaram, University of Cambridge
Angela Wanhalla, University of Otago
Stuart Ward, University of Copenhagen

To buy or to find out more about the books currently available in this series, please go to: https://manchesteruniversitypress.co.uk/series/studies-in-imperialism/

An empire of many cultures

Bahá'ís, Muslims, Jews and the British state, 1900–20

Diane Robinson-Dunn

MANCHESTER UNIVERSITY PRESS

Copyright © Diane Robinson-Dunn 2024

The right of Diane Robinson-Dunn to be identified as the author of this work has been asserted in accordance with the Copyright, Designs and Patents Act 1988.

Published by Manchester University Press
Oxford Road, Manchester, M13 9PL

www.manchesteruniversitypress.co.uk

British Library Cataloguing-in-Publication Data
A catalogue record for this book is available from the British Library

ISBN 978 1 5261 6921 1 hardback
ISBN 978 1 5261 9489 3 paperback

First published 2024
Paperback published 2026

The publisher has no responsibility for the persistence or accuracy of URLs for any external or third-party internet websites referred to in this book, and does not guarantee that any content on such websites is, or will remain, accurate or appropriate.

EU authorised representative for GPSR:
Easy Access System Europe – Mustamäe tee 50, 10621 Tallinn, Estonia
gpsr.requests@easproject.com

Typeset
by Cheshire Typesetting Ltd, Cuddington, Cheshire

For my husband, Brad, and also for my father

Contents

List of figures	*page* viii
Preface and acknowledgements	ix
Abbreviations	xiii
Notes on language	xiv
Introduction: valuing diversity in an empire of many cultures	1
1 From precarity to prominence: 'Abdu'l-Bahá and the cultivation of British–Bahá'í networks in England and the Middle East	21
2 Planting the "banner of Islam" in the "heart of the British Empire": Muslim missionaries from India solidify their new base in England during a time of crisis	89
3 Zionist debates among Jews in England take a new imperial turn	147
Conclusion: some comparisons, some reflections	233
Index	244

Figures

1.1 Lady Sara Blomfield. Copyright © Bahá'í International Community   *page* 34
1.2 'Abdu'l-Bahá during his travels to the West, 1911. Public domain, via Wikimedia Commons   37
1.3 Ethel Jenner Rosenberg and Western Bahá'í pilgrims in Acre, 1901. Public domain, via Wikimedia Commons   45
1.4 'Abdu'l Bahá's knighting ceremony, Haifa, 1920. Copyright © Bahá'í International Community   61
2.1 Kamal-ud-Din with converts and others, Woking. Courtesy of Woking Muslim Mission Heritage, www.wokingmuslim.org   91
2.2 Sadr-ud-Din, *Eid al-Fitr*, Woking, 1915. Woking Muslim Mission Heritage. Courtesy of Woking Muslim Mission Heritage, www.wokingmuslim.org   99
2.3 Kamal-ud-Din and Lord Headley, 1913. East meets West in the Unity of Islam. Courtesy of Woking Muslim Mission Heritage, www.wokingmuslim.org   106
2.4 "A Trio of Brave English Soldiers who have joined the colours of Islam," 1916. Courtesy of Woking Muslim Mission Heritage, www.wokingmuslim.org   120
3.1 Lucien Wolf, 1907. National Portrait Gallery, London   168
3.2 "Bertha Claff pictured in fancy dress for a ball in Bournemouth." Manchester Libraries, Information and Archives   192
3.3 Lord Balfour in Palestine with Zionist leaders, 1925. Seated left to right, Vera Weizmann, Chaim Weizmann, Lord Balfour, Nachum Sokolow. Public domain, via Wikimedia Commons   196

Preface and acknowledgements

This book is the product of a number of influences, beginning in the 1970s when, as a child, I accompanied my father as he did genealogical research for the Robinson side of the family, well before the internet and even the widespread use of computers. I saw how, over the years, he was able to uncover and to a certain extent recreate the lives of women and men whose numbers increased as we journeyed back in time over the generations. His findings about our ancestors, in England, the British Isles, Europe and North America, reflected much of what I already knew from reading history. Yet they also added a new dimension to it, not just in terms of providing a personal element, but in that they created opportunities to gain insights that complicated the familiar assumptions those in the present so often impose upon the past.

My father humbly approached genealogy as a "student of history," not as an academic researcher. Yet when I began my MA programme at the University of Alabama, Birmingham in the early 1990s, I found in Carolyn Conley not only a mentor in the field of English history but also a scholar who confirmed the value of archival research. In order to write her books on the topic of crime and the legal system in the British Isles, she thoroughly and painstakingly read all of the records available to her. While some of her colleagues had suggested saving time by, for example, taking random samples of court cases, she rejected that course of action. As she explained to me, an analysis based on random samples does not produce the same results and therefore does not allow for the same understanding of history as one based on an examination of all of the existing documents.

From these two influential figures I developed an appreciation for the archives and for the time and patience that it takes to research them. I am fortunate to be at the University of Detroit Mercy, in that the institution has given me the necessary support to comb the collections of primary source material relevant to my research questions. Competitive internal award monies, negotiated by our faculty union, have supported my trips to Britain and the Middle East, while the college's Language and Cultural

Training programme has given me opportunities to travel to the Far East and South Asia. I first began my series of research journeys for this project in 2009. In that year I met the Bahá'í author Robert Weinberg. I am grateful to him not only for giving me access to the library and the archival holdings at the United Kingdom National Bahá'í Centre, London, but also for his help in finding relevant sources that had been packed in storage, awaiting transport. Also of note are the collections housed in the Bahá'í World Centre, Haifa, Israel and the Afnan Library, Sandy, Bedfordshire, England. In addition, the Allenby Papers in the Liddell Hart Centre for Military Archives, Kings College, London provide insights into Palestine during and immediately after World War I and help to shed light on General Allenby's attitudes with regard to 'Abdu'l-Bahá and the Bahá'ís there.

Primary source collections consulted for Chapter 2 include the Woking Muslim Mission papers in the Shah Jahan Mosque Archives, Woking, England; the Woking Mosque files at the Surrey History Centre; and the India Office Records and Private Papers in the Asian and African Studies section of the British Library. I am thankful for assistance from Muhammad Habib at the Shah Jahan Mosque and Zahid Aziz of the Ahmadiyya Anjuman Isha'at-e-Islam Lahore (UK). The latter maintains the website of Woking Muslim Mission materials at www.wokingmuslim.org/ and has provided English translations for Urdu writings, including those from the Ahmadiyya periodicals *Paigham-e-Sulh* and *Badr*, published in British India (Lahore and Qadian).

With regard to Chapter 3, the London Metropolitan Archives (LMA); Manchester Archives, Greater Manchester County Record Office; Manchester Jewish Museum (MJM); and the Bill Williams Jewish Studies Library at the Centre for Jewish Studies, University of Manchester all contain primary source materials that speak to the research questions of this study. The LMA houses the records and papers of the Board of Deputies of British Jews, the Anglo-Jewish Association, and the Conjoint Foreign Committee that represented the two. Organized separately but also in that facility are the materials of the Federation of Women Zionists and the British Women's International Zionist Organisation. The MJM's oral history and photograph collections are of particular interest.

Outside of the UK are the Central Zionist Archives in Jerusalem and some smaller collections in New York City and Hong Kong. With regard to the CZA, I am grateful for the assistance of Rochelle Rubinstein and Masha Steiner. Both helped me to navigate the Hebrew databases, catalogues and other finding aids, and Steiner provided translations when necessary. As a result, I was able to research the papers and records of the English Zionist Federation there, which included materials of the World Zionist Organization; Jewish Colonial Trust; Jewish National Fund

(JNF); JNF Committee of England; and the British Palestine Committee. Also worthy of mention are the New York Public Library's Dorot Jewish Division; the papers of Lucien Wolf housed in the YIVO Institute for Jewish Research, Archives and Library New York, NY and the materials pertaining to Jewish communities in Hong Kong and Shanghai during the period in question, including those with links to the Middle East, England and the Zionist movement, housed in the Hong Kong Heritage Project Archives in Kowloon, China.

Finally, certain libraries, archives and special collections informed the book as a whole. In addition to the British Library and Liddell Hart Centre mentioned already, I conducted research at the Imperial War Museum London; the Middle East Centre Library and Archive, St Antony's College, Oxford; The National Archives, Kew, especially Foreign Office records; and the International Collections at the Library of Congress, Washington, DC.

Along with providing financial support for these research trips, my position at the University of Detroit Mercy has exposed me to alternative perspectives. The experience of being at a Catholic university in the United States with Jesuit colleagues has provided numerous opportunities to consider how people who espouse minority worldviews are able to reconcile them creatively with the dominant discourses and ideologies of the larger society, including those of the state. I am also fortunate to have colleagues there such as Gail Presbey, whose commitment to social justice has introduced me to new ways of approaching the dialogue between past and present. Knowing of my interest in the Middle East and postcolonial questions, in 2010 she invited me to a dinner honouring the life and work of Edward Said. The event was hosted by Meta Peace Team, a group dedicated to empowered peace making as an alternative to militarism, and there I met people who had volunteered for third-party, non-violent intervention in Israel/Palestine.

Afterwards, I decided that the following summer I would not only visit libraries and archives in Jerusalem and Haifa as planned, but also would spend time in the West Bank as well. There and in East Jerusalem I spoke with a variety of activists and others, Palestinian, Israeli, European and American. Yet I also had the opportunity to listen to some very different historical narratives while staying in a West Jerusalem bed and breakfast near the Zionist archives, as it was run by a former Israeli military officer and provided temporary housing for Jews who had left Europe to relocate in Israel. I found that engaging with a number of perspectives in contemporary Israel/Palestine to be very helpful as I navigated the different, but equally diverse, voices and complex issues surrounding the Zionist debates during the early twentieth century.

Of course, this comparative study never would have become an academic book had it not been for the many scholars who contribute to the evolution of the fields in question: English, British imperial, Bahá'í, Muslim and Jewish. In particular, I would like to thank Moojan Momen and Anthony Lee for their comments on the Bahá'í chapter and Humayun Ansari and Jamie Gilham for their comments on the Woking Muslim Mission chapter. I also appreciate the anonymous scholars consulted by Manchester University Press who provided feedback on my discussion of the Zionist debates. Also, I would like to thank the faculty in the history department at Stony Brook University, New York for their guidance and insights when I was a PhD student there during the late 1990s; Fred Weinstein's depth of knowledge in history and theory and Kathleen Wilson's understanding and approach to the fields of English and British imperial history and postcolonial studies continue to influence me. I am also indebted to Said Arjomand and William Chittick with regard to the study of Islam, particularly Perso-Islamic culture and traditions.

Many thanks to Sharon Vlahovich for volunteering her time and library science skills to check my footnotes; to Judith Oppenheimer for copy-editing the manuscript; and Mateo Six for his work on the index.

Finally, strong personal relationships have sustained me throughout the process of writing this book, and I am grateful to have wonderful friends and family members. I would like to acknowledge my dear friend and colleague Sarah Stever, with whom I can talk for hours about anything from the frivolous to the profound, and my husband, Henry Bradford Dunn, my true love and soulmate.

Abbreviations

AAII	Ahmadiyya Anjuman Isha'at-e-Islam Lahore (UK)
AJA	Anglo-Jewish Association
BDBJ	Board of Deputies of British Jews
BL	British Library
BPC	British Palestine Committee
BWC	Bahá'í World Centre
CFC	Conjoint Foreign Committee
CZA	Central Zionist Archives
EZF	English Zionist Federation
FAC	Foreign Affairs Committee
FO	Foreign Office
FWZ	Federation of Women Zionists
IOR	India Office Records
IR	*Islamic Review*
JCT	Jewish Colonial Trust
JNF	Jewish National Fund
JNFCE	Jewish National Fund Committee of England
LMA	London Metropolitan Archives
MJM	Manchester Jewish Museum
SHC	Surrey History Centre
SJMA	Shah Jahan Mosque Archives
SoW	*Star of the West*
TNA	The National Archives, Kew
UKNBC	United Kingdom National Bahá'í Centre
WIZO	Women's International Zionist Organization
WMM	Woking Muslim Mission
WZO	World Zionist Organization

Notes on language

Anglo-Jewry – Used to refer to English Jews, but also includes those in the British Isles more generally as is conventional in the field of British Jewish studies.

Bahá'í – A follower of the teachings of Bahá'u'lláh and his son 'Abdu'l-Bahá. While the Bahá'í Faith would develop into an independent world religion by the end of the twentieth century, during the period in question, it can best be described as a religious movement. It was possible, in fact, for an individual to continue to identify with the religion of their birth by becoming, for example, a "Christian Bahá'í" or a "Muslim Bahá'í."

British – Used to indicate that empire as well as its global culture and administrative system. The word also may refer to institutions of the British state such as the military, the monarchy or Parliament. While the term may include England, and for that matter the other nations of the British Isles, it is by no means limited to it or to them. The terms 'British' and 'English' are not used interchangeably.

English Jews – Used to refer to Jews who both lived in England *and* identified themselves as English.

Jews in England – Used to refer not only to English Jews, but also to Jewish Zionist organizers who lived in England, either permanently or temporarily, but did not identify themselves as English by nationality.

Jew/Jewish – The historical actors in this study who identified themselves as Jews or Jewish tended to regard this identity as cultural, ethnic and, although not necessarily, religious. Often a racial dimension was stated or accepted as well. For the Zionists among them, to be a Jew also meant having have a distinct national identity and, therefore, the responsibility to contribute to the creation of a Jewish state.

Muslim – This term is used in a broad and inclusive sense to mean anyone who believes in one God and that Muhammad is the prophet of God and identifies as a Muslim.

Palestine – My use of the word "Palestine," as opposed to "Israel" or "pre-state Israel" is not a political decision, but rather an historical one. All of the historical actors in this study speak of this region of the Middle East as "Palestine" before, during and in the years immediately following the First World War. Even the Jewish Zionists in England during this time used the terms "Jewish state" and "Jewish Palestine" when speaking of their future plans and hopes for the region.

Zionism – In this study Zionism refers to a movement organized by Jews to establish a Jewish state and associated with the World Zionist Organization, the English Zionist Federation and affiliated bodies at the very end of the nineteenth and the early twentieth centuries. While these Zionists accepted support from Christian evangelicals and others, their movement was political in nature and represents a marked departure from both Christian and Jewish Zionist efforts of the early and mid-nineteenth century.

Introduction: valuing diversity in an empire of many cultures

Valuing diversity

When I began research for this book in the late 2000s I did not intend to speak to issues of diversity or multiculturalism other than to consider the histories of three religious minorities in England, all of which had ties to the Middle East. Nor did I plan to focus on the 1900–20 period and the significant changes that took place for each during the First World War. My original approach was to delve into the collections of historical sources for Bahá'í, Muslim and Jewish communities in England during the first half of the twentieth century in order to consider and ultimately shed light upon the relationships that members of each had with the people of that country, the British government and their co-religionists or those of like mind in the Middle East. After all, British involvement in the region was at its height during that time, and adherents of each of these religious or ideological systems looked to that part of the world as a spiritual and/or cultural centre.[1]

However, while exploring organizational and official archives with the above concerns in mind, three interesting historical developments emerged, all of which occurred in the context of the First World War, or more specifically the fluctuating British–Ottoman border and eastward expansion of the British Empire in the course of that conflict. In part because of the intervention of his English supporters, 'Abdu'l-Bahá went from a precarious position under the Ottomans to a prominent one under the British in Palestine, thus setting the stage for the creation of a Bahá'í World Centre in Haifa and the eventual transformation of the Bahá'ís from a relatively unknown and intermittently persecuted movement to a major world religion. The newly created and politically vulnerable Woking Muslim Mission (WMM) established itself upon a firm foundation in the greater London metropole during the First World War, as its leaders successfully negotiated the path of simultaneously serving their faith and their government, a task made especially difficult by the British–Ottoman conflict and British advances in the

Middle East. Finally, as British occupation and administration of Palestine went from being a possibility to the new political reality, and His Majesty's government allied itself with the Zionist movement through the Balfour Declaration, Zionist nationalist debates among Jews in England took a new imperial turn.[2]

While each of these developments is interesting in its own right and contributes to the understanding of Bahá'í, Muslim, Jewish and Zionist history respectively, when considered side by side and in light of the actions of and writings produced by the people involved in those processes, certain similarities become apparent; for, despite having little or no contact with one another, the Bahá'í, Muslim and Jewish leaders in question all expressed perspectives that often seem surprisingly similar and not unlike those associated with twenty-first-century multiculturalism. Yet, while modern liberal and progressive thinkers tend to see the harmonious coexistence of people from a variety of backgrounds as a way to move forward and remedy the unjust remnants of the imperial past, these historical actors understood it as a characteristic of the British Empire itself, repeatedly calling attention to the many cultures, religions, races, languages, nations and ethnicities of the people who comprised it. They found value and meaning in a polity that could forge bonds uniting people across so many commonly accepted boundaries, and in part for this reason were willing to work with His Majesty's representatives and within the imperial system despite its shortcomings, for they were not naive or blind to abuses perpetuated by it; on the contrary, all were exceptionally aware with regard to global politics. Yet they saw great potential in certain British liberal traditions and institutions and in their ability to reconcile their own beliefs and goals with them in order to create what they imagined would be a better or more just world.

Bahá'í, Muslim and Jewish communities, networks and associations also were characterized by heterogeneity, for the women and men discussed in each of this book's chapters came from a variety of backgrounds in terms of race, class, culture and ethnicity. They hailed from different continents and spoke a number of languages. While all worked within the existing imperial power structures, which included familiar ideas about metropole–periphery relationships, they also challenged those assumptions in significant ways. Developments in the "peripheries" such as Haifa or Lahore were as important as those in the "metropole," a term that can mean England generally, but in this study usually refers to the Greater London and Manchester areas. In addition, the diversity of those communities in the metropole, in some cases to a greater degree than in the peripheries, complicates the common understanding of the former as a homogenizing influence.

The Bahá'ís, Muslims and Jews discussed in the following chapters continually challenged and complicated common assumptions with regard to

"East" and "West" as well as "metropole" and "periphery," all categories of particular interest to modern postcolonial scholars. All embraced certain ideals associated with Western liberalism, yet members of each group also identified with the East. All understood that they could be labelled as Oriental in England, yet also found in that society and/or the British Empire a certain degree of protection and a vehicle through which their communities could grow and develop and their goals could be advanced. All had certain beliefs and identities that put them outside of the mainstream in both the East and the West, giving them a unique vantage point that, combined with an interest in British liberalism and imperialism; exceptional intelligence and creativity; and the desire to serve as advisors and educators to their contemporaries, allowed them to develop unique insights into the workings of empire during the early twentieth century.

Examining their words and actions allows us to consider empire during that much-studied period in a new light, raising questions of contemporary relevance with regard to the relationship between liberalism and multiculturalism. For example, is the investigation of alternative belief systems a form of liberalism as the Bahá'ís and members of the WMM maintained? If so, does that make the otherwise reflective person who neglects the study of religions outside their own tradition dogmatic? What is the place of "whiteness" in a multicultural state and society? Is it a construct against which diversity and inclusiveness is defined, an obstacle to be overcome, as it is often understood amongst progressive thinkers today, or is it simply one aspect of human variety, no better or worse than any other and to be embraced along with the rest, as the leaders of both universalist religious movements believed?

Similar issues of contemporary relevance arise with regard to the Zionist debates among Jews in England. Is Jewishness best understood as an assimilative ethnicity, one that can exist comfortably and harmoniously among a variety of peoples and cultures and anywhere in the world? What is the relationship between liberalism and a Jewish state? Is support of it contrary to the principle of equality before the law regardless of race or religion? Or, alternatively, is such a polity necessary to protect a historically persecuted minority and a form of assimilation, given that we now live in the era of the nation-state? What obligation, if any, does the individual Jewish person who lives in a modern Western, democratic society have with regard to the State of Israel? Finally, what stand should the non-Jewish liberal in those societies take? Is criticizing that state and their own government's relationship to it an intellectual and/or civic obligation, or does the danger of arousing antisemitism outweigh any possible gains that could be made by doing so?

The purpose of this study is not to provide any sort of definitive answer to these modern questions. Nor is it to advance a particular position with regard to ongoing scholarly discussions of multiculturalism. In fact, while the historical characters who appear in the following chapters spoke of diversity and of the different races, cultures, ethnicities and religions within the British Empire, they did not use the term "multiculturalism." Along the same lines, the word "white" appeared only occasionally in their writings, and even then, it usually described a physical characteristic as opposed to a power structure, theoretical concept or even race. Still, the fact that these individuals wrestled with a number of the same issues and questions that confront us today and offered a variety of different answers and approaches to them suggests that an examination of their words and actions, in that empire of many cultures of the early twentieth century, has relevance for our modern postcolonial world.

All land has become borderland: British expansion in the Middle East during the First World War

The three historical developments, Bahá'í, Muslim and Jewish, that are examined in this study all occurred in the context of specific social and political circumstances resulting from the unstable boundaries between the British and Ottoman empires during the First World War and the expansion of the former into the Middle East.[3] This is not to say that the war caused the Bahá'í, Muslim and Jewish leaders in question to think and act as they did. Individuals are capable of interpreting, understanding and subsequently reacting to changes in their environment in any number of ways, even when those changes are beyond their control, such as in the case of shifting borders and occupying armies.[4] Still, it is helpful to discuss briefly the historical developments in question in relation to their wartime circumstances.

British–Ottoman battles in the Middle East, combined with the Ottoman sultan's declaration of jihad calling on all British Muslims, in India and throughout the empire, to relinquish their alliance to His Majesty's government and join the struggle on the side of the Central Powers,[5] meant that by early 1915 the legitimacy of all previously recognized dividing lines and spheres of influence, in terms of both human relationships and physical space, which had served to distinguish between people and places under the authority of those two governments, were called into question or openly challenged. In other words, shortly after the outbreak of the First World War and the entry of the British and Ottoman empires into that conflict, the borders between those two powers "dissolved and expanded to cover the lands" that they "once separated such that all the land is borderland."[6] Realizing that Ottoman Palestine could fall under Allied control, British ministers and politicians in Whitehall began to meet with spokesmen for the English Zionist Federation (EZF) and the World Zionist Organization (WZO) on a regular basis,[7] and in response, Anglo-Jewish men of influence who opposed that nationalist programme launched a new campaign to counter it by employing Lucien Wolf, a journalist with expertise in international affairs and contacts in the Foreign Office, to lead a Conjoint Committee representing the Board of Deputies of British Jews and the Anglo-Jewish Association.[8] Wolf and the Conjoint Committee advanced arguments that represented a new imperial turn, at least with regard to the anti-Zionist side of the debate, in that they were based on the assumption that, over the course of the war, the British imperial reach would extend into Palestine and replace Ottoman authority there.

According to their position, all future immigration, expansion and development in the region needed to be consistent with the traditions and ideals of British liberalism, both in the political and economic sense. Neither subject to legal disabilities nor dependent on preferential treatment, Jewish settlers would live harmoniously with their non-Jewish neighbours, just as people from a variety of ethnic, cultural and religious backgrounds did in England and the British Isles more generally. They would succeed through their own hard work, industry and initiative and, like the "self-made man" central to the Victorian middle-class value system hegemonic in nineteenth century England and still influential in the early twentieth century, eventually achieve an ascendancy all the more secure for having been earned rather than given. In addition, Jews everywhere would be able to look to Palestine under British rule as a continually developing cultural and spiritual centre. At the same time, they would benefit from the example set by those in England who, as a loyal and assimilative ethnicity in a liberal, multicultural imperial state, occupied what Wolf and the Conjoint Committee considered to be the acme of modern emancipated Jewry.

Just as anti-Zionist English Jews were beginning to formulate arguments in light of the possibility of British expansion in the Middle East, the founders of the WMM were contemplating how that fledgling organization, only just created in 1913, could continue to remain in England during the First World War, for British Muslims, regardless of where they happened to be in the world, whether in India or the small town of Woking, occupied a kind of borderland in that their commitment to the Allied cause and His Majesty's government remained suspect. In a misguided effort to secure the loyalty of British Muslims generally, war planners launched new offensives in 1916 against the Ottomans in the Hijaz and Sinai. Yet these initiatives exacerbated the WMM's previous difficulties while creating new ones, for not only did that organization's members have to face increasing anti-Muslim sentiment in the press and public, but the new alliance with Sharif

Hussein of Mecca and the British proximity to Islam's holy places threatened to turn what WMM leaders had understood to be a secular war, which allowed them to reconcile their faith with support of the Allied cause, into a religious one.

Yet, despite these challenges, the war years proved to be critical ones in the mission's development. What began as an unknown entity with an uncertain future at the outbreak of the First World War had become, by the 1920s, a stable and important centre for Islam in England and a launching pad from which missionaries could spread their message of a religion intended for all humanity throughout the British Empire and Europe. The Muslim soldier, both in the abstract sense and as an actual person, was central to this transformation. By serving the spiritual and religious needs of those who fought on the Western Front, the WMM was able to contribute to the war effort and thus secure the place of the mission in England throughout that conflict. In addition, discussion of the Muslim soldier, both in the past and present, allowed the WMM to remain relevant with regard to contemporary concerns, while at the same time fostering and presenting the ideal of a unified *ummah*; for while Muslims in England held a variety of opinions with regard to issues such as the Caliphate, the future of Muslim holy places and pan-Islamic politics, all could unify around the figure of the Muslim soldier and the belief that those men were deserving of respect and support.

The British expansion into the Sinai, which raised concerns for Muslims in England, also provided the historical circumstances that prompted new action on the part of Zionist Jews in that country. In early 1917, as the Egyptian Expeditionary Force moved eastwards from El-Arish to Gaza, making two unsuccessful attacks on that fortified oasis city known as the gateway to Palestine, a coterie of Jewish leaders, often referred to as the "Manchester group," began to formulate and promote a new dimension to the Zionist argument. While the idea that the Zionist movement would greatly benefit any power whose policy makers had the foresight to ally with it had been a part of the WZO's strategy and culture since the late nineteenth century, this body of Manchester-based individuals, calling themselves the British Palestine Committee (BPC) and producing a monthly publication entitled *Palestine*, initiated a new imperial turn with regard to Zionist arguments. According to their position, only a Jewish Palestine could defend and advance the interests, and thus secure the future, of the British Empire in the East. Likewise, only through the administration and institutions of that imperial power, which more so than any other was capable of ruling diverse peoples and preparing them for self-government, could the Zionist dream of an independent state and therefore the emancipation of the Jewish people be realized.

Introduction

On November 7, 1917 the Egyptian Expeditionary Force made a third attack on Gaza, and that time succeeded. Two days later, the Balfour Declaration, issued by the Foreign Secretary, Arthur Balfour, and negotiated by representatives of the EZF, particularly Chaim Weizmann, and members of the Foreign Office, War Office and War Cabinet, was made public. That declaration, and international recognition of it and of British Mandatory power in Palestine at the San Remo conference in Italy, meant that by 1920 London had become the political as well as financial centre of the world Zionist movement, with Word Zionist Organization headquarters no longer in Germany but next door to the EZF offices on Great Russell Street. That turn of events also inspired the female leaders in the above-mentioned Manchester group to create two new women's organizations: first the Federation of Women Zionists, in 1918 following the Balfour Declaration, and then the Women's International Zionist Organization, in 1920 after San Remo. The founders of these bodies expressed the belief that, as Jewish women living in England, they now had a "special responsibility" to organize other Jewish women in the British Isles and internationally so that they might mobilize themselves and their resources on behalf of female settlers in Palestine and their offspring, upon whom the future success of a Jewish state would depend. While Zionist arguments had already begun to take a new imperial turn with the formation of the BPC in early 1917, the founders of these two new bodies added a distinctly feminine and feminist element to it in the following years, for they not only understood their initiatives as an obligation stemming from their position in England, but also believed that demonstrating the critical role that female contributions played in the process of nation building would serve to elevate the status and improve the lives of Jewish women and girls both Palestine and in their home communities.

The Balfour Declaration, so important in prompting the creation of these new, English-based feminist-Zionist organizations, appeared as soon as General Edmund Allenby had secured Gaza in late 1917, yet wresting Palestine from the Ottomans proved more difficult than originally anticipated. After two unsuccessful offensives in what is today northern Jordan, months of preparation and an elaborate ruse which succeeded in giving the appearance that they would attempt a third attack in that same area, Allenby's forces launched the final battle of the Palestinian campaign on September 19, 1918 on the plains just east of the Mediterranean and south of Haifa. When that port city fell to the British four days later, General Allenby cabled London with the words "Have to-day taken Palestine. Notify the world that 'Abdu'l-Bahá is safe."[9]

From that day forward a new and mutually beneficial relationship began between that Bahá'í leader and the British administration in Palestine.

The officer in charge of Haifa operations dispatched guards to ensure the safety of 'Abdu'l-Bahá and his family, a necessary precaution given both the dangers of wartime and the pronouncement made by Cemal Pasha, the military commander and Governor-General in Greater Syria, that he should be put to death. That spiritual leader, in turn, assisted British troops facing a food shortage by donating grain from his community's surplus. Over the years that followed, 'Abdu'l-Bahá provided valuable advice to members of the new administration, including Allenby, for which he was honoured with a knighthood in 1920. With the protection and legal recognition of the British government, the Bahá'ís began to build their World Centre in Haifa. What would have appeared in 1916 to be a small, obscure sect of Shia Muslims experiencing intermittent persecution in Iran and the Ottoman Empire and in real danger of losing their leader, should Cemal Pasha's forces advance, became by the late twentieth century an internationally recognized and respected religion with an independent global administrative structure and millions of believers from around the world, a transformation made possible by the creation and subsequent development of British–Bahá'í relationships in Palestine during the First World War period.

Creating meaning by finding common ground: universalist religious movements and ideologies of imperial intersection

While the First World War may have provided the context and necessary support for the creation of new relationships between certain Bahá'í and WMM leaders, on one hand, and the British imperial state, on the other, those historical actors, nevertheless, made choices with regard to how they interpreted and reacted to changing circumstances. In order for the Bahá'í and WMM leaders to have made the decisions, assumed the roles and taken the actions that they did, their efforts first had to be rendered meaningful in culturally available terms.[10] Those individuals used their intellectual and creative abilities to sift through a myriad of ideas, representations, existing practices and dominant discourses available in the larger imperial culture and chose certain ones that shared common ground or could be harmonized with their own goals and interests.[11] This study considers the creation of these ideologies, which motivated and oriented diverse people around a common cause and provided a means through which each could understand personal experiences in relation to abstract beliefs, as social events in and of themselves.[12]

I refer to this process as the creation of ideologies of imperial intersection because, in the case of both religious movements, leaders, and eventually other supporters, focused on the areas of overlap between elements of their own core or canonical systems of meaning and certain aspects of British imperial culture, and from that place of intersection or common ground developed new, additional systems of meaning. In other words, they drew from an extensive cultural repertoire of beliefs, traditions and narratives, existing both inside and outside of British spheres of influence, in order to reconcile their own movements with the imperial context, while at the same time taking care to preserve and maintain their original core value systems. The term "intersection" is especially useful in that it conveys both the temporary or situational as well as the partial nature of the ideologies in question.[13] For the historical actors involved in these two movements understood themselves as working on behalf of a cause of global significance for future generations, which could be reconciled with aspects of the current British imperial culture but not defined by or contained within it.[14]

While the creation of ideologies of imperial intersection may sound manipulative or disingenuous, especially because it involves religious identities and beliefs, it is important to remember that the need to form systems of meaning culturally understandable to others is a basic one. Without this ability the individual would be unable to function and instead would degenerate, as Geertz famously stated, into a "kind of formless monster with neither sense of direction nor power of self-control."[15] Given that the WMM originated in the context of the Raj, with a base in England after 1913, and that after the occupation of Haifa in 1918 the central hub of the Bahá'í world fell under British control, it would have been impossible for the leaders of either one of those movements to have continued their work throughout the First World War period without engaging with the larger imperial culture of which both increasingly had become a part. In addition, Bahá'ís and supporters of the WMM did not simply decide to appreciate features of the British Empire whenever they discovered that an advantage could be gained by doing so. Rather, they built upon and contributed to fairly complex creative and intellectual processes that had begun well before the outbreak of the First World War.

As early as 1868 Bahá'u'lláh, whom Bahá'ís regard as possessing divine revelation, wrote to Queen Victoria praising that monarch for the growth of democracy and the abolition of slavery in her realm.[16] His son 'Abdu'l-Bahá, who would succeed his father as head of that community in 1892, also had great respect for certain liberal ideals and contemporary efforts to further them in both the Middle East and Europe. While he criticized the gross inequalities, exploitative labour practices and racial prejudices that existed in England and the empire, he also saw the potential for the British administration to function as a progressive force in the world, especially with regard to the protection of religious minorities. As a spiritual leader who repeatedly stressed the oneness of humankind and the need for the world's people to recognize and embrace that truth, 'Abdu'l-Bahá also appreciated the multicultural nature of the British Empire and its ability to inspire loyalties that transcended national and other commonly accepted boundaries. By the time His Majesty's officers sought the disinterested advice of 'Abdu'l-Bahá, thus initiating the development of the mutually beneficial relationships that would make the creation of a Bahá'í World Centre in Palestine possible, an ideology or system of meaning supporting the intersection between movement and empire already existed.

Like the Bahá'ís, supporters of the WMM also appreciated the ways that the British Empire could connect people from diverse backgrounds and promote certain liberal ideals, while at the same time criticizing the exploitation, poverty and racism perpetuated by it. Unlike 'Abdu'l-Bahá, however, the founders of that mission were British Indian subjects well educated in English history and traditions and, as such, they repeatedly insisted upon having the same rights and freedoms as their Christian counterparts. The most important of these included the ability to embark upon missionary efforts throughout the empire, harness the power of the pen and print culture to further their beliefs and, finally, to criticize the actions and policies of the British government without having their loyalty questioned. They understood these demands as well as their actions and goals to be in complete accordance with the principles of a British constitutionalism.

For supporters of the WMM and the Bahá'ís, the liberal traditions and many cultures of the British Empire had the potential to complement one another in such a way so as to enrich the spiritual and intellectual lives of all His Majesty's subjects, for the leaders of both believed that truth could be found in all of the major world religions, a number of which already were represented in that empire, and they took great pride in the wide variety of racial, ethnic and linguistic backgrounds among those attracted to their message, a diversity which each also understood as testifying to the attainability of world unity. The inclusive nature of these movements is reflected in the fact that previous religious identities did not need to be relinquished in order for new ones to be acquired, and English women and men identified themselves as "Christian Muslims" or "Christian Bahá'ís." Both Bahá'í and WMM leaders expressed the idea that sympathetic engagement with more than one faith tradition was, in and of itself, a form of liberalism, as doing so ran counter to rigid dogmatism of any type, religious or secular. Yet both also lamented that, despite England's historical association with liberal ideals, the vast majority of the people in that country had no interest in engaging in that type of intellectual exploration.

Like the Bahá'ís, leaders of the WMM also created what can be considered an ideology of imperial intersection even though their movement originated within the borders of the Raj, for mission founders drew from a vast cultural repertoire which included not only values, traditions, representations and discourses of the British Empire, but also those from their centuries-old and distinctly Indian Perso-Islamic heritage.[17] They discovered common ground between the two, and from that place of overlap developed a system of meaning that made new relationships with the British state and its representatives possible, thus securing the establishment of their base in the Greater London area on a firm footing during the First World War period. Perhaps the best example of this process is the way in which the leaders and most dynamic supporters of the WMM selected certain Islamic writings, primarily from the Qur'an and hadith literature, that addressed issues of war and peace and then applied those teachings to the current conflict. By doing so they presented themselves as loyal subjects of His Majesty's government and their faith as containing wisdom beneficial to British soldiers and civilians alike during a time of crisis.

Yet this loyalty was contingent upon the British government treating their religion with respect. The ideology of imperial intersection created by the leaders of the WMM was situational and therefore temporary; it needed to last only as long as the relationships it sustained. Mission founders knew that followers of Muhammad from the north-western regions of India, from which they hailed, had over the course of generations witnessed the rise and fall of a number of empires, from the eighth-century Umayyad to the Mughal, to the Sikh.[18] Just because a new Muslim missionary movement developed and functioned within the context of British imperialism did not mean that it was defined solely by that empire or contained within it. In fact, the Woking mission leaders were drawn to the London area not only because of its importance as the imperial capital but also because of its proximity to Europe and ability to serve as a gateway through which to bring Islam to the West more generally.

Discussion of the ideologies of imperial intersection created by WMM leaders and the Bahá'ís would not be complete without addressing the issue of Orientalism, which in this study refers to distorted and fantastical representations of the East, broadly defined, which served to depict Western peoples and institutions as superior and therefore to justify the inequalities of empire.[19] Familiar dichotomies include juxtaposing "Western reason" with "Eastern superstition" and presenting the West as energetic and industrious, and therefore as a force for progress helping humankind to achieve a higher level of civilization, while presenting the East, in contrast, as signifying the lethargic and stagnant. While the supposedly unchanging nature of the Orient could be romanticized, as could its perceived exoticism, even positive Orientalist images might be employed to reinforce imperialist assumptions, if not by Bahá'ís or WMM members themselves, then by their contemporaries in England and elsewhere in the empire.

Also, frequently contrasted were Western, or more specifically British, liberal democratic traditions and ideals, especially with regard to equal rights and religious freedom, with depictions of political and social relationships of the East as essentially backward and unenlightened. While Orientalist discourses often were applied to the people of a particular region, they were not necessarily bound by geographic location and could be used to express value systems and project alterity anywhere in the world. Such was the case for those two religious movements, both of which were at one time or another labelled Oriental in English society even though each had followers and other supporters living in England, many of whom had been born in that country or elsewhere in the British Isles.

Yet, despite being considered Oriental in England, both movements occupied only a marginal position in relation to the dominant power structures and ideological systems of the Eastern lands from which they originated, which they hoped to influence, or both. Hundreds of Bábís, or early Bahá'ís, were tortured and killed in mid-nineteenth-century Iran, and the Bahá'í leaders, Bahá'u'lláh and his son 'Abdu'l-Bahá, experienced exile from their homeland and eventually imprisonment in Ottoman Acre.[20] The founders of the WMM came not from the centres of power and authority in the Islamic world such as Istanbul, the area of Mecca and Medina, Cairo or even Qom but, rather, from the nineteenth-century Punjab, where Sikhs, Hindus and Christians as well as Muslims competed with one another for converts and influence. In addition, the connections that mission founders had with the controversial spiritual leader Mirza Ghulam Ahmad made them suspect amongst their co-religionists in that region.[21]

Belonging neither wholly to the East nor to the West and never entirely certain of acceptance in either, both of these movements straddled the imagined line between Orient and Occident and by doing so embodied the definition of hybridity as "less than one and double."[22] This idea presented by Homi Bhabha is particularly relevant to the Bahá'ís and the WMM in the British context during the period examined because it understands the categories of East and West not as describing any sort of authentic, preexisting conditions of essential difference but, rather, as concepts created in the context of human relationships, particularly imperial relationships. Examining the various ways in which historical actors involved with these movements engaged with Orientalism in the course of their imperial contacts helps to illustrate this hybridity. Sometimes they opposed it directly and created counter-representations, while at other times they identified with the West, or aspects of it, and reproduced their own modified versions of Orientalist discourses and images. In addition, certain characteristics associated with Western liberal democracy, in particular freedom of speech and religious tolerance, were valued or at least proved useful to supporters of these movements, not despite but because they belonged to religious minorities often labelled Oriental. Advocates of each found that liberal traditions provided a means through which they could communicate their beliefs and establish a place for their movement in English society, challenging Orientalist assumptions about a rigid dichotomy between East and West in the process.

Bahá'í and WMM leaders accepted and reproduced the Orientalist idea of a spiritual East and material West, while at the same time representing their respective movements as capable of overcoming or bridging the division between the two. Bahá'ís and Muslim missionaries both believed that while great advances had been made in the West in the realms of technology and industry, Occidentals were in dire need of the spirituality and religious wisdom that the Orient had to offer. Given this perspective, it is not surprising that English people and others from the British Isles drawn to those two movements would take considerable pride in the origins of their new-found belief system. A number of them communicated their identification with the East, and thus their own internal hybridization, by incorporating Orientalist elements into their creative self-presentation by, for example, acquiring additional Persian or Arabic names or adopting elements of Eastern dress. Both Bahá'ís and Muslim missionaries believed that as their message spread, it would initiate spiritual regeneration throughout the world, so that eventually the categories of East and West would cease to have any meaning, at least outside of the most practical and literal sense of the terms.

Creating meaning through debate: Zionist arguments among Jews in England take a new imperial turn

While considering the creation of ideologies of imperial intersection is a helpful approach to understanding the history of the Bahá'ís and the WMM in relation to the British imperial state during the First World War period, it is of limited value with regard to Zionism. Certainly, the EZF and BPC leaders found common ground between their goals and those of His Majesty's government and wove their already well-developed nationalist narrative with common British imperialist discourses, especially during and after 1917. However, while the Bahá'ís in England were of like mind in their belief in the need to support 'Abdu'l-Bahá in Palestine and share his and his father, Bahá'u'lláh's, teachings, and the supporters of the WMM could agree that the message of Islam was meant for all of humanity and therefore should be spread in the West as well as the East, Jews in England remained divided with regard to the creation of a Jewish state. Despite EZF and BPC efforts, Anglo-Jewry as a whole did not support that nationalist movement in the early twentieth century, and a number of community leaders actively opposed it. Therefore, any attempt to understand and shed light on the significance of Zionism with regard to Jews in England during this period must take into consideration not only EZF/BPC ideology and representations, as important as those were, but also the discussions and debates that surrounded them.

Like those two universalist religious movements, Jews in England on both sides of the Zionist debate found value in the diversity in the British Empire. According to the anti-Zionist position, Jewishness was one of many assimilative ethnicities that existed harmoniously alongside others. For generations, Jews had been a part of an English nation comprised of a variety of local, regional and other cultures as, or more, different from one another as they were from that of the Jewish English person. With the outbreak of the First World War and the possibility that British power would extend into Palestine, that same argument was applied to the imperial context as Lucien Wolf and his Conjoint Committee argued that the creation of a Jewish state there was not necessary. Rather, Jews could live and flourish alongside their non-Jewish neighbours in that country and even develop the area as a Jewish cultural centre in the empire and world.

The Zionist Jews in England, on the other hand, maintained that they never truly could be a part of the English, or any other non-Jewish, nation and therefore needed to form a separate, independent state. During the First World War, as British troops made their first two attacks on Gaza, Zionist discourses began to take a new imperial turn in that they presented that movement and the British Empire as in dire need of each other. Just as only a Zionist nation in the process of becoming a state could safeguard His Majesty's interests in the East, only that power with its unique appreciation of human diversity could foster the development of Jewish culture in Palestine in such a way as to prepare for eventual self-government. To those who raised the concern as to what would happen to non-Jewish Arabs who lived in the region, the Zionists expressed confidence that the British were capable of developing an Arab state as well; the two could then grow and develop side by side under British tutelage and eventually initiate together a Renaissance of Semitic civilization in the Middle East. In addition, diversity in England could serve as a model in that, just as non-English people such as the Scots or Welsh could have successful lives and careers in England, non-Jewish Arabs similarly could find a place for themselves in a Jewish state.

Both Zionist and anti-Zionist Jews saw the variety of nations and peoples in the British Empire as evidence that they too either already had or could create a place for themselves within that imperial system, and in both cases British expansion into Palestine and the subsequent policies regarding Jews there were understood as necessarily having profound consequences on the status of those in Russia and Eastern Europe. The anti-Zionists believed that a British commitment to religious and racial equality in Palestine would encourage the spread of that liberal principle to those regions where Jews still encountered legal disabilities and discrimination. Those on the Zionist side of the argument, however, saw the creation of a Jewish state, to which those experiencing persecution in Russia, Eastern Europe and elsewhere could emigrate, as the key to emancipation. While the latter argument had less to do with individual rights and more to do with what those historical actors understood as collective or national rights, they too appealed to a certain understanding of liberal ideals when they maintained that the British had always protected the rights of small nations, such as Greece in the early nineteenth century and Belgium in the early twentieth.[23]

Certain Orientalist concepts informed the debates and their imperial turn, and those who opposed Zionism portrayed it as an Eastern European "sub-nationalism," one of many that had emerged from an environment of oppression and ethnic strife and reflected the backward, unenlightened political relationships of its origins. According to this line of reasoning, rather than allow a foreign, Eastern ideology to undermine the hard-won position of Anglo-Jewry within British institutions and liberal traditions, Jewish leaders in England had an obligation to defend the principle of religious equality at home and facilitate, or at least encourage, its spread abroad, especially to places like Russia and Romania. In other words, British influence and imperial power needed to westernize the East, not vice versa. In the discourses of Wolf and the Conjoint Committee during this period, references to the East or the Orient had more to do with indicating a lack of certain values than they did with geographical location. Therefore, as long as the British government took appropriate measures to ensure the development of liberal, democratic institutions in Palestine, even that region in the Middle East could become a vehicle for Westernization as Eastern European Jews who moved there adapted to new political circumstances.

The Zionists, on the other hand, tended to promote the idea that as Jews they had certain Oriental as well as Occidental characteristics, which made those living in a Jewish Palestine under the British Crown uniquely qualified to act as intermediaries between His Majesty's government and the peoples of its eastwardly expanding empire. This hybridized sense of identity had a certain malleability that allowed it to vary depending on the context. For example, Zionist leaders sometimes found inspiration from the power of the Other or the perceived exoticism of the Eastern European Jews in the face of their critics in England who used that discourse in an attempt to undermine their efforts. Yet they also could argue that Jewish settlers, which included those from Eastern Europe, were bringing the benefits of Western civilization to a "primitive" Eastern land. Thus, while EZF or BCP members might regard an Eastern European or Russian Zionist Jew as Oriental in the English context, they would see that same person as Occidental in the Palestinian one, with positive connotations in both places. Further complicating this situationally determined use of Orientalism was that, just as with British imperialism in the East more generally, which involved the simultaneous interplay of identification and the projection of alterity on colonized subjects, Zionist Jews in England could express an affinity with the Arab-speaking, non-Jewish inhabitants of Palestine, emphasizing, for example, the need for Semitic solidarity and cooperation while at the same time working to undermine and replace the existing social and political structures in the country, and see no contradiction between the two.[24]

Chapter overview

The following chapter, Chapter 1, elucidates the relationship between the Bahá'í movement, the English people who were attracted to it and the British Empire, focusing on the early twentieth century and especially the First World War period. As British troops expanded into the Ottoman Middle East during that conflict, all three intersected in ways that would prove pivotal for Bahá'í history, marking the beginning of that persecuted movement's establishment as a major world religion. This chapter explains how individual historical actors, from the movement's leadership in the Haifa–Acre area, to the Bahá'ís in England, to, although to a lesser extent, the British officers and administrators in Palestine, were able to sift through a variety of principles, beliefs and representations culturally available to them in order to create systems of meaning that made new Bahá'í–British relationships possible. Areas of common ground included certain shared liberal, democratic ideals; a global perspective that included people from many different ethnic, racial, religious and national backgrounds; and a willingness to cross familiar boundaries between "East" and "West," even as those concepts were created and recreated in the process.

Chapter 2 explains how the WMM established a new, distinctly twentieth-century version of Islam in England, one that fostered hybridity between "East" and "West'" on multiple levels and celebrated the diversity of believers that body could attract as a result of its location in the English metropole. According to its founders, the fact that people from a variety of religious, racial, cultural and linguistic backgrounds participated in mosque events in Woking and/or declared themselves to be Muslims through the WMM's international publication, the *Islamic Review*, testified to the universality of their faith. The chapter describes how Muslims from India drew from both their own religious writings and practices, on the one hand, and certain British liberal and imperial traditions, on the other, in order to develop a system of meaning that made possible the creation of the WMM in 1913. It then goes on to explain how, in the following year when the outbreak of the First World War and British–Ottoman conflict within it threatened the organization's ability to continue its work in England, its leaders and other supporters elaborated upon their existing ideology of imperial intersection by calling attention to the ways that Islam could contribute to the war effort, focusing on the importance of the British Muslim soldier. By serving the religious needs of those men during a time of crisis, the WMM succeeded in solidifying its place in English society. As a result, it emerged from the war as both a base and a model for future missionary activity in the British Isles and Europe.

Chapter 3 examines how the Zionist debates among Jews in England took a new imperial turn as that nationalist movement became increasingly imbricated with the British state during the First World War period. Part I of the chapter introduces the reader to the terms of debate prior to that conflict, beginning by addressing how resistance to Zionism was rooted in a commitment to emancipation based on certain liberal ideals and traditions as expressed by the leadership of the Anglo-Jewish communal institutions in the nineteenth and early twentieth centuries. It also explains how the EZF served as a conduit for a new Central European nationalist culture, bringing the ideology, representations and organizational structure of early twentieth-century political Zionism to England and the British Isles. Part II of the chapter details the imperial turn taken by both Zionist and anti-Zionist Jewish leaders in England, beginning with the outbreak of the First World War, through the years immediately following the San Remo Conference. It shows how, during that time, representatives on both sides of the debate created and advanced new arguments based not only on the expectation of a British-controlled Palestine but also on the understanding of that empire, and even of English society, as characterized by diversity, as both were comprised of people with various religious, ethnic and national identities. Finally, the chapter as a whole explores the use of Orientalist ideas by both the advocates of Zionism and their opponents.

Notes

1 In this study the term "British" is used to indicate that empire as well as its global culture and administrative system. The word also may refer to institutions of the British state such as the military, the monarchy or Parliament.

While the term may include England, and for that matter the other nations of the British Isles, it is by no means limited to it or to them. The terms "British" and "English" are not used interchangeably.

2 The phrase "Jews in England" includes English Jews, but is not limited to them. A number of Jewish Zionist leaders living in England during this period had been born elsewhere and did not identify strongly, or at all, with Englishness. "English Jews," on the other hand, is used to refer to Jews who *both* lived in England and identified themselves as English. My use of the word "Palestine," as opposed to "Israel" or "pre-state Israel" is not a political decision but, rather, a historical one. All of the historical actors in this study speak of this region of the Middle East as "Palestine" before, during and in the years immediately following the First World War. Even the Jewish Zionists in England during this time used the terms "Jewish state" and "Jewish Palestine" when speaking of their future plans and hopes for the region.

3 For more on the First World War in the Middle East see Neil Faulkner, *Lawrence of Arabia's War: The Arabs, the British and the Remaking of the Middle East in WWI* (New Haven: Yale University Press, 2017); Eugene Rogan, *The Fall of the Ottomans: The Great War in the Middle East* (New York: Basic Books, 2015); Hew Strachan, *The First World War* (London: Simon and Schuster, 2003); Kristian Ulrichsen, *The First World War and the Middle East* (London: C. Hurst and Company, 2014); and *Empires at War 1911–1923*, edited by Robert Gerwarth and Erez Manela (Oxford: Oxford University Press, 2014).

4 Miguel Cabrera discusses how, even though social circumstances may provide necessary support for a particular interpretation of an experience, they do not guarantee that one possible interpretation will be chosen over another. "On Language, Culture, and Social Action," *History and Theory*, Vol. 40, No. 4 (Dec. 2001), 82–100.

5 For discussion of that proclamation and its sanction by the Ottoman Empire's religious and secular authorities see Erik-Jan Zurcher (ed.), *Jihad and Islam in World War I* (Leiden: Leiden University Press, 2016).

6 Michael Taussig, *Mimesis and Alterity: A Particular History of the Senses* (New York and London: Routledge, 1992), 248. While the quotation is apt, Taussig is not referring to this particular historical context.

7 Todd Endelman, *The Jews of Britain, 1656 to 2000* (Berkeley: University of California Press, 2002), 190; David Cesarani, "The Transformation of Communal Authority in Anglo-Jewry 1914–1940," in *The Making of Modern Anglo-Jewry*, edited by David Cesarani (Oxford: Basil Blackwell, 1990), 120; Robert Lieshout, *Britain and the Arab Middle East: World War I and Its Aftermath* (London and New York: I.B. Tauris, 2016), 198; and "The London Bureau its origins and work," Z4/40252, Central Zionist Archives (henceforth CZA).

8 These organizations, however, were not uniformly anti-Zionist. There were divisions regarding this issue, and the backlash against the representatives of the Conjoint Committee when they sent an anti-Zionist letter to *The Times* in 1917 will be discussed in Chapter 3.

9 Lady Blomfield, *The Chosen Highway* (Wilmette, IL: Bahá'í Publishing Trust, 1940), 220.
10 Gerald Platt discusses the importance of meaning with regard to action. People, especially those seeking to exert influence or effect change, must make their actions understandable to others. "Thoughts on a Theory of Collective Action Language, Affect, and Ideology in Revolution," *New Directions in Psychohistory*, edited by Mel Albin (Lexington, MA: Lexington Books, 1980), 80. For more about the critical importance of meaning with regard to other types of action see J.G.A. Pocock, *Virtue, Commerce and History: Essays on Political Thought and History* (Cambridge: Cambridge University Press, 1985); R. Ashcraft, *Revolutionary Politics and Locke's Two Treatises of Government* (Princeton, NJ: Princeton University Press, 1986), 5–6; and Gordon Wood, "Ideology and the Origins of Liberal America," *The William and Mary Quarterly*, Vol. 44, No. 3 (July 1987), 628–40.
11 Cabrera's definition of culture as "society's repertoire of interpretive mechanisms and value systems" is helpful in that we can imagine these historical actors choosing from a repertoire of possibilities. "On Language," 84. Even imagining an empire and/or a particular movement within it required creativity, as it would have been impossible for any one person to know every other person involved in that imperial system or inspired by the movement in question. Benedict Anderson makes this point with regard to the nation in *Imagined Communities: Reflections on the Origin and Spread of Nationalism* (London: Verso, 1983), 15.
12 With regard to understanding personal experiences in relation to abstract beliefs and ideology formation as a social event see Clifford Geertz, "Religion as a Cultural System," *The Interpretation of Cultures* (New York: Basic Books, 1973), 87–125.
13 As Alberto Melucci has discussed, the constructs through which individuals define themselves in relation to social movements are fluid, "rooted in the present to deal with the fluctuations and metamorphoses." Melucci, "Signs of Everyday Life," ch. 5 in *Nomads of the Present: Social Movements and Individual Needs in Contemporary Society*, edited by John Keane and Paul Mier (Philadelphia, PA: Temple University Press, 1989), 103–118, at p. 114. Also see Melucci, "The Process of Collective Identity," in *Social Movements and Culture*, edited by Hank Johnston and Bert Klandermans (Minneapolis: University of Minnesota Press, 1995), Vol. 4, 41–63.
14 My use of the phrase "ideologies of imperial intersection" should not be confused with "intersectionality" or "intersectional discrimination" as first presented by Kimberlé Crenshaw in "Mapping the Margins: Intersectionality, Identity Politics, and Violence against Women of Color," *Stanford Law Review*, Vol. 43, No. 6 (July 1991), 1241–99.
15 Clifford Geertz, "Religion as a Cultural System," 99. Also helpful is Nile Green's observation that "by recognizing religions as social construction that are made and unmade by human decisions ... we can see that religious interactions and borrowings are often partial and selective ... malleable and changeable in

doctrinal substance and organizational form," *Terrains of Exchange: Religious Economies of Global Islam* (London: Hurst Publishers, 2015), 5.

16 Bahá'u'lláh, *The Summons of the Lord of Hosts* (Bahá'í World Centre: Haifa, Israel, 2002), 88–95 and Shoghi Effendi, *God Passes By* (Wilmette, IL: Bahá'í Publishing Trust, 1944), 211.

17 Ron Geaves discusses the influence of this distinctly Indian Perso-Islamic culture on the WMM in *Islam and Britain: Muslim Mission in an Age of Empire* (London: Bloomsbury Academic, 2018), 15–33. As he notes, the term was first presented by Francis Robinson in *The 'Ulama of Farangi Mahall and Islamic Culture* (London: Hurst, 2001).

18 Geaves relates the Umayyad invasion in 711 AD in the north-western Punjab with regard to the history of Muslims in the area and therefore the WMM. *Islam and Britain*, 7.

19 Much has been and continues to be written on the topic of Orientalism since Edward Said first pioneered this rich field in 1979. Said, *Orientalism* (New York: Vintage Books, 1979).

20 For a collection of published primary historical sources detailing the persecution of the Bábís see *The Bábí and Bahá'í Religions, 1844–1944: Some Contemporary Western Accounts*, edited by Moojan Momen (Oxford: George Ronald, 1981), 69–152. For a general overview of and introduction to these leaders see Peter Smith's *A Short History of the Bahá'í Faith* (Oxford: One World, 1995) and his *An Introduction to the Bahá'í Faith* (Cambridge: Cambridge University Press, 2008).

21 They were persecuted both during and after the colonial period. See chapters 6 and 7 of Adil Hussain Khan's, *From Sufism to Ahmadiyya: A Muslim Minority Movement in South Asia* (Bloomington, IN: Indiana University Press, 2015), 128–66.

22 Homi Bhabha, *The Location of Culture* (New York: Routledge, 1994), 166.

23 This understanding of collective rights framed as national rights and capable of emancipating Jews in Palestine and Europe simultaneously is explained in Chapter 3 of this book. For discussion of that issue and the related concept of "emigrant colonization" see Ethan Katz, Lisa Leff and Maud Mandel (eds), *Colonialism and the Jews* (Bloomington, IN: Indiana University Press, 2017), especially the chapter by Tara Zahra, "Zionism, Emigration and East European Colonialism."

24 Such was the case with regard to British officials in Egypt during the late nineteenth century who could identify with the Arab Muslim man while working to undermine the power structures in that country and yet see no contradiction between the two. This process is discussed in Diane Robinson-Dunn, *The Harem, Slavery, and British Imperial Culture: Anglo-Muslim Relations in the Late Nineteenth Century* (Manchester: Manchester University Press, 2006), chapter 2, 31–69 and 207.

1

From precarity to prominence: 'Abdu'l-Bahá and the cultivation of British–Bahá'í networks in England and the Middle East

Introduction

When 'Abdu'l-Bahá first gained his freedom in 1908, after having spent forty years incarcerated in the Ottoman city of Acre, he would have appeared to be someone with little interest in or connection to either English society or British politics. While he was an "Eastern" man of noble birth, he was neither a maharaja allied with the British Empire through the system of indirect rule nor was he a British Indian gentleman pursuing a career in the Raj. Rather, he had been born in 1844 in Shia-dominated Iran during the reign of Mohammad Shah Qajar. He and his family were persecuted for their religious beliefs, and he suffered exile while still a child and then imprisonment just as he was becoming a young man. While he spoke some English, he was to a considerable extent unfamiliar with the customs and manners of that country.[1]

Yet, despite being persecuted in the East and unknown in the West, 'Abdu'l-Bahá believed that he had a message for all mankind and that London should be a "place for a great proclamation of the Faith";[2] so, in September 1911 he arrived in that city, the first stop on his tour of the Occident. It was there, in the heart of the British imperial metropole, that he spoke in public for the first time when he addressed an audience of thousands at the nonconformist City Temple in Holborn.[3] There he told the crowd that "the East and the West will understand each other and reverence each other, and embrace like long-parted lovers who have found each other."[4] Afterwards his translator described those in attendance as "breathlessly absorbed" in 'Abdu'l-Bahá's words and "in watching his every smile and movement."[5]

The success of 'Abdu'l-Bahá's trip to England had much to do with the efforts of a small but dedicated group of British people who had found meaning in his teachings and those of his father, Bahá'u'lláh, some of whom had already visited 'Abdu'l-Bahá in Palestine. Through their support and connections, 'Abdu'l-Bahá was able to visit religious, humanitarian and educational institutions, attend social gatherings and receive a steady stream of visitors. These contacts would prove valuable during the First World War, when networks of British Bahá'ís and Bahá'í sympathizers in the UK, Egypt and Palestine would work together to put pressure on their government to secure the safety of 'Abdu'l-Bahá and his community in Haifa, an area which would become the religious and administrative centre for Bahá'ís around the world as a result of the mutually beneficial relationships between that spiritual leader and the members of the new British administration in Palestine.

These new networks that crossed the commonly accepted boundaries between East and West and existed in both the metropole and peripheries of empire came into being as the result of the creative and intellectual abilities of certain historical actors of the early twentieth century, most notably 'Abdu'l-Bahá, but a number of English women and men as well. All drew from a repertoire of beliefs, values, practices and representations found in the larger culture in order to produce what this study refers to as an intersectional imperial ideology. This concept is helpful in that not all aspects of the British Empire nor even its dominant discourses needed to be reconciled with core or canonical Bahá'í beliefs, which would, in fact, have been impossible to do. Rather, individuals found areas of common ground between the two upon which they focused and elaborated, thus creating a system of meaning that oriented diverse people and made the new British–Bahá'í relationships possible. The term "intersectional" conveys both the partial overlap between religion and empire as well as the temporary and situational nature of connections that, significant though they were, especially with regard to the development of the Bahá'í movement, represent only a segment of the global history of that emerging faith. Places of convergence or harmony included liberal democratic ideals such as the importance of equality, social justice and religious toleration, in addition to valuing print culture and the ability to forge identities and bonds capable of connecting people from different parts of the world and transcending familiar national, cultural and religious divisions.

History and overview

Before discussing these networks and systems of meaning, both of which were characterized by hybridity between East and West, it is necessary first to give a brief history and overview of the Bahá'í movement, which had its roots in early nineteenth-century Iran and in the messianic traditions of *Ithná-'Ashariyyá* or Twelver Shia Islam, Iran's official state religion. It began with Sayyid 'Ali Muhammad, a man born to a family of merchants in

1819 in the southern city of Shiraz, who gained a reputation for his asceticism and piety and became known as the Báb or "Gate." The Báb was a prolific writer, and the works that he produced, especially his thousands of verses, served as proof to his followers, the Bábís, of his divine mission. They understood his book the Bayán as superseding the Qur'an in that it contained the most recent revelations of God and the laws most appropriate for that day and age.[6]

Not surprisingly, the movement generated considerable controversy, especially as the number of Bábís grew, reaching roughly 100,000.[7] While some clerics accepted his teachings and decided to follow him, bringing entire congregations into this new faith, others condemned him as an imposter and heretic. In the town of Nayriz, in the south-western province of Fars, and the city of Zanjan, in the north-west of the country, aggression against the Bábís escalated into what became urban civil wars, with the one in Zanjan lasting for eight months and involving female as well as male Bábí combatants. In 1850, the Shah's government executed the Báb before a firing squad, and his followers experienced hardships and punishments of all types, from arrest and imprisonment to exile, torture and death.[8]

During this period, a number of Bábís found refuge in and around Ottoman Baghdad. One among them, Mirza Husayn 'Ali Nuri, who had been born to a prominent family whose members occupied high positions in the Qajar state administration, and who had given up a life of privilege to follow the Báb, began to reinvigorate the movement from exile. In 1863 he told his companions about the experiences that he had years earlier while incarcerated during a wave of anti-Bábí sentiment: as he languished in chains in Tehran's notorious and foul-smelling *Síyáh-Chál* or "Black Pit," a former water cistern that had been converted to an underground prison, he began to have visions and receive revelation, discovering that he was the "One whom God will make Manifest" promised by the Báb. This new station put him at the end of a long line of divine messengers which included, but was not limited to, Zoroaster, Abraham, Moses, Jesus, Muhammad and the Báb. Mirza Husayn 'Ali Nuri became known as Bahá'u'lláh, meaning the "Glory of God." As word spread amongst the remaining Bábís, the majority of them accepted this new leader and thus became Bahá'ís.[9]

Because Bahá'u'lláh was no more willing to subordinate his beliefs to the interests of the Sublime Porte than he had been to those of the Shah's government, and because the latter had put pressure on the former to remove that spiritual leader from an area that was not only close to its own borders but also regularly visited by Iranian pilgrims travelling to Shia holy places, Bahá'u'lláh was exiled, along with a group of supporters and family members, first to Edirne or Adrianople in Turkish-speaking Eastern Europe, from 1863 to 1868, and then to the Ottoman prison fortress of

Acre on the Mediterranean coast. For the first two years in Acre conditions were so miserable and unsanitary that almost all of the seventy prisoners became ill with malaria, dysentery or typhoid, and three of them died. Yet, over time the Bahá'ís gained the respect of their captors and their situation improved. Eventually they were allowed to live under house arrest outside of the fortress, although still within the city.

The exile and then imprisonment of Bahá'u'lláh and the persecution of Bahá'ís did not stop the growth of this movement. Rather, organization and consolidation continued underground in Iran and the Ottoman Empire. New Bahá'í networks developed, while teaching activity, pursued cautiously, led to slow but steady growth and expansion. In Iran, Jews and Zoroastrians, both religious minorities in that country, began to join the ranks of the Bahá'ís as well, with roughly 10 per cent of the former and between one third and one half of the latter becoming Bahá'ís by the end of the century.[10] Meanwhile messengers smuggled letters back and forth, linking Bahá'u'lláh with his followers in Iran, and individual Bahá'ís positioned themselves along the major travel routes so as to assist those taking the arduous journey to Acre, sometimes on foot, in hopes of meeting or even catching a glimpse of their new spiritual leader. Pilgrims, who also would become carriers of "Tablets" or letters and other writings, began to appear in Acre shortly after the arrival of Bahá'u'lláh and his retinue, as did groups of Bahá'ís who had decided to leave their previous homes in order to live in or around that prison city.[11] While the Báb's followers had come from Iranian, primarily Shia, backgrounds, the message of Bahá'u'lláh had spread far beyond the borders of Iran, and new Bahá'ís included Ottoman subjects from Sunni Arab and Levantine Christian backgrounds.[12]

Within the first five years of arriving in Acre, Bahá'u'lláh penned the *Kitáb-i-Aqdas* or "Most Holy Book," which for Bahá'ís superseded the Bayán of the Báb, and letters or Tablets to prominent rulers in Europe and the Middle East, including Napoleon III of France, Pope Pius IX, the Czar of Russia, Shah of Iran, Sultan of the Ottoman Empire and Queen Victoria, informing them of his station and calling upon them to establish universal peace.[13] While he had a number of harsh criticisms for the others, his Tablet to Victoria was complementary by comparison: in it he praises her for prohibition of slave trading in the empire and the growth of democracy in England, with one of its "weightiest passages" addressed to the members of the British legislature, "the Mother of Parliaments";[14] for, like the Young Ottomans and other reformers in the Middle East, with whom Bahá'u'lláh seemed to move "in tandem," that religious leader had developed a "profound appreciation for British constitutional monarchy, parliamentary rule, and consultative government."[15] This appreciation was made possible, in part, through the assistance of his eldest surviving son,

Abbas Effendi, whose abilities in the Turkish language allowed him to serve as a liaison between Bahá'u'lláh and progressive Ottoman intellectuals from the mid-1850s onward.[16]

In addition to its democratic institutions, the British liberal principle of religious toleration had particular appeal for Bahá'ís, especially over the course of the last three decades of the nineteenth century, when the spreading networks of teachers and new believers in the Middle East and South Asia intersected with the growing imperial reach of the British state and the Bahá'ís and their expanding networks found a certain degree of protection in the peripheries of the latter. For example, in 1860s Egypt, when British influence was still limited, Iranian Bahá'ís living there endured violence, imprisonment, torture and exile to the Sudan.[17] Yet, by the 1890s, during the time of the British-dominated military-administrative system known as the "Veiled Protectorate" which had replaced Ottoman rule in 1882, the distinguished Bahá'í scholar, Mirza Abu'l-Fadl Gulpaygani, was given a position in Cairo's prestigious al-Azhar University, and a "small but dedicated" community of Egyptian converts came into being.[18]

At the end of 1885 and the beginning of 1886, roughly three years after the British occupation of Egypt, imperial expansion in south-east Asia saw the annexation of the last stronghold of the Konbaung dynasty, and with it the reduction of the former kingdom of Myanmar to the province of Burma within the British Raj, thus giving the Bahá'ís in Mandalay the same protection as was already enjoyed by those living in India. Thus, in two very distant and different regions of the world, as British imperial expansion displaced the governments of Eastern dynastic states, both of which had been contracting or losing territory over the course of the nineteenth century, members of growing Bahá'í networks came under the authority of British governing institutions and officials. When the American Bahá'í Sydney Sprague visited Mandalay in 1905, he reported finding a community of several hundred Bahá'ís, most of whom were native Burmans. He also related how an angry mob armed with sticks and stones tried to drive the resident Iranian Bahá'í teacher, Mirza Mahram, out of town, but failed to do so because of a detachment of British soldiers who arrived on the scene to disperse the crowd, with some remaining for several days to guard the house. This instance was, most likely, not the only time that a Bahá'í teacher or new convert experienced intimidation, for as Sprague noted, to become a Bahá'í in India often meant losing previous friendships and connections, a position which left individuals vulnerable to the caprice of charismatic local leaders capable of whipping an audience into a frenzy with the "white heat of hatred and fanaticism."[19]

The story of how Bahá'í beliefs were first propagated and taught in India beyond the Iranian diaspora communities is interesting in that it sheds light on the ways in which Eastern mercantile and religious networks intertwined with each other as they simultaneously wove in and out of the peripheries of the British Empire during this period, for in addition to being a spiritual leader, the Báb was born into a large extended family of merchants. His relatives, the Afnans, had built a trading empire which stretched from Baku on the Caspian Sea in Russian Azerbaijan through Shiraz, Bombay and all the way to British Hong Kong. The Bombay branch of the family owned a printing press and publishing house from which they produced Bahá'í writings, and, in hopes of generating greater understanding of and interest in that belief system, they sent word to Bahá'u'lláh in Palestine offering to pay all expenses if he would provide a Bahá'í teacher.[20]

Bahá'u'lláh then instructed the Iranian pilgrim Sulaymán Khan-i-Tunukabuni to go to Bombay for that purpose. Despite his noble background, Sulaymán Khan dressed and lived as a poor dervish and spent the 1870s travelling throughout the Indian subcontinent, in Burma and Ceylon, and teaching his faith, before moving on to the Far East. In 1877 he took full advantage of the Proclamation Durbar held in Delhi, a lavish affair which lasted for weeks and celebrated Queen Victoria's assumption of the title "Empress of India," as it provided opportunities for him to address many dignitaries.[21] As a result of his efforts and those of several prominent Bahá'ís, introduced by him to the teachings of Bahá'u'lláh, small communities of new believers began to develop in India, particularly in the urban centres of the north. As most were Persian educated, they were able to appreciate the *Kitáb-i-Íqán* (*The Book of Certitude*) and *Risálih-i-Madaniyyih* (*The Secret of Divine Civilization*), the first Bahá'í books ever to appear in print, published in 1882 by the Afnan press in Bombay.[22]

At the other end of the Afnan trading network in Azerbaijan, and other territories of the Russian Empire, Bahá'í communities grew from the 1860s onwards, with the vast majority coming from the Iranian diaspora. Many were former Bábís who became Bahá'ís as news of Bahá'u'lláh's revelation spread. Travelling merchants among them made their way into the Caucasus. Meanwhile, hundreds of Bahá'í traders and builders found both freedom from persecution and economic opportunities in the new frontier town of Ashkhabad in Russian Turkistan as it quickly grew with the construction of the Trans-Caspian railway.[23] From there Bahá'í "outposts" were established in Samarqand and Bukhara in Central Asian Uzbekistan. A small community settled in Moscow as well.[24]

As the Bahá'í networks expanded and became intertwined with local communities from Central and South Asia to North Africa over the course of the last three decades of the nineteenth century, Bahá'u'lláh and his son Abbas Effendi remained active, establishing the area in and around Acre as a critical hub both for these expanding Bahá'í networks and for their own circles of alliances and friendships with men of influence in the Ottoman Empire, especially after 1877, in which year Bahá'u'lláh was allowed to leave the prison city of Acre. Shortly thereafter he established residence in the nearby mansion of Bahji. While not repealed, his prison sentence had become a dead letter, and governors, generals and local officials all sought his presence. At the same time, he communicated "with comparative ease" with his followers in "the multiplying centers" in Iran, Iraq or Mesopotamia, the Caucasus, Turkistan and Egypt.[25] In addition to lands in the Acre area, a number of liberated Bahá'í exiles settled on lands purchased "at Bahá'u'lláh's bidding" in the Jordan Valley on the Sea of Galilee or Lake Tiberias.[26]

After Bahá'u'lláh moved to Bahji, Abbas Effendi took full advantage of the new and more lenient attitude of the state in order to maintain his family's connections throughout the Middle East and build new ones. He developed friendships with civil and religious leaders in Acre and nearby Nazareth,[27] and associated with modernizers and progressive thinkers,[28] including Midhat Pasha, the prominent Ottoman statesman and constitutionalist, who invited him to Beirut, and with Muhammad 'Abduh, the influential Egyptian scholar, jurist and legal reformer, with whom he had several interviews.[29] At the same time, he managed the inflow of pilgrims, which "continued apace,"[30] and for whom new facilities were established in Beirut to assist them on what was often a long and arduous journey.[31] Over the course of decades, the stream of travellers flowing in and out of Acre provided a critical link between this growing Bahá'í base and fellow believers in Iran, and the fact that prominent Iranian families were willing to send their daughters and sons to that prison city to marry and have children testified, as well as contributed, to the strength of the networks connecting south-western Asia with the Mediterranean region. Abbas Effendi's wife came to him in 1872 from a "distinguished family" of Isfahan, and the two would go on to have nine children, four of whom lived to adulthood. Roughly twenty-five years later, a member of the aforementioned Afnan clan left Shiraz to marry that couple's eldest daughter.[32] In addition, Abbas Effendi earned the respect of the people of Acre by giving alms to the poor, calling upon the sick and visiting the nearby al-Jazzar mosque and its attached school, where he expounded upon the Qur'an,[33] although most of his neighbours regarded him as simply a devout Muslim rather than as the son of one who received divine revelation.

By 1890, as Bahá'u'lláh was approaching the end of his life, Abbas Effendi had gained "influence and esteem" even beyond "the circle of his father's followers," according to Edward Granville Browne, the well-known Orientalist scholar and Cambridge University professor who visited both men that year[34] – a high complement, considering that that at the time of Browne's visit Bahá'u'lláh had as many followers as did the Báb, roughly 100,000. In addition, Browne described the devotion and love shown to Bahá'u'lláh as such that "kings might envy and emperors sigh for in vain"; his meeting with that "wondrous and venerable figure" at Bahji made such a profound impression upon the scholar that he could neither forget nor describe Bahá'u'lláh's face except to say that his eyes "seemed to read one's very soul."[35] Abbas Effendi's ability also to inspire admiration and confidence no doubt stemmed from the many years he spent learning from his father, whom he had served loyally as a personal assistant and secretary ever since his teenage years, when both were living together in Baghdad. In his will, Bahá'u'lláh appointed Abbas Effendi to succeed him by becoming the "Centre of the Covenant," a role that would give the new Bahá'í leader the authority to interpret and expand upon his father's teachings, while acting as an exemplar of how to live according to them.[36] Despite having several lofty titles bestowed upon him after Bahá'u'lláh died of fever in 1892, Abbas Effendi decided to go by the comparatively humble name of 'Abdu'l-Bahá meaning "Servant of Baha" or "Servant of Glory."

Under 'Abdu'l-Bahá's leadership, the movement continued to grow and, in addition to affirming his father's recognition of the ancient Iranian and Abrahamic prophets, he proclaimed Krishna and Buddha to have been divine messengers as well.[37] One of the most significant developments of 'Abdu'l-Bahá's ministry was the spread of the Bahá'í movement to the West, for while Christians and Jews had become Bahá'ís during Bahá'u'lláh's lifetime, they lived and worked in Islamic societies, within either Iran or the Ottoman Empire, and shared the language, culture and many of the values of their neighbours. Also, even though Browne had visited Bahá'u'lláh and wrote about the Bábí and Bahá'í movements, his interests were more of a scholarly and academic rather than spiritual nature. In fact, he spent more time in Cyprus with Bahá'u'lláh's enemy and younger half-brother, Mirza Yahya Nuri, known as Subh-i Azal and regarded as the true successor to the Báb by his followers the Azalis, than he did in Bahji.[38]

Abdu'l-Bahá's travels to the Occident played an important role in spreading his father's teachings to that part of the world, and often when he made a public speech in the West a list of Bahá'í principles would be given to audience members. Following his example, Western Bahá'ís reproduced these same tenets for others in their home countries and in their own literature, presentations or discussions. That list provides a brief introduction to basic or core Bahá'í beliefs. It also helps to shed light on how those involved with the movement in the English imperial metropole and elsewhere in the British Isles during the early twentieth century understood and presented it. The list is as follows:

- Each individual should independently investigate truth, putting aside historical prejudices. Thus will they find the one reality that is common to all.
- All divine religions are one; they are expressions of a single reality.
- The teachings of Bahá'u'lláh best represent the "universal religion" needed at the present time.
- Genuine religion is a powerful support for social stability: without it crime and irreligion flourish.
- For all its fruits, material civilization by itself is not sufficient to promote human progress. Only when combined with "divine civilization" and empowered by the Holy Spirit will it be the cause of genuine advance.
- Religion should be the cause of love and unity. If a particular religion only produces hatred and division then it is no longer an expression of true religion and should be abandoned.
- Religion must be in conformity with science and reason; if it is not, then it is only ignorant superstition.
- Bahá'u'lláh has come to establish the Most Great Peace. An international tribunal should now be instituted to adjudicate disputes between nations.
- The whole human race is one, all human beings are equally the children of God, the only differences between them being those of education and spiritual health.
- Religious, racial, political, national and class prejudices are destructive and based on ignorance; they cause strife and impede moral progress.
- Human progress cannot occur as long as people are still forced to struggle for their daily existence.
- Extremes of wealth and, more especially, of poverty are to be abolished, and all are to have access to the necessities of life.
- All individuals are to be equal before the law, and justice is to be securely established in society.
- Women are the equals of men and are to have equality of rights, particularly of educational opportunity. Without such equality the progress of both sexes is impeded.
- All children are to receive an education.
- There should be an international auxiliary language.[39]

Finally, it is important to note that while the Bahá'í Faith eventually would go on to become an independent world religion,[40] in part because of events and processes described in this chapter, the term "movement" most accurately describes British Bahá'í activities during the period of time in question, for during the early twentieth century and during the First World War, Bahá'ís in Britain were only loosely or informally tied to one another. They had no rituals, requirements for membership or official organization.

Rather, they shared a devotion to 'Abdu'l-Bahá and the teachings of Bahá'u'lláh and believed in the importance of unity among all religions, races and nations. Many of these early Bahá'ís remained practising Christians or involved themselves with alternative spiritual movements, for if all religions are the expression of a single reality, as the Bahá'ís believed, and 'Abdu'l-Bahá could attend the mosque in Acre without compromising his role as the "Servant of Baha," then English people could become followers of Bahá'u'lláh without abandoning previous interests or religious traditions. In fact, the terms "Christian Bahá'í" as well as "Muslim Bahá'í" or "Zoroastrian Bahá'í" all appear in the early correspondence and papers of the English communities.[41]

The transformation of this small but geographically dispersed and widely inclusive movement into a more structured and formalized religion, which would draw millions of followers from throughout the world, began under the leadership of Shoghi Effendi, 'Abdu'l-Bahá's grandson, who assumed the role "Guardian of the Bahá'í Faith" upon his grandfather's passing in 1921 and until his own death in 1957. Incidentally, he had to be called from his studies at Balliol College, Oxford in order to attend the public reading of 'Abdu'l-Bahá's will and testament, which was addressed to him. As Guardian, he made clear that "the presentation of the Bahá'í message to the world could no longer be left to individual initiative and interpretation." In addition, he dedicated himself to developing the administrative order, instructing Bahá'ís to organize themselves into spiritual assemblies, with a national assembly for Great Britain coming into being in 1923.[42]

After mid-century, certain significant demographic changes began to take place, with the vast majority of new Bahá'ís coming not from the Islamic lands where the faith originated and first developed, nor from the capitals of the West, but, rather, from areas often referred to as the "third world" or "global South" in sub-Saharan Africa, Latin America and south and southeast Asia.[43] Finally, by the end of the twentieth century, the Bahá'í Faith had become the "world's youngest significant independent religion," with roughly five million believers.[44]

'Occidentals' find meaning in the 'Orient': the first English Bahá'ís and their connections to Acre

The first interest in the Bahá'í movement in England began in the last years of the nineteenth century with two London friends: Mary Virginia Thornburgh-Cropper, an American-born widow, and Ethel Jenner Rosenberg, an accomplished portrait painter and miniaturist, originally from Bath. In 1898, Thornburgh-Cropper joined a travelling party, arranged by her lifelong friend the American philanthropist and heiress Phoebe Apperson Hearst, to visit 'Abdu'l-Bahá in the prison city of Acre.[45] After returning to London, Thornburgh-Cropper shared her new beliefs with Rosenberg, who, by the summer of 1899, became the first English person living in England to become a follower of Bahá'u'lláh.[46] Rosenberg went on to establish a Bahá'í community in the British imperial metropole, specifically the London area, and would remain at the centre of Bahá'í activity in England until her death in 1930.[47]

By taking an interest in 'Abdu'l-Bahá and his message, first introduced into England via the Apperson Hearst travelling party, Rosenberg added a further layer to her already existing relationships, while at the same time integrating herself into a small but growing international network of Western Bahá'ís. The bond that Rosenberg and Thornburgh-Cropper shared prior to the latter's pilgrimage necessarily acquired a new dimension as the two women began to see themselves not only as possessing a unique knowledge and understanding but also as responsible for spreading it among their peers, communities and associations in the London area, with the intention of reaching the people of England more generally. Rosenberg sought advice and mutual support from those who were pursing the same goals in other countries. She visited Hearst in California during the summer of 1901 and spent time in France with May Bolles, who, like Thornburgh-Cropper, was connected to Hearst through friendship and had joined the latter's travelling party to Acre. Bolles's trip to Palestine had had a profound impact on her, and afterwards she began to share her experiences and the Bahá'í teachings with those among her circle in Paris, including Rosenberg.[48] There she became friends with the first French Bahá'í, Hippolyte Dreyfus, and the American Laura Clifford Barney, her "counterparts ... pioneer workers engaged in the same important task, separated only ... by a narrow stretch of sea."[49]

Rosenberg too travelled to Acre, first for three months in 1901 and then for eight months in 1904, developing a bond with 'Abdu'l-Bahá that would inform her spiritual life and Bahá'í work in England. While in Acre, she spent her days absorbing the core principles of her new-found belief system and listening to 'Abdu'l-Bahá speak on a wide range of topics, from the nature of the soul to more practical matters of law and proper behaviour. 'Abdu'l-Bahá encouraged her to share the Bahá'í teachings in England, and the two discussed issues at length in order to prepare her for the types of questions that Christians in her home country might pose.[50] The extensive notes that she took during this time as well as later recollections of 'Abdu'l-Bahá and life in Acre became the "main substance" of the meetings that she and Thornburgh-Cropper would host, out of their homes and at the Higher Thought Centre in Kensington, in order to attract those interested in Bahá'í teachings.[51]

Rosenberg's stay in Acre allowed her, in addition to acquiring knowledge, to experience a small-scale version of a core principle that lay at the heart of the Bahá'í message, the oneness of the human race; for pilgrims came to that city from different parts of the world. In April 1904, during the celebration of the ninth day of Ridvan, commemorating Bahá'u'lláh's revelation of himself as "He Whom God will make manifest," Rosenberg recalled sitting at a table with Bahá'ís who had travelled from India, Burma, Iran, Russia, the United States and Europe. Each brought their own customs and traditions to the group, and each approached 'Abdu'l-Bahá and the Bahá'í teachings from the perspective of their own particular religious and cultural background. A number came from Muslim families, both Sunni and Shia. Others had been born into Judaism, Christianity and Zoroastrianism.

In her notes, Rosenberg recorded how this coming together of diverse people from around the world pleased 'Abdu'l-Bahá. He told his guests:

> We are all assembled under one tent ... We are all breathing one atmosphere, drinking from one cup and sailing upon one sea ... It is a very marvelous thing that such a glorious meeting should be held here in the very centre of a prison; and it is one of the great signs of the Divine Manifestation. We must speak of it everywhere and never forget it.[52]

In Acre, Rosenberg experienced the unifying power of the Bahá'í teachings, where the commonly accepted divisions of race, nation and religion seemed to dissolve under the harmonizing influence of a common bond. Such situations would have reinforced the idea that, as an English woman, often the only English person in the gathering, she had a mission or special role to play in the dissemination of the Bahá'í message in her home country. After all, 'Abdu'l-Bahá told his followers to speak of the Bahá'í principles "everywhere."

By visiting Acre, Rosenberg had the opportunity to become close not only to 'Abdu'l-Bahá, but also to the women and girls of his immediate family, thereby extending her own network of mutually supportive female friends into the Middle East, or more specifically to this group of Persian Bahá'ís living in exile and imprisoned in Palestine. Rosenberg came to know 'Abdu'l-Bahá's wife, Munírih Khánum or the "Holy Mother"; his only sister, Bahíyyih Khánum, the "Greatest Holy Leaf"; and his four daughters, Díyá'iyyih, Túbá, Rúhá and Munawar. They addressed her affectionately as "Rosie," "Rosa," or "Roser," and 'Abdu'l-Bahá called her a "firm and steadfast leaf" – a great compliment in that it associated her with Bahíyyih, who was highly revered as the daughter of Bahá'u'lláh and for her devoted service to the cause.[53] The women of the family participated in religious gatherings and discussions in Acre where they contributed their insights and interpretations, shared their experiences and helped to facilitate translation and communication with visitors.[54] Between Rosenberg's pilgrimages, they wrote to her and expressed their love, which she reciprocated, sending them English books and clothes, even corsets, and toys for the children.[55]

The bond between Rosenberg and the "Holy Family," sustained and strengthened through regular correspondence, helped her to spread the Bahá'í message in England in the face of adversity and isolation. In her letters, she confided her frustrations and difficulties, relating when teaching efforts did not seem to be yielding results or when her asthma and astigmatism worsened. In addition, because of these health problems, combined with the amount of time she now dedicated to Bahá'í work, she painted fewer portraits, which caused some financial strain. The "Holy Family," especially 'Abdu'l-Bahá and his youngest daughter, Munawar, responded with sympathy and concern, while at the same time they encouraged Rosenberg to continue her efforts to share the Bahá'í teachings. They emphasized the spiritual benefits of suffering and related some of the trials and tribulations that they, other Bahá'ís and even Bahá'u'lláh had endured as a result of persecution.[56] For example, in one of 'Abdu'l-Bahá's letters to her, known as "the Rosenberg Tablet," he wrote,

> I am aware that thou art much afflicted, and in extreme distress; but if we taste a drop from affliction's cup, the Blessed Beauty [Bahá'u'lláh] drank down a sea of anguish, and once we call this to mind, then every hardship turneth into peaceful rest, and toil into merciful bliss. Then will a draught of agony be but refreshing wine, and the tyrant's wound only a friend's most gentle balm.[57]

This encouragement seems to have helped, and by 1907 Rosenberg was physically healthy and financially stable enough to travel again to Paris, where she assisted Laura Clifford Barney in a project begun while the two women were on pilgrimage in Acre in 1904. During that time 'Abdu'l-Bahá responded to inquiries on a number of religious and philosophical issues posed to him by Barney, while Rosenberg carefully recorded the exchange, resulting in the publication of *Some Answered Questions* in 1908.[58] While in Paris Rosenberg made the acquaintance of Lady Sara Louisa Blomfield, who would become one of the leaders in the English Bahá'í movement (Figure 1.1). As Blomfield had been searching for spiritual truth and guidance for some time, a quest which led her to consider Buddhism and Theosophy as well as different interpretations of Christianity, she was delighted to learn that an English woman who had visited 'Abdu'l-Bahá happened to be staying in that city at the same time and was willing to meet her.[59]

These new female friendships and working relationships that Rosenberg was developing as a result of her dedication to the Bahá'í cause could be seen as an extension of the types of networks with which she was already

Figure 1.1 Lady Sara Blomfield.

familiar as a single, independent artist who enjoyed both financial success and critical acclaim; for Rosenberg's portrait sitters were among "the cream of London society,"[60] and each of the above-mentioned Western Bahá'í women had, in addition to a certain degree of wealth and social privilege, some connection to the art world or appreciation of the fine arts through family members or as patrons or collectors. All valued cultural and aesthetic pursuits and the cultivation of refined sensibilities and were linked to each other by individual friendships before finding common ground in the Bahá'í movement.[61] In addition, Rosenberg was familiar with the female networks in the art world, from her aunts who taught her to paint when she was young to the large communities of single women artists in late nineteenth-century London who rented or bought their own studios and apartments and who socialized primarily with each other.[62] Only by avoiding the burdens associated with having a husband and children could women of talent harness "their art practice to those moral principles of feminine purity which were perceived as unique to their class and their sexuality."[63]

While the majority of Bahá'í women did not reject marriage in pursuit of a higher calling, Bahíyyih Khánum, Bahá'u'lláh's daughter and 'Abdu'l-Bahá's sister, chose not to wed in order to concentrate her energies on furthering the cause, and she continues to be revered by Bahá'ís for her invaluable contributions during a formative period.[64] One wonders if Rosenberg did not sense a certain affinity with, or familiarity in her interactions with, that Persian lady in Acre, reminiscent of those with her unmarried, female colleagues in London – not only with regard to Bahíyyih's grace, elegance and attention to detail but in her selfless dedication to what both women would have considered to be the most noble of pursuits.[65]

Regardless of any common ground that Rosenberg may have shared with Bahíyyih or the other Bahá'í women who befriended her during the early years, she nevertheless understood herself as having the responsibility of spreading this new belief system far beyond familiar circles. Over the next decade, as more English people became Bahá'ís, small but active communities formed in London and Manchester, the members of which looked to the East for inspiration and maintained a connection with 'Abdu'l-Bahá and his family through pilgrimages, correspondence and publications. The monthly periodical published out of the United States which debuted in 1910 as the *Bahá'í News* and from the second issue onwards became the *Star of the West* kept its readers informed of developments in Acre and included copies of "Tablets" or letters written by 'Abdu'l-Bahá. English Bahá'ís who were able to do so travelled to Acre, and pilgrims' notes continued to inform teaching efforts and publications. For example, Rosenberg started working on her introductory pamphlet, entitled "Behaism," after she returned from her third pilgrimage, inspired and with fresh insights. Also, it was during that visit that 'Abdu'l-Bahá began to speak to her about issues related to the community life of the new believers.[66] In his poem entitled "To Him We Love – Late Prisoner in Acca," Edward Hall, the unofficial leader of the Manchester Bahá'ís, expressed his joy that the message of Bahá'u'lláh had found its way from the East to the British Isles:

> Bless'd be the lips that thrilled the passing winds
> That moved the palms where Syrian sunshine smiles
> And bore the peaceful sweets to waiting minds
> 'Neath oak and beech in these far-distant isles![67]

For the Bahá'ís of early twentieth-century England, the East was a part of the world with which they increasingly identified as the birthplace of their new belief system and home to their spiritual leaders, yet it was also a part of the world where their co-religionists experienced persecution. The Báb, the precursor to their prophet, had been shot by a firing squad in Tabriz in 1850, and many of his followers had suffered brutal torture.[68] Fellow Bahá'ís endured persecution not only by Iranian Shias but also at the hands of the Sunni Ottoman government. Even when they went to visit 'Abdu'l-Bahá they did so in the penal colony of Acre, described by Bahá'u'lláh as the "most desolate of cities."⁶⁹ 'Abdu'l-Bahá's living conditions and those of his guests – indeed, whether or not he could have guests – varied considerably over the years and depended upon local feeling, the extent of the influence of his enemies and the political concerns of the Ottoman officials who happened to be posted in the area at any given time. Thornburgh-Cropper recalled the precautions taken to visit 'Abdu'l-Bahá without arousing the suspicion of Ottoman authorities, explaining that the pilgrims could not go directly to Acre, but first travelled by boat to Egypt, where they spilt into groups of five before making their way to Haifa. Then, and only under the cover of the dark of night, could they complete the last leg of their journey, taking carriages along the sandy coast to the prison city.⁷⁰

During one especially difficult period, from the winter of 1907 until the summer of 1908, 'Abdu'l-Bahá was not allowed communication with the outside world. He could neither receive visitors nor send letters.⁷¹ Just when his situation looked the bleakest, and rumours had spread that soon he would be banished to the desert to meet his death, his fortunes took an unexpected turn for the better: as a result of the Young Turk Revolution in July 1908, Sultan 'Abdu'l-Hamid granted freedom to all political and religious prisoners in the Ottoman Empire. For the first time in forty years, 'Abdu'l-Bahá could leave the penal colony of Acre and do as he wished.⁷² By 1910 he had moved to Mount Carmel in the nearby city of Haifa, where he had begun to establish the spiritual and administrative centre of the Bahá'í Faith. In that same year he was ready to embark upon a journey to the West, and, after a period of ill health in Egypt, he arrived in London in 1911.

'Abdu'l-Bahá's visit to the imperial metropole: gender and social justice

The network of women who hosted 'Abdu'l-Bahá

During this period, the dominant British imperial ideologies assumed that if the status of women improved, it did so because of Western, or more specifically British or English, influences. In other words, while English people could help Eastern women by spreading Christianity, liberal-feminist ideas or Western culture in general, the process did not work in the reverse, and the females of the United Kingdom had much to lose and little to gain if gender practices or ideologies associated with the East took root in the British Isles.⁷³ Yet, when the Bahá'í movement, with its Iranian origins and leadership based in Palestine, came to the metropole during that period, it was brought not just by English women but by English women who, by any standard, would be considered

Figure 1.2 'Abdu'l-Bahá during his travels to the West, 1911.

strong, independent minded, creative, educated, resourceful and actively involved in the public sphere, both before and after becoming Bahá'ís. They took inspiration from the Bahá'í teachings on the equality of women and men, and worked towards realizing that goal in a number of ways: by spreading the message of Bahá'u'lláh, involving themselves in liberal and humanitarian causes and supporting feminist movements. 'Abdu'l-Bahá's successful visits to Great Britain, where he was able to reach thousands and visit people from a cross-section of society, had much to do with the connections and efforts of early female Bahá'ís such as Ethel Rosenberg and Sara Blomfield.

Blomfield invited 'Abdu'l-Bahá and his retinue to stay in her home at Cadogan Gardens during his time in London, and Thornburgh-Cropper put her car at his disposal.[74] Together, Blomfield and Rosenberg managed the "constant stream" of people who came to see him: Rosenberg kept a book of 'Abdu'l-Bahá's meetings, while Blomfield marshalled the processions of visitors. She described how they came all day and every day,

Ministers and missionaries, Oriental scholars and occult students, practical men of affairs and mystics, Anglican- Catholics and Nonconformists, Theosophists and Hindus, Christian Scientists and doctors of medicine, Muslims, Buddhists, and Zoroastrians. There also called: politicians, Salvation Army soldiers, and other workers for human good, women suffragists, journalists, writers, poets, and healers, dressmakers and great ladies, artists and artisans, poor workless people and prosperous merchants, members of the dramatic and musical world, all these came; and none were too lowly, nor too great [to visit 'Abdu'l-Bahá].[75]

Many had learned of 'Abdu'l-Bahá from the daily papers, which related the news of his arrival in a tone that showed both respect and interest.[76]

While Blomfield and Rosenberg took care of 'Abdu'l-Bahá's appointments, the responsibility for running the household was delegated to Blomfield's friend Beatrice Platt, who, with the help of the regular staff and 'Abdu'l-Bahá's cook Khosru, provided regular meal service for groups of up to nineteen.[77] 'Abdu'l-Bahá was grateful for their administrative work, and joked that while he had spent much of his life disobeying Sultans of empires, he was quite content to take orders from Lady Blomfield and the other women in her home.[78]

Some of the visitors to Cadogan Gardens, such as Reginald Campbell, Basil Wilberforce and Annie Besant, had already become acquainted with the teachings of Bahá'u'lláh through Blomfield and, after meeting with 'Abdu'l-Bahá, invited him to speak to their respective organizations. 'Abdu'l-Bahá gave his first public address in the West at City Temple in Holborn at the request of the Reverend Campbell, whose perspectives on Christianity Blomfield admired. Archdeacon Wilberforce, liberal, women's suffragist, grandson of the famous abolitionist and a friend of Blomfield, personally welcomed 'Abdu'l-Bahá to speak to his congregation at St John the Divine in Westminster.[79] Finally, as the president of the Theosophical Society, Besant invited 'Abdu'l-Bahá to present to the members of that organization, which he did on more than one occasion.[80]

Elizabeth Herrick and Isabel Fraser came to the service of 'Abdu'l-Bahá in Liverpool, just as Blomfield and Rosenberg had in London. When he arrived in that port city in December 1912 to begin his second trip to England, they took care of all of the practical aspects of his visit, and Herrick arranged for him to speak at the Pembroke Chapel, where she had been a member. In fact, the night before his steamer was due to dock, the two women travelled to Liverpool and, using the typewriters at their hotel, created announcements of 'Abdu'l-Bahá's upcoming address, which they then distributed to various newspaper offices and elsewhere in the city. These activities defied the conventional mores in England during that time, where, as a general rule, "respectable" women did not travel freely on their own, book hotel rooms and make their way through unknown urban spaces during the wee hours of the night. Their publicity efforts proved successful, and people from the greater Liverpool area, and even as far away as Manchester, began to assemble outside Pembroke Chapel long before 'Abdu'l-Bahá was scheduled to speak.[81]

This network of women willing and able to host 'Abdu'l-Bahá during his stay in Britain and to ensure that his message reached an audience beyond the existing Bahá'í communities, through meetings and speaking engagements, extended into Scotland with the efforts of Mrs Alexander Whyte. Despite being the wife of a minister in the United Free Church of Scotland, whose name she used rather than her own, Whyte seems to have been fairly independent minded. Like Rosenberg, she made the journey to Acre after hearing about 'Abdu'l-Bahá from her friend Thornburgh-Cropper. During his second visit to Great Britain, 'Abdu'l-Bahá stayed in Whyte's home, the manse in Charlotte Square, as a welcomed guest. From there 'Abdu'l-Bahá gave public addresses and received a number of visitors, including "many eminent citizens of Edinburgh." One such address on "the station of women" drew an audience which included both suffragists and their opponents, the anti-suffragists.[82]

Feminism and women's suffrage

Given the core Bahá'í belief that all human beings, male and female, are essentially equal and should have equal rights before the law, it is not surprising that 'Abdu'l-Bahá would support the women's suffrage movement. Still, he objected to the use of violence to achieve its goals; to use the terms of his contemporaries, he was suffragist but not a suffragette. He repeatedly called for those involved in the cause to avoid militancy, as "radicalism breeds other harms." His own gentle behaviour despite years of persecution was meant to serve as an example to his followers. In order to help explain this position to English Bahá'ís familiar with Judeo-Christian traditions, he used an example from the Bible, reminding them of how God told Moses to use "soft language" when speaking to Pharaoh.[83] 'Abdu'l-Bahá maintained that violence was a sign not of strength but of weakness, and that incendiary methods merely impeded the progress of the women's suffrage movement, a just cause which would triumph through the spiritual advancement of civilization.[84]

By rejecting militancy and emphasizing spirituality, 'Abdu'l-Bahá's position could seem similar to that of English conservatives, or even anti-suffragists, who argued that when women pursued a public political role they compromised their ability to exercise moral influence.[85] Certainly some of his statements taken out of context could be interpreted as encouraging women to take a passive rather than active role in political life; for example, his instructions that they should strive to become "channels whereby the virtues of humanity may flow like a health giving spring."[86]

However, he called repeatedly for female enfranchisement and equality in the sphere of public political life. Presenting a humorous twist on the practice of looking to nature for guidance on the proper relationship between the sexes, common in the West since the Enlightenment, 'Abdu'l-Bahá drew laughter and applause from his audience when he asked them to consider the animal and vegetable kingdoms, where both males and females enjoy equal suffrage.[87] In addition, he had good relationships with workers in the cause of women's suffrage, some of whom were also Bahá'ís. He was visited by Emmeline Pankhurst and her daughter Christabel, leaders of the militant Women's Social and Political Union (WSPU), as well as being invited to speak to the non-violent splinter group of the WSPU, the Women's Freedom League.[88] Years later, just as Europe was recovering from the carnage of the First World War, 'Abdu'l-Bahá praised the signs of female emancipation in Britain, explaining that if women had had the vote and the prestige in society that they deserved, they would have prevented the outbreak of war.[89]

Elizabeth Herrick was both a Bahá'í and a suffragette, a member of the WSPU. While she exceeded the boundaries prescribed by 'Abdu'l-Bahá when committing violence against property, her feminist activism and religious faith remained inseparable. For example, after she was arrested for smashing shop widows on Kensington High Street and sent to Holloway Prison, she insisted on being registered as a Bahá'í. While in prison, she prayed "unceasingly," repeatedly invoked the name of Bahá'u'lláh, spoke of her faith to all who would listen and even gave Bahá'í literature to the chaplain. She treated her incarceration as an opportunity to put her faith into action by working to better the situation for herself and her fellow inmates, most of whom were poor, uneducated and had no knowledge of their rights. She met regularly with the prison doctor and governor as well as the chaplain and spoke to them about the appalling conditions. As a result of her efforts, the lives of the prisoners improved in small but significant ways: their filthy cell walls were washed and each received a daily ration of fruit.[90]

Herrick was not the only female Bahá'í to become involved in the women's suffrage movement in England. Sara Blomfield and her daughters, Mary and Eleonore, contributed to that cause as well. While they refrained from militant or violent action, they took a special interest in the treatment of hunger-striking suffragettes. When Herbert Asquith's government betrayed its principles by allowing the brutal, sometimes fatal, forced feeding of these prisoners, Lady Blomfield severed her ties with the

Liberal Party.[91] She also opened a cottage on her estate as a refuge for suffragettes who had been released from prison in a dangerously weak and malnourished state. Despite the semi-official practice of re-arresting these women once their strength and health had been regained in the outside world, her guests remained safe. As Mary later recalled, while the local village policeman would "prowl around the house" on a regular basis, he made no attempt to enter.[92] Perhaps inspired by their mother, Mary, accompanied by Eleonore, made an "impassioned appeal" to King George V to put a stop to the forced feeding of suffragettes, creating a "sensation" that had the entire country talking, for, according to the *Daily Sketch*, it marked "the first time in history that so dramatic a speech had been made by a girl at the Throne of England."[93]

That article, and news of the Blomfields' activities regarding "the woman question" in general, reached Ottoman Haifa. The Bahá'ís there expressed their admiration for the heroism, fearlessness and "matchless resolution" of Mary, known to them by her Persian or Bahá'í name, "Parveen Khanum." 'Abdu'l-Bahá listened attentively as the article was read, responding with "what courage!"[94] He then wrote to Lady Blomfield instructing her to urge Mary and Eleonore to speak both inside the home and in public.[95] He expressed his hope that her "noble daughters" would one day visit Iran in order to further the emancipation of women in that country.[96]

As 'Abdu'l-Bahá's proposal that the Blomfield daughters should travel to Iran suggests, he saw the movement for female emancipation not as limited by country or region but, rather, as an effort that ought to transcend national boundaries and confining notions of "East" and "West." On more than one occasion he communicated to his British followers that Bahá'ís had been working to improve the position of women in the East for years, especially in Iran,[97] and, given that he believed female enfranchisement could be realized in Iran in the near future, it is quite likely that his invitation to the Blomfields was intended as a step toward the creation of an alliance between English and Iranian Bahá'í suffragists. In addition, he sent his own daughter Rúhá to London and Paris, and two other Bahá'í women, Zeenat and Ghodsia, to the United States, so that they would gain knowledge and experience to help them advance the cause of women's liberty in Iran and serve as examples for "Eastern women" more generally.[98]

While 'Abdu'l-Bahá expressed the idea that, overall and especially in recent years, women of the West had made more progress than those of the East,[99] which explains his interest in providing Western or Westernized female role models in the East rather than vice versa, he did not see female strength, defiance or public political activity as developing solely out of Western feminism. In this respect he differed from many Western feminists, and even Eastern feminists such as Qasim Amin.[100] During his visits to

Great Britain, he spoke to Bahá'ís and non-Bahá'ís alike about female heroism in the East, from the ancient Syrian warrior queen Zenobia, who led armies into battle brandishing her sword,[101] to the outstanding Bábí and Bahá'í women of the nineteenth and twentieth centuries who gave their lives for their religious beliefs.[102] The most notable among them was poet, philosopher, linguist, theologian and disciple of the Báb, Tahirih Qurratu'l-'Ayn, for Tahirih defied religious and secular authorities as well as accepted customs and traditions by leaving her husband and travelling throughout the country, even speaking unveiled in public in an effort to win converts to her new-found faith. She participated in Bábí politics and assumed a leadership position in Karbala.[103]

In addition to relating stories of heroic or accomplished Eastern women, 'Abdu'l-Bahá maintained that the Bahá'í movement itself, which had originated in the East, acted as a force for female emancipation, for according to the teachings of Bahá'u'lláh, true justice and the progress of human civilization will be realized only when women take their rightful place of equality alongside men in society.[104] As 'Abdu'l-Bahá explained to a gathering in Edinburgh, humanity is like a bird with two wings, one male and the other female. If one wing is dominant, the bird will fly in circles, but if both wings are equally strong, humanity will soar to a "higher dimension of human perfection."[105] In addition, he taught that with the revelation of Bahá'u'lláh a new era had dawned which eventually would bring equality and enfranchisement to all of humanity.[106]

'Abdu'l-Bahá explained to his British audience that, according to the Bahá'í belief system, not only did the progress of the human race and the elevation of the status of women go hand in hand, enabling each other, but also that female education was a critical component of both. He spoke of how women were more intuitive, receptive and intelligent than men;[107] with the right educational opportunities, they could reach their full potential, benefiting themselves and the larger society. He told his audience at Westminster and another in the village of Byfleet, just outside London, of Bahá'í contributions to female education. In Byfleet, 'Abdu'l-Bahá addressed educators and writers, explaining to them that in this modern day and age the education of the girl is *more important* than that of the boy, for while all are responsible for the care of children, the female is the "mother of the human race."[108] Yet, unlike the leaders who emerged in the wake of the French Revolution and promoted the ideal of the educated "republican mother" as a way of limiting the influence of female citizens to the domestic sphere, 'Abdu'l-Bahá maintained that education would serve as the gateway for their participation in public political life. As he told suffragists, feminists and others during his time in Britain, votes for women could be achieved through the power of reason, female accomplishments in the arts and sciences and educated mothers enlightening the next generation and teaching them about the need for justice and equality, all methods which were preferable to violence.[109]

Orientalism and elegant hospitality

Like a number of the non-violent suffragists, who also had 'Abdu'l-Bahá's support, Bahá'ís living in early twentieth-century Britain did not hesitate to use what would have been considered "ladylike" social skills in the service of their new-found beliefs. They hosted celebrations of all types: parties, receptions and dinners. These events could range from intimate gatherings of two or three people discussing spiritual matters over refreshments in the drawing room to more elaborate affairs such as the farewell party Thornburgh-Cropper threw for 'Abdu'l-Bahá, which was attended by over four hundred people.[110] Edward Hall fondly remembered elegant details from early Bahá'í meetings: red roses, afternoon tea in Miss Gamble's garden and music played, perhaps on the piano or harpsichord, by Miss Jack.[111] In the English context, the mere reference to "afternoon tea" implies an exquisite event, complete with lace napkins, delicate finger sandwiches, and scones. In addition, polite correspondence such as formal invitations and thank-you notes appear frequently among the early Bahá'í materials.

It is important to note, however, that a number of these practices generally regarded as "ladylike" in Great Britain were not necessarily gendered as feminine in the land of Bahá'u'lláh's birth or elsewhere in the Middle East, for hospitality had been integral to both Persian and Arab culture for centuries and was extended by men and women alike. Interactions in that part of the world, social and otherwise, often required the sharing of food and at the very least drinking tea, usually accompanied by some type of ritual, which could vary in length and formality depending upon the circumstances. Roses had played a role in Persian ceremonies and celebrations of all types long before they appeared at British Bahá'í events. In addition, both 'Abdu'l-Bahá and Bahá'u'lláh expressed a fondness for that flower: 'Abdu'l-Bahá sometimes carried a single rose, and Bahá'u'lláh declared his mission surrounded by roses in the garden of Ridvan. The garden itself, mentioned above by Hall, and so often associated with elegant or privileged femininity in England, from Ruskin's well-known "Of Queens' Gardens" to the fashionable garden parties of the Edwardian era, had a broader significance in the Islamic world, where it was believed to represent the afterlife awaiting the virtuous Muslim.[112] Both Bahá'u'lláh and Abdu'l-Bahá' loved to spend time in gardens, and at one point when it looked as if the latter was in danger of being hanged from the gallows, he, "to the amazement of

His friends and the amusement of His enemies" took to the garden, where he busied himself planting new trees and vines.[113]

If we consider the gracious hospitality which characterized the activities of the first English Bahá'ís as hybridized or the product of Eastern as well as Western influences – after all they looked to 'Abdu'l-Bahá as a model for proper behaviour – it becomes clear that practices which to the Western observer may appear "ladylike" and therefore confined to the private sphere in fact defied such simple categorization.[114] For English Bahá'í women, social life overlapped with public involvement and even international politics. One letter from Rosenberg to Blomfield, written in 1918, helps to illustrate this convergence of networks and circles of influence, from the private and domestic to the national and global. In it, Rosenberg not only speaks of visiting socially, inviting Blomfield to afternoon tea, but also relates her recent encounters with the British War Office in Egypt. She was trying to secure the safety of the Bahá'ís in British-occupied Haifa and requested Blomfield's help, suggesting that the latter use her connections in England to put additional pressure on British officials in the Middle East.[115]

In addition, as 'Abdu'l-Bahá recognized, the social interaction that resulted from the extension of hospitality served to educate newcomers about Bahá'í values and to foster a sense of unity and spiritual purpose among those who had already adopted that belief system, both of which contributed to the growth and development of the Bahá'í movement in Great Britain. For example, he praised Blomfield for serving "coffee, tea and sweets" in her house on Friday evenings after Bahá'í programmes, as guests were more inclined to stay afterwards, talk and ask questions when she did so.[116] Along the same lines, Blomfield opened her country house to the biblical scholar and Bahá'í, Thomas Cheyne, who previously had arranged for 'Abdu'l-Bahá to speak at Manchester College, Oxford. When 'Abdu'l-Bahá learned of the intended visit, he instructed Blomfield to make every effort to see that both Cheyne and his wife became "wholly spiritual and illuminated" during their stay.[117]

It is important to note that while 'Abdu'l-Bahá appreciated Blomfield's talents as a hostess, which had much to do with her circumstances and years of practice, this did not prevent him from recognizing her abilities outside of this realm. He advised her to take part in public life, and the two shared a podium on at least one occasion.[118] With regard to speech, he praised her courage and eloquence, in one letter stating "thou art the conqueror."[119] Believing that she possessed both the wisdom and ability to interpret the Bahá'í teachings correctly, he urged her not simply to repeat his words but, rather, to explain the movement's principles from her own perspective, knowing "assuredly that new significances will flow from thy lips!" In addition, he called upon her to undertake the formidable task of countering his enemies who led the Azali movement in Lausanne by travelling there to give "lengthy lectures" and display such "zeal, attraction, majesty and power" that they would be forced to flee, or at least be driven underground and into obscurity.[120]

English Bahá'í women such as Blomfield, for whom religious, political and social activities overlapped, experimented with incorporating Eastern, especially Persian, elements into their lives and dress, reflecting as well as contributing to their internal hybridization. For example, even though their new belief system did not require them to veil, it was not unusual for Western women to drape a light-coloured cloth over their hair and shoulders while on pilgrimage as was the custom in Acre (Figure 1.3).[121]

Figure 1.3 Ethel Jenner Rosenberg and Western Bahá'í pilgrims in Acre in early 1901. Ethel Jenner Rosenberg is seated on the far left. Shoghi Effendi, who would become the Guardian of the Bahá'í Faith in 1921, is the child sitting in the middle of the group. Laura Clifford Barney is standing on the far right.

Like the female members of the "Holy Family," Blomfield became fond of wearing "garments with long flowing lines" and a "scarf or veil ... about her head" even when in England. Her daughter describes her clothing as "not fashionable in the ordinary sense ... distinctive and individual, without being strange."[122] Similarly, Elizabeth Herrick was known as having "artistic taste in dress."[123] A number of these early English Bahá'í women, including Herrick, the Blomfields and Rosenberg, studied the Persian language, which gave them an appreciation for its poetic qualities and beauty of form as well as an understanding of the words of Bahá'u'lláh and 'Abdu'l-Bahá in their native tongue.[124] Lady Lamington wore a ring inscribed with the name of Bahá'u'lláh in Persian calligraphy, which made a striking impression, especially at dinner parties where that "simple and humble stone" of red agate became even more conspicuous in the company of the precious jewels worn by her peers.[125]

The creative self-presentation, Orientalist interests and elegant entertaining discussed in this subsection all had aristocratic as well as feminine connotations in English society,[126] and both Blomfield and Rosenberg, two of the most active Bahá'í women of the time, had aristocratic sympathies. Blomfield did not hesitate to employ her title and influence in the service of Bahá'í principles, and even the name given to her by 'Abdu'l-Bahá included the title "Khanum," the Persian equivalent of "Lady."[127] Class privileges allowed her and her daughters to contribute to the women's suffrage movement and come to the aid of its militant wing without becoming violent themselves. After all Lady Blomfield was fortunate to have an estate with a cottage that she could offer to suffragettes just released from prison, and Mary even suspected that the local policeman did not re-arrest them while in her mother's care out of deference or "respectful affection" for her.[128] Mary, who was called "the society suffragist" by the press, took advantage of her position to make a speech before the king, an opportunity not available to most British subjects.[129] While less privileged than the Blomfields, Rosenberg supported herself as a "portrait painter of London's aristocracy,"[130] and came from a family of artists who had been catering to aristocratic tastes since her great grandfather moved to Bath from Vienna in the 1780s; he painted German, French, and English royals, strongly opposed the French Revolution, and lived long enough to meet the young Victoria.

Social and economic justice

The aristocratic connections and sympathies of Rosenberg and the Blomfields in no way prevented the Bahá'í movement from appealing to British women from a variety of circumstances and socio-economic backgrounds. Even Rosenberg experienced financial hardship, especially during periods of illness.[131] The first person to become a Bahá'í in the northern part of England, Sarah Ann Ridgway, lived in a modest manner as a weaver in the Greater Manchester area.[132] Elizabeth Herrick, mentioned previously for her service to Abdu'l-Bahá in Liverpool and activities as a Bahá'í suffragette, experienced changing fortunes throughout the course of her life. When what had been a prosperous family business failed, she was forced to leave school at the age of fourteen to work long hours as an apprentice in a milliner's shop. Over time she built her own wholesale business "of which any man might be proud" and became a rare female version of the middle-class social ideal, "the self-made man," only to experience financial difficulties later in life as a result of overextending herself personally and financially in the service of social causes.[133]

'Abdu'l-Bahá met a Bahá'í charwoman during one of his trips to Britain, who showed him her rough, callous hands, to which he responded by taking them in his own and blessing them.[134] According to the still dominant or hegemonic middle-class belief system of that time, the private, feminine sphere of the home was supposed to be a place apart and a refuge from the world of work, which meant that female hands marked by any sign of physical labour were considered an unsightly source of embarrassment, something to be hidden, or at the very least ignored.[135] Yet 'Abdu'l-Bahá made a point of not only holding her hands but also telling her how pleased he was with them and even that he "loved them very much."[136] Through his words and gestures, 'Abdu'l-Bahá communicated his recognition of the value of female domestic labour during a time when that type of work remained largely unacknowledged and unappreciated in English society.[137]

While in London, 'Abdu'l-Bahá visited a group of roughly sixty women and their one hundred children at a shelter for "toiling mothers" in the Battersea area, where he walked amongst them talking, giving his blessings and distributing money. Even without full command of the English language, he seemed to have been able to win their trust. As one observer noted, while the very poor who resided there were usually suspicious of strangers, the crowd not only accepted 'Abdu'l-Bahá but also cheered him.[138] On another occasion, during a visit to Passmore Edwards Settlement, he told a group of "working women" that he loved them and that he would be no happier surrounded by the queens of the earth than he was in their presence. Furthermore, as he considered himself to be "the servant of the poor," he was their servant.[139]

The respectful affection that 'Abdu'l-Bahá showed for women who lived in poverty or whose days were spent cleaning and scrubbing was a part of his overall concern for the poor and for domestic labourers in general, male as well as female. After all, one of the core Bahá'í beliefs was that everyone should have access to the necessities of life, a principle which could be applied and appreciated in the West as well as the East. After addressing a reception in Bristol, 'Abdu'l-Bahá met with the servants at the guesthouse where he was staying, thanked them for their work and spoke of the dignity of labour.[140] On Christmas day he visited the Salvation Army shelter in Westminster, and when he began to speak the hundreds of hungry men who crowded the dining hall stopped eating and fell silent in order to listen. He praised the high moral standards of the poor and related his own experiences of poverty as well as those of Christ and Bahá'u'lláh. He then donated enough money for the shelter to serve an additional one thousand dinners on New Year's Day.[141] Giving to those in need came naturally for 'Abdu'l-Bahá, as he had been doing so all his life, even during his imprisonment in Acre when he had barely enough for himself.

While 'Abdu'l-Bahá gave generously and encouraged his followers to do the same, he also realized that charity alone could not put an end to structural economic injustices.[142] When visiting England, he was both shocked and saddened to find that a nation so wealthy could allow such terrible poverty in its midst, commenting that the rich were too rich and the poor too poor.[143] He called extreme inequalities a form of tyranny which need not exist if, for example, workers were guaranteed a share of company profits and pensions in old age.[144] One of the most important steps towards eradicating poverty, 'Abdu'l-Bahá believed, was to end the arms race, for not only do the poor suffer disproportionately in times of war, but military spending can be as much of a drain on the economy as the actual conflict.[145]

As radical as these ideas may have sounded at the time, there was also a certain conservative element to 'Abdu'l-Bahá's position on the relationship between capital and labour, at least from the perspective of socialists and other reformers for whom the spread of working-class consciousness served as a measure of progress and levelling remained an ideal; for, while 'Abdu'l-Bahá always condemned gross inequalities and stressed that workers deserved respect and comfortable lives, he also believed that hierarchies were necessary, and that just as workers should be treated fairly and with kindness by their employers, they should be "submissive and obedient" in return. Divisiveness along class lines or ill will generated by labour leaders was no more acceptable to him than the abuse of power fuelled by capitalist greed. Just as in the case of other loyalties or identities that could separate people based on ideas about race, nation or religion, the Bahá'í perspective valued unity above all else.[146]

This commitment to realizing the unity of the human race did not prevent 'Abdu'l-Bahá from noticing and appreciating differences within it, and he formed a favourable opinion of English people and their government. His understanding of what might be called the English national character was based on relationships that had developed over the years with the English

Bahá'ís who visited Acre as well as during time spent in their country.[147] He described the English as showing firmness and resolve in every undertaking, explaining that they were "not easily turned aside, being neither prone to begin a matter for a little while nor ready to abandon it for little reason."[148] He also expressed high regard for the degree of individual liberty allowed in their society, where "every person can go his own way and say what he thinks ... is king of himself." He went on to explain that such freedom of thought and speech facilitates understanding among diverse people, fostering unity and therefore progress.[149] Finally, he praised the growth of democracy in England, stating that the efforts there to "give all souls an equal and true place" – which most likely refers to both the expanding franchise during the previous century as well as the ongoing movements for continued reform – had raised the standard by which justice is measured.[150]

Over the course of the early twentieth century, from Ethel Jenner Rosenberg's first pilgrimages to Acre to 'Abdu'l-Bahá's travels to Great Britain, that leader continued to build upon a process begun by his father, for both father and son understood liberal, democratic reform as in line with modern divine revelation and took note of areas of convergence or harmony between the core or canonical Bahá'í beliefs, on the one hand, and certain values or practices found in British culture, on the other. For example, just as Bahá'u'lláh had written a letter to Queen Victoria during the nineteenth century commending her on the prohibition of slave trading in the empire, a practice also forbidden in the *Kitáb-i-Aqdas*, 'Abdu'l-Bahá became a supporter of the women's suffrage movement in the early twentieth century as an expression of the fundamental Bahá'í belief in the equality of women and men. In the case of 'Abdu'l-Bahá', however, focusing and elaborating on this and other areas of common ground between Bahá'í teachings and the culture of the imperial metropole helped to sustain bonds with a growing network of followers and sympathizers in Great Britain as both that leader and the new communities of adherents continued to find avenues of mutual identification that crossed the East–West divide and contributed to increasingly hybridized systems of meaning.

Bahá'í attitudes towards the British Empire

In the peripheries: Egypt and South Asia

'Abdu'l-Bahá's appreciation of British liberal principles was not confined to the imperial metropole, for British-occupied Egypt continued to serve as a place of refuge for members of the struggling Bahá'í minority in the early twentieth century as it had during the nineteenth century. At one point in 1904, when the situation for Bahá'ís in the then Ottoman

Haifa–Acre area became especially difficult, 'Abdu'l-Bahá managed to secure safe passage to Egypt for seventy of them and, after being released from prison in 1910, he took up residence there himself.[151] While that country did not become an official British Protectorate until 1914, the period from 1882 to 1914 is known as the "Veiled Protectorate" because of the British-dominated government and administration of that time. In fact, 'Abdu'l-Bahá told an audience at Manchester College, Oxford that when he resided in Egypt he did so "under the protection of the Khedive and Great Britain."[152]

Not surprisingly, the tradition of protection that the British provided to Bahá'ís in Egypt under the Veiled Protectorate would continue during the British Protectorate as well. As the number of Iranian Bahá'ís moving to Port Said increased towards the end of the First World War, so too did cases of discrimination and even violence against them, and when the Egyptian authorities ignored a popular sheikh who targeted them by arousing "fanaticism," the Bahá'ís turned to the British for help. In one instance, an angry, stone-throwing mob refused to disperse until it was told that cases involving the harassment of members of Bahá'í religious minority would no longer be tried in the local Egyptian courts but instead by a British military consul. As a report to 'Abdu'l-Bahá describing the persecution of Bahá'ís in Port Said concluded, until the Egyptian government could guarantee liberty and freedom to its minorities, it remained a despotism not yet ready for independence from British rule.[153]

In addition, just prior to the war and under a British-dominated administration, Egypt had become a crossroads between East and West, to an unprecedented degree, providing opportunities for Bahá'ís from either side of the imagined divide both to meet with each other and to make contacts that transcended narrow expectations associated with birth or background. Developments in transportation, from the railways to the Suez Canal to the new commercial steamships, brought increasing numbers of Westerners to Egypt, some of whom visited 'Abdu'l-Bahá while he resided there. For example, Lord and Lady Lamington happened to be travelling in the area. Also, Mrs Stannard lived in that country from 1908, when she first became a Bahá'í, until 1925, and during that time made trips to Europe, India and Haifa.[154] Elinor Hiscox took advantage of the favourable terms the government extended to British residents and initiated teaching efforts and other Bahá'í activities in Cairo, Alexandria and Ramleh throughout the 1910s.[155] While in Egypt, 'Abdu'l-Bahá welcomed all types from both East and West to his house, and pilgrims from throughout the world came to visit him there. Despite his Iranian and aristocratic background, he did not remain aloof from the ordinary people of that country, but visited the public marketplace where he conversed "heartily" in the colloquial Arabic.[156]

British Egypt had real significance for 'Abdu'l-Bahá and the Bahá'í community in Palestine even during periods when circumstances such as imprisonment or war hampered the ability to communicate with their co-religionists across the border. While confined to Acre, 'Abdu'l-Bahá spoke of the great progress made in Egypt under British rule, particularly with regard to ameliorating the condition of the poor, and observed that the people of Syria and Palestine were becoming interested in adopting Western education and practices because of the British example.[157] For years he kept abreast of developments in Egypt and maintained a relationship with the Bahá'ís there. He felt grieved when the outbreak of the First World War caused a loss of contact, and thought about them every day.[158] Yet even during the war, that country could serve as a link between Bahá'ís in the Haifa area and those in England, such as in 1915 when a follower of Bahá'u'lláh, Hussein Afnan Effendi, concluded his seven months of travel in Syria and Palestine by making his way to Cairo and from there posting a letter to Ethel Jenner Rosenberg in London, updating her on 'Abdu'l-Bahá and his community.[159]

In addition to Egypt, Bahá'í communities continued to grow in British India during the early twentieth century. In 1911, a nineteen-member teaching council was formed which organized lectures and other presentations under the auspices of universities and business associations and through reform movements, particularly the Hindu Brahmo Samaj and Arya Samaj. As in England, Theosophists provided audiences and venues for Bahá'í speakers as well. The majority of 'Abdu'l-Bahá's followers on the subcontinent were from a middle-class, educated, Persianized background. Still, a number of Parsees, or Zoroastrians native to India, in Bombay had become Bahá'ís during this period, as did at least one Sikh and one high-caste Hindu.[160]

Bahá'ís who spoke favourably of the colonial Raj in South Asia tended to do so because they valued the protection that the government could provide to religious minorities, along with the spread of British liberal ideals. 'Abdu'l-Bahá himself stated that "England has done much for India" and was appreciated by the "best of the people" there – perhaps a reference to those connected to the above-mentioned networks and reform movements.[161] The *Star of the West* (*SoW*) followed a description of an Indian princely state as "sect-beridden" and a "hot-bed of religious prejudices" with an address by 'Abdu'l-Bahá entitled "India needs these principles of toleration and liberalism," qualities that he had repeatedly associated with British rule. Another issue of *SoW* suggested a congruence between the Bahá'í principles and those of the Raj by depicting the Bahá'í movement as having helped to save the "Indian empire" from nationalism by weakening the Hindu caste system.[162]

Working towards global unity within existing power structures

Whenever nationalism threatened to divide members of the human race from one another, whether in South Asia or Europe, 'Abdu'l-Bahá condemned it in no uncertain terms. This position was communicated in his speeches and in the *SoW*. For example, while in Paris in 1911, he called attention to the absurdity that the French people seemed to care more about twenty-five of their countrymen recently killed in an accident in that city than the thousands of Italians and Arabs slaughtering each other in nearby Tripoli. He explained that such indifference to the lives of others based on nothing more than national prejudice was, like "bloodthirstiness," morally wrong.[163] He likened the drawing of national boundaries to "canine" behaviour, yet noted that even dogs do not fight for something as worthless as the ground, which is naught but our tomb, a necropolis. For three years prior to the First World War 'Abdu'l-Bahá urged the people of Europe to unite, repeating the warnings of his father, Bahá'u'lláh, about the dangers of the arms race. He described war as a tyrannous and savage practice which required cowardly leaders to send soldiers to their deaths and drained the economy, causing the most suffering among those least able to bear it, the poor.[164] In the spirit of overcoming nationalist divisions that lead to war, the *SoW* proposed an "Anthem of World Patriotism," sung to the tune of "God Save the King," which celebrates humanity as one nation and one people living together on "mother earth."[165]

Despite their own nationalist inclinations, 'Abdu'l-Bahá tended to regard the English people and the British leadership as contributing a calm and stabilizing element to European politics amid the mounting tensions prior to the First World War. He praised the English for their peace efforts,[166] and expressed hope that Britain's "just" and "noble" government would be able to intervene effectively in the Balkans in order to put an end to bloodshed in that troubled region.[167] He even treated Britain's military spending as understandable in light of the circumstances, for, while he saw worldwide disarmament as the eventual goal, he also understood that Britain could not be expected to do it alone, as "she would be at the mercy of her enemies." His description of the tense international situation by mid-1914 reflects these same sympathies: 'Abdu'l-Bahá presented militarism as a continental problem, explaining that the ever-expanding German army fuelled the already volatile French patriotism, both of which tested the usual "calm and steady nerves of the Britishers across the channel."[168]

What may seem like a contradiction between 'Abdu'l-Bahá's support of the English nation and British government, on the one hand, and his condemnation of war and nationalism, on the other, can be understood by considering the British Empire not as an extension of a narrowly defined

English nation-state but, rather, according to its ideals and scope; for, according to the contemporary dominant British imperial ideologies, and, it seems, 'Abdu'l-Bahá's experiences and view as well, the empire could serve as a progressive force in the world, spreading liberalism, tolerance and increased democracy.[169] In addition, by the early twentieth century it had become a formidable, multicultural global network that brought together people from a wide variety of racial, national and religious backgrounds.

For a small and struggling movement which sought to transform spiritually the human race to such an extent that all of mankind would one day come together in peace and harmony, the British Empire provided not only practical assistance, as described in Egypt and India, but also a means through which individuals could begin to imagine the possibility of such global unity.

For example, the popular journalist, visionary and social reformer who met 'Abdu'l-Bahá in London, William Thomas Stead, wrote an article, published in the *SoW*, about the empire as providing a beginning or foundational framework for a future worldwide "empire of peace" characterized not by English hegemony but, rather, by a shift in the "center of gravity" away from Westminster to the "outlands": decentralization would create an "elastic," loosely tied federation which might then join with other states such as the American Republic. As he explains, "The British Empire is like a picture in dissolving view. It is gradually melting into another and more brilliant picture, the Federation of the World."[170]

While the Bahá'í movement would go on to become the Bahá'í Faith and develop its own independent, global administrative structure over the course of the mid-to-late twentieth century, during roughly the same period of the British Empire's demise, the symbolic value of the latter for the early twentieth-century Bahá'ís and those they sought to reach, particularly in England, should not be dismissed, for before individuals can take even the first step towards achieving a goal, they first must imagine their intended actions in a way that will be meaningful to others in the larger society. In that respect the empire could be seen as a kind of intermediary framework, in both practical and theoretical terms, between existing local or national loyalties, on the one hand, and the forging of global identities on the other. If people could conceive of an entity that included multiple cultures, religions, ethnicities, nations and races; that crossed the continents and the oceans; and that incorporated elements of both Occident and Orient, then perhaps they were not far from recognizing the essential oneness of humankind and the need to promote unity and justice throughout the world by becoming Bahá'ís.

The modern scholar Juan Cole insightfully describes 'Abdu'l-Bahá as an original theorist of globalization, comparing his conceptualization of that process to E.P. Thompson's understanding of the formation of the English working class, for just as individuals laboured in factories, mines and railways before mobilizing themselves politically, humankind was already global in 1912. As Cole explains, "'Abdu'l-Bahá foresaw a slow and gradual realization of this globality in the succeeding decades and centuries. The global would have to be forged, as an identity for itself, in real-world struggle, compromise and realization."[171]

Thus, for 'Abdu'l-Bahá the global nature of the British Empire provided a way to communicate one of the core Bahá'í principles to his contemporaries during the early twentieth century, particularly those from England and elsewhere in the British Isles. That spiritual leader drew upon familiar concepts of English exceptionalism in order to appeal to a sense of duty or obligation to humankind. For example, in 1913, when he addressed his audience in Pembroke Chapel, he told them that as they were members of a *noble and civilized nation*, they should strive to "unfurl the flag of international peace over all the regions of the earth," all nations, religions and races.[172] Similarly, during a time when the ability to inspire colonial people to follow remained central to commonly held conceptions of the ideal "English character" and its cultivation, he explained to Tudor Pole how the English would have the opportunity to "lead the world out of its present darkness into the light of a new day."[173] His instructions to the English to protect Easterners would have brought to mind the paternalism and maternalism so often associated with imperial expansion.[174] It is important to emphasize, however, that regardless of how much the early twentieth-century Bahá'í discourses had in common with English patriotism and the dominant British imperial ideologies, they also advocated transforming them in fundamental ways, for no longer would the gross inequalities of power and resources that usually accompanied colonization be tolerated, nor would individuals be allowed to amass a fortune at the expense of thousands who starved.[175] The Bahá'í emphasis on unity sought to overcome all divisions, especially those based on the "optical illusion" of race, an approach which sought to undermine racist ideologies and practices in their various manifestations throughout the empire, from Africa to India to Australia.[176] Even 'Abdu'l-Bahá's above-mentioned advice to protect Easterners was accompanied by instructions for the people of England to unite with the French and become the "sympathetic embodiment of one nation," which, given the centuries of rivalry, would have marked a real departure from the past.[177] Finally, while 'Abdu'l-Bahá praised certain English characteristics, he also advised the people of that country to act in ways that would seem to be at odds with the stiff upper-lipped reserve and decorum which, by the early twentieth century, had become associated with Englishness and imperial rule by foreigners and natives alike.

He encouraged English people to forget their polite conventionality, which seems cold to Easterners, and instead talk without ceremony and make an effort to get to know the strangers in their midst.[178]

Of all the changes that the Bahá'ís hoped to make in the empire and in the world, none provoked as much criticism in Britain as did the idea that all major religions should be recognized and respected, particularly from certain Christians who understood their beliefs as part of an imperial civilizing mission. As one "Edinburgh reader" complained, if we accept the Bahá'í tenet of not denouncing or antagonizing any religion, then not only would Christian missionary activity cease but also the "noble list of missionary martyrs" such as Livingston would be dismissed as fanatics.[179] Other "letters to the editor" made the same argument and employed familiar imperialist language by, for example, referring to "heathenism" in colonial territories or the importance of bringing moral teaching to the "African cannibal."[180] One newspaper article even expressed concern that receptivity to the message of 'Abdu'l-Bahá would leave the British Isles open to a kind of reverse imperial missionary activity, allowing Islam, a religion associated with the peripheries of empire, to spread to the degree that "mosques and mullahs [would start] springing up all over Scotland to replace the Kirk and ministers."[181]

While the Bahá'ís had no desire to replace Christianity with Islam, they believed that the West had much to learn from the East with regard to matters of the heart. 'Abdu'l-Bahá may have considered Western civilization to be "great" and even "splendid," but he also believed that its strengths were practical and material rather than spiritual, an imbalance that had caused its people to grow "feverish" and overdriven by ambition. They needed the "spiritual physician" from the East to restore harmony and equilibrium and reawaken in them an appreciation of beauty, repose and love.[182] Perhaps these ideas are best illustrated by the observations recorded in the diary of one British Bahá'í, John Esslemont, during his pilgrimage to Palestine. In it he described how the Western Bahá'ís, particularly the American ones, caused a constant "bustle." During mealtimes they continually posed questions to 'Abdu'l-Bahá, with two or three among them taking notes to be transcribed and discussed afterwards. Esslemont reflected on how much more peaceful and devotional the atmosphere became in the wake of their departure. In contrast, the Eastern Bahá'ís who remained made no such demands and seemed content simply to be together and in the presence of their spiritual leader, sharing simple meals and enjoying the silence without any sense of urgency or awkwardness.[183] Along the same lines, 'Abdu'l-Bahá's grandson described his grandfather's silent solitude at Bahji as uplifting, a stillness with neither monotony nor ennui.[184]

While this perspective reproduces the familiar Orientalist imperialist dichotomy between a spiritual East and a material West,[185] it simultaneously challenges the corollary assumption that Western expansion necessarily leads to the advancement of humankind, for during this period popular writers such as Arminius Vambery were praising Westernization, particularly in the form of steam engines and other types of technology and high-speed transportation, for rousing the "sleepy and apathetic man in the East." Citing the lines from the English poet Matthew Arnold,

> The East bowed down before the blast
> In patient, deep distain;
> She let the legions thunder past,
> And plunged in thought again

Vambery advised "present-day Europe, in its restless, bustling activity" to "take good care not to let the East relapse again into its former indolence."[186] By ascribing a quality, a serene and much-needed Eastern spirituality, to what many Westerners perceived as merely a lack of motivation or initiative, if not a more serious defect, 'Abdu'l-Bahá and his followers challenged one of the fundamental beliefs underlying Western hegemony in the imperial context. Once again, while the Bahá'ís shared common ground with British imperial ideology, their points of departure from its dominant ideologies are as important to understanding the place that they created for themselves within the British imperial cultural system of the early twentieth century as are the more accommodating aspects of the movement. In addition, it is possible that Vambery's beliefs regarding the relationship between the East and West may have changed after he met 'Abdu'l-Bahá in Budapest in 1912, for the following year he wrote a letter expressing his deep admiration for that spiritual leader, whom he addressed as "your Excellency."[187] Finally, it is worth noting that, like their contemporaries who also spoke of the relationship between East and West, Bahá'ís understood these terms as having more to do with certain values and practices than with geographic location.[188]

As the irate letter from an "Edinburgh reader" cited earlier reminds us, 'Abdu'l-Bahá visited Scotland as well as England, and while both countries may have been considered part of the West, centres of power and their peripheries existed in the British Isles just as they did in the global empire. In certain respects, 'Abdu'l-Bahá's travel itinerary reflects these inequalities. After all, he was based in London and spent most of his time, just over fifty days, in the English capital, with brief stays, usually lasting from one to three days, in Oxford, Bristol, Liverpool and Edinburgh, while avoiding the "Celtic fringe" or Ireland, Wales and Highland Scotland entirely. His approach to the British Isles was representative of his position regarding the empire more generally in that he understood the practical benefits of working within the existing political structures, making use of his network of well-connected supporters in England and Lowland Scotland, yet at the same time he sought to spread an ideology that promoted greater equality and inclusiveness. Certainly, his followers were expected to assist in carrying out this mission in areas where he could not. For example, while in London he met a woman who had travelled from Belfast to see him. He instructed her to make herself like a spiritual "torch" causing the "illumination of Ireland," just as the Iranian Bahá'í women had done in the land of his birth.[189]

The discussion of Bahá'í attitudes towards nation and empire during this period would not be complete without mention of Edward Hall. Hall, who hailed from the Manchester area, embodied what would seem to be the tensions and contradictions of a movement that sought to promote love and harmony among the peoples of the earth, on the one hand, while simultaneously maintaining a role within the existing political structures, on the other; for even though 'Abdu'l-Bahá condemned war in general, individual Bahá'ís still were instructed to obey their governments, and in doing so Hall, "with resignation and peace of heart," joined the army and went to France.[190] While abroad he shared his beliefs in the divine revelation of Bahá'u'lláh and the need for world unity and found that his fellow soldiers, who might soon face death, tended to be more respectful and sympathetic than the civilians he had encountered previously.[191] Even his praise of German Bahá'ís was well received by comrades who, far from dehumanizing those on the opposing side, considered all involved as victims of the same war.[192]

Despite his somewhat unconventional spiritual path, when it came to the struggle to reconcile the wanton destruction and disregard for human life exhibited daily on the Western Front with faith in God and duty to one's country, Hall, like so many other English soldiers, turned to verse for consolation and self-expression.[193] In the following poem, entitled "Villers Pluich (Villers Plush) Autumn 1917," he relates his experience of the Somme region of northern France:

> A dreadful storm of fire and shell
> Illumined morn and broke its hush;
> And deadly answers round us fell
> As we looked down on Villers Plush
>
> And then with dawn the stricken scene
> Of homesteads down to ruin brought!
> What peace or business now can screen
> Or stifle memory's after thought?
>
> The scattered flesh, and pools of blood –
> The shattered walls and twisted rails –

> The shell-torn fields and roads of mud –
> Are real yet, though language fails.
>
> And still we mend with pick and spade
> The road that on to Cambrai runs;
> And still pass by in ghostly shade
> The horses, men, and rumbling guns.
>
> Whilst o'er the ridge the thing accurst
> Shrieks through the gloom, and falling near,
> Springs into flame with fiery burst
> That shocks the heart with sudden fear
>
> But God is King – and in that glare
> Was bending all things to His Will;
> It may have been that we were there
> To learn our duty better still.[194]

'Abdu'l-Bahá sent a "Tablet" or letter to Hall commending him for poetry that, by effectively depicting of the evils of war, had the potential to promote the cause of universal peace.[195]

The First World War, expansion into Palestine and British–Bahá'í relationships in the Middle East

The bond between 'Abdu'l-Bahá and the Bahá'ís in Great Britain remained strong during the First World War, despite the associated hardships that hampered communication between them. One month before the outbreak of conflict he instructed all pilgrims who had come to see him in Haifa to return home for their own safety.[196] When the Ottoman Empire entered the war on the side of the Central Powers, correspondence between Britain and Palestine was prohibited. 'Abdu'l-Bahá temporarily relocated the Bahá'í community from Haifa and Acre to Abu-Sinan, a small Druze village in the mountains of Western Galilee, in order to protect it should an allied attack come from the coast.[197] One Bahá'í described the monotony that accompanied the isolation of wartime Palestine by comparing the days to the empty, white pages of an endless blank book.[198] At one point news regarding 'Abdu'l-Bahá reached his British followers via the Bahá'í community in Tehran after an elderly and almost blind man, who was chosen in part because he would be unlikely to attract attention, made the long and perilous journey on foot from Palestine to officially neutral Iran in 1916.[199]

The following year, British Bahá'ís and Bahá'í sympathizers convinced their government to take an interest in the welfare of 'Abdu'l-Bahá and his family, who were living in Haifa at that time. Concern was initiated by an intelligence officer and admirer of 'Abdu'l-Bahá stationed in Cairo named Wellesley Tudor Pole.[200] Tudor Pole had met 'Abdu'l-Bahá in Egypt, and the latter visited the Tudor Pole's home twice in Bristol, England. Shortly before the British invasion of Haifa, Tudor Pole learned that Cemal Pasha, who was leading the Ottoman army in Palestine, had plans to put 'Abdu'l-Bahá to death.[201] After having tried unsuccessfully to interest his superiors in the matter, he convinced a fellow officer to hand-carry a letter out of Egypt and past the censors in order to alert the Bahá'ís in England.

The letter reached Lady Paget and was brought to the attention of both Lady Blomfield and Mrs Whyte.[202] These women were exceptionally well connected and, as a result, they were able to have the issue presented to the Foreign Office in a timely manner and from three different avenues, no less. Most men of the time would not have been able to do this. Yet it is also noteworthy that, despite their class privileges and involvement in the public sphere, each had to rely on a male intermediary in order to bring the matter to a decision-making body. Paget, through Lord Lamington, and Blomfield, via Lord Plymouth, brought 'Abdu'l-Bahá's predicament to the attention of Lord Balfour.[203] Whyte reached the Foreign Office through her son, who was serving as a Member of Parliament. These representations had the desired effect: Balfour contacted His Majesty's High Commissioner in Egypt, and British military authorities advancing in Palestine were instructed to treat 'Abdu'l-Bahá and his family with "all possible consideration" in the event that the British army should occupy Haifa.[204] Given the dangers of living in a war zone, combined with Cemal Pasha's public pledge to crucify 'Abdu'l-Bahá, a threat which automatically singled out that spiritual leader as a target for violence regardless of whether or not Ottoman troops reached him, the Bahá'ís and Bahá'í sympathizers who intervened on his behalf may very well have saved his life.

Mirza Ahmad Sohrab, an Iranian Bahá'í and editor of *SoW*, the Bahá'í publication for English speakers, described the British occupation of Palestine in glowing terms. While 'Abdu'l-Bahá and his followers repeatedly advocated an end to war, this invasion was regarded as an exceptional case. As Sohrab related, the sound of the British cannons brought excitement as it heralded the "glad news of the approach of our liberators."[205] In another letter, also published in the *SoW*, he described Allenby's capture of Haifa as sending an "electric wave of joy" through all of Palestine and Syria.[206] In this particular context "British" refers not just to that government or the British Isles but, in fact, to the people of a diverse and far-flung empire. Both letters mention Indian cavalrymen among their rescuers. In addition, Sohrab explained how the British military presence in Egypt and Palestine provided him with opportunities to teach the Bahá'í principles to people from throughout the world, including the Caribbean and South Asia as well as England.[207] He commented that the Black soldiers from the West Indies were especially nice and that he hoped to be able to visit them in the future.[208]

A mutually beneficial relationship developed between 'Abdu'l-Bahá and the British in Palestine. Immediately after troops entered Haifa, guards were posted to protect him and his family, and word spread that there would be "stern retribution" if any harm came to them. In addition, he was provided with the means to send and receive letters, so that he could reconnect with his followers.[209] In return, 'Abdu'l-Bahá assisted the British with their food supply shortage, for, in anticipation of future needs, had for years been instructing the Bahá'ís who had left Iran and settled on lands he had purchased in the Jordan Valley to produce a surplus of grain, which was kept in various places, from ancient Roman storage pits to, at one point, even the Shrine of the Báb.[210]

Tudor Pole continued to act as a liaison bringing together 'Abdu'l-Bahá and his followers, both in the British Isles and Palestine, on the one hand, and representatives of His Majesty's government, also in both countries, on the other. Soon after the occupation of Haifa he visited 'Abdu'l-Bahá and made every effort to work on his behalf, securing support of the British military governors in the area.[211] In addition, Tudor Pole's experience in navigating through the "maze of officialdom" meant that he could provide valuable services to the Bahá'ís of Palestine during a period of transition in that country.[212] At the same time, Tudor Pole kept the Bahá'ís at home informed of their leader's well-being and the situation in the Middle East. Acting upon Tudor Pole's advice, the "friends of 'Abdu'l-Bahá" in Great Britain wrote to Allenby, Balfour and others thanking them for his protection.[213] Of course this expression of gratitude was also a way of letting them know that British citizens had an interest in 'Abdu'l-Bahá's welfare and were aware of how he was being treated by the occupying forces.

Over the next few years, 'Abdu'l-Bahá became a valued advisor to a number of British officials, most notably the High Commissioner for Palestine, Sir Herbert Samuel; the military commander, Lord Edmund Allenby; and the military governors of Haifa and Jerusalem, Colonel Staunton and General Ronald Storrs, respectively. This role gave him considerable influence, especially considering that at the time British authorities in the area had no clear plan. As Allenby himself wrote, "I haven't the foggiest idea what is going to be the future of the Near East. Anything may happen ... All nations and would-be nations, and all shades of religion and politics are up against each other, and trying to get me to commit myself on their side ... there is need to walk warily."[214]

'Abdu'l-Bahá's counsel was sought by "all the important military personages in Palestine ... to say nothing of a constant flow of officers and men who call upon him daily."²¹⁵ Samuel revered him greatly, and Storrs, who had travelled to Haifa wishing him well on behalf of Britannia, filled a number of government posts based on 'Abdu'l-Bahá's recommendations.²¹⁶ Staunton was a "firm friend" and promised to do all he could for 'Abdu'l-Bahá and his spiritual movement. It was Allenby, however, who recommended that 'Abdu'l-Bahá should be knighted for his service to the British administration; the knighting ceremony was held in Haifa in 1920 (Figure 1.4), and while that ritual conferred upon him the right to use "Sir" before his name and KBE after it, for Knight Commander of the Most Excellent Order of the British Empire, he continued to call himself 'Abdu'l Bahá, or servant of Bahá, for he received knighthood just as he had accepted a gold medal from George V, not as a change in status but, rather, as "'a gift from a just king.'"²¹⁷

While the First World War and the expanding reach of the British imperial state into Palestine created the social and political circumstances which made the new relationships between 'Abdu'l Bahá and representatives of His Majesty's government possible, the historical context alone cannot explain why 'Abdu'l Bahá took the actions that he did. After all,

Figure 1.4 'Abdu'l Bahá's knighting ceremony, Haifa, 1920.

both he and his father had spent most of their lives defying governments, first in Iran and then in the Ottoman Empire, and suffered decades of exile and imprisonment as a result. His decision to be of assistance to the British authorities at the age of 73, just four years before his death, cannot be explained simply by the fact that they held power in the region. Rather, 'Abdu'l Bahá had, over the course of his life, found common ground between his own convictions as a Bahá'í and certain aspects of the British Empire. He had great respect for British liberal, democratic ideals and appreciated the empire's multicultural character and global scope, which facilitated exchanges between East and West and encouraged the spread of modern technological developments. While he was aware of and repeatedly criticized the injustices that the empire perpetuated, such as gross inequalities, exploitation and racism, he nevertheless found enough overlap between it and core or canonical Bahá'í principles to create an *intersectional imperial ideology* or system of meaning which allowed him to develop new relationships with British officers and administrators stationed in Palestine.

In addition, he understood that through these relationships he could have an influence on leaders within, and thus on the culture of the British Empire, for he did not hesitate to share Bahá'í teachings with those whom he met and, interestingly, he seems to a struck a chord with Allenby. The latter asked for Bahá'í literature, which the former provided, and the two men would meet for long, private discussions.[218] While serving as High Commissioner in Egypt, both he and Lady Allenby travelled to Haifa and spent New Year's Day with the spiritual leader. 'Abdu'l-Bahá took the couple to Acre, where the holy family had been imprisoned, and to the Shrine of Bahá'u'lláh at Bahji.[219] The visit to Bahji would have been especially intimate, as it is a quiet place, off the beaten path, and for Bahá'ís the most sacred spot on earth.[220]

Interestingly, Allenby's speeches, both in terms of the ideas presented and the phrases used, began to bear a striking resemblance to the words of Bahá'u'lláh and 'Abdu'l-Bahá.[221] For example, in one public ceremony held in Jerusalem in 1920, Allenby not only criticized war and the narrowness of nationalism but stressed the need, for "all peoples of the earth" to unite in order to work towards peace, harmony and "perpetual amity."[222] Certainly these statements reflected the general war-weariness of the time. Still, it is surprising that they would come from someone who willingly dedicated much of his life to the military, who was known to his troops as "the Bull" and who was celebrated for his successes as a commander and general, leading soldiers into battle in South Africa, Europe and the Middle East. One fellow officer stationed in Cairo, General Archibald Wavell, commented on how the theme of "longing for peace" seemed to appear in all Allenby's later Jerusalem addresses.[223] At the inauguration of the new buildings for the Jerusalem branch of the Young Men's Christian Association, Allenby spoke of promoting better understanding among Christians, Muslims and Jews and how the work of that organization would be "interracial, interfaith; without distinction of country or creed" and "in the interests and for the benefit of both sexes," ideas which reflect core Bahá'í principles.[224]

'Abdu'l-Bahá's practice of discussing Bahá'í beliefs with British officials, even when to do so meant introducing sensitive or controversial topics, began before the war. As one pilgrim letter from June 1914 related, just a few minutes into conversation with the commander and general of the British forces in Damascus, 'Abdu'l-Bahá voiced his support for female emancipation. He praised the Blomfields for their contribution to the women's suffrage movement in England and even produced the article about them from the *Daily Sketch* for the general to see. 'Abdu'l-Bahá's guest had no choice but to admire Mary Blomfield's "pluck and energy" in making an appeal to the king on behalf of the hunger-striking suffragettes.[225] This exchange is significant, for the dominant British imperialist discourses regarded the Eastern man as not only an obstacle to female emancipation – particularly if he had any religious orientation or connection to Islam – but a primary cause of the hardships and injustices women experienced.[226] Yet, in this case it was the bearded, turbaned man from Shia-dominated Iran who allied himself with English feminists in the face of British officials who, as a group, tended to be indifferent if not hostile to their cause.[227]

'Abdu'l-Bahá's influence over British officials and their willingness to listen to him and engage with his belief system had much to do with the mutual respect that existed, and continued to develop over the years, between the spiritual leader and representatives of His Majesty's government in the Middle East, for just as 'Abdu'l-Bahá was honoured with knighthood and sought as an advisor, he, in turn, held the British administration in high esteem, expressing admiration for its ability to promote justice and harmony in Palestine while at the same time "modernizing" and "developing" the country. He spoke of the contributions that the new "enlightened government" made in the realms of industry, commerce and agriculture and compared British rule favourably with that of the former Ottoman Empire, even likening the people of Palestine to lost sheep who had finally found a shepherd.[228] 'Abdu'l-Bahá's intersectional imperial ideology expanded to include Palestine along with Egypt, India and other parts of the world that he believed benefited from British rule. Along the same lines, one of 'Abdu'l-Bahá's most influential followers, Mirza Ahmad Sohrab, explained that not only had the British administration brought progress to the region in the form of law, education and equal opportunity, but under its continued rule Palestine would evolve to a "higher altitude of modern civilization": natural resources would be developed, new production methods would be introduced and even the "liberation of the soul" from racial and religious prejudices could be realized.[229]

In the following year Ahmad Sohrab wrote a letter published in the *SoW* which extended his praise of British rule into Egypt as well. He reported the people of the country as laughing, making money and enjoying life and described the scenery from the train on his way to Cairo as green with fertile fields. By preceding these comments with mention of soldiers and Kantara, the city of army tents which had served as a base for the Egyptian Expeditionary Force during the war, Sohrab's choice of words served to associate abundance and security with the British military presence. In fact, he noted that the local Arabic publication *Mokattam* reported how Egypt had profited from the war. He then went on to relate his experiences in Cairo in a way that presented that city as benefiting from Western influences: he stayed in the elegant Eden Palace, designed in the style of the grand European hotels, rode in carriages through the parks and enjoyed strolling along the "brilliantly lighted and crowded thoroughfares."[230]

This image of a pleasant and thriving metropolis illuminated with electricity sounds very much like the vision that 'Abdu'l-Bahá had for the Bahá'í holy places in Palestine.

In 1914 'Abdu'l-Bahá had stood on Mount Carmel and looked across the Bay of Haifa towards Acre and the nearby tomb of Bahá'u'lláh and envisioned a day when the two cities would be linked by "one mighty metropolis," with wonderful gardens, modern buildings, industries and even electricity that would illuminate the harbour and guide ships arriving from all nations. Men and women would be able to visit from "every part of the globe" and travel easily from one holy site to another.[231] Soon after the occupation of Haifa in 1918, the new British administration put policies into action that seemed almost as if they were designed to further this vision. As Tudor Pole observed, by the following year they had begun working on a railway between Haifa and Acre, improving the water supply and drainage systems in both places and erecting new buildings. In addition, they pledged to spend two million pounds to turn Haifa into a major Mediterranean port.[232]

Yet, even more important than these economic developments for the future of the Bahá'ís in the world was British support for 'Abdu'l-Bahá and his followers in their efforts to turn Haifa into an international spiritual and administrative base during the Mandate period; for the creation of the Bahá'í World Centre, which would become a place of pilgrimage visited by millions, was a critical step in the development of a global faith and a turning point for the Bahá'ís with respect to their status. They went from being regarded as a small, obscure sect of Shia Islam experiencing intermittent persecution at the hands of both the general population and the government, first in Iran and then in the Ottoman Empire, to experiencing protection under the British in a land considered holy by millions, Muslims, Christians and Jews.

In addition, as a result of British involvement in what might be considered internal Bahá'í political matters, 'Abdu'l-Bahá's grandson and handpicked successor, Shoghi Effendi, gained sole guardianship of the Bahá'í buildings and holy places in the Haifa–Acre area in 1929. The decision to intervene resulted, in part, from repeated representations made to the British government by both the Bahá'ís of London and Tudor Pole; for 'Abdu'l-Bahá's younger half-brother, Mirza Muhammad-'Ali, led a rival faction intent on assuming leadership of the emerging world religion, and his earlier efforts to convince the Ottoman authorities that his older sibling plotted against that government had led to a period of increased confinement and supervision for 'Abdu'l-Bahá.[233] When the latter died, Mirza Muhammad-'Ali made use of the local Arabic papers to appeal to Bahá'ís in Egypt and Palestine for support.[234] He, not Shoghi Effendi, had possession of the Shrine of Bahá'u'lláh, and only relinquished the keys upon the insistence of the British officer stationed in Acre at the time.[235] Had it not been for the British–Bahá'í networks in the Middle East and Great Britain and British sympathies with 'Abdu'l-Bahá and his movement, both of which developed over the course of the first decades of the twentieth century and as the result of efforts to forge new relationships based on the creation of intersectional imperial ideologies from the common ground shared by the Bahá'í belief system and British imperial culture, what eventually emerged as a major global religion would never have developed along the trajectory that it did.

Conclusion

From the turn of the century until shortly after the First World War the Bahá'ís went from what would appear to be a precarious existence as members of a little-known and often misunderstood religious minority, enduring varying degrees of persecution in Iran and the Ottoman Empire, to gaining international recognition and a secure base in Haifa roughly twenty miles away from the place where 'Abdu'l-Bahá had spent decades imprisoned. The changing political and social circumstances brought about by the war, particularly the demise of the Ottoman Empire and the expansion of the British army and government into the Middle East, provided the necessary support for the development of British–Bahá'í networks and the intersectional imperial ideologies that made them possible. These new bonds were characterized by hybridity both because they continually crossed the fictive boundaries between East and West by connecting people of the British Isles, primarily England, with those of Palestine and, to a lesser extent, Egypt, and because they depended upon systems of meaning comprised of both Oriental and Occidental elements.

This web of British–Bahá'í relationships began with a single strand or link between two people who would seem to have had little in common: Ethel Jenner Rosenberg, an Englishwoman and portrait painter in London, and 'Abdu'l-Bahá, a man of Iranian descent imprisoned in Ottoman Palestine. Rosenberg visited him on more than one occasion in search of spiritual truth and, in the process, formed a strong bond with him and members of his family. She began to see herself as part of a spiritual movement which connected her to Bahá'ís from throughout the world and invested her, as the only English person in the gathering, with the responsibility of sharing his teachings and those of his father, Bahá'u'lláh, with as many people as possible in her home country. Her decision to look to the East or to this prisoner in Acre for guidance should be understood as showing extraordinary initiative or agency on her part, for, however commonplace it might have been for single, middle-class women of the late Victorian and early Edwardian eras to involve themselves in spiritual or religious movements, including ones that were considered Eastern or outside of the mainstream such as Spiritualism or Theosophy, the steps that Rosenberg took would have been considered beyond the pale and not without risk.

Rosenberg, as well as the others in the British imperial metropole, particularly the London and Manchester areas, who became Bahá'ís, looked to the East for spiritual guidance and inspiration, working creatively to reconcile new teachings with their own cultural repertoire of values and practices, in part because they found a kind of reciprocity in the form of Easterners interested in them as well. As 'Abdu'l-Bahá told a crowd in London, East and West were like long lost lovers who had found each other. The union of Occident and Orient, and indeed all of mankind, was a central tenet of the teachings of Bahá'u'lláh, and while this position might appear to be simply a logical response to increasing Western influence and expansion, especially given that a number of nineteenth- and early twentieth-century intellectuals from Muslim backgrounds sought reconciliation between liberalism and Islam,[236] it also had the potential of alienating those influenced by growing anti-Western sentiment. After all political-religious movements of the late nineteenth and early twentieth centuries, from South Asia to the Middle East and West Africa, united people around the idea that Western influences brought moral corruption and decay. 'Abdu'l-Bahá's decision to travel to London, the very heart of the metropole of the British Empire, for the purpose of sharing his father's teachings with all who would listen and welcoming Western followers as fellow Bahá'ís was no less extraordinary in terms of agency than was Rosenberg's initial journey to find him in Acre.

When 'Abdu'l-Bahá first arrived in England in 1911, he discovered a network of British Bahá'ís who coordinated their efforts in order to ensure the success of his stay by hosting him and making the necessary arrangements so that he would be able to address crowds of thousands and meet people of influence, as well as others from all walks of life. Lady Blomfield was instrumental in this respect, opening her home and employing her extensive connections, spiritual, humanitarian, feminist and liberal. The people in Great Britain who either identified themselves as Bahá'ís or lent their support to that movement came from a variety of backgrounds, occupations and belief systems. Other than initial exposure, no single predisposing factor determined who would find meaning in this particular ideology and who would not. For example, while some Christians welcomed 'Abdu'l-Bahá to their homes or to speak in their places of worship, others regarded him with hostility and treated his message as a threat to their values and way of life. In addition, given that the man from the East or Islamic world, especially a religious one with a beard and a turban, had become a standard trope in English culture and society representing all that was backwards or barbaric with regard to gender relationships, the fact that alliances and bonds of mutual respect developed between Abdu'l-Bahá and English suffragists is remarkable in and of itself.

Prior to the First World War neither the Bahá'ís in England nor those in the Middle East could have predicted the relationships that would develop between Abdu'l-Bahá and representatives of His Majesty's government. Yet, as British military forces expanded into and occupied Palestine in the course of the conflict, both the religious leader and the country's new rulers found that they could be of assistance to one another. The system of meaning that allowed them to work together initially, expanded and evolved over the years as mutual respect continued to grow between them. 'Abdu'l-Bahá and Lord Allenby shared a particularly close bond, the former acting as a trusted advisor to the latter as well as to a number of other British officials in the area. The British government, in turn, showed its appreciation by honouring 'Abdu'l-Bahá with a knighthood and ensuring that his grandson and chosen successor, Shoghi Effendi, would assume responsibility for the Bahá'í holy places in Haifa and Acre, not 'Abdu'l-Bahá's half-brother and rival, Mirza Muhammad-'Ali. As this conflict suggests, the British did not enter a politically neutral area but, rather, a region with rival factions and interests or, as Allenby put it, "all shades" of religion and politics each vying for a commitment of support; developing an alliance with one often meant making enemies with another.

British officials who collaborated with or sought the advice of 'Abdu'l-Bahá chose to do so with the full understanding that other options and alternative courses of action were available to them. After all, 'Abdu'l-Bahá had enemies and rivals, not only his own half-brother Mirza Muhammad-'Ali and his supporters in Palestine, but also his father's half-brother Subh-i Azal, who lived in Cyprus until 1912, and his followers, the Azalis; for in 1868 when the Ottoman authorities exiled the Bahá'ís to the prison city of Acre, they sent the Azalis to confinement on the eastern coast of Cyprus. Ten years later, Cyprus fell under the control of Her Majesty's government, and these former Ottoman prisoners became British pensioners. Thus, by the time of the British occupation of Palestine at least two factions or movements, both within the realm of British rule, had already challenged 'Abdu'l-Bahá's authority as a spiritual leader, each with their own version of history and plans for the future. Such circumstances allowed for a variety of courses of action on the part of officialdom, which would have been understood, especially by the more seasoned among them.

These relationships characterized by East–West hybridity that shaped both the Bahá'í and the British experience in Palestine might never have developed in the first place had it not been for the intelligence officer and admirer of 'Abdu'l-Bahá, Wellesley Tudor Pole. From his posting in Cairo, Tudor Pole alerted the Bahá'ís in England to the dangers facing their leader during the First World War when communication between these two communities had come almost to a grinding halt. He then continued to act as a liaison between the Bahá'ís and British officialdom, both in England and in the Middle East. If we continue to use the web analogy, Tudor Pole became, for a short time, a kind of hub, re-linking networks between religious communities that had been severed by the war, until they could repair themselves, and creating new connections between expanding webs of officialdom and Bahá'í leaders. As with the other historical characters examined in this chapter, Tudor Pole may have had the support of social circumstances, the most obvious being his position in the Middle East, but these did not determine his actions. In fact, his most significant undertaking with regard to these British–Bahá'í networks, sending the initial letter to London concerning the welfare of 'Abdu'l-Bahá, was done covertly, with the sanction of neither his superiors nor the censors, a move which could have had serious consequences for his life and career.

Tudor Pole's intervention during a critical moment in the history of the Bahá'í movement reflects the position of Egypt more generally in the British–Bahá'í networks of the early twentieth century, for while England and Palestine may have been the two most important centres of activity, Egypt acted as both a gateway and a meeting place for Bahá'ís from East and West. 'Abdu'l-Bahá spent time there as well, and that country served as an example of what he and his followers considered to be the positive aspects of British rule: economic development and religious toleration. The latter proved to be especially important, as Bahá'ís experiencing or in danger of persecution in Iran or the Ottoman Empire found refuge in Port Said, where they could rely upon protection, even from mobs of angry Egyptians. As in the case of Palestine, the British officials stationed in Egypt realized that their actions did not take place in a neutral environment and that their choice to intervene on the side of the Bahá'ís, when the Egyptian courts had chosen to turn a blind eye to the matter, would antagonize the influential local sheikh who had aroused the mob in the first place, and most likely others as well.

These various British–Bahá'í' networks and alliances whether in Egypt, Palestine, England or connecting all three came into being as the result of individuals, from both East and West, who created as well as found meaning in the intersections between the tenets of this growing spiritual and religious movement, on the one hand, and British ideals, usually those associated with liberalism, on the other. Religious toleration; support for the growth of democracy, including the women's suffrage movement; and the importance of social justice; all served as places of common ground for mutual appreciation and identification upon which new imperial intersectional ideologies were formed, thus making the previously described actions possible.

In addition, the written word or print culture was valued highly in both Bahá'í and British traditions. It tended to be associated with freedom of the press in the context of liberal movements, in both East and West. In its loftier forms it became a mark of civilization and refinement, and in the Persian Bahá'í context, spiritual truth as well. Its pursuit proved to be of great practical use and a real passion for the leaders and others involved in this new movement. It kept the Bahá'ís in England and the Middle East connected with each other, their spiritual leader and the progress of the cause, primarily through correspondence and the *SoW*. 'Abdu'l-Bahá was a prolific writer, like his father before him, Bahá'u'lláh, and translations of their materials such as books, speeches and even letters served as the foundation for the Bahá'í belief system. English-speaking followers read and discussed these works, and some studied Persian as well. Finally, new believers produced their own notes, articles, pamphlets, poems and other literature for the benefit of the British Bahá'í community and others interested in or attracted to it.

In addition to the appreciation of print culture and other values associated with liberalism, the empire itself provided opportunities for historical actors to find harmony between Bahá'í beliefs and British traditions. 'Abdu'l-Bahá expressed a tempered admiration for it, particularly its ability to bring together people from different parts of the world and at times even to foster a sense of unity among them. He regarded the nationalist movements within it, whether in India or Egypt, in the same way that he viewed the nationalism that drove the arms race in pre-First World War Europe, as dangerous and divisive, obscuring the essential truths that could be found only through recognizing a common humanity. The empire, in contrast, was multinational as well as multicultural and multireligious. Even the British campaign in Palestine created opportunities for Bahá'ís there, some of whom had never left the area, to meet and befriend people from distant parts of the world, such as the Black British soldiers from the West Indies mentioned by Mirza Ahmad Sohrab. 'Abdu'l-Bahá was not blind to racism, nor to the other injustices and inequalities perpetuated by the British Empire such as exploitation of the poor, about which he spoke on a number of occasions; but, like other religious leaders, humanitarians and activists of the time, he believed in the potential for reform within and of the imperial system. In other words, the existing structures and networks need not be dismantled, at least not in the immediate future, in order for progress to take place, but instead could be employed in an effort to improve the human condition.

Discussion of the areas of overlap between British culture and the beliefs of this growing movement and the intersectional imperial ideology that developed as a result would not be complete without mention of the ways that Bahá'ís from both East and West found meaning in Orientalist ideologies. Common assumptions about the spirituality of Eastern lands and the tradition of journeying to them in search of enlightenment provided familiar context for pilgrims from the British Isles who decided to travel to Acre. Even those who stayed at home could imagine their spiritual leader uttering profound words under the "Syrian sunshine" in a land where palm trees swayed in the breeze, as in Edward Hall's poem. English Bahá'ís sometimes incorporated Iranian or Persian styles into their dress and Iranian traditions of hospitality into their social events. While Bahá'ís in the British Isles turned to the East for spiritual guidance, 'Abdu'l-Bahá praised the practical or material influences that British expansion brought to Egypt and Palestine in the form of economic investments, technology and improvements in transportation. Even occupation was described as liberating and bringing a higher level of civilization to the people of the region. As Easterners and Westerners looked to each other, both the movement and the individuals who comprised it became increasingly hybridized.

Yet, while the Bahá'ís may have found meaning in Orientalist discourses, including the dichotomy between a spiritual East and a material West, they understood the former as far more important than the vast majority of imperialists ever would have considered. Far from being a lack or absence of initiative, they regarded spirituality a necessity to human existence. The imbalances caused by decades of technological progress and industrial development in the face of spiritual stagnation had taken a heavy toll on the health of the human race. In the words of Bahá'u'lláh,

> The All-Knowing Physician hath His finger on the pulse of mankind ... We can well perceive how the whole human race is encompassed with great, with incalculable afflictions. We see it languishing on its bed of sickness, sore-tried and disillusioned. They that are intoxicated by self-conceit have interposed themselves between it and the Divine and infallible Physician.[237]

The belief that Bahá'u'lláh's message was the divine prescription sent from God for the purpose of healing the ills that afflicted all of humankind meant that, despite the mutual identification, common ground and numerous accomplishments that characterized the British–Bahá'í networks of the early twentieth century, that spiritual movement never could be contained in its entirety within the ideological and cultural framework of the British imperial system, any more than that empire was limited to furthering the Bahá'í cause. People from England and other parts of the British Isles may have found meaning in the Bahá'í teachings and discovered a number of ways to reconcile previous traditions and beliefs with new ones, and 'Abdu'l-Bahá and his followers in Egypt or Palestine may have recognized some of their own values reflected in the ideals of British liberalism, the scope of the empire and the actions of certain representatives of the British government and chosen to focus and elaborate on those places of overlap, creating intersectional imperial ideologies, yet neither the Western nor the Eastern Bahá'ís would have regarded the points of convergence between their spiritual path and that imperial system as an end in and of itself.

Notes

1 Shoghi Effendi, *God Passes By* (Wilmette, IL: Bahá'í Publishing Trust), 1944, 279–80.
2 *'Abdu'l-Bahá in London: Addresses and Notes of Conversations* (London: Unity Press, 1912), 53. Afnan Library, Sandy, Bedfordshire, England.
3 One contemporary estimated that two thousand were in attendance. Last page of "'Abdu'l-Bahá in Britain," under the subdivision "(Isabel Fraser in 'Everywoman,' Dec./Jan. 1915/16)," B10 in the archives held at the United Kingdom's National Bahá'í Centre, Rutland Gate, London (henceforth UKNBC). Another reported three thousand. Robert Weinberg, *Ethel Jenner Rosenberg: The Life and Times of England's Outstanding Bahá'í Pioneer Worker* (Oxford: George Ronald, 1995), 136.
4 "'Abdu'l-Bahá's first address in the West," City Temple, London, 1911, B11, UKNBC.

5 "Private Memorandum," notes by Wellesley Tudor Pole on the passing of 'Abdu'l-Bahá, London, Dec. 5, 1921, 5. Major Tudor Pole folder, UKNBC. Also see Brendan McNamara, *The Reception of 'Abdu'l-Bahá in Britain: East Comes West* (The Netherlands: Brill), 2021.

6 Peter Smith, "Part One: The Bábí Religion, 1844–53," *A Short History of the Bahá'í Faith* (Oxford: Oneworld Publications, 1997), 13–47.

7 This estimate comes from Smith, *Short History*, 89.

8 For a detailed discussion of the activities of the Báb and his followers see *The Dawn-breakers: Nabil's Narrative of the Early Days of the Bahá'í Revelation*, translated from the original Persian and edited by Shoghi Effendi (Wilmette, IL: Bahá'í Publishing Trust, 1970). Also see Abbas Amanat, *Resurrection and Renewal: The Making of the Bábí Movement in Iran, 1844–1850* (Ithaca and London: Cornell University Press, 1989); Hasan Balyuzi, *The Báb: The Herald of the Day of Days* (Oxford: George Ronald, 1973); *A Traveler's Narrative: Written to Illustrate the Episode of the Báb by 'Abdu'l-Bahá (nee Abbas Effendi)*, translated by Edward G. Browne and first published in 1891 (London: Cambridge University Press, 1975); and S. Effendi, "First Period Ministry of the Bab 1844–1853," in *God Passes By* (Wilmette, IL: Bahá'í Publishing Trust, 1971), 3–88.

9 Robert Stockman estimates that by the 1870s roughly 90 per cent of Bábís had become Bahá'ís. *The Bahá'í Faith: A Guide for the Perplexed* (London: Bloomsbury Academic Press, 2013), 100.

10 Stockman, *Guide for the Perplexed*, 101.

11 According to Eunice Braun, some of his followers who had not been sentenced to Acre even approached the Ottoman authorities offering to pay all transportation costs if they could allowed to accompany their leader. Braun, *A Crown of Beauty: The Bahá'í Faith in the Holy Land* (Oxford: George Ronald, 1982), 57. For reference to or discussion of these developments, see Smith, *Short History*, 58–62, 92; S. Effendi, *God Passes By*, 197–8; and David Ruhe, *Door of Hope: The Bahá'í Faith in the Holy Land* (Oxford: George Ronald, 1983), 29, 73.

12 The 100,000 estimate is from Smith, *Short History*, 89. He also gives an overview of the spread of Bahá'í beliefs during Bahá'u'lláh's lifetime, which in addition to Iran and the Ottoman Empire included India, Burma, Russian Turkistan and Caucasia, 92–4. Stockman relates that it had spread to Indonesia and China as well, *Guide for the Perplexed*, 102.

13 Smith, "Bahá'u'lláh" and "The writings and teachings of Bahá'u'lláh," *A Short History*, 51–73 and Shoghi Effendi, "Second Period: The Ministry of Bahá'u'lláh 1853–1892," S. Effendi, *God Passes By*, 89–234. See also Hasan Balyuzi, *Bahá'u'lláh the King of Glory* (Oxford: George Ronald, 1980).

14 Bahá'u'lláh, *The Summons of the Lord of Hosts* (Bahá'í World Centre: Haifa, Israel, 2002), 88–95. The quotation is from Bahá'u'lláh's grandson, Shoghi Effendi, *God Passes By*, 211. The first use of the phrase "Mother of Parliaments" is usually attributed to the British statesman John Bright.

15 Juan Cole, *Modernity and the Millennium: The Genesis of the Bahá'í Faith in the Nineteenth-century Middle East* (New York: Columbia University Press, 1998), 76.
16 Necati Alkan, *Dissent and Heterodoxy in the late Ottoman Empire: Reformers, Bábís, and Bahá'ís* (Istanbul: The Isis Press, 2008), 22 and 222. Also see Alkan's "The Young Turks and the Bahá'ís in Palestine," in *Late Ottoman Palestine: The Period of Young Turk Rule*, edited by Yuval Ben-Bassat and Eyal Ginio (London: I.B. Tauris, 2011), 259–278.
17 Momen, *The Bábí and Bahá'í Religions*, 257. Also see, *Stories from the Delight of Hearts: The Memoirs of Haji Mirza Haydar-'Ali*, translated by A.Q. Faizi (Los Angeles: Kalimat Press, 1980), first published in Persian in Bombay in 1913.
18 Smith, *Short History*, 92. While one Bahá'í was sent to the Sudan in 1888, in general the community prospered. Juan Cole, "Rashid Rida on the Bahá'í Faith: A Utilitarian Theory of the Spread of Religions," *Arab Studies Quarterly* (Summer 1983), 276–91. In addition, British authorities would come to the aid of persecuted Bahá'ís in Egypt in the early twentieth century, as will be discussed later in the chapter.
19 This story and these observations were related by the American Bahá'í Sydney Sprague in his *A Year with the Bahá'ís in India and Burma* (London: Priory Press, 1908), 16, 27–8 and 34, quotation at p. 28.
20 Bombay was, in fact, a centre for Muslim print culture. K. Humayun Ansari, "Pickthall, Muslims of South Asia, and the British Muslim Community of the Early 1900s," in *Marmaduke Pickthall: Islam and the Modern World*, edited by Geoffrey Nash (Leiden: Brill, 2017), 13.
21 Hasan Balyuzi, "The Nobleman of Tunukabun Conqueror of India," *Eminent Bahá'ís in the Time of Bahá'u'lláh* (Oxford: George Ronald, 1985), especially 120–4 and Peter Smith, *Bábí and Bahá'í Religions: From Messianic Shi'ism to a World Religion* (Cambridge: Cambridge University Press, 1987), 193.
22 Also see William Garlington, "The Bahá'í Faith in India: A Developmental Stage Approach," *Occasional Papers in Shaykhi, Bábí and Bahá'í Studies*, vol. 2, 1997 (www.h-net.org/~bahai/bhpapers/india1.htm) and Smith, *Short History*, 92–3.
23 The first Bahá'í temple or house of worship in the world was built in this city in 1907.
24 For reference to and discussion of the spread of Bahá'ís into these areas of the Russian Empire see, S. Effendi, *God Passes By*, 195; Smith, *Short History*, 89, 93–4; Graham Hassall, "Notes on the Babi and Bahá'í Religions in Russia and Its Territories," *Journal of Bahá'í Studies*, Vol. 5, No. 3, 41–80, 1993; and *The Bahá'ís of Iran, Transcaspia and the Caucasus*, vol. 1, edited by Soli Shauar (London: IB Tauris, 2011).
25 S. Effendi, *God Passes By*, 193–5, quotation at p. 195. Also see Ruhe, *Door of Hope*, 49.
26 Ruhe, *Door of Hope*, in the Acre area 103, 104, 120, 209 and in the Jordan Valley 53, 208; "at Bahá'u'lláh's bidding," S. Effendi, *God Passes By*, 194.
27 S. Effendi, *God Passes By*, 193, 242.

28 Juan Cole, "Globalization and Religion in the Thought of 'Abdu'l-Bahá," in *Bahá'í and Globalisation*, edited by Margit Warburg, Annika Hvithamar and Morten Warmind (Denmark: Aarhus University Press, 2005), 55–76.
29 S. Effendi, *God Passes By*, 193, 242. In addition, Abbas Effendi had much in common with the progressive Turkish intellectuals Namik Kemal and Ziya Pasha, both of whom supported and recommended him to Midhat Pasha. See Necati Alkan, "Midhat Pasha and 'Abdu'l-Baha in 'Akka," *Bahá'í Studies Review*, vol. 13, 2005, 1–13, reference at p. 9–10.
30 Ruhe, *Door of Hope*, 51 quotation at p. 52.
31 S. Effendi, *God Passes By*, 195.
32 Ruhe, *Door of Hope*, 41, 56.
33 Ruhe, *Door of Hope*, 45, 62.
34 Ruhe, *Door of Hope*, 55, from *A Traveler's Narrative*, ed. Browne, Vol. II, xx, vi.
35 Browne, quoted in *Traveler's Narrative*, ed. Browne, Vol. II, xxxix–xl. For more on Browne's relationship with the Bábís and Bahá'ís see Hasan Balyuzi, *Edward Granville Browne and the Bahá'í Faith* (London: George Ronald, 1970) and *Selections from the Writings of E.G. Browne on the Bábí and Bahá'í Religions*, edited by Moojan Momen (London: George Ronald, 1987).
36 Alessandro Bausani, *Religion in Iran from Zoroaster to Bahá'u'lláh* (New York: Bibliotheca Persica Press, 2000), 394.
37 Smith, "'Abdu'l-Bahá," in *Short History*, 74–87; S. Effendi, "Third Period: The Ministry of 'Abdu'l-Bahá 1892–1921," *God Passes By*, 235–320. See also, H. Balyuzi, *'Abdu'l-Bahá: The Centre of the Covenant of Bahá'u'lláh* (London: George Ronald, 1971). The reference to his neighbours' perception of him in Acre is from Smith, "'Abdu'l-Bahá", 74–6.
38 Over the course of the twentieth century the Azali movement would decline to the point of being forgotten almost completely. William Miller, "The Vice Regency of Subh-i-Azal" and "The Schism between Two Brothers," *What Is the Bahá'í Faith* (Grand Rapids, MI: William Eerdman, 1977), 32–47.
39 Smith, *Short History*, 86–7.
40 Stressing the essentially independent nature of the Bahá'í Faith has become a point of no small importance to many modern Bahá'ís and Bahá'í scholars. As the introduction to William Hatcher and Douglas Martin's book explains, "The new faith is a distinct religion, based entirely on the teachings of its founder, Bahá'u'lláh. It is not a cult, a reform movement or sect within any other faith, nor merely a philosophical system. Neither does it represent an attempt to create a new religion syncretistically by bringing together different teachings chosen from other religions." Hatcher and Martin, *The Bahá'í Faith: The Emerging Global Religion* (Wilmette, IL: Bahá'í Publishing Trust, 2002), xxxiii.
41 Phillip Smith makes many of these same points in his explanation as to why in the beginning of the Bahá'í Faith in Great Britain, it resembled a millenarian movement more closely than it did an independent religion. "The Development and Influence of the Bahá'í Administrative Order in Great

Britain, 1914–1950," *Community Histories: Studies in the Bábí and Bahá'í Religions*, Vol. 6, edited by Anthony Lee and Richard Hollinger (Los Angeles: Kalimat Press, 1992), 153 and 161.
42 Smith, "Development," *Community Histories*. The quotation is on page 163. However, the entire essay traces what Smith describes as the transformation from an inclusive Bahá'í movement to an exclusive Bahá'í religion, 153–211.
43 Smith, *Bábí and Bahá'í Religions*, 170 and Smith, *Short History*, 10. The fact that modern Bahá'ís come from many different ethnic backgrounds and more than two hundred countries is often noted by both Bahá'ís and Bahá'í scholars. For example, Youli Ioannesyan, *The Development of the Bábí and Bahá'í Communities: Exploring Baron Rosen's Archives* (London and New York: Routledge, 2013), 1.
44 Cole, *Modernity and the Millennium*, 13–14.
45 Ibrahim Kheirella, a Syrian of Christian background who had become a Bahá'í in Cairo, moved to Chicago where, during the mid-1890s, he began to teach classes about his new belief system, reaching hundreds in the Chicago-Kenosha, Wisconsin area. One of his students, Louisa Getsinger, then travelled throughout the US in an effort to further spread these teachings. It was Getsinger who first spoke of 'Abdu'l-Bahá to Hearst. Weinberg, *Ethel Jenner Rosenberg*, 35; Hatcher and Martin, *Emerging Global Religion*, 52, 54; S. Effendi, *God Passes By*, 256–7; Smith, *Short History*, 95. Kheirella's version of the Bahá'í teachings later was rejected by 'Abdu'l-Bahá. For more on Kheirella see L.C.G. Abdo, "Religion and Relevance: The Bahá'ís in Britain 1899–1930," PhD thesis, SOAS, University of London, 2003, 40–3. This thesis was published as Lil Osborn, *Religion and Relevance: The Bahá'ís in Britain, 1899–1930* (Los Angeles: Kalimat Press, 2014).
46 While often Thomas Breakwell is regarded as the first English Bahá'í, he could not have discovered the teachings until the summer of 1901. Abdo, "Religion and Relevance," 86.
47 Weinberg, *Rosenberg*, 29–40, 47, 75 and O.Z. Whitehead, *Some Bahá'ís to Remember* (George Ronald: Oxford, 1983), 17–20. Phillip Smith describes her as the "dominant personality and unofficial leader" of the British Bahá'ís in the early years, "Development and Influence," 155. Also see Osborn, *Religion and Relevance*.
48 May Ellis Maxwell, detailed biography published in *A Compendium of Volumes of the Bahá'í World, I–XII, 1925–1954*, ed. Roger White, compiled on behalf of the Universal House of Justice, Haifa, Israel, 516–28. Also see May Maxwell (nee Bolles), *An Early Pilgrimage* (Welwyn, UK: George Ronald 1969).
49 Weinberg, *Rosenberg*, 87.
50 While there was and continues to be speculation that Rosenberg was of Jewish descent, her great grandparents were married in Bath Abbey and had their children christened in the Church of England. Weinberg, *Rosenberg*, 6.
51 Weinberg, *Rosenberg*, 47–58, 64, 73–7, quotation at p. 77.
52 Rosenberg's notes from Acre, 29 April 1904, UKNBC.

53 Weinberg, *Rosenberg*, 56, 65–6 and 71. "Firm and steadfast leaf" comes from a translation of an unpublished Tablet (letter) from 'Abdu'l-Bahá to Rosenberg, housed in the Research Department, Bahá'í World Centre, Haifa, Israel (henceforth BWC). As Weinberg notes, pp. 71 and 295, this translation has not been approved officially by the current Bahá'í administration.
54 Weinberg, *Rosenberg*, 55–7 and Whitehead, *Some Bahá'ís*, 19.
55 Weinberg, *Rosenberg*, 65–6.
56 Weinberg, *Rosenberg*, 64–6, 69–71, 78–82.
57 Another unpublished Tablet (letter) from 'Abdu'l-Bahá to Ethel Rosenberg, BWC. Unlike the previous one, the translation of this letter was, as Weinberg notes, "authorized," *Rosenberg*, 81 and 296.
58 London: Kegan Paul, Trench, Trubner & Co Ltd.
59 "Sitarih Khánum (Sara, Lady Blomfield), a brief account of her life and work by her daughter, Mary Basil Hall," 1939, 96, UKNBC. The story of Lady Blomfield's encounter with the Bahá'í Movement is recounted in the beginning of her *The Chosen Highway* (Wilmette Illinois: Bahá'í Publishing Trust, 1940), first pages. Also see Weinberg, *Rosenberg*, 87–8, 91–3, 95–6.
60 For four generations the Rosenbergs of Bath had made careers from rendering the likeness of aristocrats and royals. For an overview of this family's artistic accomplishments over the course of four generations see "The Rosenbergs of Bath," 1–13. Quotation at p. 27. Weinberg notes her financial success and her "circle of rich and influential friends" (p. 28) and the galleries where she exhibited as including the Royal Academy of Art (pp. 25–7). All in *Rosenberg*.
61 The links of friendship among these women prior to learning of 'Abdu'l-Bahá were: Rosenberg and Thornburgh-Cropper; Thornburgh-Cropper and Phoebe Hearst; and Phoebe Hearst and Mary Bolles, the mother of May.
62 Weinberg, *Rosenberg*, 19–20.
63 Deborah Cherry, *Painting Women* (London: Routledge, 1993), 46, quoted in Weinberg, *Rosenberg*, 19–20.
64 Bahiyyih would assume responsibility for affairs in Haifa when 'Abdu'l-Bahá's successor, Shoghi Effendi, left, sometimes for months at a time, in the 1920s. Smith, *Bábí and Bahá'í Religions*, 116.
65 See Marjorie Morten, "A Tribute to Bahíyyih Khánum," *Bahá'í World*, Vol. 5, 1934, 181–5.
66 "Behaism: Its Ethical and Social Teachings," UKNBC; 'Abdu'l-Bahá, *Some Answered Questions*, Collected and translated from the Persian by Laura Clifford Barney, Newly revised by a Committee at the Bahá'í World Centre (Wilmette, IL: Bahá'í Publishing, 2014), 159; "Love is the Foundation of Everything," from the notes of Miss Ethel J. Rosenberg, London, England, taken in Acre, Jan. 1909, in *Star of the West* (henceforth *SoW*), Vol. 7, No. 11, 107–8; Weinberg, *Rosenberg*, 106–8.
67 "Poems by Edward Theodore Hall (1879–1962)," p. 6, B13, UKNBC. Also reprinted in Weinberg, *Rosenberg*, 120–1. Smith refers to Hall as the unofficial leader of the Manchester community in "Development," *Community Histories*, 156.

68 Douglas Martin has traced the history of the persecution of the Bahá'ís by the Iranian government from the Qajar and Pahlavi dynasties through the creation of the Islamic Republic in *The Persecution of the Bahá'ís of Iran, 1844–1984* (Ottawa, ONT: Association for Bahá'í Studies Press, 1984).
69 The quotation is from Bahá'u'lláh's *Kitab-i Mubin*, quoted in Cole, *Modernity and the Millennium*, 59.
70 Blomfield, *Chosen Highway*, 235–6. Weinberg, *Rosenberg*, 36–7.
71 While restrictions had been relaxed after 1887, new developments including shifting political alliances within Ottoman politics meant that after 1901 'Abdu'l-Bahá's incarceration within the walls of Acre was renewed. During this difficult period from 1901 to 1908 'Abdu'l-Bahá wrote ninety letters or "Tablets" a day. S. Effendi, *God Passes By*, 264, 267 and Ruhe, *Door of Hope*, 63 and 66.
72 Weinberg, *Rosenberg*, 101–2. Shoghi Effendi notes that many of the ministers, pashas and officials who were enemies of "the Faith," were executed after the revolution, *God Passes By*, 272.
73 This issue is explored at length, especially in the first three main chapters of my *The Harem, Slavery and British Imperial Culture* (Manchester: Manchester University Press, 2006).
74 Reference to Thornburgh-Cropper's car in Weinberg, *Rosenberg*, 130.
75 The reference to a "constant stream" and the description of 'Abdu'l-Bahá's visitors are quotations by Blomfield from Isabel Fraser, "'Abdu'l-Bahá in Britain," typed copy of an article published in *Everywoman*, Dec. 1915/Jan. 1916, B10, UKNBC.
76 Wellesley Tudor Pole, "'Abdu'l-Bahá in London," *SoW*, Sept. 27, 1911, 3–4.
77 The reference to Rosenberg's "interview book" and Platt's responsibilities as well as general information about 'Abdu'l-Bahá at Cadogan Gardens is from Hall, "Sitarih Khánum," 8–10, UKNBC.
78 Weinberg, *Rosenberg*, 149.
79 Basil Wilberforce became a "much revered and beloved friend" to Lady Blomfield, who treasured the "many beautiful letters" he sent her. Hall, "Sitarih Khánum," 7, UKNBC.
80 "'Abdu'l-Bahá's first Public Address in the West (at the City Temple, London, Sept. 1911)," B11, UKNBC; "'Abdu'l-Bahá in London," 45, B4, UKNBC; Fraser, "'Abdu'l-Bahá in Britain"; Hall, "Sitarih Khánum," 6–7; Tudor Pole "Private Memorandum," Dec. 5, 1921, 5, UKNBC.
81 "Elizabeth Herrick," a short biography with no author and no date, most likely written between 1908 and 1914, UKNBC.
82 Fraser, "'Abdu'l-Bahá in Britain".
83 These quotations come from the translation of Tablet (letter) 17 written by 'Abdu'l-Bahá in Haifa to Sara Blomfield, Oct. 14, 1914, UKNBC. While the letter may have been addressed specifically to Blomfield, the advice in it was intended to be shared.
84 The reference to 'Abdu'l-Bahá telling a suffragette that violence is for the weak is in "With 'Abdu'l-Bahá in London: extracts from the letters written by Mirza

Ahmad Sohrab, 16 Dec. 1912," *SoW*, March 2, 1913, 5. On more than one occasion he expressed the belief that militant methods would retard the progress of the women's suffrage movement. This reference is from a letter written by a Bahá'í in Haifa to "Dear friends," presumably the English Bahá'ís, June 23, 1914, UKNBC.

85 For arguments of those against women's suffrage see Brian Harrison, *Separate Spheres: The Opposition to Women's Suffrage in Britain* (London: Croom Helm, 1978), especially 75–8.

86 "'Abdu'l-Bahá's address to a women's meeting in Edinburgh," 1913, 5–7, B12, UKNBC.

87 Isabel Fraser, "'Abdu'l-Bahá at Clifton England," *SoW*, March 21, 1913, 5. This same idea is expressed in "Teachings of Bahá'u'lláh from Discourses Given by 'Abdu'l-Bahá in London and Paris," *SoW*, April 9, 1912, 4.

88 Letter from Florence Underwood to Lady Blomfield asking her to thank 'Abdu'l-Bahá for speaking to the Women's Freedom League and for his advocacy of the cause, Jan. 4, 1913, UKNBC. The president of this organization referred to 'Abdu'l-Bahá as an "Eastern Master" after his address to an audience at the Westminster Palace Hotel, "Talk by Mrs. Despard," in Fraser, "'Abdu'l-Bahá in London," *SoW*, Jan. 19, 1913, 9. References to Mrs Pankhurst and her visit in the above-mentioned letter from June 23, 1914 and in Fraser, "'Abdu'l-Bahá in Britain."

89 Tablets (letters) from 'Abdu'l-Bahá to Lady Blomfield, July 29 and May 16, 1919, UKNBC. "Tablet from 'Abdu'l-Bahá to Alice Ives Breed, Nov. 17, 1918," *SoW*, April 28, 1919, 39.

90 "Elizabeth Herrick," UKNBC.

91 For discussion of the Liberal government's betrayal of its own principles with regard to the women's suffrage movement see "The Women's Rebellion" and "The Pankhursts Provide a Clew," in George Dangerfield's *The Strange Death of Liberal England* (New York: Capricorn Books, 1935), 139–213 and 364–88.

92 Hall, "Sitarih Khánum," 5, 16.

93 Letter from a Bahá'í in Haifa, June 23, 1914, UKNBC.

94 Letter from a Bahá'í in Haifa, June 23, 1914, UKNBC; letter from Isabel Fraser to Lady Blomfield, Oct. 8, 1913. Mary's Persian name also appears as "Parvine Khánum," along with the Persian names of her mother, Nouri Khánum, and sister, Vardiyeh Khánum, in letter No. 1 of the translated Tablets (letters) of 'Abdu'l-Bahá to Lady Blomfield, Oct. 1911; and on an unidentified timeline. All in UKNBC.

95 Tablet (letter) from 'Abdu'l-Bahá to Lady Blomfield, 1919, Haifa, UKNBC.

96 Tablet (letter) from 'Abdu'l-Bahá to Sara Blomfield, Oct. 14, 1914, Haifa, UKNBC (translated by M. Ahmad Sohrab).

97 For example, he made this point in "'Abdu'l-Bahá's address to a women's meeting in Edinburgh," 1913, 7–12 and in his Tablet to Lady Blomfield, Oct. 14, 1914, both in UKNBC; and in his address at Westminster Palace Hotel, Fraser, "'Abdu'l-Bahá in London," *SoW*, Jan. 19, 1913, 8.

98 'Abdu'l-Bahá to Blomfield, Oct. 14, 1914.

99 "Teachings of Bahá'u'lláh from discourses given by 'Abdu'l-Bahá in London and Paris," *SoW*, April 9, 1912, 4.
100 Qasim Amin, *The Liberation of Women and The New Woman: Two Documents in the History of Egyptian Feminism*, translated by Samiha Peterson (Cairo: American University of Cairo Press, 2000).
101 The story of Zenobia was told by 'Abdu'l-Bahá to a group of visitors, Bahá'í and non-Bahá'í, at the Blomfield residence in London. *'Abdu'l-Bahá in London: Addresses and Notes of Conversations* (London: Bahá'í Publishing Trust, 1982), 103–4, first published in 1912 "through the good offices of Lady Blomfield."
102 "'Abdu'l-Bahá's address to a women's meeting in Edinburgh," 1913, UKNBC.
103 "'Abdu'l-Bahá's teaching described by Dr. Kelman," Jan. 1913, UKNBC. For a collection of articles by both Eastern and Western writers who have praised her as a role model with regard to female emancipation see *Táhirih in History: Perspectives on Qurratu'l-'Ayn from East and West*, edited by Sabir Afaqi (Los Angeles: Kalimat Press, 2004). Among them is an article written by 'Abdu'l-Bahá, "Jináb-i Táhirih," 3–13. Also see Abbas Amanat, "Qurrat al-'Ayn: The Remover of the Veil," *Resurrection and Renewal*, 295–331 and Martha's Root's biographical study, *Táhirah the Pure* (Los Angeles: Kalimat Press, 1981), and Smith, *Short History*, 25, 34. For discussion of the important role that women played in the growth and development of the Bahá'í Faith, both in the West and the Middle East, as well as gender issues from the feminine divine to women's suffrage in the writings of Bahá'u'lláh and Abdu'l-Bahá, see Juan Cole, "'Women Are as Men': Gender in the Making of the Bahá'í Religion," *Modernity and the Millennium*, 163–87.
104 One of 'Abdu'l-Bahá's lectures was even entitled "The Equality of Women," Jan. 2, 1913 at Essex Hall, London, invitation/announcement in UKNBC.
105 "'Abdu'l-Bahá's address to a women's meeting in Edinburgh," 1913, UKNBC.
106 Reference to the commencement of a "new era" for women and the teachings of the Báb and Bahá'u'lláh is in "'Abdu'l-Bahá's Teaching described by Dr. Kelman," Jan 1913 and reference to "this is the day of justice," equality and enfranchisement is from "'Abdu'l-Bahá's address to a women's meeting in Edinburgh," 1913, UKNBC.
107 "The New Religion: How the Bahá'í Movement Is Drawing Londoners back into the Churches," unidentified newspaper clipping in UKNBC and "Teachings of Bahá'u'lláh from Discourses Given by 'Abdu'l-Bahá in London and Paris," *SoW*, April 9, 1912, 4.
108 Fraser, "'Abdu'l-Bahá in London" and a record of 'Abdu'l-Bahá's sayings during his stay in Byfleet in Sept. 1911 kept by Miss Schepel and Miss Buckton, *Abdu'l-Bahá in London: Addresses and Notes of Conversations*, 85, 90, quotation at p. 91, UKNBC.
109 "With 'Abdu'l-Bahá in London: Extracts from Letters Written by Mirza Ahmad Sohrab, Dec. 19, 1912," *SoW*, March 2, 1913, 5. "'Abdu'l-Bahá's Address to a Women's Meeting in Edinburgh," 1913. In addition, 'Abdu'l-Bahá stressed the importance of equality between men and women in personal conversations as

well as public addresses. "Notes after Conversations with Abbas Effendi," in the file entitled "Account of a Visit to the Master," 1906, UKNBC.
110 Weinberg, *Rosenberg*, 138–9. Invitation in UKNBC, 1911.
111 E.T. Hall, "Retrospect of the Manchester Bahá'ís," 1913, 7, UKNBC. While the document focuses on the Manchester Bahá'ís, this particular reference relates to a visit to London. Certainly, men could appreciate and take part in these "feminine" entertainments, for it was Hall who brought the red roses to the Bahá'í gathering.
112 The word for paradise or heaven in Arabic, *jinnah*, also means garden.
113 S. Effendi, *God Passes By*, 269.
114 Even in the purely English context, the idea of separate private domestic and public political spheres is problematic, for feminists had been challenging patriarchal power by yoking public and private together for decades. See, for example, Philippa Levine, *Feminist Lives in Victorian England: Private Roles and Public Commitment* (Oxford: Blackwell, 1990).
115 Letter from Rosenberg to Blomfield, Jan. 23, 1918, UKNBC.
116 Tablet (letter) No. 8 from 'Abdu'l-Bahá to Blomfield, Aug. 21, 1912, UKNBC.
117 Tablet (letter) No. 16 from 'Abdu'l-Bahá to Blomfield and "'Abdu'l-Bahá in London," UKNBC.
118 The occasion was a presentation on Bahá'í beliefs and pacifism in Caxton Hall, Westminster. Blomfield opened with a half-hour talk on "An Account of the Peace Ideas of the Bahá'ís" followed by 'Abdu'l-Bahá's "A Message to the Pacifists." Invitation to the event, Jan. 1913, UKNBC.
119 Translated Tablet (letter) No. 8 from 'Abdu'l-Bahá to Lady Blomfield, Aug. 1912, B5, UKNBC.
120 In addition, Blomfield helped to link the Bahá'ís of England and 'Abdu'l-Bahá by reporting to him on that community and relaying his instructions to them. Translated Tablets (letters) from 'Abdu'l-Bahá to Lady Blomfield, quotations from letter No. 3, Jan. 4, 1912, Switzerland. Also see letters No. 7, July 15, 1912; No. 15, Feb. 24, 1914, Haifa, Syria and No. 18, May 16, 1919, Haifa, Palestine. All in UKNBC.
121 Weinberg, *Rosenberg*, after 88. British male Bahá'ís sometimes did the same with the fez. For example, see the picture from the 1919 pilgrimage to Haifa in Momen, *Esslemont*, between pages 22 and 23.
122 Hall, "Sitarih Khánum," 9–10, UKNBC.
123 "Elizabeth Herrick," UKNBC.
124 In addition to Rosenberg's translation abilities, the Blomfield daughters studied that language as well. Summary of letters from Lady Blomfield to 'Abdu'l-Bahá, July 30, 1912, 3, and "Herrick." UKNBC.
125 Shoghi Effendi's Diary, Dec. 24, 1918, Acre/Haifa, UKNBC.
126 While the aristocracy had been in decline in English society and politics for many years and was on the verge of becoming marginalized (see Dangerfield, "Their Lordships Die in the Dark," *Strange Death*, 30–7 and David Cannadine, *The Decline and Fall of the British Aristocracy* (New York: Vintage Books, 1999)), by the early twentieth century many of these types of practices and values had

spread to the rising middle classes, for example, the gardens of the growing suburbs. See Alun Howkins, "The Discovery of Rural England," *Englishness, Politics and Culture, 1880–1920* (London: Bloomsbury Academic, 2014), 66–88.
127 Like "Lady," the title "Khanum" originally was associated with a certain rank or status, but by this period had come to be used more broadly.
128 Hall, "Sitarih Khánum," 16.
129 Letter from a Bahá'í in Haifa, June 23, 1914, UKNBC.
130 Weinberg, *Rosenberg*, 26–8, quotation at p. 28.
131 Weinberg, *Rosenberg*, 65, 69.
132 Madeline Hellaby, *Sarah Ann Ridgway* (Oxford: George Ronald, 2003).
133 "Elizabeth Herrick," UKNBC.
134 Untitled document in UKNBC, London, Dec. 24, 1912.
135 Anne McClintock discusses the gender politics of hiding female domestic labour in *Imperial Leather: Race, Gender and Sexuality in the Colonial Contest* (New York: Routledge, 1995), 98, 141, 160–2, 293.
136 Untitled document written in London and dated Dec. 24, 1912, UKNBC.
137 Despite their large numbers, domestic servants remained un-unionized and isolated, both physically and socially, from the emergence of an increasingly self-conscious and politically organized working-class. Female domestic servants, like housewives, tended to be ignored as workers by both the government and society. For discussion of the inequalities and difficulties experienced by both see Leonore Davidoff, "Mastered for Life: Servant and Wife in Victorian and Edwardian England," *Journal of Social History*, Vol. 7, No. 4 (1974), 406–28.
138 L. Heron-Oliphant, "'Abdu'l-Bahá at the Cedar Club, London, Jan. 2, 1913," *SoW*, Feb. 7, 1913, 9.
139 Fraser, "'Abdu'l-Bahá in Britain," *Everywoman*, Dec./Jan. 1915–16, UKNBC.
140 Ibid.
141 Contemporaries estimated the crowd at the Salvation Army to be between seven hundred and a thousand people. This shelter visit is related in a number of sources in the UKNBC, including: Fraser, "'Abdu'l-Bahá in Britain" and in Fraser, "'Abdu'l-Bahá at the Salvation Army Shelter, London, England, Christmas Night, 1912," *SoW*, Feb. 7, 1913, 1–8. Even after being released from prison, 'Abdu'l-Bahá continued to live in "Spartan simplicity" as Tudor Pole described in his letter to the editor of the *Daily Mail* (date on the original looks like 5/12/1912), UKNBC.
142 Mary Hanford Ford, "The Economic Teaching of 'Abdu'l-Bahá," *SoW*, March 21, 1917, 1–7.
143 Wellesley Tudor Pole, *Writing on the Ground* (London: Neville Spearman Ltd., 1984), 146 and Fraser, "'Abdu'l-Bahá in Britain."
144 "Teachings of Bahá'u'lláh from Discourses Given by 'Abdu'l-Bahá in London and Paris," *SoW*, April 9, 1912, 5 and "Strikes: 'Abdu'l-Bahá's words to Mme. Dreyfus-Barney," *SoW*, March 21, 1919, 15.
145 "If the power of love and peace become predominant, their effects will be greater than the power of hate and war: 'Abdu'l-Bahá comments on war in

Europe, from the diary of Mirza Ahmad Sohrab," *SoW*, Oct. 16, 1914, 180 and "The Way to Universal Peace: Extracts from the Diary of Mirza Ahmad Sohrab, May 1914," *SoW*, June 24, 1916, 41–3.

146 "Teachings of Bahá'u'lláh from Discourses Given by 'Abdu'l-Bahá in London and Paris," *SoW*, April 9, 1912, 5; "Strikes: 'Abdu'l-Bahá's words to Mme Dreyfus-Barney," *SoW*, March 21, 1919, 14–16; Isabel Fraser, "'Abdu'l-Bahá at Clifton England," *SoW*, March 21, 1913, 6; "'Abdu'l-Bahá's address in Edinburgh, Jan. 1913," UKNBC; "'Abdu'l-Bahá in Canada," newspaper clipping in UKNBC; Tablet from 'Abdu'l-Bahá to John Craven in E.T Hall's, "Retrospect of Manchester Bahá'ís," Haifa 1919, 12, UKNBC.

147 "Some Teachings of 'Abdu'l-Bahá Abbas from Discourses Given in London and Paris," March 2, 1912, *SoW*, first page.

148 "Tablet to the Bahá'ís of England from Abdu'l-Bahá," *SoW*, June 5, 1911, 6.

149 "Towards Spiritual Unity" (dialogue between 'Abdu'l-Bahá and Rev. Campbell originally printed in the *Christian Commonwealth*), *SoW*, Sept. 27, 1911, 5. 'Abdu'l-Bahá also contrasted English freedoms with the lack of freedom in the East broadly defined. Arthur Cuthbert, "'Abdu'l-Bahá in London," *SoW*, Oct. 16, 1911, 6.

150 "'Abdu'l-Bahá's First Address in the West," City Temple, London, Sept 1911, UKNBC. The working classes were enfranchised in 1867, and the movement for women's suffrage was ongoing.

151 Weinberg, *Rosenberg*, 73.

152 He lived in Egypt for eleven months in 1910–11 and again in 1913, "Lecture on Bahaism at Manchester College," Jan. 4, 1913, *Oxford Times*, UKNBC. Mirza Ahmad Sohrab's diary from the time that he lived in Egypt with 'Abdu'l-Bahá, from July 1 to Sept. 30, 1913, offers additional insight into this period and reflects upon that country's importance to Bahá'ís from East and West. It has been published under the title *'Abdu'l-Bahá in Egypt* (London: Rider and Co., 1930). Also see *The Master in Egypt: A Compilation*, edited by Ahang Rabbani (Los Angeles: Kalimat Press, 2021). For more about the history of Egypt with regard to the increasing British presence see Timothy Mitchell, *Colonizing Egypt* (Cambridge: Cambridge University Press, 1988); William Welch, *No Country for a Gentleman: British Rule in Egypt, 1883–1907* (New York: Greenwood Press, 1988) and Ahmad Turbiyyn, al-fasl al-khamis, "Misr min Ihtilal Baritani ila Thawra," *Tarikh Misr wa al-Sudan al-Hadith wa al-Mu'asir* (Beirut: Muwassasat al-Risala), 1994.

153 "Verbatim Copy of report to His Holiness Sir Abdul Baha Abbas by A.C. Saad, Judge, Native Courts, Egypt. Report on the persecution of the Bahá'ís in Port Said." The document is not dated, but since it refers to 'Abdu'l-Bahá as "Sir," it would have to have been during 1920–1, UKNBC.

154 Lord and Lady Lamington's visit in Alexandria is mentioned the following year in an unidentified journal of 'Abdu'l-Bahá's visit to London, Dec. 25, 1912, UKNBC. Reference to Stannard from the "Diary of Mirza Ahmad Sohrab," Ramleh, Egypt, Oct. 29, 1913, *SoW*, Sept. 27, 1916, 101.

155 The *SoW* relates the teaching and other Bahá'í activities of Elinor Hiscox in Cairo, Alexandria and Ramleh from roughly 1911 until at least 1920. Elinor Hiscox, "Mashrak-El-Azkar Contribution from Cairo, Nov. 30, 1916," *SoW*, Jan. 19, 1917, 169; "Tidings from Egypt – Word from Elinor Hiscox," *SoW*, April 9, 1917, 22–23; "Diary Letters of Shoghi Rabbani," Feb. 14, 1919, *SoW*, 50.
156 "'Abdu'l-Bahá in Egypt," *Bahá'í News*, Nov. 23, 1910, 2–4; Mohammed Yazdi, "'Abdu'l-Bahá in Egypt," *Bahá'í News*, Jan. 19, 1911, 4–10; and "From the Diary of Mirza Ahmad Sohrab, Ramleh, Egypt, Oct 29, 1913," *SoW*, Sept. 27, 1916, 105.
157 "Notes after Conversations with Abbas Effendi," March 1906, UKNBC.
158 'Abdu'l-Bahá,' "To the Believers of Egypt," *SoW*, July 13, 1919, 142.
159 Cairo, April 17, 1915, UKNBC. In both this letter and 'Abdu'l-Bahá's statement regarding those interested in adopting Western practices and education, just the word "Syria" is used. However, it is clear from the context of Bahá'í correspondence during this period that the word refers to greater Syria or the general region which included Palestine.
160 Smith, *Short History*, 92–3 and *Bábí and Bahá'í Religions*, 194.
161 "Notes after Conversations with Abbas Effendi," March 1906, UKNBC.
162 "'Once the principles of the Bahá'í movement are known in India, it will spread like wildfire!' Extracts from the diary of Mirza Ahmad Sohrab," Jan. 1914; "India needs these principles of toleration and liberalism, extracts from the address delivered by 'Abdu'l-Bahá in New York City, Dec. 1912," and N.R. Vakil, "The Work in India," all in *SoW*, April 9, 1914, 19–22. Also, M. Holbach, "The Breaking Down of Caste," from the *Christian Commonwealth*, in *SoW*, April 28, 1914, 40. 'Abdu'l-Bahá learned of Bahá'í activities in British India through Bahá'í teachers and the press. At least two Indian publications were sympathetic with that movement "letter from Dowlat, Bombay, India, Dec. 4, 1915," *SoW*, Feb. 7, 1916, 160 and "'Abdu'l-Bahá in London," UKNBC.
163 "Let There Be Peace: Talk by 'Abdu'l-Bahá given in Paris, France, Nov. 23, 1911 during the War between Italy and Tripoli," *SoW*, Sept. 27, 1916, 106.
164 "Universal Peace: Questions Asked and Answers Given by 'Abdu'l-Bahá Abbas, from the Diary of Mirza Ahmad Sohrab, May 11–14, 1914," *SoW*, Aug. 1, 1914, 115–17; Tablet from 'Abdu'l-Bahá, "No sane person can at this time deny the fact that war is the most dreadful calamity in the world of humanity," *SoW*, Dec. 31, 1914, 243–5; the diary of Habib Mu'ayyad; Ahang Rabbani, "'Abdu'l-Bahá in Abu-Sinan," *Bahá'í Studies Review*, 2005, 75–103.
165 "Anthem of World Patriotism," *SoW*, Oct. 16, 1914, 182.
166 Isabel Fraser, "'Abdu'l-Bahá Addresses Pembroke Chapel Liverpool, England, Sun. Dec. 15, 1912," *SoW*, Jan. 19, 1913, 5.
167 "A World Religion and Universal Peace," *Plain Truth*, Jan. 1913, UKNBC; "Lecture on Bahaism at Manchester College," *Oxford Times*, Jan. 4, 1913, UKNBC; Isabel Fraser, "'Abdu'l-Bahá in London," *SoW*, Jan. 19, 1913, 10.

168 "Universal Peace: Questions Asked and Answers Given by 'Abdu'l-Bahá Abbas, from the Diary of Mirza Ahmad Sohrab, May 11–14, 1914," *SoW*, Aug. 1, 1914, 116.
169 Obviously, having national or imperial ideals and putting them into practice are not one in the same. Gandhi, for example, could admire British ideals but still oppose that empire for its unjust practices. Rajmohan Gandhi, *Gandhi: The Man, His People, and the Empire* (Berkeley: University of California Press, 2007). His famous quotation about having "fallen in love" with certain ideals of the British Empire is at p. 185.
170 "W.T. Stead on 'Empire of Peace'," *SoW*, Aug. 1, 1911, 18–19.
171 Cole, "Globalization and Religion," 58 and 68, quotation at p. 58; and E.P. Thompson, *The Making of the English Working Class* (London: Victor Gollancz, 1963).
172 "World Religion and Universal Peace," *Plain Truth*, Jan. 1913, UKNBC.
173 Tudor Pole, *Writing on the Ground*, 147.
174 'Abdu'l-Bahá, "Farewell Words to Europe," *SoW*, Dec. 31, 1911, 6. Kathryn Tidrick has explored the relationship between the concept of an English national character and the belief that English people had an obligation or duty to the colonized peoples of the empire. Tidrick, *Empire and the English Character* (London: I.B. Tauris, 1990).
175 "Strikes: 'Abdu'l-Bahá's Words to Mme Dreyfus-Barney," *SoW*, March 21, 1919, 14–16. While this particular reference appears in 1919, 'Abdu'l-Bahá presented this position during his travels to Great Britain.
176 "'The world is at the threshold of a most tragic struggle,' Stirring Talk by 'Abdu'l-Bahá from the Diary of Mirza Ahmad Sohrab," *SoW*, Sept 27, 1914, 164 and "Notes on the Early Days of the Bahá'í Faith in London (Written at the request of the National Spiritual Assembly, March 1942)," in "History of the Faith in the U.K. file," UKNBC.
177 "Farewell Words to Europe," *SoW*, Dec. 31, 1911, 6.
178 "Some Teachings of 'Abdu'l-Bahá Abbas: From Discourses Given in London and Paris," *SoW*, March 2, 1912, 4.
179 Letter to the editor from "An Edinburgh Reader," Jan. 1913, stray newspaper article from UKNBC. This attitude is not unusual among Christian missionaries and those who sympathized with them. For the Bahá'ís "threatened to be their greatest rivals in the field of conversions" and "proved a great hindrance" to their efforts. Moojan Momen, "Early Relations between Christian Missionaries and the Bábí and Bahá'í Communities," *Studies in Bábí and Bahá'í History*, Vol. 1, edited by Moojan Momen (Los Angeles: Kalimat Press, 1982), 49–82. The first quotation is at p. 68, and the second one at p. 69 and refers to an article in a March 1917 edition of the *Church Missionary Review*.
180 Two letters to the editor of the *Edinburgh Evening Dispatch* from W.A.D.S., Jan. 16 and 23, 1913, UKNBC.
181 "'Abdu'l-Bahá in Edinburgh," *Edinburgh Evening News*, Jan. 9, 1913, UKNBC.

182 While these ideas were expressed by 'Abdu'l-Bahá on a number of occasions, these particular references come from "'Abdu'l-Bahá in Edinburgh," *The Scotsman*, Jan. 8/9, 1913; "Dr. Kelman on the Bahá'í teachings," introduction and "Address of 'Abdu'l-Bahá on International Language," Jan. 1912. All in UKNBC.

183 From the diary of Dr Esslemont, Nov. 1919, in Moojan Momen, *Dr John Ebenezer Esslemont* (London: Bahá'í Publishing Trust, 1975), 16–17, UKNBC.

184 "Diary Letters of Shoghi Rabbani Written to Mirza Ahmad Sohrab in America," *SoW*, April 28, 1920, 54.

185 In reality, spiritual and secular movements and ideologies operated within both England and India during this period, complicating and problematizing this imagined dichotomy. Peter van der Veer provides an analysis of this process in *Imperial Encounters: Religion and Modernity in India and Britain* (Princeton: Princeton University Press, 2001).

186 Arminius Vambery, *Western Culture in Eastern Lands; a Comparison of the Methods Adopted by England and Russia in the Middle East* (London: John Murray, 1906), 2.

187 The original letter in Arabic is in the archives at the Bahá'í World Centre, Haifa, Israel.

188 'Abdu'l-Bahá objected to the imaginary boundaries that separate East and West and divide humanity, calling them "superstitions" and noting that birds and other animals had no regard for these fictitious barriers. This idea is repeated frequently and appears, for example, in "The Most Great Peace," *SoW*, Aug. 20, 1914, 132.

189 Letters from Mirza Ahmed Sohrab, London, Dec. 22, 1912, UKNBC. There were some Bahá'ís in Ireland during the early twentieth century. One in particular, George Townshend, who had been born in Dublin and served as Canon of St. Patrick's Cathedral in that city, would emerge as an important Bahá'í leader. David Hofman, *George Townshend: Hand of the Cause of God* (Oxford: George Ronald, 1983).

190 Edward Theodore Hall, "Letter from England," Manchester, Dec. 22, 1916, *SoW*, Dec. 31, 1916, 161. During the First World War he served in the Labour Corps in France and the Canadian Forestry Corps.

191 Foreword to "Poems by Edward Theodore Hall (1879–1962)," first page and E.T. Hall, "France 1917," in "A Retrospect of Manchester Bahá'ís," 10, UKNBC.

192 "News from England, Letter from E.T. Hall to Mr. Remey, Manchester, Nov. 14, 1920," *SoW*, Dec. 30, 1920, 274.

193 Paul Fussell has analysed the intersections between poetry, specifically that of the English soldier, and history in the context of the Western Front during the First World War. *The Great War and Modern Memory* (New York: Oxford University Press, 1975).

194 "Poems by Edward Theodore Hall (1879–1962),", 13, UKNBC.

195 'Abdu'l-Bahá praised another of Hall's wartime poems, "The Woods of Blavincourt," in Hall, "Haifa 1919," in "A Retrospect of Manchester Bahá'ís,", 11–12, UKNBC.

196 "'Abdu'l-Bahá Dismisses all Pilgrims," *SoW*, Oct. 16, 1918, 133.

197 They remained in Abu-Sinan from Sept. 1914 until May 1915. "'Abdu'l-Bahá in Abu-Sinan: September 1914–May 1915," Ahang Rabbani, *Bahá'í Studies Review*, 13 (2005), 75–103.
198 "Doors of the Holy Land Open – Recent Letters from Mirza Ahmad Sohrab," *SoW*, Nov. 4, 1918, 1. "Tell Everyone Now Is the Time to Teach and Spread the Cause! Letters from Lua Getsinger," *SoW*, Oct. 16, 1915, 89–90.
199 Roderic and Derwent Maude, *The Servant, the General and Armageddon* (Oxford: George Ronald, 1998), 40–3, 50.
200 Tudor Pole could be considered a Bahá'í sympathizer in that he believed the movement had "an important part to play in the religious regeneration of the world." Tudor Pole, *Writing on the Ground* (London: Neville Spearman Ltd., 1984), 164. Also, as Abdo notes, Tudor Pole became a Bahá'í for a short time, Abdo, "Religion and Relevance," 79.
201 Maude, *The Servant*, 6–9 and "A Recent Letter from the Holy Land, Haifa, Oct. 19, 1918," *SoW*, Dec. 31, 1918, 178.
202 Tudor Pole also wrote a letter to Rosenberg while in hospital in Alexandria expressing concern for the safety of 'Abdu'l-Bahá, and asking the Bahá'ís to send cables urging their government to protect him. Dec. 22, 1917, UKNBC.
203 Balfour met with advisors regarding this matter, including Lord Curzon. Curzon had already encountered the Bahá'í movement during his time Iran in 1889–90 and expressed sympathy with it. In fact, Curzon's *Persia and the Persian Question* has been described as "in many ways, the most penetrating analysis of the religion of Bahá'u'lláh penned in the nineteenth century." Momen, *The Bábí and Bahá'í Religions*, 247.
204 Letter to Lord Lamington from the Foreign Office, Jan. 31, 1918, UKNBC. The Foreign Office also assured Lamington that 'Abdu'l-Bahá was in good health and being well cared for, Sept. 30, 1918, UKNBC.
205 Sohrab, "Letter to Mr. Joseph H. Hannen," Haifa, Sept. 26, 1918, *SoW*, Nov. 4, 1918, 142. Sohrab lived with and acted as secretary to 'Abdu'l-Bahá in Palestine and travelled with him in Europe and the US.
206 "Letter from Mirza Ahmad Sohrab to the Editor of the *Christian Commonwealth*, London, Haifa, Dec. 2, 1918," *SoW*, Jan. 19, 1919, 189.
207 The Indian army formed the bulk of the forces there and in Mesopotamia. Rob Johnson, *The Great War and the Middle East* (Oxford: Oxford University Press, 2016), 48.
208 "Letter from Mirza Ahmad Sohrab, at Cairo Egypt, to the Bahá'í Friends in America," Jan. 1, 1919, *SoW*, March 2, 1919, 217–19. Eugene Rogan notes that the battlefields of the Middle East were often the most international, with soldiers from Australia, New Zealand, multiple ethnicities in South Asia and North Africa, France and regions throughout the British Isles. Rogan, *The Fall of the Ottomans: The Great War in the Middle East* (New York: Basic Books, 2015), xvii.
209 Tudor Pole, *Writing on the Ground*, 154 and letter from Tudor Pole to Rosenberg, Nov. 4, 1918, UKNBC.
210 "Abu-Sinan," 75–6 and Maude, *The Servant*, 40–1 and 123. Reference to shrine of the Báb is from Stockman, *Guide for the Perplexed*, 124. Lady

Blomfield relates that because of a surplus of corn, 'Abdu'l-Bahá had been able to feed the poor of Palestine during 1914–18 as well. Blomfield, *The Chosen Highway* (Wilmette, IL: Bahá'í Publishing Trust, 1940/1967), 210.
211 Letter from Tudor Pole, Haifa, Dec. 17, 1918, UKNBC.
212 "Letter from Sohrab at Cairo, Jan 1, 1919," *SoW*, March 2, 1919, 219.
213 Letter to the Bahá'ís from Tudor Pole, March 20, 1919, UKNBC. Letters from "the friends of 'Abdu'l-Bahá" in Great Britain to Balfour, Allenby and Sir Arthur Money, the Chief Administrator in Jerusalem, all in March and May 1919, UKNBC.
214 Letter from Allenby to General Vaylan, Allenby Papers, March 2, 1919, Liddell Hart Centre for Military Archives, Kings College, London.
215 Tudor Pole, "Private Memorandum," Dec. 5, 1921 and Leroy Ioas Papers, 1919, US Bahá'í National Archives.
216 Tudor Pole, "Private Memorandum" from his notes on the passing of 'Abdu'l-Bahá, London, Dec. 5, 1921. "How the Door of Communication Was Opened: Letter from Mirza Azizollah Shirazi, Haifa, to Mirza Mahmood Bayhir Khan Shirazi, Tehran, Iran – the first Tablet received in Egypt, Haifa Palestine, Sept. 25, 1918," *SoW*, July 13, 1919, 128–30 and 141.
217 Quote from Maude, *The Servant*, 130 and "The Knighting of 'Abdu'l Bahá," *SoW*, Dec. 21, 1920, 266. Not surprisingly, 'Abdu'l-Bahá's passing the following year drew comments of praise and sympathy from a number of British leaders such as Viscount Allenby, High Commissioner for Palestine; General Sir Arthur Money, formerly Chief Administrator of Palestine; and Winston Churchill, the Secretary of State for the Colonies. The funeral itself was a triumphal procession of ten thousand, which not only included the secular and religious leaders, but men, women and children from all backgrounds. "The Passing of 'Abdu'l-Bahá, from His Family, Haifa," 1921–2, 11, 19–20, UKNBC and "Private Memorandum," notes by Tudor Pole on the passing of 'Abdu'l-Bahá, Dec. 5, 1921, 1, UKNBC. Also see his obituary notice in *The Times*, Nov. 30, 1921.
218 Tudor Pole, "Visit to 'Abdu'l-Bahá Abbas at Haifa and Acre, on the 25th, 26th, and 27th Feb., 1919," UKNBC. This document was labelled "Secret" and "Not for publication, but for the private guidance of the friends in England." Perhaps for political reasons, Allenby did not want his interest in Bahá'í beliefs to be known widely.
219 Momen, *Dr John Esslemont*, 18.
220 Shoghi Effendi wrote in his diary about a time when 'Abdu'l-Bahá brought a group of seven Australian aviators to the shrine of Bahá'u'lláh at Bahji. He taught them the basic Bahá'í principles beforehand. Upon approaching the shrine, they removed shoes and hats out of respect, and as they left a rosewater blessing was sprinkled on their heads. Dec. 24, 1918, UKNBC.
221 Maude has made this observation, *The Servant*, 129.
222 Allenby's speech dedicating the Jerusalem YMCA, April 1933, Allenby papers, Liddell Hart Archive, Kings College, London, 3/5, 3–5.
223 Biographical detail about Allenby by General Sir Archibald Wavell, Commander in Chief, GHQ, Cairo, 1, May 1940, Allenby Papers 7/1/30, Liddell Hart Centre for Military Archives, Kings College, London.

224 The speech is dated April 1933 and is with the Allenby Papers, 3/5, 1–2, Liddell Centre, Kings College, London.
225 Letter from a Bahá'í in Haifa to "Dear friends," June 1914, UKNBC.
226 Robinson-Dunn, *Harem, Slavery, and British Imperial Culture*.
227 For example, two of the most important British statesmen of the late nineteenth and early twentieth centuries, Lord Cromer, who acted as the "uncrowned king of Egypt," and Lord Curzon, who served as Viceroy of India, were so vehemently opposed to women's suffrage that they formed what came to be known as the "Curzon-Cromer combine." "Uncrowned king" comes from Welch, *No Country for a Gentleman*, xi. Reference to their anti-suffrage combine is from Constance Rover, *Women's Suffrage and Party Politics in Britain, 1866–1914* (London: Routledge and Kegan Paul, 1967), 171–3.
228 Marion Weinstein, "Declares Zionists Must Work with Other Races: Leader of Bahaism Believes Neutral Government Like British is Best for Palestine at Present," *SoW*, Sept. 8, 1919, 196; "First Tablet Revealed for Bahá'ís of Iran since Opening of Doors of Holy Land," *SoW*, Dec. 12, 1918, 170; "Recent Tablet to Lotfullah Hakim," *SoW*, July 13, 1919, 138; "Letter from Mirza Ahmad Sohrab to the Editor of the *Christian Commonwealth*, London, Haifa, Palestine, Dec. 2, 1918," *SoW*, Jan. 19, 1919, 191–2; "Letter from Shoghi Effendi to W. Tudor Pole," Dec. 17, 1918, *SoW*, Jan. 19, 1919, 195–6; and Tudor Pole "Visit to 'Abdu'l-Bahá" Secret, 1919.
229 "Letter to Editor of the *Christian Commonwealth*, Dec. 2, 1918," *SoW*, Jan 19, 1919, 190–1.
230 "Letter from Mirza Ahmad Sohrab," Jan 1, 1919, *SoW*, March 2, 1919, 217–21, quote at p. 218.
231 Ruhe, *Door of Hope*, 130–1 quoting from Esslemont, *Bahá'u'lláh and the New Era*, 252–3.
232 Tudor Pole, "Visit to 'Abdu'l-Bahá ... Feb., 1919," 1.
233 Stockman, *Guide for the Perplexed*, 109.
234 Smith, *Bábí and Bahá'í Religions*, 119.
235 Tudor Pole and the London Bahá'ís first contacted Sir Herbert Samuel, the High Commissioner for Palestine, about this matter in 1922. Cable to the Commissioner from the Bahá'í Assembly, London, May 29, 1922, UKNBC and letter from Tudor Pole to the same, May 31, 1922, London, UKNBC. Ruhe, *Door of Hope*, 112–13.
236 See Albert Hourani's *Arabic Thought in the Liberal Age, 1798–1939* (Cambridge: Cambridge University Press, 1962). Also, for an in-depth analysis of the complex relationship between the ideas of Bahá'u'lláh and 'Abdu'l-Bahá and the various intellectual currents of the nineteenth-century Middle East, which included liberal, reformist and constitutional movements as well as religiously based ideologies, see Cole, *Modernity and the Millennium*. Chapter 2, "Bahá'u'lláh and Ottoman Constitutionalism," 49–78, is particularly interesting in light of issues explored in this study.
237 *Gleanings from the Writings of Bahá'u'lláh*, translated by Shoghi Effendi (Wilmette, IL: Bahá'í Publishing Trust, 1952), 213.

2

Planting the "banner of Islam" in the "heart of the British Empire": Muslim missionaries from India solidify their new base in England during a time of crisis[1]

Introduction

In early 1913, the same time that 'Abdu'l-Bahá visited England in order to propagate the Bahá'í teachings, Khwaja Kamal-ud-Din, a lawyer-turned-missionary from Lahore, coordinated the reopening of the Shah Jahan mosque and the debut of the Woking Muslim Mission.[2] The WMM is unprecedented in that, for the first time, Muslims from the East, or "peripheries" of empire, established an institution in the English "metropole" with the intent of converting Westerners to Islam. Certainly Muslims from the Raj and elsewhere in the world had lived and practised their faith in that country since at least the early nineteenth century,[3] but the spread of their faith had never been a goal, and even those who attended the Shah Jahan mosque prior to Kamal-ud-Din's resurrection of it were instructed, in no uncertain terms, to maintain their distance from the larger society in which they lived, keeping the division between colonized and colonizer intact.[4] William Henry Quilliam was able to convert fellow Britons to Islam during the Victorian period. However, his status as a prominent, respected and White Liverpool solicitor gave him certain privileges and protections not available to Muslims from South Asia or the Middle East, and even so his community experienced continual harassment and violence at the hands of local members of the population.[5]

Kamal-ud-Din also encountered hostility from the local townspeople when he first arrived in Woking. His turban immediately identified him to the residents of that small town as an outsider, and some who objected to the very presence of the WMM were determined that it be "nipped in the bud" by measures including cutting off the food supply to the mosque.[6] While these threats ultimately came to naught, apprehensions of what might happen in this new place would have been daunting, at least during the first year of operation. After all, Kamal-ud-Din was from a part of

India characterized by religious diversity who understood well how easily differences of belief could lead to violence and how quickly those with minority views could become targets. His initial move was what many would consider to be both a sacrifice and a "leap in the dark," for at the age of forty-three he left a successful career and comfortable life for an uncertain future and relatively Spartan accommodation in a place that, despite his language skills and knowledge of the British government and its institutions, still could feel very much like an "alien country." In addition, he experienced London as a "place of trial" inhabited by irreligious or only nominally religious people who cared little for spiritual matters and instead busied themselves in "a strange way."[7]

Despite these various challenges, and having arrived in Woking with only two companions, his personal secretary and a man he had met aboard ship, Kamal-ud-Din began to build a new centre for Islam in England. The missionary leader made every endeavour to reach the people of that country, Muslim and non-Muslim alike.[8] His gave his first public address at Speakers' Corner in Hyde Park and made himself available for anyone interested in learning more about his faith. He appeared at events organized by philosophical and literary organizations and nonconformist religious groups. Each week he led traditional congregational prayers on Fridays for his brethren in London and delivered a sermon at the mosque on Sundays, with the latter designed to appeal to those who came from Christian backgrounds.[9] Within a year Kamal-ud-Din succeeded in attracting Muslims living in Great Britain, both those born into the faith and converts, who became galvanized by the Khwaja and the WMM and, as a result, began to organize additional Islamic associations in the Greater London area (Figure 2.1).[10]

In order for Kamal-ud-Din and his early supporters to have established this new community and mission in England, they first had to make their intentions meaningful in terms culturally recognizable to themselves and others. This process is reflected on the pages of the *Islamic Review* (*IR*), the WMM's monthly journal beginning in early 1913 and produced for an English-speaking readership in England and throughout the empire.[11] That publication, like the words and actions of WMM leaders, was made possible by what this study understands as an ever-evolving, intersectional imperial ideology created, and recreated, as individual historical actors sifted through and drew from a vast cultural repertoire of existing practices and beliefs, including Islamic texts and traditions, British liberal ideals and the example of others who operated within the framework of empire. Central to this system of meaning was the conviction that British Muslims could and should take advantage of existing rights with regard to freedom of the press, speech and religion so as to spread their faith,

Figure 2.1 Kamal-ud-Din with converts and others, Woking.

influence their government and strengthen their communities, just as British Christians had been doing for generations. It also maintained that Islam was relevant to the modern world and, because it was intended for all of humanity, it was not only applicable to the people of the West but was needed by them.

This is not to say that everyone involved with the WMM agreed on specific issues. There was considerable diversity of opinion, especially when it came to pan-Islamist politics. Rather, it is to say that Kamal-ud-Din and, later, Maulvie Sadr-ud-Din, his missionary colleague from India, imam and co-editor of the *IR*, succeeded in creating discourses, both through their own individual efforts and by careful selection, which balanced the concerns of their various co-religionists with those of the larger English society and the British government, thus enabling the establishment of that missionary organization and, subsequently, new conversions to Islam. This ability to accommodate diverse perspectives created a new type of religious organization in the British Empire, one in which Muslims from the East succeeded in establishing a mission in the Western metropole in which hybridity was a goal, an expected and positive development, with regard to both the interior lives of individual believers and the composition of the community more generally. While Christian missionaries from England had done much to encourage the development of new cultures of religious hybridity in India since the early nineteenth century, the WMM, itself as a product of these earlier exchanges, represents the first time that this process developed in the opposite direction, an endeavour fraught with complications and thus requiring delicate navigation.[12]

The outbreak of the First World War in the year immediately following the WMM's debut created new difficulties for an organization still in the early stages of development. In addition to disrupting travel and post, the conflict demanded the attention of civilians as well as soldiers, leaving most people with little time or inclination to consider the merits of a new belief system.[13] The greatest challenge for the new mission, however, was the entry of the Ottoman Empire into the war on the side of the Central Powers during the autumn of 1914 and the subsequent declaration of jihad made in the name of Sultan Mehmed V. While the vast majority of British Muslims, including those associated with the WMM, did not follow the Caliph's call and instead chose to remain loyal to His Majesty's government, the fact that the First World War pitted Muslim against Muslim and expanded into the Ottoman territories of the Middle East, putting a number of Islam's most important cultural and religious sites in a precarious position if not immediate danger, created considerable tension for individual believers and within the WMM community. The already formidable task of attracting and unifying Muslims from diverse cultural and linguistic backgrounds and specific religious traditions and political leanings was complicated further as wartime developments provoked a variety of opinions and reactions among them. At the same time, the mission leadership had to contend with people in English society and the British government who viewed their organization with new suspicion and as even a possible threat to national security.

Given these new difficulties, the WMM founders could very well have chosen to return to India for the duration of the war with the intent of relaunching their organization at a more opportune time. They also could have looked for another place in the empire or world to pursue missionary activity. However, despite the availability of alternative courses of action, they chose to remain in Woking during those early and especially trying years and, as a result, the WMM emerged from that period as a strong, stable centre for Islam not only in the British Isles but also Western Europe more generally. By the time of the Paris Peace Conference, its leaders deemed the WMM to be such a success that they used it as both model and resource in order to expand missionary efforts into Central and Eastern Europe, most notably with the opening of the Berlin Muslim Mission in 1922, where Sadr-ud-Din served as the imam.

This transformation of the WMM from a budding, but still somewhat inchoate, endeavour prior to the outbreak of the First World War to an organization solidly established in the Western metropole by the time of peace negotiations was made possible by the ability of the mission's leaders and most dynamic supporters to add a new aspect to their ever-evolving ideology of imperial intersection, one which presented their faith as of great value to the war effort. According to them, Islam provided what Christianity could not, a religion offering His Majesty's government, soldiers and subjects divine guidance for waging war in the most practical and ethical manner possible, which, if followed, would bring ultimate victory and a just and lasting peace. The Muslim soldiers, both in the abstract sense and as actual human beings, played a central role in ensuring that the WMM would remain in England. Those who attended the Shah Jahan mosque and events held there gave the mission a new legitimacy in the eyes of a sceptical public, while the funeral and burial services provided for those who perished as the result of battle on the Western Front helped His Majesty's government to counter ongoing German propaganda efforts to convince British Muslims that the Allied cause was contrary to their faith. Finally, while believers drawn to the mosque and mission may have had different opinions regarding the British–Ottoman conflict and the expansion of the First World War into the Middle East, all could find common ground in their shared respect and admiration for the British Muslim soldier and could support WMM efforts to serve their religious needs.

Origins in British India

While WMM leaders sought to create and present an inclusive version of Islam, one free of any type of factionalism or specific regional identity and therefore capable of orienting Muslims from a variety of backgrounds and traditions as well as attracting Westerners, and were to a great extent successful in doing so, it is, nevertheless, important to discuss briefly the emergence of Ahmadiyya Islam in the Indian Punjab and the relationship between that historical development and the expanding British imperial state; for that movement's founder, Mirza Ghulam Ahmad, had considerable influence on Kamal-ud-Din, particularly during the latter's student days in Lahore. In addition, the missionary impulse to spread the Muslim faith in England, central to the WMM's purpose and self-definition, can be found in the teachings of Ghulam Ahmad and reflects the unique religious-political climate of the post-1857 Punjab in which both men, despite being of different generations, struggled to reconcile Muslim traditions with new British imperial and Christian evangelical influences.[14] Finally, briefly considering the British-Indian and Ahmadiyya context which shaped Kamal-ud-Din's early life not only contributes to a better understanding of that leader and thus the WMM but also offers a glimpse into the variety of ways that Muslims from privileged or elite backgrounds could adapt to changing circumstances, creating new networks and reconfiguring old ones in the context of British expansion and ascendancy.

Mirza Ghulam Ahmad was descended from a long line of Muslim aristocrats whose lands north-east of Lahore and the authority to govern them with considerable autonomy were acquired during the reign of the first Mughal emperor, Babur, in the sixteenth century. The rise of Sikh power in the Punjab during the late eighteenth and early nineteenth centuries, however, dealt a devastating blow to the family. One by one they lost the villages on their estate, and the final Sikh conquest of their lands in 1802 forced the surviving family members into exile. They were allowed to return in 1818, but only under the condition that Ghulam Ahmad's father should serve with his brothers in the army of the new emperor, Maharaja Ranjit Singh. In return, they received pensions and control of some of their former villages.

Whatever feelings of loyalty Ghulam Ahmad's relatives might have had for their new Sikh rulers would have been tenuous at best. After all, they regained only a fraction of their former wealth and power and had been obliged to fight fellow Muslims during campaigns in Kashmir, Peshawar and Multan. It is not altogether surprising, then, that the family would gravitate towards the Raj as it expanded into the region and annexed the Punjab in 1849. Ghulam Ahmad even described his father as awaiting British rule "like a thirsty person who longs for water." After the outbreak of the sepoy rebellion eight years later, the family provided infantry and cavalry units to assist the British, with Ghulam Ahmad's brother leading what would become a division of General Nicholson's 46th Native Infantry. Still, the land grant received as a reward for their contribution was not nearly enough for the family to live as they had prior to Sikh ascendancy, so when Ghulam Ahmad came of age during the mid-1860s, he took a position as a reader in the British-Indian court of Sialkot.[15]

Like Ghulam Ahmad, Kamal-ud-Din also came from a prominent northern Indian Muslim family whose members had served the short-lived empire of Maharaja Ranjit Singh before allying themselves with the expanding Raj, although they were more inclined towards educational and judicial rather than military pursuits. Kamal-ud-Din's grandfather, the well-known poet 'Abdur Rashid, acted as the Cadi or chief Muslim judge of Lahore when that city was the Sikh capital, and his brother helped to make education available to Muslims throughout the Kashmir and Jammu region. Kamal-ud-Din attended Forman Christian College, also in Lahore, and received honours and administrative appointments from institutions of higher education in the area, including the Punjab University, established by the colonial administration of the Raj, before serving as a lawyer in the British Chief Court of the Punjab.[16]

Not only did the extension of British imperial power into northern India impact upon the careers, networks and alliances of Kamal-ud-Din, Ghulam Ahmad and their families, but the unique cultural and intellectual milieu created by the shifting borders and a growing British presence in the Punjab played a critical role in shaping the religious lives and missionary efforts of both leaders; for in a part of the world where Hindu, Muslim, Sikh and Christian communities all lived in close proximity to one another and political and religious identities remained inseparable, disruptions, first Sikh and then British, to existing Muslim power structures compromised the status of traditional religious authorities, thereby creating opportunities for new leaders to emerge, revive centuries-old debates and initiate religious reform.[17] As a result of these changes, the *Munazara*, or place of Muslim religious debate, previously confined to the rarefied spaces associated with the royal courts of Lahore and Fatehpur Sikri during the period of Mughal ascendancy, broadened to include a much larger segment of the population.[18] In addition, the increasing number of evangelical missionaries who took advantage of their expanding state by travelling from the British Isles to the northern Punjab for the purpose of converting as many people as possible to Christianity made the need for Muslims to reinvigorate their own faith seem all the more urgent.[19]

As young men, both Ghulam Ahmad and later Kamal-ud-Din encountered Christian missionaries who influenced their lives and beliefs. By the time Ghulam Ahmad arrived in Sialkot to serve as a court reader for the British government, that city already had become a major centre of evangelical activity and, in the course of developing his ideas, he engaged in religious dialogue and debate with Christian missionaries, which exposed him to "new modes of thought." In addition, his position that Jesus Christ survived the crucifixion and travelled to Kashmir where he later died of natural causes has been interpreted by modern scholars as a reflection of the rivalry between Christianity and Islam in India, as what would become an Ahmadi tenet also served to undermine the teachings of evangelicals in the colony.[20]

Ghulam Ahmad was known for his anti-Hindu polemics as well as his anti-Christian ones, and some of his earliest publications were created for the purpose of rallying Indian Muslims against the rise of the Hindu revivalist groups Arya Samaj and Brahmo Samaj, both of which also developed in the context of Christian missionary activity in India.[21] Conversely, Kamal-ud-Din fell under the influence of missionaries while a student at Forman Christian College, to the extent that he almost converted to that faith. In fact, he very well may have done so had it not been for his relationship with

Ghulam Ahmad and attraction to the developing Ahmadiyya movement. Later in life he would explain his decision to spread Islam in England as based, in part, upon the desire to atone for having almost renounced the religion of his birth.[22]

Like the evangelicals who, prior to the Charter Act of 1813, had appealed to their government to prevent the East India Company from denying Christian missionaries access to the subcontinent, Ghulam Ahmad associated his cause with the British liberal traditions of freedom of religion and speech. While the administration of the Raj often fell short of the liberal ideals so often used to justify its existence, he nevertheless praised the British system for allowing "'everyone not only to profess and practice but also to preach and propagate his own religion.'"[23] He even related a vision he had of himself standing on a minaret in London and "elucidating the truth of Islam in a very argumentative discourse in the English language" and then catching a large number of white birds, a scene which he interpreted to mean that one day his words would reach the people of that country and result in new converts.[24] As early as 1892 Ghulam Ahmad and his followers formally declared the intention to spread their beliefs beyond northern India, to Europe, including England, and throughout the world, and in his book published the following year he invited Queen Victoria to embrace Islam.[25] He launched a monthly English-language journal, *The Review of Religions*, in 1902, published from Qadian and edited by Kamal-ud-Din.[26] He believed that not only would his efforts result in the spreading of his faith to the West but an Islamic renaissance would begin in London and then emanate outwards from that capital city of the British Empire.[27]

Certainly, freedom of speech and religion would be issues of no small importance to any religious reformer, especially one like Ghulam Ahmad who had aroused the ire of traditionalists and more established Muslim authorities by, in 1891, proclaiming himself to be a *muhaddath*, or one to whom God speaks directly. Ghulam Ahmad's exact status, however, would become a subject of debate for the Ahmadi community after his death in 1908, and then again after the passing of his successor, Nur al-Din, six years later, for he had not only referred to himself as a *muhaddath* but also as a *zilli nabi* or non-law-bearing prophet; *mujaddid*, a renewer or divinely chosen reformer of the faith; a *mahdi*, guided one; and as the *masih-i maw'ud*, the messiah or return of Christ.[28] The latter three titles tended to be understood by his followers as indicating someone destined to revive and purify Islam. In addition, because Ghulam Ahmad expressed himself in a style rooted in certain mystical and Sufi traditions which valued subtlety, ambiguity and the use of contradiction, his writings allowed for different ways of interpreting his spiritual status. As a result of differing viewpoints on this issue, as well as conflicting personalities, the Ahmadiyya movement split into two factions in 1914. The Qadiani branch, named for Qadian, a town just outside Lahore, base of support and birthplace of Ghulam Ahmad, revered the leader as a prophet, although one of lesser importance than Muhammad. The Lahori branch, on the other hand, maintained that Ghulam Ahmad was a reformer or renewer of Islam but not a prophet, a position which put them closer to Sunni orthodoxy.[29]

This conflict within the Indian Ahmadiyya community came to a head just after Kamal-ud-Din had officially opened the doors of the WMM, so in 1914 the Khwaja, as he also was known, entrusted the new mission to Sadr-ud-Din, and left Woking for Lahore. There, Kamal-ud-Din worked to reconnect with his loyal base of supporters, many of whom were English-educated Muslim men tied to the Raj through official positions, titles of honour or both.[30] He then stayed to lend his expertise and assist in the development of the Lahori branch of Ahmadiyya Islam, thus laying the foundation for future relationships between this newly organized or reorganized community in India and the WMM, to which he returned after two years.[31]

Not all WMM members, however, sympathized with the Lahoris when the Ahmadiyya movement split in 1914. One of Kamal-ud-Din's assistants during the early days of that organization, Chaudhry Muhammad Sayal, sided with the Qadianis and left Woking to start a separate mission in London. Still, most Muslims in Britain downplayed or ignored this sectarian conflict, relying upon the resources of both missions,[32] and the Shah Jahan mosque remained the centre of Islam in England, even drawing followers from William Henry Quilliam's former Liverpool-based Muslim community.[33] The WMM possessed greater resources and reached more Britons than Sayal's London Muslim Mission, which struggled to attract converts and even attendees for events.[34] For these reasons the WMM, not the London Muslim Mission, is the focus of this study.

Throughout the chapter, I refer to the WMM as a "Muslim" movement as opposed to an "Ahmadiyya Muslim" or a "Lahori Ahmadiyya Muslim" movement. This choice of words is not to contest the practical and intellectual influences that the life and teachings of Mirza Ghulam Ahmad had on Kamal-ud-Din and other members of the WMM. Nor is it to deny the continued connections between the Lahori community in India and the WMM after the Ahmadiyya split.[35] Rather, it is to engage with the way that members of the WMM understood and represented themselves in Britain and in the English-language press during the First World War period, for in their publication, the *IR*, they did not describe themselves as "Ahmadi" or as belonging to the "Ahmadiyya" movement, but instead simply used the word "Muslim."[36] In addition, most converts were unaware of the WMM's Ahmadi roots, believing themselves to be a part of Sunni Hanafi Islam.[37]

Celebration of global diversity

The WMM's reluctance to embrace a factional identity is consistent with the mission's emphasis on the unifying force of their faith. After all, its leaders and most dynamic members focused on commonalities shared by all Muslims and extended open arms to their co-religionists from throughout the empire and world regardless of their political beliefs, the particular version of Islam they practised or the labels that they had assumed or been given, whether Shia, Sunni or Wahhabi. Even when Kamal-ud-Din believed 'Abdu'l-Bahá to be the "Head of the Bábí religion" he, nevertheless, invited that spiritual leader to the Shah Jahan mosque and to join the community for *Asr* prayers on the grounds that he "is after all the son of a Muslim, and used to be a Muslim."[38] In addition, Kamal-ud-Din and other members of the WMM participated in, and in some cases helped to establish, Muslim organizations in the London area, including the Central Islamic, Anglo-Ottoman and British Muslim societies, which gave them opportunities to engage with their co-religionists of different views and backgrounds.[39]

Reports of events at the Shah Jahan mosque related with pride the global diversity at that place of worship, where Arabic, English, Hindustani and Persian all might be heard. One describes the festival of *Eid al-Adha* as attended by a "sprinkling of Muslims from Persia and Egypt" and representatives from "nearly every corner of Arabia and Africa."[40] Another praised the unifying force of Islam, as demonstrated by the crowd gathered on the lawn of the mosque during *Eid al-Fitr* (Figure 2.2):

> White and black, brown and yellow, men from the east and west, north and south ... from "subject" races and men from "ruling" races, princes and peasants, civilians and military men, in short men, and women too, of various places, rank and nationalities stood shoulder to shoulder.

On that day, four hundred people took part in the festivities, and hundreds more came from the town to watch.[41] Photographs taken of these types of events further helped to communicate the ideal of a unified world which challenged Orientalist assumptions as boundaries between "East" and "West" were crossed, and fashionable European-style hats, dresses and tailored suits appeared among majestic turbans and flowing kaftans.[42]

Such gatherings testified to the diversity that characterized both the Islamic world and the British Empire, for while the belief in one God and in Muhammad as the prophet of God may have drawn Muslims from different

Planting the "banner of Islam"

Figure 2.2 Sadr-ud-Din, *Eid al-Fitr*, Woking 1915.

backgrounds to Woking, most would not have been in the London area in the first place if not for some connection to institutions of empire, political, economic or educational. Because of its unique and, in certain respects, privileged location in the metropole, events at the Shah Jahan mosque drew crowds resembling a microcosm of the *ummah* from the peripheries and beyond them. Yet this degree of heterogeneity was not typical of the majority of Muslim communities in the world. With regard to the Indian Ahmadis, for example, many of the early followers, especially those in rural areas, came to the movement not because of its intended global outreach or even sophisticated arguments but, rather, because of its regional character: in it they found familiar spiritual practices which reflected their own backgrounds combining "folk Sufi, Sunni, [and] Punjabi" traditions.[43] The extraordinary diversity of WMM gatherings and its visual impact was expressed perhaps most poetically by William Henry Quilliam, the former Liverpool solicitor and convert who led a small community of believers in that city during the late nineteenth century, when he explained that, despite his many years of living and travelling amongst Muslims in Europe, Asia and Africa, never had he "witnessed a more picturesque" scene than that of a recent *Eid* ceremony at the Shah Jahan mosque, upon which his "visual organs feasted in delight."[44] Soon after establishing the WMM, Kamal-ud-Din had succeeded in the goal he originally set for himself when he first visited Woking, which was to transform that abandoned place of worship into a "Mecca in the West," or a hub capable of drawing believers from nations throughout the world.[45]

Within the first two years of its creation the WMM attracted over one hundred converts[46] and, as people from England and other areas of the British Isles began to accept Islam, thereby extending mission networks more deeply into that region of the world, the Woking community became both increasingly hybridized and more firmly established in the metropole. "Western" Muslims frequently incorporated "Eastern" elements into their lives and dress. Often, they adopted Arabic names to be used interchangeably or combined with their given ones, such as "Ameena Mubarkah Alice Welch" or "Noor-ud-Din Harris," as a way of consciously embracing and communicating more profound internal transformations. These new believers acted as an important link between the WMM and English society. Initially, they defended the Woking community against townspeople who objected to the reopening of the mosque. They also helped to make curious visitors feel welcome and comfortable, a service which brought additional members to the fold. As Kamal-ud-Din explained to his brethren in Lahore, when English people came to gatherings at the mosque, they were able to talk more freely and mix more quickly with WMM members from their own country.[47]

Despite what would seem to be an elite bias based upon the disproportionate number of aristocratic and upper-middle-class converts and the professional success of Indian Muslim supporters, Kamal-ud-Din and other contributors to the WMM took pride in the fact that their community transcended divisions based upon not only nation, race and ethnicity but also class.[48] A description of another *Eid* celebration explains a kind of "democratic socialism" inherent in Islam as evidenced by the egalitarian nature of ceremony and seating arrangements at the mosque. At that particular event His Highness the Aga Khan of India arrived late. Yet, despite his status and the fact that he frequently lunched with His Majesty the King of England and Emperor of India, as he had done only a few days prior to his visit to Woking, no attempt was made to postpone the ceremony for him. When he arrived, he humbly sat in the back with ordinary soldiers. The report relates that the convert Lord Headley, who was also known in Muslim circles as Saifur-Rahman Sheikh Rahmatullah Farooq, sat in the back as well, although if he had remained in the faith of his birth he would have had his own pew.[49]

WMM supporters also expressed concern for the poor and the oppressed and hopes that they too could be empowered through the spread of Islam. One described the successes that the organization had had in converting English people of different social backgrounds, from royalty to labourers, noting that while their faith welcomed all classes, they had not yet been "fortunate" enough to gain converts from among the very poor, those who starve or live "hand to mouth."[50] Members of the WMM sometimes compared the destitute of England to the Shudras, or the lowest caste of India, relating how both could be elevated and made equals through Islam. Kamal-ud-Din expressed similar sentiments, and in a sermon given at the Woking mosque he combined religious beliefs in the value of equality, compassion and charity with contemporary socialist language by stating "Is not capital sucking the very blood of labour and trying to take his pound of flesh from the bleeding breast of the workman?"[51]

While the use of this particular phrase has antisemitic overtones in that it calls to mind Shakespeare's *Merchant of Venice*, in which the Jewish moneylender Shylock demands a pound of flesh from his client for defaulting on a loan, Jews were welcomed at the mosque and encouraged to visit, as were people from all backgrounds and religious persuasions. Notices for Friday prayers and Sunday lectures invited non-Muslims to attend and even encouraged "friendly controversy" and "healthy criticism" amongst people from different faith backgrounds.[52] A series of talks at the mosque about the relationship between Christianity and Islam drew crowds of interested Christians, as intended.[53] In addition, those involved with the WMM repeatedly described or referred to Judaism and Christianity as "sister faiths" of Islam, as all three monotheistic religions stemmed from the Abrahamic tradition. Each year WMM members made an extra effort to encourage Jews and Christians to join them for *Eid al-Adha*, when they commemorated Abraham's willingness to sacrifice his son. The *Woking Herald* covered one such event, noting the presence of Jews, Catholics, "Church and Chapel people" (a reference to Anglicans and dissenting Protestants) and even Hindus, concluding that "probably no sacred building other than the Mosque would have these elements united in the service."[54]

As the reference to Hindus suggests, the Woking community did not limit itself to the Abrahamic tradition when it came to welcoming people with other belief systems and finding common ground with them. Kamal-ud-Din maintained that, like Judaism and Christianity, Hinduism also was a "sister religion" of Islam, and that just as he regarded certain portions of the Bible as the word of God, he also considered the Bhagavad Gita as "my joint property with my Hindu brethren." Along the same lines, he expressed cherishing feelings for Krishna and Ramachandra not unlike those he had for Moses and Jesus, both of whom he respected as prophets.[55] Others representing the WMM added Buddha and Zoroaster to the list of those who communicated the message of God to mankind.[56] Confucius might be mentioned as well, usually as an enlightened teacher, but sometimes as a prophet.[57] Finally, on at least one occasion Socrates, Jesus and Hussain were grouped together as the world's three greatest martyrs.[58] Leaders and others who helped to create the developing intersectional imperial ideology of the newly established WMM did so by engaging with intellectual and religious traditions available to them in the larger British, and especially British Indian, imperial culture; in the organization's small library one could find, in addition to the Qur'an and other Muslim core or canonical writings, the essays of Thomas Babington Macaulay, novels of Charles Dickens, Hindu religious texts and Theosophist publications.[59]

This intellectual openness on the part of the WMM supporters, however, does not mean that they regarded all perspectives as equally valuable, for they understood Muhammad as the last prophet at whose feet followers of all other religions and belief systems could come together:

> The Yogi and Swami, Rishi too,
> Bow to Allah the One.
> And Christian and Buddhist and Hindu
> Unite when day is done
> Together to pray and together repeat,
> At the feet of Muhammad East and West meet.[60]

After all, the WMM was a missionary organization created for the purpose of winning converts, and, according to its discourse, only by becoming a Muslim could an individual be truly universal. As much as Judaism and Christianity were praised as sister religions, they also were criticized for their exclusivity, the belief in themselves as a "chosen people" in the former and the conviction that salvation comes through Christ alone in the latter.[61] Yet, not surprisingly, what WMM members considered imperfections or shortcomings of both faiths, as well as those of other world religions, could be remedied through that organization's teachings. As one *IR* article explains, Judaism remained encumbered by "stiff chains of ritual." Christianity, on the other hand, went too far in the opposite direction and, like Buddhism, tended towards the "impractical ... abstruse and dreamy." Yet both Jews and Christians could find a "happy mean" by embracing Islam.[62]

Countering Orientalism with Occidentalism: a response to Christian missionaries

Members of the WMM had a complicated relationship with Christian missionaries, characterized by the dynamic interplay of identification and the projection of alterity. As noted previously, Kamal-ud-Din almost converted to that faith while a student at Forman Christian College in Lahore. Through that experience he came to understand both the potential power of missionary work as well as its methods, which he later decided to apply in the reverse. After all, if people from the imperial metropole could travel to the peripheries of empire to teach their religious beliefs, why then couldn't Punjabis make their way to England for the same reason? If Muslims could be convinced or, as in his case, almost convinced, to reject the teachings of Muhammad, couldn't Christians be persuaded to accept that prophet as an extension of the religious beliefs they already held?

Members of the WMM looked to Christian missionary practices and accomplishments as a model of what their own movement could become. As one prominent WMM supporter and contributor to the *IR* explained, the "Christian missionary system is a wonderful organization," for not only did it have "colossal wealth at its disposal" but it had the backing of powerful states, an "army" of preachers and countless well-organized societies and institutions such as primary schools, colleges and hospitals. In addition, Christians had their literature translated into many languages and brought it to every corner of the earth.[63] Finally, they took advantage of new developments in technology, from the use of steamships and railways to improved printing presses, in order to spread their faith. Now was the time for Muslims to do the same.[64]

Kamal-ud-Din used Christian missionaries as an example when requesting support from fellow Muslims in Lahore. In an attempt to gain funding for a project to translate and publish the Qur'an in English, he remarked on the mental effort that Christians devoted to their cause and lamented that while their clergymen were "printing the Bible in tens of millions and throwing it around," Muslims remained comparatively silent even though potential converts were asking to read their holy book.[65] Similarly, in a report justifying his expenses, Kamal-ud-Din explained the need for extending hospitality to English converts who came to Woking in order to study and learn more about Islam. Doing so was not charity, as none was poor and some were "quite affluent," but, rather, a means of strengthening a budding community. Such expenses were negligible, he added, especially when compared to the "huge amount of money" that Christian missionaries willingly spent in India, even just to convert a single "street cleaner."[66]

As Kamal-ud-Din and other members of the WMM found themselves teaching their faith primarily to people from English Christian backgrounds, they accommodated themselves to beliefs, practices and expectations of those potential converts. For example, they stressed the common bond both faiths shared with regard to progressive revelation and used terms with which Christians would be familiar by, for example, referring to the Qur'an as the "Islamic Bible" and the Shah Jahan mosque as a "Muslim church." Shoes could be worn during prayer if they were clean, and while women who visited from India and other parts of the world where they were accustomed to veiling continued to do so, there was no such expectation for English converts.

Yet, despite the various ways that WMM members accommodated and identified with Christians and looked to their missionaries as role models, ultimately, they regarded workers in that cause as adversaries who must be countered and overcome at every turn. WMM leaders continually complained that Christians distorted and maligned Islam for the purpose of maintaining loyal congregations at home and winning converts abroad. In addition, when they extended their mission activities to Muslim lands, they became like modern-day Crusaders. Editors and others supportive of the WMM regularly took to the pages of the *IR* to respond to Christian criticisms of their faith by, for example, reproducing debates in the form of letter exchanges or refuting specific statements made by prominent religious leaders.

Often, they adopted the very missionary discourse used to discredit Islam and then modified it to the degree that it could be employed against Christianity instead. Discussions of gender proved particularly useful in this respect, as the West was not without its own gender-based inequalities and injustices. For example, a reviewer of the Christian missionary book *Our Moslem Sisters* maintained that such publications depicting the oppression of females under Islam were created as a form of propaganda intended to help recruit women for organizations such as the "Zenana Mission," a programme always in need of female volunteers who might be able to bring their faith to the private quarters of Muslim and Hindu and households in India where men outside of the immediate family were not permitted. The reviewer goes on to say that while scenes in that book in which females appear as "beasts of burden" carrying heavy loads may exist in Muslim Indian slums, women are equally overburdened with physical labour in the sweatshops, match factories and rolling mills of East End London.[67] Other articles relate how the spread of Islam in the West will liberate females from their subjugated state, as misogynistic beliefs perpetuated by Christian authorities will cease to exist, such as the idea that woman caused original sin.[68] Along the same lines, another WMM supporter and regular contributor to the *IR* presented the position that the Christian tendency to criticize the practice of polygamy stemmed not from the desire to protect the fair sex, as missionaries and others so often claimed, but, rather, from a deeply rooted dislike of women inherent that religion. The author then went on to explain that the laws limiting a man to only one wife came from the same impulse that encouraged men to distance themselves from females in general by idealizing monastic and celibate life.[69]

These types of representations reversing common "Orientalist" tropes and stereotypes could be seen as an "Occidentalist" response. As the reviewer of the aforementioned book explained, while Christian missionaries so often blamed the closed and backwards "Oriental mind" when their teaching efforts failed to yield results, they remained unaware of how their own understanding of Christianity was distorted and encumbered by "Occidentalism," or the very same "Occidental polytheistic tendencies which induced" their "forefathers to accept Jesus for Zeus and Mary for Venus."[70] WMM missionaries and writers for the *IR* often referred to the "Occidental mind" as obscured from truth, employing images such as clouds, mist or tarnish to describe it. For example, Kamal-ud-Din explained to his followers that "strenuous efforts" would be required to "disillusionize the Occidental mind from the clouds of calumny and slander" that prevented it from seeing true Islam.[71]

Other common reversals of familiar Orientalist discourses include depicting Christianity as the "religion of the sword" and the systems of labour perpetuated by modern Western powers as akin to slavery. Those who wanted to call attention to acts of violence committed by Christians found no shortage of examples, from the Crusades and the Spanish Inquisition of previous historical periods to more recent atrocities in Tripoli or the Balkans.[72] Alternatively, while English abolitionists, reformers and others denounced slavery as fundamentally contrary to their own values, associating it with the barbarism of previous eras of European history and the "backwardness" of the Islamic world, past and present, supporters of the WMM drew attention to the ongoing exploitation of labour in various forms in the West, including that which accompanied imperialism, for European expansion in Africa, Asia and the Middle East often had profoundly negative consequences on the original inhabitants, reducing them to, as one *IR* contributor commented, a state of "serfdom."[73]

It is important to note, however, that despite efforts to counter the dominant "Orientalist" discourses by presenting "Occidentalist" alternatives, writers for the *IR* and others who contributed to the mission of the WMM repeatedly emphasized their belief that Allah recognized no such man-made categories and that they hoped first to bridge and then eventually eliminate this perceived divide. Missionaries from India referred to Woking and the Shah Jahan mosque as a gateway through which they could reach hearts and minds in the West.[74] Conversely, Britons who embraced Islam spoke of reorienting or opening themselves to influences from the East. The idea of Orient and Occident joining together in harmony, fellowship and mutual respect is perhaps most effectively communicated by a photograph of the convert Lord Headley and Kamal-ud-Din standing together side by side with hands clasped, under the caption "East meets West in the Unity of Islam" (Figure 2.3). In fact, Headley, who regarded Kamal-ud-Din as a close friend, spiritual brother and role model, first suggested the creation and dissemination of this portrait as a way of dispelling the widespread belief embodied in Rudyard Kipling's oft-quoted phrase "East is East and

Figure 2.3 Kamal-ud-Din and Lord Headley, 1913. East meets West in the Unity of Islam.

West is West and never the twain shall meet."[75] Given the larger missionary and imperial context, the binary thinking reproduced when WMM supporters employed Occidentalist discourses as an answer to the dominant Orientalist ones would have to have been understood as but a temporary side effect of a process that one day would unify all of humanity, rendering such divisions and their labels meaningless.

One of the most common Orientalist tropes, adopted, modified and then reversed, was the idea that missionaries faced the challenge of teaching their faith to people who held antiquated beliefs belonging to previous, less developed eras in human history. For some time, Christian missionaries from the British Isles had depicted those they encountered in Africa, India and the Middle East in such a manner. With the establishment of the WMM, Muslim missionaries did the same. Sometimes these types of representations appeared in an informative or light-hearted manner, such as when *IR* articles explored the history of popular English Christmas holiday customs. One related the "heathen origin" of the Yule log, describing how it had been used to honour the Norse gods Thor and Odin and how similar practices once were employed in fire- and sun-worshipping rituals. It also explained the tradition of hanging mistletoe as originating with the ancient Druids, who did so to welcome or extend a "kiss of greeting" to the fairies of the forest.[76]

Similarly, although on a more serious note, contributors to the WMM and the *IR* repeatedly emphasized the importance of believing in the oneness of God and the humanity of Jesus, and defined Christians who subscribed to the doctrine of the Trinity, a tenet of the Church of England and other denominations in the British Isles, as polytheists and therefore idolaters.[77] This position reversed the more familiar discourses of Christian missionaries who understood idol worship and polytheism as existing either in the pagan world of the ancient Mediterranean, known to them through the Old Testament, or in colonial territories, where they encountered what they considered to be heathen fetish objects, but not in their own churches.[78] As Abbas Ali Baig, one of the original founders the Woking Mosque Trust, explained to a crowded London lecture hall, the two "sister religions" of Christianity and Islam had much in common and seemed to differ only because the former had become corrupted by pagan influences, including the belief in the Trinity.[79] One of the editors of the *IR* even expressed hope that the day would come when including "*Trinitarians* in the fold of Christians" would be a "crime."[80] Yet, just as Christian missionaries continually expressed the conviction that through their efforts the light of the truth would shine in the East and in the dark regions of their empire's peripheries, members of the WMM believed that they could reach the people of the metropole and help to put the English and other Britons on the straight path. By spreading Islam, they could do for Westerners of the twentieth century what their prophet and exemplar Muhammad had done for the inhabitants of the Arabian Peninsula during the seventh: destroy the idolatry "into which Jews, Christians, and heathen had equally fallen."[81]

Like the Trinity, WMM supporters regarded the belief in Christ's crucifixion and the rites commonly associated with it as remnants from a less civilized era in human history, with some of the harshest criticisms coming not from Indian missionaries but from Britons who had embraced Islam. For example, the Scottish-born convert John Yehya en-Nesr Parkinson called the Christian Eucharist a form of ritual cannibalism, varieties of which could be found throughout heathendom, and explained such practices as stemming from the actual cannibalism of prehistoric times.[82] The following year Parkinson once again took up the theme of the crucifixion, this time in a two-part article published in the *IR* entitled "The Type of the Red Heifer." In it he explains how, in the ancient world, sacrifices of both animals and human beings took place on all continents, as ritual formed "the thought-structure of savages" and "reason was only awakening in the cradle of Time."[83] He then goes on to discuss the crucifixion of Christ in this context and in relation to ancient Jewish and pagan sacrificial ceremonies, speculating that they too were rooted in even earlier traditions, perhaps long-forgotten cults dedicated to animal deities, possibly a cow goddess.[84] Similarly, Lord Headley called Christ's death upon the cross a story of human sacrifice that has no place in the twentieth century as it "savours of … Druidical horrors" and "dates back to the days when primeval savages attempted to propitiate angry deities."[85]

Such pagan influences combined with subsequent generations of religious authorities who misunderstood the teachings of Christ meant, according to WMM supporters, that Britons were in real need of Muhammad's message. Contributors to the *IR*, regularly outlined the erroneous thinking behind common contemporary Christian beliefs and practices, from alcohol consumption to doctrines regarding sin and salvation, with one concluding that because of that religion's "untenable dogmas … alien to human nature," it had become a "dead-letter" incapable of protecting its followers from the increasingly powerful forces of atheism and materialism.[86]

Yet, by recognizing Muhammad as the "Comforter" promised to them by Jesus and embracing Islam, Christians could reinvigorate their faith and come to understand its true ideals.[87] Similarly, while much of the Bible had been invented by human beings, it, nevertheless, contained spiritual verities which could be revealed and understood when supplemented by the Qur'an.[88]

In addition, British Christians were not far from realizing, as Lord Headley and other converts insisted, that one could simultaneously be a good Christian and a good Muslim.[89] The editors of the *IR* regularly related instances in which Christians expressed some sort of admiration of or affinity for Islam, reinforcing the idea that more conversions could be expected in the near future, at least as long as the WMM continued its work. Such reports were not confined to any particular denomination. One might refer to the Church of England, as in the case of an article about the vicar of Brixton who caused controversy by announcing to his congregation on Easter Sunday that he did not believe in the bodily resurrection of Christ.[90] Others might, for example, make note of how a Catholic man expressed a greater sympathy with Islam than any form of Protestantism or include a paper presented by an English Quaker praising aspects of Islam.[91]

The press and print culture

As the above examination of the WMM's relationship with Christianity and the discourses of Christian missionaries indicates, the *IR* played an important role in providing a platform for the development, presentation and dissemination of Muslim counter-narratives.[92] In fact, one of the primary reasons why Kamal-ud-Din decided to launch the monthly periodical in 1913 was as an answer to *The Moslem World*, a quarterly produced under the auspices of the Nile Mission Press and the Christian Literature Society for India, for he and other English educated Muslims in the empire often read that publication for its coverage of current events and issues of cultural interest in Muslim lands. Yet, in doing so, they continually exposed themselves to articles with a strong bias against their faith, depicting it as, at best, an obstacle to be overcome. The Khwaja envisioned an alternative journal which would provide news and intellectual stimulation from the perspective of the Muslim rather than Christian missionary, thus connecting followers of Muhammad from diverse backgrounds, while at the same time showing the Muslim religion in a positive light and in such a way so as to generate interest in it among people from other faith traditions.

Yet Christian missionaries were not the only ones perpetuating negative representations of Islam: so too did journalists, especially when their articles served to defend Foreign Office policy decisions based upon assumptions of Muslim alterity. In an effort to check such tendencies and provide alternative ways of understanding their co-religionists in the international context, WMM supporters monitored and engaged with the English-language press, either through letters to their editors or articles of response in the *IR* or both.[93] For example, prior to the First World War, writers for the *IR* frequently called attention to the relative lack of coverage when it came to reporting atrocities committed against Muslims in the Balkans, as compared to the interest generated when Christians in that region experienced persecution, a bias that seemed to go hand in hand with government policies favouring the Czar's regime over that of the Sultan. A series of articles in the *IR* during that period warned of the difficulties that might result if the British press, people and government continued with this anti-Turkish position.[94] It is important to emphasize, however, that these types of criticisms or suggestions were always presented in the most unconfrontational manner possible, as a way that members of the WMM could use their intimate understanding of both Islam in general and the specific concerns of Indian Muslims to assist His Majesty's representatives with the "arduous and delicate" task of harmonizing the various interests, peoples, races and creeds that comprised the British Empire;[95] as Kamal-ud-Din explained in the first issue of the *IR*, that empire was like a living organism that depends upon the "complete fusion of it various components" for health, stability and vigour.[96]

For a number of British-educated Indian Muslim leaders, including those involved with the WMM, the future of the Ottoman Empire became an issue of real concern. As one of the few remaining, and by far most significant, Islamic powers in a world that had witnessed Western imperial expansion into Muslim lands from Africa, to the Middle East, to South Asia, the strength and integrity of that empire had considerable emotional as well as political significance. Muslims in India and the London–Woking area organized themselves into a wide range of political organizations and pressure groups, most notably the Central Islamic and Anglo-Ottoman societies, through which they pursued Ottoman-oriented, pan-Islamic goals in an effort to stem the decline of the *ummah*. Some pan-Islamists, members of an older generation and led by the statesman and trustee of the mosque Syed Ameer Ali, worked through British institutions and according to constitutional methods, while a younger generation influenced by the prominent international writer and activist, Jamal al-Din al-Afghani, tended to have more anti-Western and, in the case of India and Egypt, nationalist leanings.[97] Kamal-ud-Din welcomed believers of different political persuasions and shades of pan-Islam and maintained a kind of middle ground by both warning fellow Muslim subjects of the Raj that sedition was prohibited by their faith while at the same time insisting that they had every right to criticize government policy.[98]

In response to accusations of disloyalty by members of the press and the public, Kamal-ud-Din responded by explaining that Muslims of the Raj were neither slaves nor serfs but, rather, fellow subjects who served the state and paid taxes just like any Christian or Jewish subject in the empire and that, therefore, they had a legitimate right to voice their disapproval of government policy.[99] In "An open letter to the Prime Minister," published in the *IR*, Kamal-ud-Din stresses the inherent sympathy between Islam and British constitutionalism. In it, he begins by explaining that even if Indian Muslims had no previous knowledge of English history or that country's political traditions, they still would know well how to be simultaneously loyal subjects and critical of their government, for Muhammad had instructed his followers to obey those in authority *and* inform rulers of wrongs done by them. To behave in such a manner was a duty, a meritorious act and even a type of jihad, or holy struggle, possibly because of the courage it might require. Like so many other British subjects in the empire, His Majesty's Muslims had no difficulty in understanding the proper relationship between ruler and ruled as one characterized by rights and obligations on both sides. While the ruled may be required to obey laws and pay taxes, they could expect, in return, the protection of life and property and the right "to see our feelings respected and our susceptibilities not ignored." After all, Christians regularly criticized the government, and Christian organizations frequently intervened on behalf of their co-religionists abroad. Shouldn't Muslims be able to do the same without having their loyalty questioned?[100]

Kamal-ud-Din would continue to maintain Islam's affinity with constitutionalist principles and contract theory, as he explained in his book *India in the Balance*, published almost a decade after his "open letter":

> From a *Muslim point of view* [italics mine] the rulers and the ruled are parties to a contract, under which it is the former's duty to look to the safety of the life, property and general interest of the latter, and the latter's to pay the taxes lawfully demanded and submit to authority.[101]

By participating in public political print culture, asserting their rights as British subjects, and entering into debates with their critics, Kamal-ud-Din and other supporters of the WMM engaged in well-known liberal and Enlightenment traditions. They insisted repeatedly upon the importance of rational dialogue and debate, so that audiences would be free to consider the merits of different belief systems and then make up their own minds. As one convert and contributor to the *IR* explained, with all the conviction and flair of any number of English writers or orators who had championed the causes of a free press, free speech, or reform,

> We have planted our banner in the fields of England ... Our principal weapon is the pen, our organ the *Review*. It is war, but what we destroy are not human lives, but wrong ideas.[102]

Also tapping into English liberal and Enlightenment ideals, while at the same time asserting the rightness of their mission, Kamal-ud-Din expressed the belief that because the *IR* and the WMM had begun to correct misperceptions about their faith and teach it on "these soils of freedom and liberty," soon millions in Great Britain would become Muslims as well.[103]

In pursuit of that goal Kamal-ud-Din wrote over one hundred books, pamphlets and other missionary materials, which eventually "penetrated all the nooks and corners of the British Isles."[104] Both he and Sadr-ud-Din, co-editor of the *IR*, repeatedly emphasized the critical importance of that periodical, and of the written word more generally, to the work of the WMM. As Kamal-ud-Din explained to his co-religionists in India, because most people in England worked long hours, they had very little free time to dedicate to independent thought by, for example, discussing ideas or attending lectures. Instead they found a newspaper that they considered trustworthy, read it before work in the morning, and adopted the beliefs and opinions expressed in it as their own.[105] Therefore, continuing to produce a regularly appearing Muslim journal that engaged with contemporary issues of interest as well as more literary, religious or cultural concerns could not be more vital to the cause. Similarly, Sadr-ud-Din urged fellow Muslims to contribute financially or otherwise to the *IR* and to the translation of books and missionary writings by explaining that the "only means of finding access to the otherwise impenetrable heart of the West is through a large volume of inspiring and illuminating literature."[106]

Publishing from the imperial metropole allowed the WMM to reach a global as well as a Western audience. As Kamal-ud-Din reported to his co-religionists in Lahore, "we can propagate Islam in the whole world while sitting in London."[107] Within the first year the *IR* had a circulation of three thousand in England and India,[108] with additional copies sent regularly to contacts from West Africa to the Far East.[109] The WMM donated subscriptions to major libraries throughout the empire and beyond its borders as well as to interested non-believers. Soon after its debut, the periodical held a "virtual monopoly" with regard to the British Muslim press,[110] and over the course of the period studied it became the most widely circulated Muslim publication in the world. Material from the *IR* appeared monthly in Urdu under the title *Isha'at-i Islam*, and sections, or in some cases entire issues, were translated into Arabic, Persian, Malay and Esperanto. The use of different languages, including English, reflects the WMM's mission to reach and eventually unify all of humanity with the message of Islam. Given this universalist approach, it is not surprising that the editors would take an interest in Esperanto, as that language was invented during the nineteenth century for the purpose of facilitating communication and therefore understanding amongst the peoples of the world.[111] For the editors of the *IR*, engaging with multiple languages was, like publishing from the London area, a way to reach an international audience. As they told their co-religionists when appealing for support, "put forward your utmost effort to keep the flag flying topmast high in the heart of the British Empire, in the greatest city of Christendom, and in the forefront of the world."[112]

As the above discussion indicates, for the creators of the WMM the primary appeal of the imperial metropole had to do with its ability to serve as a kind of launching pad, or place from which Indian Muslims could reach, in addition to the English, millions of others who resided in the peripheries of empire and even beyond it. In that respect WMM supporters should be understood as working within existing British power structures, including the commonly accepted understanding of centres and peripheries associated with them, while simultaneously challenging certain imperialist assumptions. In fact, due to developments in transportation, communication and the technology of print culture, none of which existed independently of larger imperial processes, it was possible for individuals to convert without ever having to travel to the metropole, or the London–Woking area.¹¹³ As the editors of the *IR* explained to their readership, the only action required to become a Muslim was to send a letter or signed declaration form in which the new believer testified to the "Unity of God" and the "brotherhood of man, as preached by all the prophets from Adam and Abraham down to Moses, Jesus, and Mohammad." WMM organizers testified to a "stream" of such letters "pouring in every week," although a "steady trickle," is perhaps the more apt analogy.¹¹⁴ Still, conversion was possible via print culture alone.

The WMM and the First World War

New challenges

So far, this chapter has focused on the emergence of the WMM in the Woking–London area, and the intersectional imperial ideology that made it possible. Critical to that system of meaning was a belief in the importance of establishing a base in the English metropole and of certain liberal ideals, particularly with regard to religious toleration, free speech and a flourishing print culture. WMM supporters understood Islam as broad, inclusive and as necessary to the well-being and spiritual growth of Westerners as it was to Easterners. These basic components of the WMM's ideology originated within certain Muslim communities of the British Raj and they continued to be discussed, represented and used to inform the actions of the Woking missionaries throughout the period examined in this study. With the outbreak of the First World War, however, the WMM was presented with new challenges, to which its leaders and most dynamic supporters responded by elaborating and building upon the organization's existing or foundational ideology in such a way so as to make their continued presence and efforts in England meaningful and therefore possible during a time of crisis.

The First World War was a shock to the organizers of the WMM, as it was to others in the British Isles, empire and world. When Kamal-ud-Din decided to create the mission in 1912 and the mosque officially opened its doors in the following year there was no way that supporters could have predicted the series of events that would lead to the eruption of hostilities in Europe and the British declaration of war on August 4, 1914. The Ottoman Empire's entrance on the side of the Central Powers complicated matters considerably. Not only did it mean that British Muslim soldiers might be obligated to oppose their co-religionists on the battlefield, but, with the declaration of jihad or holy war in the name of Sultan Mehmed V in November of that year, they were called upon to take up arms against the Allies. In response,

British war strategists pursued policies that resulted in the expansion of the conflict into the Middle East, both from Mesopotamia, or modern Iraq, and Egypt, believing that the loyalty of the empire's Muslim subjects could be secured by a show of strength in the form of decisive victories in places of historical, cultural and religious significance for Islam.[115]

These developments, however, created additional difficulties for British Muslims who understood their faith as requiring loyalty to a just government but not one that was hostile or antagonistic to their religion. In other words, their support was not unconditional and depended upon that government's willingness to respect the sensibilities of its Muslim subjects, the definition of which could vary depending upon the individual, a diversity of opinion which reflected the essentially heterogeneous nature of those connected to the WMM in thought as well as area of origin and cultural background. Some expressed concern that the war should remain secular in nature, usually meaning that holy places would remain undisturbed and that British leaders would show sensitivity and tact with regard to the Caliphate.[116] One person in particular, the English convert Marmaduke Pickthall, became such an outspoken critic of British foreign policy that contemporaries dubbed him the country's "most loyal enemy."[117]

In order for the WMM to stay, and to continue missionary work in the metropole, its leaders and others who represented it had to walk a fine line, maintaining their integrity as Muslims, on the one hand, which was necessary in order to play a meaningful role in the lives of their co-religionists in the capital, while on the other hand demonstrating loyalty to the British Empire. The latter task was made all the more difficult by the fact that the overwhelming majority of people in English society, including those serving in the government, had very little knowledge of Islam or of the WMM, and some among them regarded the organization as suspect if not subversive. During a period fraught with tension and uncertainty, even the most seemingly innocuous words or actions on the part of WMM leaders risked unintentionally alienating fellow Muslims, the British government or both – at a time when doing either would have had dire consequences for that organization's future, for any opposition from their co-religionists would have undermined the unity so central to the message and purpose of the WMM. Likewise, because the Defence of the Realm Act gave the government sweeping powers during the war, the authorities easily could have disbanded it in the interest of national security.

Given the dramatic change in circumstances, it would not have been unreasonable for WMM leaders to have decided to cease activity in Woking. They could have chosen to return to India until after the First World War, or of have left England altogether and found another way to serve their faith or different place from which to teach non-Muslims. In addition, even if missionaries did not have to worry about the new political–religious issues raised following the Ottoman Empire's entrance into the war on the side of the Central Powers, they still would have had to struggle with the challenge of trying to convince people in Great Britain to put aside current concerns in order to contemplate questions of religious truth. As Kamal-ud-Din wrote to his contacts in Lahore, the mission "cannot draw public attention for some time … The war has turned all thoughts towards itself. No one has any room left in his mind to think about anything else."[118] Even media outlets that previously had covered WMM activities in England lost interest after the outbreak of hostilities in 1914.[119]

However, the leaders and most dynamic members of the WMM responded to these new and trying circumstances by creating an additional dimension to their already existing intersectional imperial ideology, one that concentrated on Muslim contributions to the British side of the struggle and the unique ability of Islam to provide divine guidance for waging war both ethically and successfully and ensuring lasting peace in the future. The *IR* reported in 1917, "Islam is able to assume the burden of these days, and no other religion is able."[120] WMM members focused and elaborated on areas of common ground between the needs of an empire at war and the core or canonical texts and traditions of their faith.

Central to this evolving system of meaning was the Muslim soldier, as both a historical and a contemporary figure, with photographs of the latter appearing in the *IR*.[121] In the context of WMM wartime discourse and activity this figure helped to orient believers who held diverse political views: for, regardless of how individual Muslims may have felt about the conflict or specific foreign policy decisions, all could agree that their brethren in uniform deserved respect and support. In addition, by attending to the religious needs of those men and their families, the WMM publicly and repeatedly demonstrated its loyalty and importance to king and country and forged new relationships with the British government, particularly the War and India Offices. Finally, by drawing attention to the Muslim combatant, past and present, representatives of the WMM found a way for their organization to remain relevant during wartime while maintaining a distance from the political minefield of ongoing developments in the Middle East.

The Woking Mission and Muslim soldiers at war

Shortly after the outbreak of the First World War, leading members of the WMM voiced their support for British Muslim soldiers, while also acknowledging the tension and sense of internal conflict caused by the knowledge that their co-religionists fought on opposite sides of that struggle. In September 1914, at a meeting held at the Shah Jahan mosque, Lord Headley and Sadr-ud-Din proposed to issue a resolution offering "wholehearted congratulations" to British Muslims at the front, expressing "delight" that they were fighting on the side of "honour, truth and justice." It was approved unanimously, translated, and given to the Commander of the Indian Army Corps, General James Willcocks, to be distributed among the troops.[122] Following the publication of that resolution in the *IR* is a passionately patriotic article by Headley in which that influential convert explains how the very same spirit that filled Muhammad when he was forced to draw his sword in battle centuries ago now animates comrades in arms from throughout the empire who oppose German aggression and fight "shoulder to shoulder," Muslims, Christians, Hindus and Jews.[123] Three months later, after the Ottoman entrance into the war, Sadr-ud-Din spoke at a similar meeting, also held at the Woking mosque and this time open to the public, in which he explained that, because of the bonds that unite believers throughout the world, British Muslims sympathize or "feel for" the "Turks" and that it is "a matter for great regret" to see the followers of Muhammad pitted against one other. Nevertheless, he continued, because Islam teaches loyalty, "we must serve his Majesty the King, whose subjects we are."[124]

By providing funeral and burial services to fallen Muslim soldiers, the WMM performed a solemn role, one which allowed them to serve both their faith and their government at the same time without contradiction: for those who perished needed to be buried according to Islamic laws and customs shortly after death, and to do otherwise would have been considered a grave injustice to the individuals, their families and the *ummah* more generally, a possibility which German propagandists used to their advantage. In an effort to weaken morale and encourage defection, the Nachrichtenstelle für den Orient, or German Intelligence Office of the East, produced leaflets in "Oriental languages," most likely Urdu and Arabic, alerting Muslims fighting in France that the British government had improperly disposed of the bodies of their slain brethren. These materials were dropped into the trenches, and in at least one case the propaganda had the optimum desired effect, inspiring a group of soldiers from northwest India, members of the Afridi tribe, to desert their regiment and rejoin the fight on the German side. Meanwhile British censors struggled to keep any hint of such rumours from reaching the civilian population on the subcontinent.[125] In light of these circumstances, it became imperative for representatives of His Majesty's government to secure provisions for proper Muslim funeral and burial arrangements as soon as possible and in relatively close proximity to the Western Front, services which the WMM was positioned to provide.

In October 1914 the statesman and trustee of the Shah Jahan mosque, Abbas Ali Baig, put his colleagues in government in touch with the acting imam, Sadr-ud-Din, regarding the issue of funeral and burial rites.[126] The following month, the first Muslim to die from wounds while serving at the front, Ahmad Khan of the Indian Expeditionary Force, expired en route from France to England. His body was transported by "motorhearse" to the Woking mosque and arrived enshrouded in the Union Jack. He was buried soon afterwards, and Sadr-ud-Din performed a "brief and simple ceremony" while a cluster of mourners faced Mecca, offering silent prayers.[127] Sadr-ud-Din incorporated elements of British military as well as Muslim religious ritual in these burial ceremonies, including the presence of a firing party to provide a last volley over the grave, a practice not commonly observed for Indian soldiers.[128]

Bodies of fallen Muslim soldiers would continue to arrive in Woking throughout the war years, for whom a small cemetery was created, and that community was never far removed from the conflict.[129] As one worshipper explained, within "eighty miles of where we prostrated ourselves in humble and solemn adoration … cannons were belching forth fire and destruction and human beings were engaged in murderous and fratricidal strife."[130] The miseries of trench warfare gradually became known to the people of that small town, just as they did elsewhere in the country. One convert wrote to his brethren expressing *Eid* greetings while also describing his conditions, noting the "Foul smoke" around him and the flow of even "fouler gases" on a field "reeking and sodden with slaughter."[131] In the English tradition of ironic understatement, one Woking resident sent a postcard from the front relating how soldiers were busy "making themselves comfortable" in dugouts.[132]

The majority of Muslim soldiers who fought on the fields of France and became ill or wounded were taken to the Kitchener Indian Hospital in Brighton on England's south coast. The facility opened in January 1915, and in April of that year the commanding officer in charge of running the institution, Colonel Seton, invited Sadr-ud-Din to visit. This was no ordinary hospital, as it included the Royal Pavilion complex, a palace originally built for the Prince Regent (later King George IV) as a place to entertain while enjoying the seaside. The structure usually is described as an over-the-top orientalist fantasy, which includes a variety of Eastern styles, broadly defined, from its riot of onion domes and interior columns designed to look like palm trees, to rooms decorated in chinoiserie with giant sculptures of serpents and winged dragons that take the unsuspecting visitor by surprise.

Yet Sadr-ud-Din's experience of the pavilion was spiritual and, not surprisingly, Muslim oriented in nature. While he acknowledged the attractions that it offered the tourist or sightseer, to him the inclusion of Moorish and Mughal-inspired architectural features testified to the skill, resources and overall sublimity of Islamic civilizations and their contributions to humankind. His mind was drawn to details that went unnoticed by most: the crescent and star set upon columns in the interior dome, and Arabic calligraphy testifying to the oneness of God and facing the direction of Mecca. He explained how these images imparted a "sanctity" to the atmosphere where Muslim soldiers had the "proud privilege" to convalesce.[133] Sadr-ud-Din may have encountered an extravagant orientalist structure, but he chose to focus on those aspects of it that had meaning for him as an imam and missionary living in First World War England. Because of that particular perspective, the non-Muslim Indian patients there, of which there were many, went unmentioned in his account.

The people of India, and especially those of the Punjab, made a significant contribution to the war effort in terms of both troops and resources, and that colony was of vital importance to the British government.[134] In that respect, certain interests and concerns of the WMM dovetailed with those of Whitehall. After all, the founder of the mission came from the Punjab region of India and the organization's leaders continued to maintain strong links with their base of support on the subcontinent, especially in and around Lahore. In fact, the discourses of the *IR* during the First World War which emphasized the comradery, cooperation and mutual respect that soldiers of the empire had for each other as they struggled together for the same cause could sound similar to those of the Viceroy of India, Lord Hardinge. The *IR* reproduced Hardinge's words along with King George V's message to the Princes and peoples of India praising them for their devotion.[135] In addition, both leaders of the Woking community and prominent statesmen, including Arthur Balfour, David Lloyd George and Lords Cromer and Curzon, contributed to the Indian Muslim Soldiers' Widows and Orphans War Fund.[136]

Expressions of gratitude for Indian soldiers serving in the war appeared on the pages of the *IR*, such as in "The Gift of India," a poem by Sarojini Naidu, the feminist and activist who would later become president of the Indian National Congress. In it, she assumes the voice of a kind of spiritual or mythical mother of all Indians who

> yielded the sons of my stricken womb
> To the drum-beats of duty, the sabres of doom.

The work goes on to relate the grief and anguish of this great mother whose offspring lie dead on the "blood-brown meadows of Flanders and France," as well as her pride in the sacrifices they have made. It concludes by urging the reader not to forget the martyred sons of India.[137]

Lesser-known figures contributed similar poetry and prose. The English Muslim convert Alice Mobarikah Welch also speaks of maternal heartache and despair in "India, as here," in "A Cheer from the British Muslims to our Indian Troops in France." As its title suggests, her tribute has a more rousing and patriotic tone than Naidu's poem, and in the first verse she offers a hearty welcome to the Indian soldiers who have come to "help to save the flag Our Empire holds so dear."[138] With all of Welch's imperial patriotism, and no mention of parental woes, either maternal or paternal, Eric Hammond sent his "Salutation to Indian Soldiers" to the IR in hopes that some of those soldiers might read and feel gladdened by an expression of English appreciation for their chivalry, loyalty, prowess and courage, all of which "draped the Empire in a robe of glittering glory."[139] Finally, a poem by "Ameena," entitled "England's Debt to India," tells the English reader to be grateful not only for the sacrifice of Indian soldiers in battle, or "Human flesh and blood in fray," but for "the soul of India's teachings" or the message of the Woking Muslim missionaries. The poet goes on to say how she hopes that they will "shake off worn out dogmas" and exchange them for "the higher view."[140]

Muslims in uniform appeared regularly at Woking mosque services and events, sometimes addressing an audience, and their contribution to the war effort gave the community a new visibility and legitimacy.[141] Observers and journalists would comment on the visual contrast between, for example, the "king's khaki" and the flowing robes of the other worshipers, or the presence of "Tommies'" caps interspersed among the red fezzes.[142] One *Eid al-Fitr* held on the lawn of the Shah Jahan mosque in 1915 attracted considerable attention, with three to four hundred Muslim attendees, including a contingent of forty to fifty soldiers who had recently arrived from the Western Front, one hundred onlookers and the press. The London *Daily Graphic* reported that the soldiers "arrested the greatest interest on the part of the spectators," noting that one who had been wounded recently and therefore walked with difficulty and the aid of a stick received "a special cheer."[143] A press reluctant to report on issues unrelated to the war now had reason to cover WMM events, and the IR could draw attention to the British Muslim soldiers that the Mission served (Figure 2.4).

While members of the WMM had experienced opposition to their very presence in Woking even as late as the spring of 1914, the Muslim contribution to the war effort gave its leaders new-found confidence that they would be accepted and even appreciated by the local community. After lunch on the day of the *Eid* celebration, they planned a carefully ordered procession through the town with uniformed soldiers leading the way. As one WMM member related, the "garb worn by Indian Muslims – their splendid regalia, their turbans, their golden cloaks, and a variety of shoes – created a source

Figure 2.4 "A Trio of Brave English Soldiers who have joined the colours of Islam," 1916. Inside front cover of the *Islamic Review*, September 1916.

of particular attraction for the residents of Woking." The same WMM member even went on to emphasize how comfortable the people of the town had made them feel. The march began in the Moslem cemetery, wound through the main shopping streets and proceeded to the railway station before concluding at the Shah Jahan mosque.[144] The ability of the members of the WMM to establish a secure place for themselves in Woking within the first few years of its opening and to attract converts from England and other parts of the British Isles, who, in turn, extended the networks of the WMM more deeply into the metropole, cannot be separated from the First World War context and the role that the organization played in serving the needs of British Muslim soldiers. In fact, as attendance at mosque events grew during the war years, it also became increasingly hybridized, with greater numbers of Occidentals identifying with what they considered to be an Oriental belief system and mixing with new arrivals from the East, or soldiers who had made the long journey in order to serve the needs of His Majesty's military in the West.

The ability of Islam to "assume the burden of these days": teachings on just war and lasting peace

The members of the Woking Muslim community expressed support for the British war effort and for the idea that those who fought on that side were fighting on the side of honour and for a just cause, yet a number of them maintained that Islam could have prevented the outbreak of war in the first place. Others understood the war as the consequence of a civilization that had made great technological advances but had lost its moral foundation in the process. According to them, while Christianity had proven itself incapable of stopping the conflict or even countering the forces of materialism and atheism that led to it, including the ideology of "survival of the fittest," Islam could fill that spiritual void and bring peace amongst races and nations. Furthermore, Westerners had become arrogant and indifferent to the suffering of the poor in their own societies and the exploitation of colonized people in the East. The war, then, was a punishment from God as well as a lesson showing the Europeans the error of their ways and warning the rest of the world not to follow their example.[145]

While the Woking Muslims and other contributors to the *IR* may have wished that Islam had spread throughout Europe in time to prevent the outbreak of the First World War, they nevertheless understood war as an inevitable aspect of the human condition, and one for which their faith was particularly well equipped, providing invaluable guidelines and ethics. Christianity, in contrast, was presented as putting the British and Europeans in general at risk during a time of great danger, for the principle of turning the other cheek or taking a pacifist stance was depicted as sentimental naivety at best, and dangerous irresponsibility at worst.[146] Yet to wage war without an ethical system rooted in religion led to atrocities and wanton violence, causing the suffering of innocent civilians. Not surprisingly, the Germans tended to be blamed the most on this count, although contributors to the *IR* refrained from ridiculing or dehumanizing them through abusive speech – as was common in the British press at the time – calling such violent discourse "unethical."[147] Finally, the quest to develop ever more efficient and effective technology for the purpose of killing, maiming and disfiguring, often on a grand scale, which Christian, European governments had been pursuing even before the outbreak of the First World War, was at the very least morally questionable if not a blatant manifestation of aggression, to which Islam was opposed. As Pickthall related in a London address, "What Muslim ever came near to inventing poisoned gas, or building Dreadnoughts, or even dreamt of a gun with a range of more than eighty miles."[148] Yet technology used in an ethical way to protect and defend was not only compatible with Islam but a result of it. As one article in the *IR* explains, the fleet upon which the existence of the British Empire and English lives and liberties depends has been made possible by Muslim inventions such as the compass, and even the word "Admiral" originally came to the English from the French corruption of the Moorish use of the Arabic "*Amir-ul-bahr*," or commander of the sea.[149]

While certainly a number of bishops and other members of the clergy in England rejected passivism and spoke of the British role in the First World War as a moral obligation, *IR* contributors regarded their position as an essentially Islamic one and even as expressing the true Muslim, rather than Christian, spirit.[150] One piece in *IR* juxtaposes an excerpt from a public address given at Marble Arch by the bishop of London with passages from the Gospel of Jesus and the Qur'an, showing that while the bishop advocates the protection of the weak against the invading Germans and the Qur'an gives permission to fight the oppressors, the Gospel instructs its followers to "love thy enemies."[151] Similarly, an article entitled "The Qur'an and War" reproduces a number of passages from that book in order to show that it, not the Bible, provides a guide for humanity in the event that war becomes inevitable.[152]

Along the same lines, in the first of a series of lectures given on Sundays at the Shah Jahan mosque entitled "The Present War and the Prophet of Islam," Kamal-ud-Din explained to his audience how, in deciding to go to war, the leaders of His Majesty's government were acting not as Christians but, rather, as Muslims; for just as Muhammad had had to protect himself and his small community from enemies intent upon destroying them, the German invasion of Belgium endangered the safety of the "English nation." In both cases self-preservation required violence; history was repeating itself. With regard to recent discussion of war in the House of Commons, Kamal-ud-Din stated,

> Sir Edward Grey and the Prime Minister, in their historic speeches to vindicate their actions, have simply vindicated the Holy Prophet Muhammad ... Mr. Asquith, with all his Nonconformist conscience, has been forced to put the Sermon on the Mount behind his back and follow the Lord of Islam.[153]

According to the leaders of the WMM, God had provided humanity with a role model for the ideal soldier and general in the person of Muhammad, and the words and actions of this "warrior prophet" were as relevant to the British in the twentieth century as they had been to the Muslims of the Arabian Peninsula during the seventh. Members of the Woking Muslim community called attention not only to Muhammad's military prowess, but also to his ability to engage in combat without compromising his tender and compassionate nature. As a result of this balance, he was able to act with justice and mercy even after defeating his enemies, forgiving them rather than seeking revenge. As Kamal-ud-Din later explained, Muhammad was a "brave soldier, a dauntless veteran, and yet so meek, so loving and so kind."[154] He had the necessary "moral spirit" to win wars, but he neither relished victory nor glorified violence. Rather, he regarded going to battle as a duty. Defending life and property of a struggling community under siege was an obligation to be met with selflessness and courage.[155]

In addition, the *IR* editors included articles explaining how Muhammad and his successors gave specific instructions regarding the treatment of civilian populations during war, which, if followed, would have prevented much of the destruction, pain and suffering that Europeans, particularly the Belgians, were experiencing, for in addition to sparing women, infants and the ill, Muhammad told his soldiers not to demolish the dwellings of unresisting inhabitants, nor their means of subsistence, nor trees of fruit or palm – words that, according to Scottish convert John Yehya en-Nesr Parkinson, "should be written across Europe in letters of gold."[156] Kamal-ud-Din discusses how Muhammad and others elaborated upon these basic directives by sparing all non-combatants – instructions that the Germans should have had; and how Abu Bakr, the first Caliph, recognised in Sunni Islam as the successor to Muhammad, told his troops not to destroy the fields or any products of the earth, not to kill the cattle, to take only what is necessary and leave the monasteries in peace. Kamal-ud-Din then reflects upon the "devastation and vandalism" in Europe and the fate of Reims cathedral and the city of Louvain.[157] Similarly, a self-described "English Muslim Lady," Haneefah Bexon, laments that "so-called Christians" in Europe have no respect for the dwellings of women and children, the means of existence, nor even the fruit trees, but are instead destroying everything which might be beautiful.[158]

One article presents the idea that the instructions given by Lord Kitchener, the British Secretary of State for War, to members of the British Expeditionary Army departing for France and Belgium in 1914 were the result of Islamic influences, for Kitchener urged each soldier to act with courtesy, consideration and kindness; to never loot or destroy property; and to resist the temptations of wine and physical intimacy with women, concluding with the words "Do your duty bravely. Fear God. Honour the King." The author of the article considers Kitchener's "commendable words" not as simply his own ideas but, rather, as a direct result of his previous exposure to Muslim culture and therefore a "fine tribute to Islam." After all Kitchener had many opportunities to come into contact with Muslim practices and beliefs during his previous postings in Egypt, the Sudan, South Africa and India, and by the outbreak of the First World War his imperial military career was well known in England. The article goes on to relate similar directives given by previous Muslim leaders, putting Kitchener in the company of the Caliph Abu Bakr and the tenth-century Moorish ruler al-Hakim ibn al-Rahman. It concludes by explaining that these various injunctions from military leaders in the course of history all emanate from the "large soul" of Muhammad and reflect his message.[159]

Islamic teachings were meant not only to serve as a guide for generals and military leaders, but also to improve the moral character of soldiers, thus enabling them to fulfil their duties to the utmost of their ability and in such a way as to benefit society as a whole, for drunken combatants committed atrocities against civilians.[160] Not only did Islam forbid the consumption of alcohol, but it required believers to abstain from food and drink from sunrise to sunset during the month of Ramadan. This practice was praised for building "patience, fortitude, and endurance" as well as resoluteness of character – all qualities necessary for anyone engaged in warfare. One *IR* article even suggests that the fast should be a part of military training.[161] The prohibition of alcohol, combined with soldiers who had greater "moral control" as the result of fasting, would reduce the number of "war-babies" and unwed mothers.[162] Similarly, another article contrasts the Caliph Omar, who felt such "anxiety" and concern for the "moral purity" of both his soldiers and their wives and the burdens of temptation that they may feel that he made certain never to separate them for more than four months at a time, with the laxity of modern European governments that tend to accept even prostitution as a "necessary evil" of war.[163]

IR contributors repeatedly stressed the idea that the First World War was essentially a moral and spiritual struggle. While materialism and the arms race may have caused the outbreak of war, weapons alone could not end it. Rather, the soldiers, generals and even members of the civilian population, women and men, had to have the necessary framework and "moral spirit" to ensure a lasting peace: Islam provided both.[164] Muslims fighting at the front wrote of the miseries of war and the hope that their faith would soon spread, putting an end to bloodshed and suffering and bringing unity to mankind. One wrote of being surrounded on all sides by the "grim spectacle of death" yet being able to imagine the future when "the battle-song of Islam swelling into a mighty paean of triumphant glory" would bring peace and hope, and people from all nations in the world would stand "hand in hand."[165] As Pickthall told his war-weary audience in July 1918, hosts of men and women, particularly in England, realized "in face of this great world-calamity, that something has been wrong in the religion and the thought of Europe." Thousands spoke of establishing a league of nations to end war, yet we needed to look no further than Islam: "We Muslims are a league of nations – count the nations in this room."[166] Here Pickthall referred to the diverse backgrounds of those drawn to the imperial entrepôt to illustrate his point.

To summarize, when, prior to 1914, missionaries often had to defend their faith against Westerners who regarded it as a religion of the sword, there would have been no reason for them to introduce topics such as the ways that Islamic teachings might be applied to military training, or Muhammad's activities as a general. However, after the outbreak of conflict in the summer of 1914, the larger imperial culture changed profoundly as wartime concerns quickly became central to it. In response, WMM leaders began to focus on Islamic texts and traditions that offered guidance for just war and lasting peace, including those that related to the cultivation of the ideal combatant. They repeatedly expressed praise and admiration for British Muslim soldiers and offered support to them and their families by providing religious services and, in some cases, funds. The conspicuous presence of men in uniform at the Shah Jahan mosque, in turn, helped to give the WMM credibility and legitimacy in English society during that difficult period. Thus, in the context of the First World War, the "Muslim soldier" should be understood as a rich, multilayered and multidimensional concept of central importance to an evolving intersectional imperial ideology which oriented diverse individuals and made the continued existence of the WMM in the metropole and the relationships that sustained it meaningful and therefore possible.

Modified Orientalism and representations of the Middle East during wartime

Discussion of that imperial ideology and its adaptation to wartime changes would not be complete without considering representation of the Middle East during that period. Given the WMM's concern with the war effort and in highlighting Muslim contributions to it, combined with the fact that the *IR* was created, in part, for the purpose of covering contemporary issues of interest to fellow believers, one would expect that publication to address the expansion of the war into the Middle East. After all, not only had a region of considerable significance to Islam become a major theatre of conflict, but Muslims there played a decisive role in Allied victories, most notably during the Arab Revolt, 1916–18, when Bedouin soldiers attacked the Ottoman garrison at Mecca and then advanced northwards while British forces provided aid from the sidelines. Yet the *IR* remains silent with regard to these and other ongoing wartime developments in the Middle East. Orientalist poetry romanticizing the Arabian desert as a place both solemn and wild where "dissension is not heard" and one can enjoy sunny breezes and the sight of "slowly moving tents" from atop the "camel's patient pad" replaced discussion of more pressing matters.[167] Even a series of articles that did, in fact, represent conflict in the Middle East dealt not with the events of the twentieth century but, rather, those of the seventh.[168]

Like Western Orientalists, the writers and editors of the *IR* preferred the past to the present when depicting the Middle East. There is, however, one critical difference between Western Orientalism and what can be understood as a modified form of Orientalism employed by WMM supporters. While the former concentrated on the ancient Middle East in a way that overshadowed the later Muslim and Arab contributions to and even presence in the region, thereby justifying imperialist expansion, WMM discourses focused instead on the medieval and early modern periods, when both the religion and culture of Islam flourished and produced a golden age of Islamic civilization.[169] Yet both types of Orientalism served to shift attention away from contemporary realities in that part of the world.

The use of Orientalism, whether in the form of focusing on past eras in human history or romanticizing the desert, served an important function for the WMM during the First World War: it helped the mission to promote a sense of unity amongst Muslims from a variety of backgrounds and traditions, both those in the Greater London community who attended events at the Shah Jahan mosque and believers throughout the empire and world who read the *IR*, by representing the Hejaz, or Muslim holy land, while at the same time avoiding any mention of the battles in and around it.[170] This contrast between the ideal of an undivided *ummah* that the WMM worked both to portray and to create and the far more complex and even violent reality is perhaps most dramatic when considering a sermon given by Kamal-ud-Din in the historical context in which it appeared in the *IR* in November 1917. Despite the fact that tens of thousands of Arab tribesmen and Ottoman troops had been fighting against each other for almost a year and a half, Kamal-ud-Din chose to focus on Mecca as he experienced it in 1914, as a place so harmonious and full of love that not even a single policeman was needed to maintain order, causing him to wonder if the kingdom of God had come from heaven to "bring that heterogeneous assembly under its peaceful arms."[171] The issue immediately following that article begins with a full-page photograph of Medina looking both majestic and serene. With its medieval walls, mosque and minarets all set against a desolate backdrop without a single person in sight, the reader easily could forget the armed conflicts that pitted Muslim against Muslim in the Hejaz.

In addition, the modified form of Orientalism used by the WMM must be understood in the light of the current political climate. As conflict with the Ottoman Empire intensified during the war, so too did anti-Muslim sentiment in the British press.[172] The trustees of the Shah Jahan mosque may have been "staunch Empire-loyalists," but they still were viewed with suspicion by the Foreign Office, which kept surveillance over what one official called the "Woking Mosque gang." Even the widely respected British Muslim statesman and Anglophile Syed Ameer Ali was referred to as a fanatic.[173] Had the editors of the *IR* chosen to report on contemporary conflict in the Middle East and happened to mention, for example, the Indian Muslim soldiers who had refused to fight their brethren upon arrival in Basra, a watchful Foreign Office could have considered the mere act of making that news available to a British Muslim readership a form of treason.[174]

Further complicating matters was the fact that a number of those associated with the WMM actively opposed the Arab revolt and the British government's role in it. They too, perhaps not surprisingly, were monitored by the authorities. Men like Kidwai and Pickthall, both regular contributors to the *IR*, would not have been content to see events on the Arabian Peninsula reported by that periodical in a neutral manner. While both professed their loyalty to His Majesty's Empire and understood themselves as obligated to support the British war effort, they also made their Turkish and Ottoman sympathies well known through other venues and publications. For example, in a letter to the editor of *The Nation*, Kidwai suggested that Sharif Hussein should be executed for treason. Similarly, Pickthall, who also considered that Muslim leader to be a traitor, contributed a letter to the *Saturday Review* on the Arab Revolt that Foreign Office reports called "a masterpiece of enemy propaganda."[175]

As the success of the Arab Revolt and its spread northward beyond the original Hashemite leaders prompted British war planners to advance the Egyptian Expeditionary Force eastward and launch a series of attacks on the fortified oasis city of Gaza, *IR* editors approached the issue of Palestine's future with similar caution. At a meeting held under the auspices of the Central Islamic Society in June 1917 to express objection to the creation of a Jewish state in Palestine under the suzerainty of a Christian government, Kamal-ud-Din voiced concern about the fate of Muslim holy sites there, particularly that of Al-Aqsa Mosque, should the Zionists decide to rebuild Solomon's Temple.[176] Yet, when coverage of that meeting and speech appeared in the *IR* two months later, all overtly political content had been removed. References to the question of who would rule Palestine were omitted, and the remaining text, which focuses on the particular suitability of Muslims to serve as guardians to the world's holy places, sounds more like the familiar missionary discourses regarding the broad-mindedness of their faith rather than an attempt to enter ongoing debates or to influence British policy in the Middle East. In fact, at one point Kamal-ud-Din's speech leaves that region altogether, drawing instead from the history of the Mughal Empire in South Asia and the syncretic tendencies of Perso-Islamic culture with regard to the Hindu majority there, as he explains that because the Qur'an enjoins believers to accept the message of "every great spiritual leader in any corner of the world," "millions of temples, pagodas and Shrines consecrated to numberless gods, goddesses, and demi-gods, teeming with valuable golden and marble images and idols have survived the most successful rule of Islam."[177]

Considering this speech in its larger context illustrates Kamal-ud-Din's diplomatic and situational approach with regard to a controversial topic and matter of importance both to fellow Muslims and to the British Empire. It therefore helps to shed light on the political sophistication and finesse required of the WMM leadership in order to ensure that their organization remained in the metropole and continued to serve the needs of a diverse and politically aware community of believers during the First World War despite the many challenges of that period, including those resulting from British expansion into the Middle East.[178] When the Balfour Declaration was issued in November 1917, the WMM did not respond as a body, even though members and other supporters expressed opposition to it through the Central Islamic Society and other pressure organizations in the Greater London area. While Kamal-ud-Din would return to the subject of Palestine and address other controversial topics such as the Caliphate[179] after the war, during that conflict he seems to have followed his own advice first given in 1914. As he told fellow Muslims then, "there is a time and place for everything," and while they were entitled to assert their rights, complaints should be postponed, at least for the time being.[180]

Conclusion

In certain respects, the creation of the WMM seems like the logical, almost inevitable, outcome of historical developments within the global culture of British imperialism. After all, Christian missionaries had been travelling to India ever since 1814 for the purpose of teaching their faith and winning converts, and, as British power extended into the northern Punjab in 1849, the region from which Kamal-ud-Din and his supporters hailed, the increased Christian presence in the area sparked a number of arguments, debates and creative exchanges among people from different religious backgrounds. Muslims had lived in the British Isles since the eighteenth century, and Muslim missionary activity in that country, initiated by Quilliam, a Liverpool solicitor-turned-convert, began in the late 1800s. It would seem to be only a matter of time before Muslims from India or other 'peripheries' of the empire would make the journey to England to share their beliefs.[181]

While the above statements are true, it is important also to acknowledge that Kamal-ud-Din and his early supporters were exceptional. The vast majority of Muslims in the empire did not leave their homes and former lives in the pursuit of creating a "Mecca of the West." Such a course of action had no precedent and fell outside of common expectations, even with regard to the most devout and energetic believers. It also challenged the dominant imperial discourses of the day, which presented missionary activity, like cultural and intellectual life generally, as originating in the metropole and then spreading to the peripheries. The decision to travel from India to England in order establish a Muslim mission must, then, be understood as supported by the existing social and political circumstances, but at the same time as a novel approach to understanding the relationship between Islam and the British Empire. The founders of the WMM valued certain British liberal ideals, particularly those regarding the freedom of speech and the press and religious toleration, and saw in the metropole, with its flourishing print culture and ability to draw diverse people from a variety of different cultural backgrounds from around the world, great potential for spreading Islam in the West and regenerating the already existing *ummah*.

Kamal-ud-Din and his early supporters were able to create the WMM because they found certain places of compatibility between their faith and the empire, and from those areas of common ground they developed what this study understands as an ideology of imperial intersection. This is not to say that they supported the empire unconditionally or ignored injustices perpetuated by it. Rather, Kamal-ud-Din had a fairly sophisticated understanding of the relationship between British Muslim subjects and His Majesty's government, one that was rooted simultaneously in both constitutional principles and devotion to their faith. A just government that respected the sensibilities and needs of the Muslims it ruled was owed their loyalty, and, like their Christian counterparts, those individuals had the right to express their opinions with regard to its policies and practices. In fact, to offer advice and criticism was described as form of jihad, not because it sowed sedition or led to militancy but, rather, because it was a solemn duty that required a certain moral fortitude.

An ideology of imperial intersection made possible the creation of the WMM in 1913, yet it did nothing to prepare its founders for the new and profound challenges the mission would encounter the following year. With the outbreak of the First World War and British–Ottoman conflict, WMM leaders faced increasing anti-Muslim sentiment in the press and public; suspicion on the part of the government; and a Muslim community in the Greater London area whose members held a variety of different opinions regarding the correct response to British foreign policy decisions, especially as the theatre of war expanded into the Hejaz and Palestine. In order to continue the work of the mission in England and foster unity amongst believers in that country, WMM leaders focused on the Muslim soldier, both as an ideal and as an individual whose religious needs they served. Kamal-ud-Din and others also presented their faith as relevant to wartime concerns by relating stories of Muhammad as a soldier and general and explaining how only Islam could provide humanity with divine guidance for waging war in an ethical manner, one that eventually would bring both military success and lasting peace. In other words, as the larger British culture changed with the outbreak of the First World War, WMM leaders and members responded to that change by sifting through the religious teachings in their cultural repertoire, particularly from the Qur'an and hadith literature, in order to add a further dimension to their already existing ideology of imperial intersection. It is ironic to reflect upon the fact that while missionary leaders may have come to England with a message of peace and unity and hoping to dispel negative beliefs about Islam, including the perception of it as a "religion of the sword," they soon found that remaining in that country hinged upon their ability to serve the war effort.

After weathering the challenges of the First World War, the WMM went on to play an instrumental role in the development of a new Europe-wide Muslim and missionary culture. Soon after peace negotiations, plans were under way for the creation of a Berlin Muslim Mission based on the Woking model and led by Sadr-ud-Din. Like the WMM, the Berlin Muslim Mission issued a monthly periodical, *Die Muslimische Revue,* and cultivated an inclusive, ecumenical form of Islam.[182] The two organizations maintained a connection with each other and with their supporters in India, and together served as a clearing house for news and other information of importance to Muslims throughout Europe during the 1920s. Their efforts between the wars centralized European Islam and gave it a platform for international exposure, linking new converts and Muslim communities from "Spain to Poland and from England to the Balkans."[183] At the same time, Woking remained the centre of Muslim activity in Britain for almost three decades, with the *IR* dominating the British Muslim press until the 1950s.[184] These post-war developments testify to the success of the WMM in creating a new type of Islam in the West, one that was characterized by a greater degree of diversity and hybridity than had existed prior to 1913.

Notes

1 This phrase is from a letter by convert John Yehya en-Nesr Parkinson read aloud at the first public meeting of the British Muslim Society held at the Shah Jahan mosque, Woking and printed in the Woking Muslim Mission's publication the *Islamic Review* (*IR*), Jan. 1915, 8.

2 Kamal-ud-Din accepted the patronage of Sultan Jahan, the Begum of the Central Indian princely state of Bhopal, who, after travelling to London in 1911 to attend the coronation of George V, decided to resuscitate the mosque funded by her mother, Shahjehan, in 1889 in the nearby town of Woking. Sultan Jahan would become the "primary benefactor" of the WMM and

Kamal-ud-Din was "in effect" an "emissary of the state" of Bhopal. Siobhan Lambert-Hurley, *Muslim Women, Reform, and Princely Patronage: Nawab Sultan Jahan Begum of Bhopal* (Routledge: New York, 2007), 57.

3 As early as 1860 a group of Yemeni sailors who settled in Cardiff's Tiger Bay area registered a house for use as a mosque. Nahid Afrose Kabir, *Young British Muslims: Identity Culture, Politics and the Media* (Edinburgh: Edinburgh University Press, 2010). See also, Mohammad Siddique Seddon, *The Last of the Lascars: Muslims in Britain 1836–2012* (Leicestershire: Kube, 2014); Fred Halliday, *Britain's First Muslims: Portrait of an Arab Community* (London: I.B. Tauris, 2010); and Humayun Ansari, *The Infidel Within: Muslims in Britain since 1800* (Oxford: Oxford University Press, 2018). Ansari notes hundreds of Muslims visiting England in the early 1600s (p. 30). By the late nineteenth century Muslim communities were established in Liverpool and in Woking, although neither lasted into the early twentieth century. See the section on "Islam in England" in Diane Robinson-Dunn, *The Harem, Slavery, and British Imperial Culture* (Manchester: Manchester University Press, 2006), 154–96; Ron Geaves, *Islam in Victorian Britain: The Life and Times of Abdullah Quilliam* (Leicestershire: Kube, 2010); and Jamie Gilham, *Loyal Enemies: British Converts to Islam, 1850–1950* (Oxford: Oxford University Press, 2014).

4 The building could not be used to disseminate religious materials, win converts or celebrate marriages between Muslim men and English women. In other words, despite the mosque's presence on English soil, Islam would not become a part of English society, so that the "social distance between the dominant and subject people and the *status quo* could most effectively be maintained." K. Humayun Ansari, "The Woking Mosque: A Case Study of Muslim Engagement with British Society since 1889," *Immigrants and Minorities*, Vol. 21, No. 3 (2002), 7. Leitner's rules are also in Ansari, *Infidel Within*, 138–9.

5 They were pelted repeatedly with stones, eggs, mud, garbage and, on one occasion, pork blood sausages. A female convert was assaulted in the street more than once, and four were injured when some "'ruffians'" tried to force their way into the mosque during the celebration of Eid al-Adha. Geaves, *Islam in Victorian Britain*, 64–7. Last reference at p. 67.

6 Olive Zaitun Howell later recalled that when the WMM first arrived, the "inhabitants of Woking had no desire for Islam ... they were determined that at all costs it must not be allowed to thrive – it must be nipped in the bud. [...] First refuse to supply food for the mosque people. Next cut all people off if they go to the place." Quoted in Gilham, *Loyal Enemies*, 208.

7 The quotations "leap in the dark" and "alien country" are from Al-Qidwai, "Haji Khawaja Kamal-ud-Din," *IR*, Oct. 1916, 434–5. The quotations "place of trial" and "strange way" are from *Badr*, Jan. 9, 1913, 2, translated and put online by the Ahmadiyya Anjuman Isha'at-e-Islam Lahore (UK) (AAII) (www.wokingmuslim.org/history/kh-beg/1912.htm#9jan13-p2) and discussed by Ron Geaves in *Islam and Britain: Muslim Mission in an Age of Empire* (London: Bloomsbury Academic, 2018), 97. Jamie Gilham relates instances of "small-scale local opposition" to the mosque in *Loyal Enemies*, 208.

8 Kamal-ud-Din contacted the Muslim advisor to the Council of the Secretary of State for India, Abbas Ali Baig, for help in obtaining the mosque, and Baig, along with other prominent Indian statesmen including Syed Ameer Ali, used their London connections to secure the building and form a trust for the property. The trust formed in 1913 held the title deeds of the mosque. Geaves, *Islam and Britain*, 99 and "To the Memory of Khwaja Kamal-ud-Din," *IR*, Jan.–Feb. 1962, 4. Both Abbas Ali Baig and Syed Ameer Ali were trustees.

9 His availability and contact information first appear in the *IR*, April 1913, 65. Friday prayers, services and lectures were held at 39 Bedford Place at Russell Square, London. During First World War the mission had a "London Muslim Prayer House" in Lindsey Hall, Notting Hill Gate. Mentioned in Jamie Gilham, "Marmaduke Pickthall and the British Muslim Convert Community," in *Marmaduke Pickthall: Islam and the Modern World*, edited by Geoffrey P. Nash (Leiden: Brill, 2017), 55.

10 Geaves, *Islam and Britain*, 110.

11 The full title was *Muslim India and the Islamic Review* from 1913 until 1914, when it was changed to the *Islamic Review and Muslim India*, Khwaja Kamal-ud-Din and Maulvie Sadr-ud-Din, eds. Woking, England: The Woking Muslim Mission.

12 Nile Green relates that the arrival of Protestant missionaries in India resulted in a hybridity that would influence the organization of the Islamic missionary movements. He specifically mentions Woking in a list of "hybrid organizations." Green, *Terrains of Exchange: Religious Economies of Global Islam* (London: Hurst Publishers, 2015), 37. The book as a whole discusses globalized processes and "chain reactions of dynamic and generative exchange," p. 284. Ansari, "The Woking Mosque," explains how for the WMM the "aim was to integrate Islam and Muslims organically into the fabric of British society" (p. 12). Islam had to be "indigenized" to prosper and missionaries had to "[tread] delicately" (p. 8).

13 Geaves, *Islam and Britain*, 114.

14 For discussion Christian–Muslim exchanges in this context more generally see Nile Green, "Evangelicals: Missionary Catalysts, Muslim Responses," *Terrains of Exchange*, 43–140.

15 Ghulam Ahmad's family history is discussed in much more detail in Adil Hussain Khan, *From Sufism to Ahmadiyya: A Muslim Minority Movement in South Asia* (Bloomington: Indiana University Press, 2015), 21–7. Also, Geaves, *Islam and Britain*, 43–4. The quotation is from Mirza Ghulam Ahmad, *Star of the Empress* (Qadian: Diyal-Islam, 1899), 3.

16 *Eid Sermons*, xiv, Surrey History Centre (henceforth SHC) and "To the Memory of al-Hajj Khawaja Kamal-ud-Din," *IR*, Dec. 1949, 5.

17 Khan makes this point with regard to the British disruptions to the existing Muslim power structures, and certainly the same could be said of the rise of the Sikh empire as well. Khan, *From Sufism to Ahmadiyya*, 5.

18 Gajendra Singh, "Throwing Snowballs in France: Muslim Sipahis of the Indian Army and Sheikh Ahmad's Dream, 1915–1918," *Modern Asian Studies*,

Vol. 48, No. 4, 2014, 1024–67. Reference on pp. 1040–1. Green, *Terrains of Exchange* notes that by the mid-nineteenth century these *Munazarat*, or public religious debates in India, attracted tens of thousands of people (p. 26).
19 As Khan has explained, for Muslim leaders in post-mutiny Punjab, reform efforts served as a way of "addressing the religious and political turmoil of the colonial experience." *From Sufism to Ahmadiyya*, 1.
20 Khan, *From Sufism to Ahmadiyya*, 28, 43. Also see, Avril Powell, *Muslims and Missionaries in Pre-Mutiny India* (London: Curzon Press, 1993). During the years 1881–1901 the Christian population in the Punjab increased from 5,000 to 42,000. Avril Powell, "Contested Gods and Prophets: Discourse among Minorities in Late Nineteenth-century Punjab," *Renaissance and Modern Studies*, Vol. 38, No. 1 (1995), 40. Cited in Geaves, *Islam and Britain*, 45 and 185.
21 Khan, *From Sufism to Ahmadiyya*, 6, 36.
22 From the Lahore Ahmadiyya publication *The Hope Bulletin*, April 2013, 12–13.
23 Sanyal, *Devotional Islam and Politics in British India: Ahmad Riza Khan Barelwi and His Movement, 1870–1920* (Oxford: Oxford University Press, 1996), 50. Originally from Yohanan Friedmann, *Prophecy Continuous: Aspects of Ahmadi Religious Thought and Its Medieval Background* (Berkeley: University of California Press, 1989), 34.
24 *The Review of Religions*, Dec. 1913, 522. Also, in Gilham, *Loyal Enemies*, 126 and Geaves, *Islam and Britain*, 47.
25 Sadia Saeed, "Imperial Ideologies, Transnational Activism: Questioning the Place of Religious Freedom from British India," *Comparative Studies of South Asia, Africa and the Middle East*, Vol. 36, No. 2 (2016), 229–45 and Geaves, *Islam and Britain*, 52. Gelvin and Green note that from the 1880s Ghulam Ahmad "took advantage of the culture of cheap print introduced by missionaries and reformists to announce his message of revelation to the world." James Gelvin and Nile Green (eds), *Global Muslims in the Age of Steam and Print* (Berkeley: University of California Press, 2014), 14. See also, Iqbal Sevea, "The Ahmadiyya Print Jihad in South and Southeast Asia," in *Islamic Connections: Muslim Societies in South and Southeast Asia*, edited by Michael Feener and Terenjit Sevea (Singapore: Institute of Southeast Asian Studies, 2009), 134–48.
26 That periodical found its way to Quilliam and other prominent converts from the British Isles, some of whom would contribute to it. However, those Western Muslims did not regard Ghulam Ahmad as a prophet but, rather, connected with fellow believers in Qadian on the basis of Islam more generally. Geaves, *Islam and Britain*, 85–6, 94, 96.
27 Geaves, *Islam and Britain*, 43.
28 The term *zilli nabi* is noted in Geaves, *Islam and Britain*, 37. Ghulam Ahmad's use of the other four terms is related in Khan, *From Sufism to Ahmadiyya*, 6, 41–3.

29 Khan, *From Sufism to Ahmadiyya*, 64–78. Khan explains that this split had much to do with the politics of personalities and that most people who joined the Ahmadiyya movement were not interested in debate but, rather, in "spiritual satisfaction" corresponding with their Punjabi cultural backgrounds (p. 68).

30 Kamal-ud-Din had always had colleagues and supporters from among English-educated Muslims of the Raj. For example, in "The Khawaja as I Knew Him," *IR*, April–May, 1933, 135, Sheikh Mushir Hussain describes an incident in Lucknow in which the more traditional members of the Muslim *ulema* wanted to silence him, but were overruled by the young, English-educated men.

31 Khan, *From Sufism to Ahmadiyya*, 72. Jeremy Shearmur notes that Kamal-ud-Din was one of the "inner circle" of the Lahore Ahmadiyya movement, although still non-sectarian in Woking. Shearmur, "The Woking Mosque Muslims: British Islam in the Early Twentieth Century," *Journal of Muslim Minority Affairs*, Vol. 34, No. 2 (2014), 165–73, at 170.

32 Geaves, *Islam and Britain*, 115–22, 170. Geaves discusses some of the similarities and differences between the London Muslim Mission and WMM with regard to beliefs and approach on pp. 111–19 and 164.

33 Gilham, *Loyal Enemies*, 119 and 173. Geaves relates that the WMM filled a void for British converts who had been inspired by Quilliam and that it became the main hub for Britain's Muslim population, *Islam and Britain*, 99, 107. Gilham explains that even Quilliam's Liverpool Muslim Institute could be considered more successful in attracting Britons to Islam than the London Muslim Mission, for despite the relative lack of resources of the former and the "arguably tougher late-Victorian and Edwardian periods" in which it operated, the Liverpool Muslim Institute still secured roughly 300 British converts. In contrast, in 1915, only seven of the Qadiani's 3,000 converts worldwide were made in England. Gilham, *Loyal Enemies*, 173–4 and 139–141.

34 Even later, after the Qadiani "London Mosque" was opened in 1926 with a capacity for 200 people and a hall for lectures "delivered in competition with those at Woking," the London events were "never as well attended" as the Woking ones. Gilham, *Loyal Enemies*, 140.

35 These influences and connections have been well documented by Zahid Aziz in *The True Succession: Founding of the Lahore Ahmadiyya Movement* (Lahore: Ahmadiyya Anjuman Lahore Publications, 2014).

36 Humayun Ansari explains that members of the WMM never claimed to be Ahmadi and, in fact, "emphatically time and time again" denied rumours that they were. He also maintains that, despite Kamal-ud-Din's attraction to the Ahmadiyya movement while a student in Lahore, that leader never actually accepted its doctrines. Ansari, "The Woking Mosque," 13. Later, in 1927, the imam of the Shah Jahan mosque declared on the pages of the *IR* that the WMM was not an Ahmadi organization and rejected the idea of Mirza Ghulam Ahmad as a prophet, equating Ahmadi with Qadiani. "Correspondence: Is Woking Mosque Ahmadi?" *IR*, Aug. 1927, 299. Ghulam Ahmad's words occasionally were reproduced by members of the WMM, as Gilham notes

in *Loyal Enemies*, 201. Yet this was rare and did not lead to the creation of sectarian identities in the Woking community.
37 Jamie Gilham, "Marmaduke Pickthall," 57.
38 *Badr*, March 20, 1913, 9–11, translated and put online by the AAII (www.wokingmuslim.org/history/kh-mosque-second.htm). This quotation reflects some confusion on the part of Kamal-ud-Din with regard to the Bahá'í movement. See the "History and Overview" section in Chapter 2 of this book. The *Surrey Advertiser*, Jan. 25, 1913, 6 also reported on 'Abdu'l-Bahá's visit to Woking. Woking Mosque file 942.2, Wok.28, SHC.
39 These organizations and the networks of those who belonged to them had political as well as spiritual dimensions and were used by Muslims in Britain who hoped to influence government policy. Ansari, "The Woking Mosque." Also see "The Woking Mosque and Muslim Mission" in Ansari's *The Infidel Within*, 126–34. The British Muslim Society was established in 1914 by Kamal-ud-Din under the presidency of Lord Headley. That body met regularly in Woking and London. This modernist and ecumenical approach had roots in certain Lahori Ahmadiyya teachings. Shearmur, "The Woking Mosque Muslims," 170. It is also worth noting that the WMM had methodological roots in the *Mu'tazalite* tradition of rationalistic theology, as did other Islamic modernist leaders including Sayyid Ahmad Khan, Muhammad Abduh, Mirza Ghulam Ahmad and Sayyid Amir Ali. All were staunch protagonists of the freedom of the human will and of human responsibility; of religion being in accordance with reason; and of parity of reason and revelation in discovering religious truth. For example, see Christian Troll, *Sayyid Ahmad Khan (A Reinterpretation of Muslim Theology)* (New Delhi: Viking, 1978).
40 Abdul Qayum Malik, "The Festival of Eid-Udha at the Mosque, Woking," *IR*, Nov. 1917, 447.
41 Al-Qidwai, "The Eid-ul-Fitr," *IR*, Sept. 1915, 447–8.
42 Sept. 1915, first page; Nov. 1915, first page; Sept. 1917, first page.
43 Khan, *From Sufism to Ahmadiyya*, 68.
44 Quilliam wrote this article under the name Haroun Mustapha Leon, "The I'd-ul-Fitr in England," *IR*, Sept. 1915, 445. Short clips of religious ceremonies, celebrations and festivals held outside of the Woking mosque and on the lawn have been documented and preserved on film by the cinematic newsreel company Pathé News: "Moslem Celebration" (1910 [sic]–19); "Moslem Festival – Qurban Bairum" (1914–18); "Islamic Ceremony in England" (1914–18); "The Feast of Sacrifice at Woking Mosque" (1919); "The Feast of Ramzan," 1920; "Muslim Festival-Woking" (1920–29). They are held in the British Pathé archive and can be viewed online at www.wokingmuslim.org/film/index.htm.
45 Kazi 'Abdu l-Haqq, "The Mosque at Woking: A Miniature of Mecca in the Days of the Pilgrimage," *IR*, July 1930, 242 and *The Hope Bulletin*, April 2013, 15.
46 *Eid Sermons*, xv, SHC. This number most likely includes converts made prior to 1913, for example those who learned of Islam through W.H. Quilliam and later gravitated to the WMM.

47 Reported by Kamal-ud-Din and printed in *Paigham-e-Sulh*, May 1914, 1. Translated and put online by the AAII, www.wokingmuslim.org/history/1914/May14.htm.
48 Ansari describes Kamal-ud-Din, Syed Ameer Ali, Abdullah Yusuf Ali and Mushir Hussein Qudwai, all of whom were connected to the WMM as "among the leading lights of the emerging Indian professional upper middle and landed classes." "The Woking Mosque," 4. Lord Headley was very active and influential in the WMM, bringing others within his circle into the fold. Interestingly, both he and Lady Cobbold were attracted to the egalitarianism of Islam. Haifaa Jawad, *Towards Building a British Islam: New Muslims' Perspectives* (Continuum: London, 2012), 60 and Shearmur, "The Woking Mosque Muslims," 168.
49 "The Eidulzuha and How We Celebrated It," *IR*, Nov. 1915, 566.
50 "The *Islamic Review and Muslim India* Its Object Accomplished," *IR*, March, 1915, 110. Shearmur notes that many converts drawn to the WMM came from the upper-middle class and the "minor aristocracy," but at least one, John Parkinson, worked in a factory. "The Woking Mosque Muslims," 167.
51 "Gospel of Peace Sermon given at the Woking Mosque *Eid-ul-Fitr*," July 10, 1918, *IR*, Aug.–Sept. 1918, 309.
52 *IR*, Aug. 1915, 385–6 and Dec. 1916, 529.
53 W.A. Lloyd, "The Mutual Relation between Islam and Christianity," *IR*, Feb. 1914, 54–6.
54 "Muslim Festival at the Woking Mosque," *Woking Herald*, Nov. 5, 1914. Reprinted in *IR*, Dec. 1914, 557.
55 Speech given by Kamal-ud-Din to the Central Islamic Society, London, in "Sister Religions," *IR*, Nov. 1916, 519.
56 Khalid Sheldrake, "Islam and the Occident," *IR*, Feb. 1914, 67 and "Christianity or Christ," *IR*, May 1914, 149. Buddha and Krishna are included along with Christ and Muhammad in Al-Qidwai's list of "prophets and holy men" in "Intoxicants in Islam," *IR*, April 1917, 144.
57 For reference to him as a prophet see "The Free Religious Movement," *IR*, Dec. 1916, 561–2, 4.
58 Sheikh Kidwai, "The Three Great Martyrs of the World," *IR*, Jan. 1919, 33.
59 The books from this early period are in the Shah Jahan Mosque Archives, Woking, England (SJMA). Most of the WMM materials, however, were destroyed in the 1960s. Incidentally, Francis Robinson discusses the Hindu, Sikh and Christian elements of Mirza Ghulam Ahmad's teachings in "Prophets without Honour? Ahmad and the Ahmadiyya," *History Today*, Vol. 40, No. 6 (1990), 42–7, 942.2, Wok 17, SHC.
60 Ameen Neville Whymant, "At the Feet of Muhammad," *IR*, Nov. 1914, 482.
61 Al-Qidwai, "The Spirit to Win," *IR*, Sept. 1915, 473 and Shaikh Mushir Hosain Kidwai's opening speech at the meeting of the Central Islamic Society, London, in "Sister Religions," *IR*, Nov. 1916, 514.
62 Al-Qidwai "Islam, A Happy Mean between Christianity and Judaism" *IR*, Feb. 1915, 70–3, quotations at p. 70.

63 Al-Qidwai, "Haji Khwaja Kamal-ud-Din," 434.
64 Nile Green has related the use of imperial technologies and Protestant missionary organizational forms by Muslim missions in late nineteenth- and early twentieth- century India in *Terrains of Exchange*, 20–6, 285.
65 Report of Khwaja Kamal-ud-Din printed in *Paigham-e-Sulh*, March 12, 1914, 2, translated by the AAII and put online at www.wokingmuslim.org/history/1914/mar14.htm.
66 Report of Khwaja Kamal-ud-Din printed in *Paigham-e-Sulh*, May 26, 1914, 1, translated by the AAII and put online at www.wokingmuslim.org/history/1914/may14.htm.
67 "Review. Our Moslem Sisters. Edited by Samuel Zwemer," *IR*, June, 1913, 191–4, quotation at p. 191.
68 Al-Qidwai, "The Eid-ul-Fitr," 450.
69 Shaikh Kiwi, "Women under Different Social and Religious Laws," *IR*, Sept. 409–19.
70 "Review. Our Moslem Sisters," 191.
71 "A Quaker on Islam," *IR*, Aug. 1913, 245.
72 For example, "The Religion of Toleration and the Religion of the Sword," *IR*, April 1913, 52–9, presents Islam as the former and Christianity as the latter.
73 "Political and Religious Liberties," *IR*, June 1915, 290. No author is mentioned for this article. It may be the work of one of the editors, Kamal-ud-Din or Maulvie Sadr-ud-Din. With regard to these types of arguments associating slavery with Islam see Robinson-Dunn, *The Harem, Slavery, and British Imperial Culture*.
74 For example, Khalid Sheldrake uses the term "gateway" in "The Mosque at Woking," *IR*, Oct. 1914, 438.
75 From a letter in Urdu by Kamal-ud-Din that appeared in the Lahori publication *Paigham-e-Sulh*, 27 Jan. 1914, 1. Both reports have been translated and put online by the AAII at www.wokingmuslim.org/photos/is-rev-east-meets-west.htm and www.wokingmuslim.org/history/1914/jan14.htm.
76 "Christmas Origins. Curious Traditions and Beliefs Concerning the Genesis of Popular Customs of Christians," *IR*, Jan. 1915, examples at pp. 51–4.
77 For example, Dudley Wright, "Islam and Idolatry," *IR*, July, 1916, 305. Also see "The Problem of Human Evolution," *IR*, Jan., 1918, 37.
78 It was not, however, uncommon for Christian missionaries to employ discourses projecting alterity onto the labouring poor in English cities in towns. Susan Thorne has discussed this process with regard to the early industrial period in "The Conversion of Englishmen and the Conversion of the World Inseparable," in *Tensions of Empire: Colonial Cultures in a Bourgeois World*, edited by Frederick Cooper and Ann Laura Stoler (Berkeley: University of California Press, 1997), 238–62.
79 His address was given under the auspices of the Central Islamic Society, "Sister Religions," *IR*, Nov. 1916, 512–25, reference at p. 524. Baig, like Mirza Ghulam Ahmad, was descended from a family of Muslim aristocrats who had contributed to the establishment of the Mughal Empire by Babur in the

sixteenth century. For more on Baig see his obituary in the *IR*, "In Memoriam," March 1933.
80 *IR*, June 1915, 304. As this quotation suggests, the Woking Muslims understood that not all Christians believed in the Trinity, and the position of Unitarians and other Christians who stressed the human nature of Christ, in both past and present, are explored in the *IR*. See, for example, "A note from the 'Unitarian Monthly,'" *IR*, June 1915, 283–4, and "Was Christ God or Man?" *IR*, Oct. 1916, 455–7, reproduced from *The Clarion*.
81 Wright, "Islam and Idolatry," 307.
82 John Parkinson, "Sin Bearers," *IR*, April 1916, 173–80.
83 John Parkinson, "The Type of the Red Heifer," *IR*, June 1917, 241–7 and July 1917, 305–9, 1917. Quotation at p. 306. This quotation refers specifically to Hindu practices, but reflects the overall attitude and tone of the author with regard to all of the ancient traditions discussed.
84 Ibid., 243–5.
85 Lord Headley, "Eli, Eli, Lama Sabachthani," *IR*, Aug., 1915, 387, 388.
86 Quotations from *IR*, April 1915, 165.
87 "The Promised Comforter," *IR*, May. 1915, 217–18. Also see "Prayer A Diet – Words of Jesus Realized in Islam," 501–2 and "Atheism in Europe," 531–2, *IR*, Oct. 1915.
88 "How the Bible was Invented," *IR*, May, 1915, 254–65 and another article by the same title, by M.M. Mangasarian, *IR*, Nov. 1916, 508–11. The need for the Qur'an as a supplement is from "Eternal Hope," *IR*, March 1913, 51.
89 Gilham, *Loyal Enemies*, 134.
90 Bertrand Tadorna, "Resurrection (?) [sic] or Resuscitation. The Rev. A.J. Waldron and the Resurrection of Christ," *IR*, Aug. 1914, 314–16.
91 "Christendom and Islam," *IR*, July, 1916, 333 and "Islam (Paper read by Mr. J.F. Holden in the Friends' Adult School at Folkestone)," *IR*, Aug. 1913, 246–52.
92 Humayun Ansari notes that the *IR* served as the "primary vehicle for the expression and dissemination" of the WMM's views. "From Woking to the Western Front: Muslims, the First World War and the *Islamic Review*," unpublished paper, AlWaleed Centre, Edinburgh University, Sept. 23, 2013, 4.
93 They engaged with local publications in and around the Woking area and those intended for national and international audiences. Some of the most frequently mentioned ones were, in addition to *The Times*, the *Surrey Herald*, *Woking News*, *Manchester Guardian* and the *African Times and Orient Review*.
94 The last point has been made by Ansari in "From Woking to the Western Front," 6–7.
95 The quotation is from Al-Qidwai, "The Powers and Turkey," *IR*, May 1914, 170. Prior to the war, WMM leaders were able to "line up" what Ansari calls "an impressive cast of tactically valuable British establishment 'front men' in their effort to defend the integrity of the Ottoman Empire," including Lords Mowbray, Morley, Lamington and Newton. Ansari, "The Woking Mosque," 10.

96 Feb. 1913, 4. After all, Kamal-ud-Din and the other early leaders and founders of the WMM were very much a part of the British Muslim establishment and imperial enterprise as Ansari explains in "The Woking Mosque," 4.

97 See Ansari, *The Infidel Within*, 92–3, 126–34 and "The Woking Mosque." The Central Islamic Society was called the Pan-Islamic Society from 1903 until 1920 and greatly influenced by the anti-imperialist Indian Muslim leader Mushir Hussain Kidwai. The Turcophile Anglo-Ottoman Society was founded in 1913. Duse Muhammad Ali was a prominent pan-Islamist and activist in early twentieth-century London. Both men were associated with Kamal-ud-Din and the WMM. Marmaduke Pickthall also was involved in these organizations. Gilham, *Loyal Enemies*, 219–20. Also see Azmi Özcan, *Pan-Islamism: Indian Muslims, the Ottomans and Britain, 1877–1924* (Leiden: Brill, 1997).

98 In 1913 Kamal-ud-Din warned that "sedition and anarchical movements were strictly prohibited in Islam," in response to inflammatory speeches given by Muslims in India who opposed British policies in the Balkans. Quoted in Ansari, "From Woking to the Western Front," 13–14.

99 That argument is presented in "The Estrangement of the Mohammedans," *IR*, March 1913, 47–8 and Kamal-ud-Din, "An open letter to the Prime Minister," *IR*, June 1913, 164–7. Initially Kamal-ud-Din wrote the entire content of the *IR* before including contributions from English converts and others. Shearmur, "The Woking Mosque Muslims," 167 and Gilham, "Marmaduke Pickthall," 55.

100 *IR*, June 1913, 165–6, quotation at p. 165. Other testaments to Muslim loyalty to that government published in the *IR* include "The Peace of Islam," Dec. 1913, 235 and "the Viceroy's reply to the Muslim deputation in Delhi, India," May 1914, 190–2.

101 Kamal-ud-Din, *India in the Balance: British Rule and the Caliphate* (Woking: Islamic Review, 1922), 110, 8382/15, SHC. A copy is also held in the archives of the Shah Jahan mosque.

102 John Parkinson, "War Waged by Our *Review*," *IR*, July 1918, 266.

103 "To My Brethren in Islam," *IR*, Dec. 1916, 572–3. A common assumption among members of the WMM was that thousands, if not millions, of men and women in England were already Muslims at heart, they just did not realize it. For example, this idea is expressed also by Abdul Qayum Malik, "New Adhesions to Islam," followed by letters from new converts, *IR*, Feb.–March 1917, 87.

104 Arslan Bohdanowicz, "To the Memory of Al-Hajj Khawaja Kamal-ud-Din 1870–1932," *IR*, Dec. 1949. Bohdanowicz mentions over 100 books, while the nook and corner quotation comes from Dr. Yemeni, President of the Burma Anjuman Isha'at-i-Islam, Ragoon. Both at p. 8. These quotations refer to Kamal-ud-Din's writings over the course of his lifetime.

105 Khwaja Kamal-ud-Din's reports published in *Badr*, March 6, 1913, 12–14 and *Paigham-e- Sulh*, April 14, 1914, 2–3, both translated by the AAII and put online at www.wokingmuslim.org/work/assessment-1913.htm and www.wokingmuslim.org/history/1914/mar14.htm. In addition, the idea that public opinion is a "great power" in the West, but one that is easily misguided, is

expressed in the introduction to a paper presented at the Sixth Congress of Religions in Paris and reprinted in the *IR*, Aug. 1913, 339.
106 "The Clarion Call of Islam to Muslims," *IR*, Nov. 1917, 486.
107 Reports by Khwaja Kamal-ud-Din published in *Paigham-e-Sulh*, March 22, 1914, 1; and April 14, 1914, 2–3, translated and put online by the Lahore Ahmadiyya Movement for the Propagation of Islam (Ahmadiyya Anjuman Isha'at-e-Islam Lahore), www.wokingmuslim.org/history/1914/mar14.htm.
108 Gilham, *Loyal Enemies*, 127, 136.
109 Report by Kamal-ud-Din to the Ahmadis in India and published in *Paigham-e-Sulh*, Jan. 22, 1914, 1, translated and put online by the Lahore Ahmadiyya Movement for the Propagation of Islam, www.wokingmuslim.org/history/1914/jan14.htm. According to Kamal-ud-Din, by 1917 the *IR* had already proven itself to be a "great educator" in South and West Africa. "The Clarion Call," 485.
110 The reference to the free supply is from *Eid Sermons at the Shah Jehan Mosque, Woking, England, 1931–1940*, 9–10, 07831/2/4, SHC. British Muslim press is from Ansari, "From Woking to the Western Front," 4.
111 As Sheldrake, who contributed several articles in Esperanto to the *IR*, explained, that language "'strives for the breaking down of these unnatural barriers of colour, creed and caste that keep mankind in a perpetual state of armed suspicion of their neighbour." *IR*, Feb. 1914, 488–90; Gilham, *Loyal Enemies*, 156.
112 "To all Muslims: the 'IR.' Ideals-Efforts-Results," *IR*, Feb. 1917, 108. This same quotation is used by Kamal-ud-Din in Nov. 1917 in "The Clarion Call," 488.
113 The WMM could be considered a part of what Gelvin and Green have called a "Muslim print revolution" that occurred in the first decades of the twentieth century and was led by charismatic and reforming Muslims who created "information hubs" in cities that previously were not centres of Islamic learning. Gelvin and Green, *Global Muslims*, 12–13.
114 "Notes," *IR*, Dec. 1914, 529–30. "A steady trickle" is the phrase used by *The Hope Bulletin*, April 2013, 26, to describe conversions during this period.
115 See Eugene Rogan, *The Fall of the Ottomans: The Great War in the Middle East* (New York: Basic Books, 2015).
116 These sentiments were expressed by J. Parkinson, "Turkey and the Crisis," *IR*, Dec. 1914, 589; al-Qidwai, "Turkey and Great Britain," *IR*, Jan. 1915, 36–7; and by the well-known British Muslim statesman and supporter of the WMM Syed Ameer Ali, first in a letter to the editor of *The Times* and then reproduced in the *IR*, June 1915, 285. That same issue reported the London Islamic Society's resolution expressing "annoyance irritation and alarm" that non-Muslims were discussing the Caliphate. That reference is also on p. 285.
117 Gilham, *Loyal Enemies*, 2. Gilham has noted that "Pickthall was a rather lone voice of public political dissent within the Woking-centred British Muslim community during the war" (p. 225), as "most British Muslims connected with the WMM fell into line" (p. 214). For Gilham's discussion of British Muslim patriotism during the First World War along with Muslim voices of dissent, see *Loyal Enemies*, 213–32.

118 Report written by Kamal-ud-Din in August 1914 and published in Lahore in *Paigham-e-Sulh*, the Lahore Ahmadiyya newspaper, Sept. 1914, 1, 4. Translated and compiled by Dr. Zahid Aziz, "Muslims in Britain and the Start of the First World War," 6, SHC 7-, 942.2, www.wokingmuslim.org/work/ww1/woking-ww1-web.pdf.
119 Geaves, *Islam and Britain*, 113–14. Here Geaves refers to letters written by Sayal of the London Muslim Mission. However, the statements expressed are of a general nature and apply equally to the experience of the WMM. One, in fact, refers to the editor of the *Woking Herald* as interested only in war news.
120 This quotation comes from "Islam and Modernism," an address given by Marmaduke Pickthall to a crowded lecture hall under the auspices of the Muslim Literary Society, Nov. 29, 1917 and reproduced in the *IR*, Jan. 1918, 10.
121 "Trio of Brave English Soldiers who have joined the colours of Islam," frontispiece of the Sept. 1916 issue and "'Brothers in Faith and Arms' – Sergeant Bertram/Khalid Sheldrake and Sergeant Omar Richardson," frontispiece of the Vol. 6 No. 2, Feb. 1918 issue. Gilham has referenced both of these images in *Loyal Enemies*, 154 and 156.
122 "A Resolution," *IR*, Oct. 1914, 421. This was a British Muslim Society meeting.
123 Lord Headley, "Comrades in Arms," *IR*, Oct. 1914, 421–3, quotation at p. 422. Ideas about war forging bonds and overshadowing religious differences between Christian and Muslim soldiers, and to a lesser extent Hindus as well, are repeated by members of the Woking Muslim community throughout the period. For example, in the British Muslim Society's President's Address, also given by Lord Headley, *IR*, Jan. 1915, 16.
124 "The British Muslim Society. Public meeting in the Mosque, Woking," *IR*, Jan. 1915, 6–7. Similarly, in his address as president of that society, Lord Headley stated that it "is deeply to be regretted that Muslims should have to be opposed to Muslims, but it cannot be helped." "British Muslim Society. President's Address," *IR*, Jan. 1915, 12.
125 *Indian Voices of the Great War: Soldiers' Letters, 1914–18*, edited by David Omissi (London: Palgrave Macmillan, 1999), 371 and Indian war correspondence, British Library (henceforth BL). Cited in Rachel Hasted, "Remembrance and Forgetting: The Muslim Burial Ground, Horsell Common, Woking and other Great War Memorials to the Indian Army in England," 2016, 8, 6, 942.2, SHC. Singh, "Throwing Snowballs in France," 1024–67, discusses how, when Indian Muslim soldiers in France expressed support for the mutineers or sympathy for the Ottoman Empire in their letters, they did so through coded messages so as to avoid the notice of the censors. The reference to that German office is at pp. 1031–2 and the one to the soldiers' letters is at pp. 1055 and 1061. Finally, Andrew Jarboe has discussed both the German propaganda and British efforts to counter it and why the latter were ultimately more successful in "Propaganda and Empire in the Heart of Europe: Indian Soldiers in Hospital and Prison, 1914–18," in *Empires in WWI: Shifting Frontiers and Imperial*

Dynamics in Global Conflict, edited by Jarboe and Richard Fogarty (London: Bloomsbury Academic, 2014), 107–35.

126 Letter from Baig dated Oct. 23, 1914 and attached to Minute 18023/1914 in BL, India Office Records, L/MIL/7/17232: 1914–19, from Hasted, "Remembrance and Forgetting," 10.

127 The discussions between Sadr-ud-Din and representatives of the British government regarding the cemetery took place in early Nov. 1914, and on Nov. 5th Ahmad Khan's body arrived at the mosque. "Indian Soldier Buried at Woking," *IR*, Dec. 1914, 534.

128 Hasted, "Remembrance and Forgetting," 11.

129 The cemetery was created in 1915, within walking distance of the mosque and with the same Indo-Saracenic features. It was considered important enough by the India Office that the government surveyor suggested calling upon the military authorities to seize the property by force if any difficulties in obtaining it occurred. T. Herbert Winny to Sir Abbas Baig, trustee of the WMM, BL, India Office and Oriental Collections, IOL/L/SUR/5/8/8. The relationship between Sadr-ud-Din and British officials, however, was not without tension as Hasted explains in "Remembrance and Forgetting," 11–12. There is also a file on the Muslim Cemetery Woking in the India Office Surveyor's records, 1915–17, 942.2 Wok 23a, SHC. The issue is first introduced in "Current Events" and "The Proposed Muslim Cemetery," *Woking Herald, IR*, Dec. 1914, 532–3.

130 Haroun Mustapha Leon, "The I'd-ul-Fitr in England," *IR*, Sept. 1915, 447.

131 John Parkinson, "Eid Greetings," *IR*, Oct.–Nov., 1918, 355. Gilham, *Loyal Enemies*, 147, has made the point that perhaps the increase in the number of converts, particularly male converts, from 1914 (four women) to 1916 (seven men and seven women) reflected a new preoccupation with death and the search for meaning brought about by the war.

132 The postcard is from "somewhere in Palestine," dated June 1917 and is housed in the file of mosque images, SJMA, Woking.

133 "A Visit to Brighton," *IR*, April 1915, 166–7, quotation at p. 167. For a description of the hospital and the measures that the administration took to accommodate dietary and other restrictions based upon religion, caste and tribe see *A Short History in English, Gurmukhi & Urdu of the Royal Pavilion, Brighton, and a Description of it as a Hospital for Indian Soldiers* (King, Thorne & Stace, 1915), IOR/L/MIL/17/5/2313, BL, India Office Records.

134 Initial Indian contributions were documented in the Oct. 1914 issue of the *IR*: two speeches given from the proceedings of the Viceroy's Council, an Announcement by the Secretary of State for India and an article in *The Times*, 428–31. Andrew Jarboe relates the resources and funds that flowed out if India and contributed to the war effort, noting that that colony supplied more soldiers than any other colony or dominion in the British Empire and that the Punjab provided the bulk of those soldiers. Jarboe, "Propaganda and Empire," 107.

135 "The Devotion of India," *IR*, Oct. 1914, 428–31. The comparison of WMM discourses to those of Hardinge is from Ansari, "From Woking to the Western Front," 10.

136 Sadr-ud-Din and Shaikh Kidwai, both associated with the Woking mosque, served on this fund committee of the Islamic Society. For more about the fund, including lists of contributors and money raised, see *IR*, Dec. 1915, 656–8 and Oct. 1916, 475–80. Ansari relates how this charity was launched by Duse Muhammad to pursue an anti-colonial agenda as well as how little support it received in English society. Ansari, *The Infidel Within*, 96–7 and "From Woking to the Western Front," 11–12.

137 Sarojini Naidu, "The Gift of India," *IR*, March, 1916, 139.

138 *IR*, Dec. 1914, 596.

139 *IR*, Aug. 1915, 412.

140 "England's Debt to India," *IR*, May 1915, first page.

141 For example, when Captain Abdur Rahman Stanley Musgrave addressed a public meeting of the British Muslim Society at the Woking mosque, *IR*, Jan. 1915, 5.

142 The first quotation is from a *Daily Express* article, July 11, [1918] cited in *IR*, Aug.–Sept. 1918, 299, and the second from the *Pall Mall Gazette*, Sept. 17, [1918] cited in *IR*, Oct.–Nov. 1918, 354.

143 "Mohammedan Festival at Woking: Indians and the War," *Daily Graphic*, Aug. 14, 1915.

144 Reported to Muslims in Lahore and reproduced in *Isha'at-i Islam*, Sept. 15, 1915, 393–5, translated and put online by the AAII, www.wokingmuslim.org/work/id-ul-fitr-1915.htm.

145 These arguments and aspects of them are expressed in a series of articles in *IR* by Al-Qidwai: "Two Lessons from the War," June 1915, 278–82; "The Spirit to Win," Sept. 1915, 472–9; "The Eidulzuha and How We Celebrated It," Nov. 1915, 563–7; "The Mercy for the Worlds," Feb. 1916, 56–62; "The War and God," April 1916, 159–79; and "A Miraculous Fish," April 1918, 161–8. Also, in "The Present War. Civilization and Religion," Oct. 1914, 417–21 and Khalide Sheldrake, "Thoughts of a Muslim Soldier," Nov. 1915, 590–1.

146 For example, the anti-passivist article "Mistaken Mercy: Sentimentalism, on the Wane," *IR*, Sept. 1917, 355–60. "Turning-the-other-cheek" is from *IR*, Nov. 1915, 602.

147 For discussion of German atrocities see Lord Headley, "The Tender Mercies of the Wicked are Cruel," *IR*, Nov. 1915, 599–602. For reference to both German atrocities and the violence of the British press see "The Ethics of War," *IR*, Nov. 1914, 509–10.

148 With regard to the issue of aggression and defensive war see "Command to Kill," *IR*, Aug. 1917, 352 and Sept. 1917, 368–80. The quotation from Pickthall is from "The Kingdom of God: An Address to London Muslims," *IR*, July 1918, 285. For both instructions from the Qur'an forbidding the slaying of the innocent and comments on the savagery of modern twentieth-century warfare see "War Waged by Our 'Review,'" *IR*, July 1918, 255–6.

149 Shaikh M.H. Kidwai, "Woman under Different Social and Religious Laws," *IR*, Sept. 1916, 416. Translation mine.

150 "The Prophet, by an English Muslim," *IR*, Aug., 1917, 316 and discussion of quotations from several bishops in "Mistaken Mercies," *IR*, Sept. 1917, 355–360.
151 "The Qur'an, the Gospel of Jesus, and the Bishops of London and Chelmsford," *IR*, July 1917, 266.
152 "The Qur'an and War," Dec. 1914, 535–44.
153 Delivered on Aug. 10, 1914, and published in the *IR*, Sept. 1914, 384–6, quotation at p. 385.
154 "Glimpses from the Life of the Prophet," *IR*, Jan. 1917, 30.
155 Also see the following in *IR*: "Muhammad Victorious," Jan. 1915, 2–4; "The Spirit to Win," Sept. 1915, 472–9; and the following three writings by Marmaduke Pickthall: "The Holy Prophet as an Example," Dec. 1917, 497–500; "The Kingdom of God, an Address to London Muslims," July 1918, 285 and "The Prophet's Character," Dec. 1918, 429–31.
156 "The Man," *IR*, Jan. 1918, 21.
157 "Muhammad a Real Warrior," *IR*, Jan. 1917, 25–6.
158 "The Beauties of Islam by an English Muslim Lady," *IR*, Feb. 1918, 60.
159 "Maxims of War. Abu Baker, the First Muslim Caliph, and Lord Kitchener," *IR*, Sept. 1914, 396–8. Kitchener also is praised for his wisdom in forbidding the use of "the life consuming-element" at the front in "The Miracle of Wine by Jesus Christ," *IR*, Feb. 1915, 81.
160 Salman, "The Prophet by an English Muslim," *IR*, Aug. 1917, 317.
161 "Ramadan," subsection "Military Discipline and Fasting," *IR*, July 1917, 292.
162 "The Institution of Fast in Islam," *IR*, Aug. 1915, 389–91 and Al-Qidwai, "Some Social Problems and the War," *IR*, July 1915, 343–6.
163 "Soldiers and Morality," *IR*, Sept. 1914, 392–3.
164 Al-Qidwai, "How to Win the War," *IR*, Aug. 1915, 392–6 and "The Moral Spirit," *IR*, Oct. 519–26, 1915.
165 Abdul Aziz (James Peach), "The Voice of Allah," *IR*, May 1918, 197. Similar sentiments are expressed in "The Dawn" by Khalid Sheldrake, Muslim and Sergeant in the 10th Battalion, London Regiment, *IR*, Oct. 1916, 452–3.
166 Marmaduke Pickthall, "The Kingdom of God. An Address to London Muslims," *IR*, July 1918, 287–8.
167 Quotations are from Ameena, "A Spirit in Prison," *IR*, Nov. 1914, 499. Also see, Mubarakah Alice Welch, "Give Us Islam," *IR*, May 1916, 206 and "El Ameen," by An Admirer of Islam, *IR*, Nov. 1915, 584–5.
168 Beaumont Hill, "The Arab Advances," *IR*, Dec. 1914, 572, 572–6; "The Arab Victorious," *IR*, Dec. 1914, 613; "The Path of the Arab," *IR*, Aug. 1914, 339–43 and "The Arab Wakes," *IR*, Sept. 1914, 398–402.
169 For example, S.H. Leeder, "The Debt of Civilization to the Arabs," *IR*, Feb. 1916, 62–70 and March 1916, 109–18.
170 While Ghulam Ahmad was not able to make the hajj, and the *jalsa salana* or annual gathering that he initiated in Qadian has been understood by some Ahmadis to have superseded it, this idea does not seem to have been promoted through the WMM. Khan, *From Sufism to Ahmadiyya*, 79.

171 "Mecca in the Days of Pilgrimage: Prayer of Abraham and Its Fulfilment," 461–8, references and quotations at pp. 465 and 467.
172 Ansari, "Pickthall," 32.
173 The reference to "staunch Empire-loyalists" is in Ansari, "From Woking to the Western Front," 6, as is the term fanatic, 14. "Woking Mosque gang" is from The National Archives, Kew, FO371/4233, 141286, Undated minutes, [1919], cited in Gilham, *Loyal Enemies*, 228. Gilham also notes that most of the "establishment figures" in the WMM were "staunchly patriotic Tories" (p. 215), but that all British Muslims were considered suspect by the authorities (p. 217).
174 Ansari, "From Woking to the Western Front" reference to Basra at p. 15. Ansari describes the period from January 1916 until the end of the war as a period of censorship for the *IR* in that only limited reporting of the war effort was permitted.
175 Pickthall's letter appears under the title of "The Revolt of the Arabs," *The Saturday Review*, Dec. 8, 1917, 461–2. Discussion of Kidwai and Pickthall is in K. Humayun Ansari, "Pickthall, Muslims of South Asia," 31, 36–7, quotation from the Foreign Office (FO) report at p. 37. Kidwai's article in *The Nation* is mentioned in Y.D. Prasad, *The Indian Muslims and World War I* (New Delhi: Janaki Prakashan, 1985), 113. FO interest in Kidwai is also related in Ansari, "From Woking to the Western Front," 14–15.
176 The speeches from that meeting have been reproduced in the booklet "Muslim Interests in Palestine," published by the Central Islamic Society and put online by the AAII, www.wokingmuslim.org/books/mus-pales/mus-pales-t.pdf.
177 "Muslim Interest in Palestine: Muslim; the Best Guardian of World's Holy Places," *IR*, Aug. 1917, 319–22, quotations at pp. 320–1. The same point was made by Kamal-ud-Din in his pamphlet "Ethics of War," in which he explained how Muslim rulers on the South Asian subcontinent have, for centuries, contributed to the establishment and maintenance of Hindu temples and shrines, from Kashmir to the Deccan (p. 10). The pamphlet was published by the WMM and literary trust and is housed in the SJMA.
178 For more on the tensions and dilemmas experienced by British Muslims with regard to issues of loyalty and identity during the First World War period see Humayun Ansari, "'Tasting the King's Salt': Muslims, Contested Loyalties and the First World War," in *Minorities and the First World War: From War to Peace*, edited by Hannah Ewence and Tim Grady (London: Palgrave Macmillan, 2017), 33–61.
179 Humayun Ansari refers to this "web of pressure group organizations," including the Anglo-Ottoman society, in "The Woking Mosque," 7553/6/2, SHC, quotation at p. 10. He relates British Muslim support of the Khalifat movement after the war in Woking and elsewhere in the empire in "From Woking to the Western Front," 10–20 and in "Pickthall, Muslims of South Asia," 26, 35–7, 40. Also noted in Gilham, "Marmaduke Pickthall," 61–2 and Ron Geaves, "Abdullah Quilliam (Henri De Léon) and Marmaduke Pickthall: Agreements and Disagreements between Two Prominent Muslims in the

London and Woking Communities," in *Marmaduke Pickthall: Islam and the Modern World*, edited by Geoffrey Nash (Leiden: Brill, 2017), 72–88, at p. 87.

180 Report written by Kamal-ud-Din in August 1914 and published in Lahore in *Paigham-e-Sulh*, the Lahore Ahmadiyya newspaper, Sept. 1914, 1, 4. Translated and compiled by Dr. Zahid Aziz, "Muslims in Britain and the Start of the First World War," 6, www.wokingmuslim.org/work/ww1/woking-ww1-web.pdf.

181 As Clayer and Germain have observed, "In a globalized colonial context, the defence of Islam in South Asia had to start at the very heart of the European metropolis." Nathalie Clayer and Eric Germain (eds), *Islam in Inter-war Europe* (New York: Columbia University Press, 2008), 27.

182 Eric Germain, "The First Muslim Missions on a European Scale: Ahmadi-Lahori Networks in the Inter-war period," in *Islam in Inter-war Europe*, edited by Nathalie Clayer and Eric Germain (New York: Columbia University Press, 2008), 89–188, at p. 98; *Eid Sermons*, xvi, SHC.

183 Germain, "First Muslim Missions," 117–18, quotation at p. 118. In addition, Clayer and Germain have described the early Ahmadiyya missions in Europe as the "forerunners of today's Islamic transnational nongovernmental organizations." Clayer and Germain, "Part I Muslim Networks in Christian Lands," *Islam in Inter-war Europe*, 22–30, quotation at p. 27. See also Umar Ryad, "Salafiyya, Ahmadiyya, and European Converts to Islam in the Interwar Period," in *Muslims in Interwar Europe: A Transcultural Historical Perspective* (Leiden: Brill, 2015), 47–87. Arslan Bohdanowicz notes that soon after the First World War Kamal-ud-Din's influence began to spread beyond England to almost all of Europe, especially in France, Germany and Belgium, with at least one pamphlet translated into Polish. "To the memory of al-Hajj Khawaja Kamal-ud-Din (1870–1932)," *IR*, Dec. 1949, 8.

184 Ansari notes that it was not until roughly 1944 that the centre of Muslim activity shifted from Woking to central London, "The Woking Mosque," 21. Ansari relates its symbolic importance on the first page and p. 7. Reference to the *IR* is in his "From Woking to the Western Front," 4. Through the WMM and the dissemination of the *IR*, thousands of people declared themselves to be Muslims between the wars. See Gilham, *Loyal Enemies*, 141, 173–5 and Geaves, *Islam and Britain*, 117. For more on Muslim networks in Britain between the wars, see Ansari's "Making Transnational Connections: Muslim Networks in Early Twentieth-century Britain," in *Islam in Inter-war Europe*, edited by Nathalie Clayer and Eric Germain (New York: Columbia University Press, 2008), 31–63.

3

Zionist debates among Jews in England take a new imperial turn

While the phrase "imperial turn" has been invested with a number of meanings in modern historiographical discussions, especially with regard to postcolonial studies,[1] in this chapter it refers to a particular type of imperial turn taken by historical actors themselves in England during the First World War period: as that conflict destabilized the previously accepted borders in the Middle East, both Jewish leaders who supported Zionism and those who opposed it began to reconceptualize and present their respective positions based on the assumption that Palestine would soon fall under British control. Shortly after the outbreak of war, the anti-Zionists, as represented by a Conjoint Foreign Committee linking the predominant communal institutions of Anglo-Jewry, advocated a policy of liberal imperialism, political and economic, in that region, maintaining that such a course of action was both in line with British values and traditions and preferable to supporting the creation of a Jewish state. For the Zionists, on the other hand, the new imperial turn came in 1917, when a British Palestine Committee, along with others connected to the English Zionist Federation and World Zionist Organization, began to promote their nationalist programme as inextricably linked to the interests of the British Empire. As the Zionist debates took a new imperial turn during the First World War, Jewish leaders on both sides of that issue formulated and advanced arguments based upon an understanding of the British Empire as characterized by diversity, particularly with regard to the many cultures, ethnicities, nations and religions that existed within it. Also mentioned, although to a lesser extent, was the variety of races of and languages spoken by the people who comprised it.

In order to comprehend what exactly was new about the imperial turn that these Zionist debates took during the course of the First World War, it is necessary first to understand the terms of debate prior to the outbreak of that conflict, including the relationship that both sides had previously with His Majesty's government and the British Empire. Part I of this chapter is dedicated to addressing those issues. The section begins by showing how both the initial rejection of Zionism and later arguments formulated against it were rooted in certain Anglo-Jewish and British liberal traditions and ideals. Chief among them was the conviction that freedom of religion and equality before the law could and should serve as the foundation to Jewish emancipation both at home and abroad. This part of the chapter then relates the debut of political Zionism in English society, or the belief that Jewish emancipation could not be achieved through the pursuit of individual rights but, rather, by securing the collective rights of the Jewish people through the establishment of a sovereign Jewish state. The Zionist argument is presented to the reader primarily by discussing the activities of and materials disseminated by the EZF during the 1900–14 period, when that body served as a conduit of WZO culture, thereby introducing thousands of Jews in England and the British Isles to that new Central European nationalism.

Part I: Prior to the First World War: establishing the terms of debate – Anglo-Jewish liberalism and Zionist nationalism

Anglo-Jewry,[2] liberal traditions and the British state

The emancipation of Jews in England technically began in 1656 under Oliver Cromwell, when, having been banished in 1290 by Edward I, they were once again permitted to live and practise their religion in that country. While still subject to legal disabilities, those restrictions were not specific to Jews but applied to all who chose not to become members of the Church of England, including Catholics and dissenting Protestants. This period known as the "resettlement" was followed by a relatively smooth process of acculturation over the course of the eighteenth century. During the nineteenth century Jews gained equal rights in an incremental or piecemeal fashion, beginning in the 1830s with admission to the bar and the franchise. By the 1840s, they were no longer subject to legal restraints with regard to land ownership, worship or entry into the professions, and in 1858 Lionel de Rothschild became the first professing Jew to serve as a Member of Parliament.[3] The issue of emancipation sparked debate amongst gentiles, not so much out of concern for Jewish people but, rather, because of the ways in which their legal status could be used to define the English nation and the institutions governing it. While Whig reformers advocated equality for religious minorities in an effort to advance the cause of individual rights and liberties vis-à-vis the Church and Crown, high Tory conservatives who defended a hierarchical, monarchical, Christian state and nation regarded maintaining Jewish disabilities as an important part of a bulwark against the rising tide of liberalism.[4]

In this context of emancipation politics, the Board of Deputies of British Jews (BDBJ) emerged, establishing itself on a permanent basis in 1836.[5]

That body, the purpose of which was "nothing less than the conciliation of the Jewish and British worlds," proclaimed itself to be the only legitimate institution for communication and mediation between the Jewish community and the various departments of state. It operated on the municipal and national levels and assumed responsibility for watching over the interest of Jews throughout the empire. It also acted as a pressure group working behind the scenes to influence government policy.[6] Outwardly, the Board allied itself with Whiggish liberalism, intervening to ensure that Jewish rights were respected and deliberately choosing a name that would associate it with the London Board of Dissenting Deputies.[7]

In terms of internal politics, however, the BDBJ functioned as an elite "old boys club," an organization dominated by members of the Anglo-Jewish *haute bourgeoisie* intent on preserving their place of privilege in communal life. While, in theory, all Jewish congregations in the British Empire could elect representatives to serve on the Board, in practice, deputies came from the wealthiest London synagogues, the city's most influential banking and brokerage families, and were chosen more by arrangement or nomination than by election.[8] Together the Board, dominated by the banker and philanthropist Sir Moses Montefiore, and the Chief Rabbinate, occupied by his close associate Nathan Adler, formed the "twin pillars" that maintained established hierarchies and communal control for decades.[9] While the contradiction between the ideals of liberalism and the exclusive nature of the Board did not go unnoticed by contemporaries, the contrast was less glaring to the Victorians than it would be to later generations.[10] After all, at mid-century most English people could not vote, much less hold high government office, regardless of whether or not religious tests remained in place; as one Jewish man from Whitechapel is reported to have replied when asked to subscribe to the campaign for Jewish emancipation, "If Rothschild wants to get emancipated, let Rothschild pay for it."[11]

Jews who did take an interest in such issues and contributed to early and mid-nineteenth-century public discourse usually presented themselves as "Englishmen of the Jewish faith," entitled to the same liberties and privileges accorded their fellow countrymen, Quaker, Unitarian or otherwise, who followed a creed outside of the Anglican Church.[12] This understanding of Jewishness as a religious rather than national identity informed their associations in the Middle East as well. Montefiore may have contributed to the well-being of his co-religionists in Palestine and even helped to establish Jewish settlements there, but he did so for philanthropic and sentimental reasons.[13] Similarly, when immigrants from Eastern Europe brought Chovevei Zion, an organization dedicated to creating independent Jewish agricultural colonies in Palestine, to England during the late nineteenth century, a number of Anglo-Jewish elites looked favourably upon and supported it because of a traditional sense of connection with the Old Yishuv; for the Zionism it promoted was historical, religious and spiritual, not political.[14]

The appearance of Chovevei Zion was not the only, nor was it the most significant, change affecting Anglo-Jewry during the late nineteenth century. Just as emancipation and embourgeoisement had been achieved broadly and the image of English Jews as modern, universalist and patriotic had been secured, what became known as the "Jewish Question" emerged in contemporary political discussions, particularly with regard to issues concerning immigration, empire and race.[15] For the first time Jews were depicted as foreign or Other to the English nation, a status that prior to the 1870s had been reserved for the French, Catholics and colonized peoples but not applied to the small number of generally acculturated Jews in Britain.[16] This new projection resulted in part from the belief that the large number of Russian and Eastern European Jewish immigrants who had begun to settle in London and other cities would, like the urban poor in general, contribute to the degeneration of the nation, thus rendering English people unfit to rule an empire.[17] Jewish leaders responded by attempting to slow immigration and Anglicize the new arrivals, while at the same time defending them against antisemitism. With regard to the latter, they often used the same language of race and empire as did their opponents, contributing to the redefinition of Jewishness in late nineteenth-century England as not only a religion but a race and ethnicity as well.[18]

At a time when the English nation was being redefined in terms of empire, Jews could find themselves distrusted for having wealth or influence as much as for living in poverty or struggling with hardships.[19] As a small number had achieved considerable success through banking, brokerage and international trade in the City of London and subsequently gained admission into English "high society" during the late nineteenth century, opinion makers expressed fear that a plutocracy had corrupted the nation, allowing Jewish financiers to dictate foreign policy resulting in problematic entanglements such as the Boer War. Even Benjamin Disraeli, who had been baptized into the Church of England as a child and therefore was not Jewish by religion, was charged with racial alterity. For example, his perceived leniency towards the Ottoman sultan after receiving news of atrocities committed against Christians in Bulgaria and even his decision to proclaim Queen Victoria as Empress of India were attributed to a "Semitic sensibility" characterized by an un-English tolerance or even proclivity for "Oriental despotism."[20]

In addition – although not unrelated – to "the Jewish Question" with regard to the English nation and the British Empire during the latter part of the nineteenth century was the decision of the BDBJ, in conjunction with the newly created Anglo-Jewish Association (AJA), to advocate for Jews abroad. The AJA, founded in London in 1871 after the Franco-Prussian war disrupted the work of the French Alliance Israelite Universelle, proclaimed its purpose to be the defence of "Jewish interests throughout the world," and by 1872 it had established additional branches in Manchester, Liverpool and Birmingham. Initially the BDBJ opposed that international outlook as a threat to the status of Jews as loyal British subjects. However, after the Foreign Secretary, Lord Derby, officially welcomed communication with AJA representatives, the Board decided to ally itself with that organization so as not to become sidelined in an area of importance to His Majesty's government. As a result, in 1878 the BDBJ and the AJA created a Conjoint Foreign Committee (CFC) which linked the two bodies and served as a lobby to the Foreign Office (FO). The BDBJ repeatedly emphasized its commitment to prioritizing loyalty to the British government and, in turn, FO representatives regarded it and the CFC as legitimate sources of information and consulted with them regarding matters of concern to Jews in foreign countries.[21] Like the BDBJ, the AJA and CFC were dominated by the Anglo-Jewish elite.[22]

To summarize the relationship between Anglo-Jewry and the British state during the nineteenth century was both dynamic and complex. How Jews were regarded or presumed to fit into the larger polity had as much to do with the understanding of the nation at any given time as it did with a people who were identified and identified themselves according to various combinations of religion and ethnicity.[23] As the true or correct nature of the English nation was debated, especially along partisan lines, so too was the position of Jews with respect to it. Furthermore, the same arguments were not just repeated over the decades but were modified and even refashioned in relation to ongoing historical developments, from the influx of Eastern European immigrants to new imperial and foreign policy concerns. By the end of the century the BDBJ and AJA, organizations which reflected and maintained established communal hierarchies, worked together through the CFC and under the assumption that Anglo-Jewry had reached a pinnacle of achievement and, therefore, served as model for the progress and advancement of Jews around the world.[24] It was in this context of heightened international awareness, a top-down internal communal organizational structure and a continually contested nation, with the latter necessarily rendering emancipation ambiguous and unstable, that Theodor Herzl first arrived in London to introduce a new type of Zionism to English Jews.[25]

The debut of political Zionism in England and the EZF as a conduit for a new nationalist culture

Theodor Herzl's first visits to London

On a foggy evening in November 1895 Theodor Herzl made his way through the "endless streets" of Kilburn, London to pay a call on the leading litterateur of Anglo-Jewry, Israel Zangwill. Later Zangwill would recall that a "blackbearded stranger knocked at my study door," introduced himself and said "help me to rebuild the Jewish state."[26] As a result of that first meeting, Herzl was able to present his ideas to English audiences, thus initiating what would become a new phase in Zionist activity in England.[27] During two trips to London, the first in November 1895 and the second in July 1896, Herzl met with community leaders, addressed a dining society for Jewish professionals and spoke to a large crowd at the Jewish Working Men's Club. His seminal work, *The Jewish State*, became available in England in 1896, just two months after the original German version appeared in Vienna.[28]

What distinguished Herzl's ideas from those of previous Zionists in English society was his purely political approach. Unlike supporters of Chovevei Zion, whose connection to Palestine was religious, sentimental or historical, the national polity Herzl proposed did not necessarily require any particular cultural corollary, whether traditional or modern. His beliefs were rooted in his own observations and experiences as an upper-middle-class, assimilated, German-speaking Austrian Jew who had studied law at the University of Vienna and worked there, and then in Paris, as a journalist. While he had encountered antisemitism previously, during the mid-1890s he came to the conclusion that its occurrence was neither an aberration nor a soon-to-be-eradicated remnant from a bygone era but, rather, a "permanent and inexorable" part of European society. Therefore, the only recourse that Jewish people had was to create a sovereign state for themselves, one that would be recognized by other sovereign states.[29]

When Herzl presented these ideas to Anglo-Jewish communal leaders, he was regarded with disdain. After all, his political Zionism was based on the rejection of the path to emancipation that was central to their own position in English society and relationship with the British state, a model they valued as an ideal to be emulated by Jews throughout the world. In their view, Herzl dismissed the important work that had been done by the BDBJ and generations of Jewish leaders while at the same time threatening to undermine the current status of their community by giving credence to the position of antisemites who argued that Jews had divided loyalties and therefore never could be trusted as fellow countrymen.[30] His attempts to woo London plutocrats were met with a cool response, a "studied silence."[31] Other critics were more outspoken, such as the president of the AJA, Claude Montefiore, who made his opposition clear both in that body and in the press, or the Chief Rabbi, Herman Adler, who called the idea of a Jewish state an "egregious blunder" and an "absolutely mischievous project."[32]

Herzl's proposal did not receive any more support from the Chovevei Zion or the Jewish masses in England than it did from communal leaders in that country. The Chovevei Zion rejected Herzl's political approach as too radical, which, according to that body's organ, *Palestina*, put the "smooth working" of Jewish colonization in Palestine in jeopardy. It went on to call this new form of Zionism a "difficulty ... as unexpected as it is embarrassing."[33] Sales of Herzl's book were poor.[34] Even the immigrants who cheered for him when he visited London's East End did so because they thought that he would "save them from anti-immigrant sentiment," not because they welcomed his ideas.[35] Most Jews who were members of the working classes or labouring poor were too busy with their own daily struggles to devote time or energy to additional causes, and those who did decide to become politically active tended to gravitate not towards Zionism but, rather, socialism, with its promise of economic benefits.

The fact that the vast majority of English Jews were either indifferent or opposed to the idea of a Jewish state after Herzl's first two visits can be explained, in part, by the ways in which his nationalist ideology reflected the distinct political circumstances and structures in the land empires of Central and Eastern Europe: the Russian, German and Austro-Hungarian. In the Russian Empire, where most Jews lived during that time, enduring legal disabilities and intermittent violence under an autocratic regime, liberal arguments about individual rights and freedoms had limited impact. However, the concept of Jewish collective rights framed as national rights gained ground within those multi-ethnic, multicultural imperial systems during the late nineteenth century, especially in urban centres such as Berlin and Vienna.[36] In addition, the ongoing Zionist projects in Palestine can be understood as a form of "emigrant colonization," promoted by the German and Austro-Hungarian governments at the time. That term refers to a type of imperial reach that did not involve annexation of new territories nor the governance of people who lived in them but, rather, the creation of closed, non-assimilative colonies of settlers within existing states – usually in Africa, South America or, as in the case of Zionism, the Ottoman Middle East – who acted as a "civilizing influence" abroad and at the same time maintained connections with Europe. Thus, while in England Jews with nationalist sympathies outside of the realm of His Majesty's government might be regarded as having divided loyalties that necessarily compromised their patriotism and therefore right to be considered part of the English nation, in the Eastern European context, Jewish nation building could take place both at home and in Palestine simultaneously, and in such a way that efforts on both fronts would reinforce each other and elevate the status of Jews overall.[37]

Despite the inherent difficulties of introducing the concept of political Zionism into an English context, Herzl did gain a small group of "loyal and energetic followers" there.[38] They included, in addition to Zangwill, the journalist Jacob de Haas; the journalist and publisher Leopold Greenberg; the solicitor Herbert Bentwich; and the clothing manufacturer Joseph Cowen. Herzl's supporters tended to be upwardly mobile, middle-class men who had distinguished themselves professionally or in business. Though often descended from immigrant parents or grandparents, they lived in suburban north London, as opposed to the immigrant enclaves of the East End. Some among them, including Zangwill and Greenberg, were a part of a community of Jewish intellectuals who dined at the Maccabeans club and resided in the district designated by London's NW6 postal code.[39] Yet, despite having talent, influence and ambition, their "birth and wealth were too humble to qualify them for membership" in the upper echelons of Anglo-Jewry who dominated the institutions of communal life.[40] Certainly, there were exceptions to these generalizations, most notably the "contentious Romanian-born" Moses Gaster, who supported "all manner of dissident causes," and Francis Montefiore, a great-nephew of Sir Moses Montefiore.[41]

New Zionist institutions

In 1897 Herzl founded the World Zionist Organization, and in that same year eleven Jews from Great Britain who had been drawn to his ideas travelled to Basel, Switzerland to attend that body's inaugural congress. There, delegates agreed upon the Basel Program, which states as follows:

> Zionism seeks to establish a home for the Jewish people in Palestine secured under public law. The Congress contemplates the following means to the attainment of this end: 1) The promotion by appropriate means of the settlement in Palestine of Jewish farmers, artisans, and manufacturers; 2) the organization and uniting of the whole of Jewry by means of appropriate institutions, both local and international in accordance with the laws of each country; 3) the strengthening and fostering of Jewish national sentiment and national consciousness; and 4) preparatory steps toward obtaining the consent of governments, where necessary, in order to reach the goal of Zionism.[42]

While the WZO remained committed to the idea of a Jewish state, believing that it would create the conditions allowing the Jewish people to truly flourish, as well as provide the only real defence against antisemitism,[43] an approach which distinguished it from previous Zionist activities in Europe as it had in England, the authors of the Basel Program carefully avoided the word "state." Instead, they used the German *Heimstätte*, which connotes a kind of "dwelling place" or "homestead" and was chosen precisely because of is vagueness. After all, Palestine was a part of the Ottoman Empire at the time, and the Zionist Congress had no wish to antagonize that government. In fact, the words of the Basel Program were selected only after much deliberation, as they were meant to unify the diverse viewpoints within the Congress and present the movement in a favourable light to the international community, especially to the leaders of sovereign states with whom WZO representatives planned to negotiate.[44] Herzl himself would travel from one great power capital to another, including that of the Ottomans, between 1896 and 1904, offering the loyalty of the Jewish people to any that would support "a national home secured by public law."[45]

Shortly after the Congress in Basel and the establishment of WZO, the Jews in England who supported this new type of political Zionism became part of an organized international movement based in Central Europe with key financial institutions in the City of London. In 1899 the EZF, which despite its name would include supporters throughout the British Isles, was created as a branch of WZO. In that same year the Jewish Colonial Trust (JCT) formed, followed by the Jewish National Fund (JNF) in 1901. Both were English limited liability companies that issued shares with the permission of the British Treasury and served to facilitate Jewish colonization in Palestine.[46] The JCT, also known as "the Zionist Bank," would provide loans and other banking services to those settlers through its subsidiary, the Anglo-Palestine Company, with branches throughout Palestine.[47] By donating to the JNF, private individuals could pool their money in order to purchase tracts of land for Jewish immigrants to "settle" and thus turn into "the inalienable property of the Jewish people."[48]

After two more Congresses in Basel, the WZO held its fourth Congress in 1900 in London, and EZF members welcomed fellow Zionists, most of whom had travelled from Central and Eastern Europe. While there, Herzl spoke of England in glowing terms, and in a way intended to arouse and mobilize the people of that country. As he told his audience, from "this place the Zionist movement will take a higher and higher flight ... England the great, England the free, England with her eyes fixed on the seven seas, will understand us."[49] Yet, despite high hopes, the Congress proved to be merely a transient event, having little or no impact on its host country.[50] The disbanding of the Chovevei Zion two years later, which allowed the EZF to redefine the meaning of Zionism in English society in political and national – as opposed to religious or sentimental – terms also failed to generate widespread interest.[51] Despite new developments since Herzl's first visit to London, the majority of English Jews were not any more enthusiastic about the prospect of a Jewish state in the early twentieth century than they had been in the late nineteenth.[52]

Zionist attempts at negotiation with the British government in the years immediately following the London Congress proved to be just as disappointing.[53] Herzl's meetings with Joseph Chamberlain, the Secretary of State for the Colonies, resulted in two failed efforts to create a Jewish homeland in British imperial territories. The first was to be at Al-Arish, on the Mediterranean coast of the Sinai Peninsula, but was vetoed by Lord Cromer, the British Agent and Consul-General in Egypt, in 1902. The following year Chamberlain proposed an area in the British East Africa Protectorate, and when Herzl presented the idea before the sixth WZO Congress, as a temporary asylum for Jewish refugees, a bitter dispute ensued which almost spilt the movement.[54] After WZO delegates eventually agreed to send an investigatory committee to East Africa, the British government, in response to pressure from white settlers, offered far inferior lands than originally suggested; predictably, the committee rejected the plan.[55] Finally, while Arthur Balfour had a genuine interest in the issue and even invited the future WZO leader Chaim Weizmann to visit him at election headquarters in a Manchester hotel in 1906, the meeting had no immediate impact on government policy and the two would not meet again until after the outbreak of the First World War.[56]

The pre-First World War period usually is regarded as a time of frustration and failure for the EZF, by contemporaries and modern historians alike. EZF organizers had hoped to win over both the Jewish masses and the communal institutions of Anglo-Jewry, but they did not come close to achieving either goal. Internal divisions and incessant squabbles plagued that body's leadership and hampered its effectiveness.[57] While anti-Zionists continued to present arguments explaining their opposition to the creation a Jewish state, they did not consider the EZF to be enough of a threat to mount any sort of campaign or organized strategy to counter it. Instead, they chose to let it flounder, assuming that the movement would eventually die of its own accord.[58]

The WZO leadership also remained unimpressed with the EZF during the pre-First World War period and expressed both shock and disappointment at the latter's inability to generate the expected support from English Jews, especially in terms of fundraising. JNF headquarters, Die Hauptbureau des Judischen Nationalfonds, in Cologne called it "simply humiliating" that the place for which Herzl had such high hopes ranked tenth in fundraising, below even Romania, where Jews' continual struggles with persecution, poverty and antisemitism were well known in Zionist circles. Similarly, in

1912 collections from one "second rate town in Russia" surpassed those for all of England, and while the following year brought a slight rise in contributions, fund organizers still considered the amount to be paltry in light of the size of England's Jewish population, the wealth and status of some among them and the fact that the JNF was chartered in that country.[59] After all, the JNF had "its seat" in London,[60] and while many European Zionists had to work with some degree of discretion or even secrecy, the movement appeared to be the weakest in the very place where its institutions were protected by law.[61] In early 1914 representatives from JNF headquarters travelled to London from Germany to address this ongoing problem in person, echoing similar sentiments and adding the opinion that, given that the British Empire had "conquered a greater part of the world," fundraising for colonization should be easier in England, not more difficult.[62]

This contrast between the ability of English Jews to contribute to the Zionist movement and their general unwillingness to do so, made all the more glaring by the sacrifices and struggles of their counterparts in Europe, did not prompt any real intellectual response from EZF leaders during the period in question. None offered sophisticated or analytical approaches to addressing the inherent tensions between the ideals of British liberalism with its emphasis on individual rights and the Zionist understanding of emancipation in terms of collective or national rights, nor did they attempt to find common ground with regard to colonization schemes. They were, as modern historians have observed, "ideologically uncreative," making "'virtually no independent contribution to Zionist theory.'"[63] At best they rejected certain WZO practices inapplicable to English society, such as the system of "self taxation" that worked well in the Austro-Hungarian Empire – in part because there it could be enforced.[64] Platitudes about supporting Zionism as a moral obligation for Jews, or that democracy entailed duties as well as rights, replaced more rigorous thought.

WZO *culture via the* EZF

Yet, while EZF leaders may have lacked the ability or inclination to advance Zionism intellectually, they nevertheless played an important role with regard to Zionist culture in England during the pre-First World War period, for they served as a conduit through which a continually evolving European-based movement that was simultaneously nationalist and international could reach Jews in England and elsewhere in the British Isles.[65] By maintaining a link with headquarters in Central Europe, primarily through correspondence and the regular world congresses,[66] and then engaging in activities at home such as the dissemination of Zionist materials and urging fellow Jews to contribute to the cause, the EZF reproduced WZO culture: its organizational structure, fundraising mechanisms, beliefs, symbols, language and visual dimension.[67] Understanding these processes sheds light on the history of Zionism in England and provides the necessary context to examine the new imperial turn taken by the EZF during the First World War.

The "shekel system," created by WZO leaders prior to the second world congress in 1898, provides an early example of this new Zionist culture. Because the term *shekel* is the Hebrew word for the coins paid by the ancient Israelites to maintain their temple in Jerusalem, those who purchased *shekelim* from the WZO during the nineteenth and twentieth centuries could associate their support for this modern nationalist movement with an ancient connection between the Jewish people and that part of the world. In addition, through this system individuals gained the right to vote for and become delegates to future WZO congresses. As *shekelim* were relatively inexpensive, EZF members hoped to involve the Jewish masses in the movement through this initiative.[68] Volunteers went from door to door canvassing, especially during certain times designated as "shekel day" or "shekel week." One EZF bulletin in 1908 urged workers in the cause to "put their shoulder to the wheel" and sell as many *shekelim* as possible, so that England would rank high in the next WZO congress returns.[69]

EZF supporters also worked to secure donations to the JNF, or Keren Kayemeth L'Israel in Hebrew. Soon after that limited liability company was established in the City of London in 1901, a special JNF Committee of England (JNFCE) was created with "commissioners" based all around the United Kingdom.[70] Through that body, Britons could make contributions and buy shares in the JCT. Because shares were not expected to increase in value for some time, JNFCE workers presented them as a moral investment to be made out of a sense of "honour" rather than for financial gain.[71] This spiritual dimension of fundraising, or the non-material link that donations were believed to generate between Jewish people and the Zionist colonization project, remained a key aspect of WZO ideology reproduced by the JNFCE.[72] One advertisement, for example, called upon "every Jew" to contribute to the fund, expressing the hope that each would come to cherish the ideal of the "regeneration of his people in Palestine."[73]

Despite the use of the word "his" in the above quotation, JNFCE workers appealed to women and girls as well as men and boys, and no Jew was considered exempt from contributing to the fund, no matter how modest their means or how small their donation.[74] In 1900 a group of supporters collected coins for the cause by parading through the streets of London and Hyde Park carrying home-made Zionist flags and accompanied by a band. One participant later recalled hearing the clang of "coppers" hitting the bottoms of the wooden fund boxes as the new national anthem

"Hatikvah," or "The Hope," played.[75] In the following year, just after the fifth congress, the JNF began to create what would become the iconic WZO fund box associated with the slogan "a penny a day is the JNF way."[76] Most were small, blue-and-white wooden or tin containers with a Star of David on the side. Instituted by WZO leader Hermann Schapira, they were modelled on the idea of the *pushke* or charity box traditionally placed in synagogues, but by the eighteenth and nineteenth centuries found in homes and other secular spaces. JNF headquarters encouraged placing boxes in Jewish homes as a way of arousing "self-denying zeal" for the cause amongst family members, especially the children.[77]

Zionists reported distributing thousands of fund boxes throughout the British Isles, from Dublin, Edinburgh and Cardiff to Manchester and London, during the years prior to the First World War. The JNFCE considered the boxes to be the "most important and most promising" means of obtaining donations and hoped to put at least one in every Jewish home and business in Great Britain. As one member explained, "a Jewish family seldom refuses one if it is offered in the proper manner."[78] In an effort to reach less settled or itinerant Jews, workers for the cause approached the owners of boarding houses and restaurants who served a Jewish clientele and urged them to display WZO boxes in prominent locations. In addition to whatever arguments they may have made about the need for a Jewish state, they also promised practical support in the form of recommendations and advertising.[79]

Fundraising specifically for Jewish agricultural settlement became "one of the most developed aspects of the Zionist project," and, following the lead of the WZO, the EZF provided different ways for individuals to contribute depending upon their financial ability:[80] for six shillings a single olive tree could be planted in Palestine; for two pounds, a *dunam* of land, or the area that a team of oxen ploughed in a day (a little over one fifth of an acre), could be secured. In 1910 EZF leaders passed a resolution vowing to call upon every Jew in Great Britain to give at least £2 towards colonization.[81] While fund organizers might request as much as 10,000 *dunams* from wealthy philanthropists or societies, they considered 100 *dunams*, or a *nahalah*, to be a reasonable and appropriate amount to ask of the middle classes. Because the Hebrew word *nahalah* could mean inheritance as well as property or estate, the JNFCE's "*Nahalah* campaign" suggested the fulfilment of an ancient Jewish birthright as well as a present-day call to purchase land. One couple responded both to it and to the ongoing encouragement to integrate financial support for the Zionist movement with Jewish family life by gifting a *nahalah* on their silver wedding anniversary.[82]

The newly invented tradition of commemoration through donation had become a part of WZO culture since at least the creation of the first

"Golden Book" in 1901. That volume, kept at JNF headquarters and displayed at WZO congresses and other Zionist events, contained the names of people who had given £10 or more to the land fund. Donors also received "handsome," "artfully designed" certificates,[83] as did those who contributed thirty shillings for the purchase of five olive trees. These objects were meant to be treasured as a material reminder of the profound, even spiritual, connection that individual contributors now had with the ongoing effort to build a Jewish state in Palestine. For example, the image on one such "olive tree diploma" effectively communicates the idea that, like the JNF trees, Jewish settlers were establishing roots in Palestine that would last for generations: a bearded man educates a boy on the significance of the holes that the latter has just dug for new plantings, while rows of young saplings and a cluster of mature adult trees form the backdrop for the figures.[84]

These certificates are an example of the visual dimension of WZO culture, which helped to orient EZF supporters around the cause and complemented written materials, such as circulars, leaflets and pamphlets, also sent from head offices in Central Europe. Often, images were linked to fundraising instruments, and in addition to the popular representations of Theodor Herzl and the Wailing Wall, agriculture appeared as a common theme.[85] Illustrated telegraph forms, like JNF stamps and postcards, provided an inexpensive and practical way of introducing the Jewish nationalist movement and presenting it in a positive light to people who might not be inclined to read, or otherwise educate themselves, about it. They sold for five pence and could be used to send a message anywhere in Great Britain or the colonies. One, for example, features a hearty, robust farming couple carrying agricultural tools and products and surrounded by leaves and fruit. The image suggests abundance through labour, reflecting the contemporary Zionist discourses which described "rich harvests" brought about by the "ardent and patriotic devotion" of Jewish settlers.[86]

Slide shows also became a way of visually connecting supporters and potential supporters to the Zionist cause, and by 1908–9 the EZF's propaganda committee had twenty-two speakers available to present lantern slide lectures in "every corner of the U.K." That year talks were scheduled in London, Oxford, Bradford and Leeds in England; Swansea in Wales; and Dublin in Ireland. The images, obtained through the WZO, depicted "pioneer work" in Palestine.[87] One photograph of Jewish farmers with baskets of fresh oranges after a successful harvest complements lectures printed and circulated by the EZF in pamphlet form during the previous year. In that publication, "The Physical and Political Conditions of Palestine," speakers discussed the agricultural capacity of the country and produce specific to Mediterranean lands, such as oranges and olives, and commented on the ease with which Jewish settlers, despite having hailed from considerably cooler regions in Russia and Eastern Europe, nevertheless possessed an innate racial vitality and "powers of acclimatization," enabling them to uproot and thrive in their new environment.[88] As important as agriculture was to the Zionist project, it also was understood as a foundation for other developments including the establishment of educational institutions, and when EZF speakers showed pictures of schools in Palestine they appealed to their English audiences by explaining that Anglo-Jewry was known and respected in that part of the world for its support of education.[89]

In 1911, the EZF propaganda committee acquired the latest technology in visual entertainment, the new "in vogue" cinematograph, which they used to show films produced by the WZO and JNF.[90] Like the lectures and slides, these films were meant to educate the Jews of the British Isles about the benefits of Zionism and to foster a connection to a part of the world that most would never visit. The principal films were "Embracing Jerusalem," "Tiberius," "The Jewish Agricultural Station," "Bezalel School" and "Haifa."[91] Together they presented a kind of historical and geographical survey of Palestine, albeit a selective one, featuring ancient ruins and modern developments as well as regional variations from cities and towns to mountains, deserts, plains and the Mediterranean coast. In them, Zionism appeared as a progressive force helping to improve the country through initiatives in agriculture, education and the arts. According to the overarching narrative, the newly purchased JNF properties and Jewish settlements, such as those in and around Lake Tiberius, represented a continuation of a Jewish nation whose people had lived in Jerusalem and surrounding areas for millennia and whose buildings, or at least the remains of them, still could be found.

Yet, as Jews critical of WZO's political Zionism frequently observed, these historical connections did not, in and of themselves, require a Jewish state. After all, Jews had been free to live, work, worship, visit and otherwise maintain a bond with the land of their ancestors for centuries without one. Therefore, part of propaganda work involved promoting educational activities that would help supporters to reimagine the last roughly 1,800 years of human history, between the destruction of the Second Temple in Jerusalem in 70 CE and the establishment of WZO in their own lifetimes, as only a brief gap in a much larger scheme, or, to use the words of the well-known Zionist leader Moses Gaster, "merely a temporary phase in the evolution of Jewish history."[92] To that end EZF organizers supplied affiliated societies with readings, syllabi and pre-prepared course lectures on WZO history and theory and facilitated the study of Hebrew as a living language. The latter was especially important in allowing individual Zionists to internalize the belief in a shared national bond that spanned both the miles and the centuries: as propaganda materials related how spoken Hebrew was becoming a part of everyday life amongst Jewish settlers in Palestine, a practice not seen since antiquity, Jewish Britons studying the innovative *Ivrit B'Ivrit*, or Hebrew in Hebrew, method could imagine how they too belonged to an ancient people connected by a common language and undergoing a kind of revitalization, a process which would eventually bring about the founding of a new and internationally recognized state.[93]

Zionism's Orientalist dimension

Despite these various efforts on the part of the EZF, the vast majority of Jews in Great Britain still rejected or remained indifferent to Zionism during the pre-First World War period, and those who actively opposed it sometimes employed Orientalist discourses by depicting Zionism as a product of Russian and other Eastern European despotic regimes, an un-Enlightened, backwards form of nationalism that had no place in English society or modern, Western democracies more generally. EZF leaders, however, found inspiration in the support that Zionism had among Eastern Europeans. As Paul Goodman, one of the early leaders in that organization recalled, while he and his colleagues laboured in the EZF offices in Whitechapel, or as he put it, the "drabness" of the "London Ghetto," the larger Zionist movement had its "head office in Vienna, its intellectual centre in Germany, and its man-power in Russia."[94] This observation was followed by a rousing description of Zionism as a "revival of the dry bones, the awakening of a people" that stretched from the East End of London to the towns and villages in the Russian Pale of Settlement. He took pride in the spectacle of the "crowds of *Ostjuden*," or Eastern Jews, who visited England for the 1900 WZO conference finely dressed in their "native garb,"[95] and while antisemites might have depicted the Jewish immigrant neighbourhoods of East End London as an "Oriental sphere" or a "domestic enclave of Otherness" existing within England's borders,[96] EZF workers looked to those same parts of the city as having great potential to become bastions of support not despite but because of the area of origin of their inhabitants.[97] Occasionally they even spoke of putting their hope in the "East" in an intentional play on words indicating the East End and Eastern Europe simultaneously.

More than any other WZO figure, Theodor Herzl came to embody an Orientalist ideal. Goodman describes him as having an Eastern aura after his recent trip to Istanbul and "Messianic glamour" when he spoke in England at the Jewish Workingmen's Club in 1896. His "sonorous voice with the soft Viennese accents of his German" kept the audience spellbound, while his presence was that of "an Oriental monarch of majestic stature, with large eyes and black flowing beard."[98] Over the years, his appearance has been likened to a number of formidable Eastern figures, from an ancient Assyrian king to a well-kempt prophet.[99] In addition, Herzl's Orientalism, real or imagined, had great appeal, even helping to reconcile what was essentially a modern Western nationalist movement with more traditional forms of Judaism, for the images of Herzl that appeared on the propaganda materials of the WZO and the EZF, with his long beard and dressed almost entirely in black, called to mind the "old, pious Eastern-type" Jew, a social figure that would have been culturally recognizable to the audience those organizations sought to reach.[100]

The Orient and Occident or East and West are, of course, relative terms with regard to both culture and geography, and while European Jews might be depicted as having Oriental characteristics or tendencies in England, those same individuals could appear as Occidental in relation to the Arabic-speaking peoples of the Middle East. Examining efforts directed by WZO and supported by the EZF to relocate struggling Jews from the Yemen to the Jewish "settlement" or "colony" of Petach Tikva in Ottoman Palestine in 1913 provides a means to shed light on some of the tensions and contradictions surrounding both the multiple – and not always congruous – layers of Orientalist ideology within the movement and the simultaneous identification and projection of alterity that accompanied Zionist colonization before, during and after the First World War. At the same time, considering this particular project allows for a glimpse into the types of networks necessary in order for supporters of the EZF to contribute to a successful programme in Palestine prior to British occupation of that country and the Balfour Declaration, for these individuals relied upon the initiative and guidance of JNF and WZO leaders in Central Europe, the cooperation of Ottoman officials and the support of a number of non-Zionist Jews in the British Isles. In fact, when the "Yemenite committee" first met in Great Britain to discuss this issue, the majority of attendees were motivated by humanitarian concerns rather than nationalist goals.[101]

The idea of providing the means through which Jews from the Yemen might settle in Palestine was first adopted by JNF leaders in Cologne and then communicated to the JNFCE, where the plan was embraced with enthusiasm. The JNFCE then, in turn, established a special Yemenite fund and committee – actually two committees, one in London and one in Leeds, the members of each assuming the responsibility of making an "urgent appeal to English Jews." They contacted the editors of popular newspapers and journals and distributed pamphlets and other WZO materials in Hebrew, Yiddish and English on that topic. In addition, supporters approached local rabbis, urging them to inform their congregations of the need for funds and to include the difficulties facing Jews from the Yemen in upcoming sermons. As a result of efforts by the JNFCE in Great Britain as well as the JNF more generally, within a year donations reached £11,000, exceeding the amount needed for a new wave of relocation to begin.[102]

Through the JNF, with its administrative headquarters in Cologne and it seat as a limited liability company in the City of London, supporters in Great Britain, Europe, the Middle East and elsewhere in the world could pool their resources, thereby allowing hundreds of Jewish families living in the Yemen to uproot themselves and move to the colony of Petach Tikva. Some arrived to find newly built cottages waiting for them, while others resided in temporary barracks until their homes could be completed.[103] Given that most of these Yemenis already possessed artisanal and agricultural skills of use in the Middle East generally and were willing to work for low wages, supporters saw their migration as a way of replacing the non-Jewish labourers in the new colonies.[104] As members of the JNFCE branch in Manchester explained, because the Jews from Yemen were industrious, modest and useful, they would be able to compete successfully with the existing pool of Arab labourers, thus helping to put the "agricultural colonisation in Palestine upon a firm foundation."[105]

While the Zionist leaders who coordinated this resettlement programme may have done so with the goal of making the colonies more "Jewish" and less "Arab," they found the Yemeni Jews to have a number of Arab tastes and sympathies. After all, these new arrivals had lived in the Arab world and spoke Arabic as a first language. An Arab culture and heritage belonged to them as much as it did to their neighbours who came from Muslim or Christian backgrounds. The affinity that Yemeni Jews shared with Arab Palestinians in their midst became a cause for concern among Western Zionists who feared that these new colonists would succumb to what they perceived as the negative influences of town life in Palestine, particularly idleness and a sense of self entitlement or, as one EZF document described it, the prevalence of a "*'Schnorrer'* atmosphere." While there doesn't seem to have been any formal effort to restrict their movement or confine these Jewish settlers to the colonies, JNF organizers expressed concern that the Yemenis who laboured on the land "should be preserved" from the "demoralizing atmosphere" of the Palestinian towns.[106]

In an effort to encourage these new colonists to drop the customs and habits associated with their previous lives and instead acquire those of Ashkenazi Jews, or at least what JNF organizers believed those customs and habits ought to be, the JNF created a contest which rewarded recent migrants from the Yemen whose homes projected conventional middle-class respectability as defined in Western (which in this context included Central European) terms. JNF judges visited the Yemeni section in the colony of

Petach Tikva to award prizes for the best-kept houses. The contest itself, as well as the structure of the cottages, precluded traditional Arab domestic sensibilities which valued privacy and plain, even imposing, exteriors to mark the division between the intimacy of family life and the public sphere.

Orderly front yards fully visible to all passers-by were meant to replace the traditional Middle Eastern enclosed courtyard, rooftop terrace or walled garden. Even wooden fences, which obstructed the view of the family home only slightly, were pronounced by the JNF judges as making a "very bad impression." As they explained, when the Yemeni Jews built those structures to enclose their property, "the whole charm of the well planted gardens is effaced for Europeans." Judges awarded first prize to a resident whose methodically arranged yard and weed-free front path created what they described as an "agreeable" exterior view. They regarded the house that they placed second as appealing but nevertheless inferior because the variety of vegetables and flowers planted made the "picture somewhat many coloured." Overall, the more established residents of Petach Tikva felt satisfied with the positive influence that the contest had on their new neighbours.[107] By 1918 a writer for the organ of the EZF, *The Zionist Review*, would describe the colony as a great achievement and an example of the transformative power that the Judean colonies were having on Palestine; European or Western characteristics such as regular streets, attractive houses and trim gardens were all presented as signs of progress and modernization, implying superiority to the labyrinthine streets and traditional homes of Arab cities and towns.[108]

While the contest itself was not a British initiative, JNFCE contributors and those who kept themselves informed of developments in Petach Tikva would have had no difficulty seeing the similarities between the bourgeois values of the contest criteria and those of their own society, for both EZF and WZO leaders came primarily from the middle classes and embraced similar values, assumptions and prejudices.[109] Just as the JNF judges preferred the house that communicated structure, order and self-discipline over the more colourful and expressive garden of the second prize winner, middle-class English men and women of the period valued the image of respectability, a carry-over from the previous century, which favoured restraint and conformity over creativity. In fact, the weedless front path mentioned by the JNF judges could be considered analogous to the freshly scrubbed stoop, a hallmark of those who held conventional "Victorian values," for not only did both lead the visitor to the threshold of the front door, but each remained visible to the rest of the neighbourhood and required regular care and maintenance beyond what is necessary for practical use alone.

The WZO-led and the EZF-supported efforts to relocate Yemeni Jews to the colonies of Palestine and instil them with Western, middle-class values of hard work, conformity and respectability reflect an Orientalist anxiety on the part of those Zionist leaders that their European nationalist project was in danger of becoming too Arab influenced. After all, the line between "Jew" and "Arab" could be blurred considerably in Palestine. Arabic-speaking Jews had lived in that region for centuries, and prior to 1914 the elites among them served as mediators between Jewish settlers and the existing population, often advocating for a more inclusive, less narrow version of Zionism.[110] In the Jewish colonies, the sight of Jews and Arabs working side by side both wearing a combination of "Eastern" and "Western" clothing was not uncommon, and Jews from the second Aliyah, or wave of immigration between 1904 and 1914, became some of the most forceful advocates of creating a joint Jewish–Arab commonwealth.[111] In the light of these realities, WZO/EZF efforts on behalf of the Yemeni Jews should be understood as a project which allowed the Zionist leadership to replace existing Arab labourers with Jews whose own attachments to Arab culture they believed could be erased under European tutelage. Like Western, imperialist discourses with regard to the Middle East more generally, Jewish Zionists in Europe found in the Yemeni Jews a "degenerate yet improvable" people who could become modernized and civilized through their efforts.[112]

Part II: After the outbreak of the First World War: both sides of the debate take a new imperial turn

The Anglo-Jewish case for liberal imperialism in Palestine as a British alternative to Zionism

Jewish ascendancy and Jewish culture

Prior to the outbreak of the First World War, neither the EZF nor the WZO had any influence on British imperial or foreign policy. As explained previously, plans for establishing a Jewish homeland in Al-Arish and East Africa came to naught, as did Chaim Weizmann's meeting with Arthur Balfour in 1906. Even as late as 1913, the British Foreign Office treated the WZO representative Nahum Sokolow with barely polite indifference, as more of a nuisance than a potential ally.[113] However, after the Ottoman Empire entered the war in October 1914, members of His Majesty's government began to consider the possibility of expanding the British sphere of influence in the Middle East and, as a result, Zionist leaders started to make headway in Whitehall, cultivating support amongst government ministers, civil servants and politicians.[114] By the end of that year Weizmann was meeting with future Prime Minister David Lloyd George and Foreign Secretary Balfour. In Weizmann's second interview with Balfour, eight years after the first, the statesmen not only expressed his interest in Zionism, as he had earlier, but pledged his support for that "great cause."[115]

Anglo-Jewish leaders opposed to Zionism who had been content to let what appeared to be a temporary and ineffectual movement wither and die of its own accord prior to the First World War suddenly were confronted with the very real possibility that the EZF would find support in His Majesty's government as the latter had new interests in the Middle East. Such an alliance would bypass the vast majority of Jews in Great Britain and the established communal institutions which claimed to represent them, both of which the EZF had failed to "win over" despite their efforts over the course of the past fifteen years.[116] Of even greater concern, however, was the fear that a British government committed to the creation of a Jewish state in Palestine would threaten the rights and status of Jews in England and other parts of the empire and undermine any future attempts to achieve equality for Jews in Eastern Europe, particularly during eventual peace negotiations. As a result of the dramatic changes brought about by the First World War, opposition to Zionism, as represented by the BDBJ and the CFC linking that body to the AJA, developed and advanced new arguments advocating a form of British imperialism in Palestine based upon liberal principles, both political and economic, as the preferable alternative to the nationalist programme.

According to this position, the Zionists needed to relinquish their commitment to the creation of a Jewish state in Palestine, at least for the time being, as any legal privileges granted to Jews would, in turn, discriminate against the non-Jewish inhabitants of the region, a course of action that would be politically disastrous for the British Empire as well as morally questionable. Zionist nationalism, as it stood, was offensive to democratic and Muslim sentiment around the world. Not only would the "Bedouins" fight against British efforts to advance it, they "would perhaps be right" to do so.[117] Furthermore, as one BDBJ letter explained to the Zionist leader James de Rothschild, it was "inconceivable" for His Majesty's government or, for that matter, "any Christian government in its senses" to support policies that would put the Christians and Muslims of Palestine at a disadvantage, especially considering the large number of followers of both religions in the empire.[118]

Rather than trying to impose the WZO programme on British institutions, Jews instead should trust His Majesty's government to make "proper arrangements" for colonization in Palestine, "whether through the medium of companies or otherwise."[119] As Lucien Wolf (Figure 3.1), head of the CFC, explained to Weizmann, the existing British charter companies "almost always specifically excluded religious or racial privileges."[120] Wolf,

Figure 3.1 Lucien Wolf, 1907.

who had been hired as the executive secretary and director of the CFC at the start of the war because of his contacts in the FO, diplomatic skills and expertise in international affairs, dominated that body during this period to such an extent that, unless otherwise indicated, all references to the position of the CFC should be understood as that of Wolf, and vice versa.[121] While the CFC supported Jewish emigration to Palestine on the basis of religious equality, or according to the British "spirit and traditions," it also was prepared to fight "tooth and nail" against efforts to create a charter company specifically for Jews, or any other Zionist scheme designed to give them preferential treatment.[122]

However antagonistic such statements may have sounded, they were tempered with regular assurances that Jewish settlers would not need to have any institutional or legal benefits to ensure their eventual ascendancy in Palestine, for they were a "progressive, industrious, and law-abiding population" already in possession of the knowledge, values and abilities that would allow them to contribute substantially to a new colonial enterprise.[123] In fact, the Jewish immigrants living in Palestine already were involved in the very types of activities that His Majesty's government would want from colonists in a newly acquired territory: they were building settlements, draining swamps and importing "modern" or European technologies and methods. In short, they were doing what imperialists of the time would call "civilizing work." If they continued such efforts under the auspices of the British government or colonizing institutions attached to it, they would rise of their own accord and be respected as a result. As one BDBJ document, produced in the context of a particularly difficult period of negotiation with Zionist leaders, explains, only by engaging in "true competition" with their neighbours would Jews in Palestine be regarded as "deserving of success."[124] As long as Jewish settlers took advantage of the opportunities given to colonists under a British system, the Zionists would not have to demand special privileges for them: those privileges would "come of themselves."[125]

Once Jewish ascendancy was secured in Palestine, over a period of years and as the result of hard work in a competitive environment, efforts to create a Jewish state could begin. Wolf made this case repeatedly to Zionist leaders, especially in 1915–16. He explained that the rift between Zionist and non-Zionist Jews in England was based on a "difference of method," not opinion.[126] Similarly, he told Weizmann that the CFC did not expect advocates of a Jewish state in Palestine to abandon their future plans, just to "hold them in abeyance" so that British Jews might work in concert to address more immediate concerns. A politically opportune moment to resume Zionist efforts would arise after the "necessary work of peaceful penetration" had been achieved.[127] Patience would be rewarded, Wolf maintained, and if the Zionists proceeded "prudently and slowly," "ultimate success" would be "all the more certain and solid."[128] As the CFC's "Statement on the Palestine Question," agreed upon in May 1917, explained,

> If the Jews prevail in a competition based on perfect equality of rights and opportunity, they will establish their eventual preponderance in the land on a far sounder foundation than any that can be secured by privileges and monopolies.[129]

This argument assumes, and therefore also advances, economic liberalism, as it champions political equality, for just as the "self-made man," according to the concept popularized by Samuel Smiles, succeeded in a laissez-faire economy without aristocratic privilege but, rather, as a result of his own thrift, initiative and hard work, Jewish settlers in Palestine would rise as a group in the absence of legal or institutional privileges by relying upon their skills, knowledge, industry and general good habits. These middle-class values and the "entrepreneurial ideal" with which they were associated became hegemonic during the Victorian period and continued to have widespread appeal in the early twentieth century. In addition, the English Jews engaged in Zionist debates had plenty of examples of upward mobility in their own communities from which to draw inspiration: from business and professional men who had moved out of the East End immigrant enclaves to the north London suburbs to members of the banking and brokerage families whose fathers or grandfathers had been self-made, thus allowing them to regard their internal plutocracy as a meritocracy.[130] Yet, just as the establishment of an Anglo-Jewish elite did not happen overnight but took generations to come into being, the rise of Jewish settlers in Palestine could be expected to take time as well, and it is likely that Wolf and the others who advocated ascendancy as an alternative to the WZO programme were more interested in finding common ground with the Zionists in order to present a united front during the war and the eventual peace negotiations than they were in creating a Jewish state.[131]

In the spirit of finding common ground with the EZF, members of the BDBJ and CFC entertained the idea of encouraging the development of Jewish "cultural nationalism." After all, the non-Zionist leaders of Anglo-Jewry already had historical, institutional and sentimental ties to Palestine.[132] According to that vision, the region would become a centre of Hebrew language and literature, drawing scholars and students from around the world, and the Jew of the Diaspora who travelled there would not only encounter "genuine" Jewish "types," such as the rabbi, artist or farmer, but also discover the "Jew-within-himself."[133] This open-ended approach to the future of Palestine had the advantage of avoiding, at least for the time being, some of the more contentious issues surrounding Zionism, such as who would qualify for inclusion in that new polity and what would happen to the status of Jews who lived elsewhere.[134] Time and time again Wolf, the CFC and other Anglo-Jewish leaders protested that when Zionists spoke of Jews as a separate "homeless" nation who never could assimilate fully into the societies in which they lived, they emboldened the antisemites who routinely made the very same argument; Zionist theories "endanger[ed] their position as free citizens of the British Empire."[135]

In contrast, the CFC's concept of cultural nationalism that emerged in the context of Zionist debates during this period dovetailed neatly with that body's presentation of Jewishness as a loyal and assimilative ethnicity existing harmoniously within the English nation and the British Empire, both of which were essentially multicultural. When the Zionist Moses Gaster described Jews as "like the Irish" in that they could never become "English by nationality," Wolf countered by distinguishing between different types of nationalisms: he explained that while Irish, like Polish and Finnish, nationalism was characterized by a desire for political independence, the Jews were more like the Scots and the Welsh, whose nationalism was primarily ethnic and cultural. He then went on to explain that ethnological diversity existed not only along the lines of nation and religion but, in fact, amongst the seemingly homogeneous English population, as the residents of every county in the country possessed their own unique characteristics. Still, those differences in no way prevented them from coming together as a nation, as "real national assimilation can, and does, exist side by side with religious, social and even racial differences."[136]

Westernizing the East

These ideas were developed further in a speech contrasting "inclusive" Western European nationalisms with "divisive" Eastern European ones. In it the speaker, who is not identified but most likely is Wolf, presents Great Britain as a place where the Jew can assimilate and feel loyalty to the state "without compromising his own non-political ethnographic peculiarities or religious identity." For the Jew

> is as much a Briton as the Scotchman, the Irishman, the Welshman or even the Yorkshireman and the Devonian, who (in their ethnographic characteristics) often differs from the average Englishman, and among themselves, even more than the assimilated Jew.[137]

It was not unusual for CFC or BDBJ members to express the idea that Jewish and English culture, character and values had much in common.[138] It should be noted that in the above quotation, the term "Irishman" refers to the individual who is able to reconcile his ethnic background with loyalty to the British state and empire, as opposed to the Irish nationalist invoked by Gaster.

Not only did Wolf and the CFC reject the position put forth by Gaster that, like the Irish, Jews were marginalized and alienated from the larger polity and, therefore, in need of their own independent nation, but also he used the Irish example to turn the tables on the Zionists, likening their plans for Jews in Palestine to the history of the Ulster Scots in Ireland. Echoing the previously mentioned list of aggrieved nations, he went on to say that if the great powers of the world were to approve of a Zionist project which would expropriate land from the native population, then they also would have to condone the "Ulsterification" of Ireland, the "Prussification" of Prussian Poland and the Russification of Finland.[139] The impact that pursuing illiberal policies in Palestine would have on foreign leaders became an issue of great concern for Wolf and the members of the CFC who considered working towards the eradication of the legal disabilities suffered by seven million Jews in Eastern Europe to be that body's primary responsibility. Soon after the outbreak of the First World War and the creation of a British–Russian alliance, the CFC began to look forward to the opportunities that peace negotiations would bring to institute the principle of religious equality in that part of the world. However, at the same time, they also feared that Zionist demands for a Jewish state would undermine their efforts and "shipwreck" the entire process.[140]

In the interest of improving the lives of Jews in Eastern Europe and protecting the existing rights of those in the West, the CFC sought to convince the Zionists of the value of understanding Jewishness as an assimilative ethnicity within a liberal state. According to Wolf and others, Jewish emancipation in Western Europe ought to be recognized both as a "splendid achievement" and as intertwined with progress more generally. As one letter from the CFC explained to Rothschild, as the "ghetto doors opened" over the course of the sixteenth through the nineteenth centuries, Jewish leaders contemplated their beliefs and options and came to the conclusion that their religious communities did not belong to a separate nation, and that their connection to Palestine was eschatological rather than political. This pronouncement was made formally in 1804 for the Jews of France, Italy, Holland and South Germany and was repeated in England. Considering this history, any attempt on the part of Western European Jews to promote Zionism would endanger their rights and invite justified reproach.[141] Along the same lines, BDBJ members contemplated their own history in the light of English liberal traditions, including the fact that the celebrated Whig politician and historian Thomas Babington Macaulay had made the case that when Britain's Jews declared themselves to be neither a nation within a nation nor a separate, cosmopolitan group, they disposed of the last obstacle standing in the way of full political and civil enfranchisement.[142]

The CFC maintained that because of differing political and social circumstances, the Jews of Eastern Europe had not made progress to the same degree as had their counterparts in the West, yet they would do so eventually and already had begun to take some important first steps in that direction by participating in the universities and trade unions. Perhaps after a generation or two Russian Jews would have the same rights as those in Britain or France.[143] Yet this important struggle for emancipation was, if not in its infancy, at least in a vulnerable state and could easily be derailed by Zionist demands. As Wolf explained to Nahum Sokolow, former Secretary General of the WZO and soon to be an instrumental figure in the negotiations surrounding the Balfour Declaration, if Jews were granted special privileges in Palestine, the consequences would be "disastrous" for their efforts to obtain equal rights elsewhere, particularly in Poland and Galicia, where the belief that the Poles and Ruthenians required special privileges served to justify the oppression of Jews.¹⁴⁴ In other words, as Wolf wrote to Rothschild the following year,

> It is all very well for Dr. Weizmann to say that the Jews in Russia and Romania must work out their salvation in their own way, and leave the Zionists in Palestine to do the same. But, one cannot divide Jewish responsibility in this easy way. If Russian oppression of the Jews is wrong, Jewish oppression of non-Jews, or even discrimination between Jews and non-Jews in Palestine cannot be right. We must either denounce both or accept both.¹⁴⁵

Similarly, the CFC expressed concerns that the Zionists intended to "expropriate the Arab population" of Palestine, noting that when antisemites made a similar proposal with respect to Jews in Poland, it was condemned around the world.¹⁴⁶

Members of the BDBJ as well as the CFC kept a close watch on Eastern Europe, which for them included a variety of independent states, neutral territories and disputed war zones in addition to the Russian, Austro-Hungarian and Ottoman empires. They monitored the treatment of Jews in those regions who encountered varying degrees of discrimination and persecution, and intervened on their behalf whenever possible. Because Russia was both a home to millions of Jews living under disabilities and a centre of Zionist activity, BDBJ and CFC members were concerned particularly with developments there. They received periodicals from Russia including the Russian Jewish weekly *Razsvet*; the Hebrew publication *Hazefira*, printed in Warsaw but circulated widely in Russia; and the more mainstream *Dien* and *Vedomosti*. Their "agent" kept tabs on the turbulent politics in the capital from his base across the Baltic Sea in Stockholm, where he also received reports from the Jewish press bureau. Issues of interest to BDBJ and CFC members included the actions of the Duma; the number of Zionists who won seats in the Petrograd Commune; and the spread of sympathy for a Jewish state amongst Russian Christians.¹⁴⁷ Wolf especially was concerned more about the emancipation of Jews in Russia and Eastern Europe than about the future of Palestine.¹⁴⁸

He and the CFC repeatedly petitioned His Majesty's government on their behalf. The CFC sent letters, memoranda and reports alerting British officials to injustices endured by Jews in Russia and Eastern Europe. Concerns could range from the lack of civil rights or unfair treatment to mass expulsions, pogroms and wholesale massacres. CFC and BDBJ members introduced these issues into conversations and meetings, and on at least one occasion Wolf brought a Russian visitor with him to the FO to provide a first-hand account of Jewish suffering in the eastern war zone.¹⁴⁹ In some cases appealing to the government resulted in immediate success, such as in 1915 when, after contacting the FO to protest the expulsion of Jews in the Polish war zone, the practice ceased.[150]

When addressing statesmen about the topic of Jews in Russia during the First World War, the CFC remained exceedingly careful and framed humanitarian arguments in terms of national interest as well as justice.[151] For example, in one meeting with Balfour, Wolf described the ongoing persecution of Jews in Russia as not only a "scandal" and a "plague spot on our civilization" but also a real danger, a threat to the good reputation of Britain and its allies, for if atrocities in Russia continued, "the enemy," or the Central Powers, could use the resulting negative press and public opinion to its advantage. Even before introducing this issue in conversation, Wolf reassured Balfour that the CFC and the bodies it represented approached "all questions connected with the war as Englishmen." In fact, after the outbreak of the war, the committee passed a resolution stating that while its members had no reason to believe that there would be any dissonance between Jewish and Allied goals, if it should arise, that body would subordinate the former to the latter in order to serve the "political interests of our native country."[152] In an effort to ensure that the CFC would not inadvertently come into conflict with His Majesty's government regarding that sensitive issue, the committee sent reports to the FO requesting formal approval even of fairly noncontroversial statements and activities.[153]

According to Wolf and the CFC, efforts to promote equal rights for Jews and non-Jews in the areas of the world impacted upon by the war, whether in Russia or Palestine, served the Allied cause. As he explained to the Foreign Secretary, Lord Robert Cecil, in 1915, if the British government lent its support to the liberal elements in Russia working towards Jewish emancipation, it would secure sympathy from the United States, maintain the stability of the Anglo-Russian alliance and contribute generally to British "fighting power."[154] The following year, Wolf met with statesman and diplomat Viscount Lord Bryce, and the two agreed upon the importance of finding ways to help British, Russian and French liberals to connect across national boundaries so that they might work together to advance the cause of religious equality, while at the same time strengthening the bond among those three democratic allies.[155] With regard to the French, Wolf and the CFC cultivated relationships with individuals, like-minded organizations and government leaders. Roughly six months after Wolf returned from a successful trip to Paris, which included meeting with Prime Minister Aristide Briand, the BDBJ received a passionate letter of support from Joseph Reinach, the well-known statesman, Dreyfusard and journalist, pledging his commitment to opposing Zionism in the name of patriotism and liberty:

Zionist debates

J'ai été toute ma vie le défenseur de toutes les libertés de conscience; philosophe et, dans le vrai sens du mot, homme de pensée libre, je resterai l'apôtre de la liberté. Le patriotisme est le premier devoir ... Je suis l'adversaire résolu du Sionisme.[156]

According to Wolf and the CFC, while liberalism crossed national boundaries, served the Allied cause and acted as a progressive force both for Jews and humanity more generally, Zionism was a backwards, isolated movement that had nothing to do with either Judaism or British interests. It was one of many secular Eastern European "subnationalities" that had developed as a response to persecution in the Russian, Austrian and Ottoman empires. Jews who continued to advocate Zionism even after moving to the West resisted assimilation with their fellow citizens, Jew and non-Jew alike. They were "refugees" who created colonial enclaves for themselves, in England and elsewhere, which allowed them to remain "in sentiment and aim ... part and parcel of the communities of their origin."[157] In one letter to the FO Wolf warned that if His Majesty's government negotiated with "foreign Jews," or the Zionists instead of the "duly elected representatives" of the British Jewish community, meaning the CFC and the bodies it linked, then a "great injustice" and perhaps even a "very serious mischief" would result.[158]

Yet, ironically, according to this argument, the very Eastern European tendencies that disqualified Zionist leaders from advising the FO also served as evidence that Jewish settlers would wholeheartedly support British imperial institutions based on liberal principles in Palestine, for Jews were "instinctively the most assimilative of peoples." Their invention of Zionism as a means of adapting to the harsh political climate of the Eastern European empires merely testified to their ability to embrace constitutional nationalism if given the right environment and opportunities.[159] In other words, while the pogroms, Russification and Slavophile movements of the 1880s bred Zionist sympathies amongst Jews, the experience of equality would generate new allegiances and values, and even those who had moved from Eastern Europe to Palestine would soon become grateful and loyal to the British Empire.[160]

"Semitic solidarity" and "the key to the East": Zionists in England imagine a Jewish Palestine under British tutelage

Negotiations in government and the new imperial turn

Despite the repeated arguments and appeals made by Wolf and the CFC, representatives of the British government continued to meet with Chaim Weizmann and other Zionist leaders just as they had been doing since shortly after the outbreak of the war.[161] Originally from the Jewish Pale of Settlement in the Russian Empire, Weizmann had been a part of the WZO's inner circle prior to moving to England in 1904 to take a research post at Owens College, Manchester. Because he invented a fermentation process that converted the starch found in potatoes and corn to acetone, a key component in the production of cordite or smokeless gunpowder, he was able to provide valuable assistance to the Allied war effort. Weizmann, who also was known for his charm, eloquence and understanding of the British administration, sought to parlay his achievement into securing a commitment of British support for the creation of a Jewish state in Palestine, and while Lloyd George and others later liked to present the idea that the Balfour Declaration was a reward for that contribution, Weizmann knew that he had to appeal to future British interests as well.[162]

In an effort to convince statesmen to support the Zionist programme, he and other EZF and WZO spokesmen "played several cards at once." They argued for the strategic importance that Jewish settlers loyal to the British Empire would provide in the region. Weizmann especially was aware of the Orientalist myths in English culture, both anti- and philo-Semitic, and how they might be used to serve the Zionist cause. Relying upon stereotypical and even fantastical beliefs about Jewish power in the world, while at the same time grossly exaggerating Jewish support for the WZO, he maintained that taking a pro-Zionist stance would help to draw the United States into the war on the side of the Allies and prevent the Russians from signing a separate peace. He increased pressure by warning that if the British government did not act quickly, the advantage could go instead to the Central Powers, for the German government had already made overtures to WZO leaders and Zionism was, after all, an Austrian idea. Finally, he invoked humanitarian concerns and Christian evangelical beliefs.[163]

While Weizmann did not share those beliefs, he nevertheless was aware of the strong romantic and biblical attachment that the idea of restoring the Jews to the Holy Land had for a number of Christians, both inside and outside of the government. Individual Christians had contributed to the JNF since its founding, and Zionist publications made mention of those who attended the congresses and watched the proceedings with interest. Even before the establishment of the WZO, English evangelicals had looked to the expansion of British influence in the Eastern Mediterranean as an avenue through which they could realize biblical prophecy.[164] This possibility had great appeal to both the Foreign Secretary, Arthur Balfour, and Prime Minister David Lloyd George. The latter related how, as a child, he knew far more about the kings of Israel than he did about those of his own country, and in his memoirs he referred to modern Palestine as Canaan, the biblical name of that region before its conquest by the Israelites.[165]

Lloyd George, Balfour and the liaison officer for Middle Eastern affairs, Mark Sykes, all were sympathetic to the Zionist programme for a combination of reasons, sentimental and strategic, and just as British troops in Egypt were poised to move eastwards towards Palestine, the government officially opened communications with the EZF/WZO.[166] Yet others in the War Cabinet and elsewhere in the administration opposed a Zionist alliance; the Secretary of State for India, Edwin Montagu, presented a particularly passionate and compelling argument. As a Jew, he had experienced at first hand the antisemitism of those who assumed he necessarily had divided loyalties and, therefore, never could be trusted fully. He reacted to EZF/WZO proposals with "horror," explaining to Lloyd George that "all of my life I have been trying to get out of the ghetto" and now it seems "You want to force me back there." Montagu regarded support for the Zionist programme in the FO as a "blow" to loyal Jewish Britons like himself, delivered in a misguided effort to "set up a people which does not exist."[167]

Both Montagu and Lord Curzon opposed an alliance with the Zionists on the basis of their practical experience and knowledge of imperial rule. Montagu pointed out that such a decision would cause alarm amongst Indian Muslims.[168] Curzon, who was a part of the coalition cabinet, had previously served as Viceroy of India and was known for his extensive travels and understanding of Eastern affairs, protested on the grounds that Palestine simply was not large enough to support both the existing non-Jewish, or Christian and Muslim Arab, population and the creation of a new Jewish state.[169] Yet in the political-bureaucratic process in which power and status trumped experience, expertise and, in many cases, sound argument, the objections of Curzon, Montagu and others, including those on the ground, were dismissed easily, while Balfour was able to get the proposal for a British declaration of sympathy with Zionist aspirations adopted with relatively little effort.[170] Two days after the Egyptian Expeditionary Force led by Edmund Allenby successfully attacked the fortified city of Gaza, the gateway to Palestine, that promise famously came in the form of a letter from the Foreign Secretary to Lord Rothschild:

> Foreign Office,
> November 2nd, 1917
>
> Dear Lord Rothschild,
>
> I have much pleasure in conveying to you, on behalf of His Majesty's Government, the following declaration of sympathy with Jewish Zionist aspirations which has been submitted to, and approved by, the Cabinet.
>
> "His Majesty's Government view with favour the establishment in Palestine

of a national home for the Jewish people, and will use their best endeavours to facilitate the achievement of this object, it being clearly understood that nothing shall be done which may prejudice the civil and religious rights of existing non-Jewish communities in Palestine, or the rights and political status enjoyed by Jews in any other country"

I should be grateful if you would bring this declaration to the knowledge of the Zionist Federation.

Yours,
Arthur James Balfour (signed)[171]

During that same year, as members of government debated with one another about the proper course of action and the Egyptian Expeditionary Force gradually made its way eastwards towards Palestine, from Al-Arish in the Sinai to Gaza, Zionist arguments presented in England began to take a new imperial turn. In early 1917 Israel Sieff, Harry Sacher and Simon Marks, all friends of Weizmann and known as the "Manchester group" among EZF members and other Zionists, formed the British Palestine Committee in order to "interest English people, English men and women in the idea of a Jewish Palestine under a British Crown";[172] or, in other words, as stated on the masthead of the committee's new publication, *Palestine*, "to reset the ancient glories of the Jewish nation in the Freedom of a new British Dominion in Palestine."[173] Over the course of the next few years, or the remainder of the First World War period, as the British became increasingly entrenched in that region of the world and committed to shaping its future, Zionism was reconceptualized and presented publicly in England as a form of British patriotism, the support of which was, therefore, a "double obligation" on the part of His Majesty's Jewish subjects. For only a "Jewish Palestine" could defend the Suez Canal, create a commercial and cultural bridge to the East, and demonstrate British moral authority by liberating an oppressed nation. Likewise, only British imperial institutions were capable of providing the political and administrative framework that would foster the development of a viable, independent Jewish state and therefore the emancipation of the Jewish people.[174] Adding this new dimension to the Zionist position in early twentieth-century England, a line of argument which posited the need for a special relationship between the Jewish people and the British imperial government for the best interest of both, was facilitated and, in fact, made possible by the multifaceted and protean nature of Zionism itself.[175]

This new imperial turn can be seen perhaps most dramatically in the way that Zionists regarded the general public in England over the course of the war. During the early years of the First World War, EZF leaders acted with understandable caution. In a political climate in which Jews could become targets of violence merely for having German-sounding names,[176] drawing attention to a nationalist movement, especially one that kept its headquarters in Central Europe, envisioned its homeland in the Ottoman Empire and had entertained the prospect of realizing the Zionist dream with the backing of the German state, could be dangerous.[177] In 1914 the JNFCE cancelled its annual "flag day" celebration, replacing it with a less overtly political "flower day," during which flowers in the Zionist colours of blue and white were sold instead.[178] While the EZF leadership decided not to cancel "*shekel* day" the following year – after all, it considered the sale of *shekelim* to be among "the most urgent of our duties" – the monthly bulletin issued by that organization warned workers in the cause not to engage in any public displays or "outdoor manifestations" that might be considered inappropriate in a nation at war.[179]

Yet, in 1917 after the issue of the Balfour Declaration, EZF leaders no longer shied away from public attention or downplayed the political nature of their movement. Rather, they celebrated it and sought to inform as many English people as possible about its goals and new alliance with the British government. Organizers booked popular venues such as the Pavilion Theatre in Whitechapel, London's Royal Albert Hall and the Manchester Hippodrome and decorated them with the blue and white flags previously deemed too controversial for sale. There they held "mass meetings" packed from "floor to roof" in which Zionist leaders and British statesmen shared the podium, on occasion Balfour himself. James de Rothschild told a cheering crowd at the Hippodrome that Britain was like a "foster-mother" to "the new-born Jewish nation," and Mark Sykes addressed an audience of thousands at the London Opera House, stating that it might be the "destiny of the Jewish race to be the bridge between Asia and Europe, to bring the spirituality of Asia to Europe and the vitality of Europe to Asia."[180] At that and similar events participants sang the Zionist anthem "*Hatikvah*" as well as "God Save the King"[181]

A political ideology that had been considered suspect or even subversive could now be reconceptualized and presented as intensely patriotic. Previous hopes for Zionist colonization under the aegis of the Ottoman Porte were abandoned, seemingly without a second thought, and EZF members referred to the advance of General Edmund Allenby and his troops as the "liberation of Palestine."[182] That body began to produce and disseminate thousands of flyers, pamphlets and other written materials intended to educate English people about the compatibility between Zionist goals and British interests in the Middle East.[183] One report depicted Jews welcoming the British into Palestine in particularly vivid terms. It describes them as "ablaze with joy," weeping with happiness and carrying "their deliverers," the British soldiers, shoulder high. Lest there be any doubt as to the intentions and feelings behind such displays, the document notes that demonstrators carried signs with phrases such as "long live Allenby" or "long live the British liberating army."[184]

By the time of the EZF annual conference, held in early 1918, speakers already had become adept at weaving together British imperialist with Zionist nationalist tropes and beliefs. These two ideologies dovetail almost effortlessly in the image of a Mediterranean traveller approaching the "doors of the Orient" evoked in the address given by Samuel Tolkowsky, the Zionist leader who soon would serve on behalf that movement's delegation to Versailles. While the idea of leaving the comfortable familiarity of the West may have seemed like a daunting prospect to his largely British and European audience, listeners could take comfort in learning that the region's "first Jewish outposts," or buildings of Tel Aviv, were visible from the sea.[185] In Zionist discourses the seaside typically was depicted as a "site of regenerative power" for Jews both in that city and in nearby Haifa.[186] The choice of the word "outpost" is significant, as it implies that Jewish settlements were neither independent communities nor were they simply a part of the patchwork of Palestine's diverse population: rather, they belonged to a larger imperial entity and served to extend its power to remote or frontier areas. In addition, both that term and the image of a ship reaching the shore would have called to mind Britain's formidable history of seafaring imperialism.

For centuries, men and women from the British Isles had journeyed by ship to colonial outposts throughout the world from the Americas to Africa, South Asia and the Far East, and by the First World War period steamship travel to the south-eastern shores of the Mediterranean had become increasingly common. A sense of anticipation upon approaching what was imagined to be the strange and exotic world of the Orient lying on the other side of that sea was not unique to Zionist discourses. For example, one First World War sergeant from the Midlands recalled how, as the SS *Indarra* advanced towards the Alexandria docks, the "smell of the East" came to him over the water. This phrase should not be regarded as simply negative or dismissive, as he later goes on to describe Alexandria, a city much like Tel Aviv with regard to its role as a Westernized "outpost," in very favourable terms. Rather, it serves to indicate a kind of palpable alterity, thereby dramatizing the transition from the intercultural space of ship and sea, usually referred to as the "oceanic interculture" in the context of Atlantic world history, to the Orient.[187]

In Tolkowsky's conference address, Tel Aviv appeared not only as an imperial outpost but also as an oasis of civilization in an otherwise dirty and backward part of the world: a model of "western cleanliness and hygiene" with broad, tree-lined streets, well-built houses and flowering squares. In contrast, he described nearby Arab Jaffa as a "town of dust and evil smells in summer and of mud and evil smells in winter."[188] These images would have called to mind similar, popularly held beliefs about the gulf between the way of life in the hill stations and other English enclaves of British India and the spaces inhabited by the general population. Yet, at the same time, this type of discourse would have been as recognizable to the European Zionists in the audience as it was to Britons familiar with standard representations of empire; for Tolkowsky's address reflects the beliefs of the WZO leaders who understood advancement in Palestine in terms of both Jewish settlement in that country and the degree to which settlers reproduced the lifestyles and value system of the Western European bourgeoisie. His reference to the yards and gardens surrounding the recently constructed houses in Tel Aviv as evidence of progress in the region echoes the previously discussed JNF contest designed to encourage newly arrived Jews from the Yemen to create domestic exteriors characterized by neat and orderly arrangements in full view of passers-by. Similarly, the prized photographs of Tel Aviv circulated by European Zionists before the war "boasted clean, wide streets, lined with white-washed buildings, with no trace of commotion."[189]

As the first true or "original 'Zionist city,'" peopled with Hebrew-speaking but not necessarily religious Jews, Tel Aviv had special significance for those inspired by Herzl's vision. Its name comes from the Hebrew translation of his novel *Altneuland* or "old new land." In that language, "*Tel*" means ruins and "*Aviv*" means spring.[190] If Palestine was a land of ruins that had not flourished since antiquity, as communicated in Zionist representations of that country, the recent Jewish settlements were the spring or the renewal of life. Herzl assured his followers that the Zionist cities of the future would have the familiar bourgeois pleasures of Europe, like salt pretzels and café society, yet also they would become modern, secular "bastions of high culture and sophisticated cooperativism" with cityscapes that combined elements of the Occident and Orient.[191] In the same year that Tolkowsky delivered his speech to the EZF conference, that body's publication, *The Zionist Review*, described the Judean colonies including Tel Aviv as

> nothing less than a revolution, these villages with their regular streets, their attractive-looking houses, their trim gardens, their motor-pumps and water-pipes, their green fields and plantations stretching as far as one can see. To realize that, you have only to contrast them with what was in Palestine before they came. There is no reason in the nature of things why within a few miles of Jaffa one should find modern houses and hotels, motor-engines, a great wine-cellar, and so forth.[192]

By 1918 EZF members could imagine recent construction on the coast of Palestine as simultaneously the start of a revolutionary new society sprung from the ruins for the Jewish people and a British imperial frontier stronghold. In fact, in the following year Nahum Sokolow related how Colonel Claude Conder described the increase "in civilization and prosperity" in that country as helping to provide an "outpost" for English interests in Egypt.[193]

A necessary nationalism in a diverse, eastwardly expanding empire

English interests in Egypt, of course, depended upon ensuring continued and uninterrupted access to the Suez Canal, and the ability of Ottoman forces to launch an attack on it in early 1915, albeit unsuccessfully, was interpreted by British military authorities as indicating the need for British expansion into lands eastward of that waterway. In this context, Zionist publications depicted a Jewish Palestine as the key to protecting that important and vulnerable area. The loyalty that settlers would feel towards the world power responsible for helping them to build a national homeland would guarantee their unwavering devotion to the defence of the region on its behalf. With the continuing growth of that population, Britain soon would gain a strong dominion ally.[194] One BPC article put this argument in particularly vivid terms by likening the Suez Canal to the jugular vein of the British Empire. It explained that, just as nature protects the essential parts of the human body, statesmen responsible for designing the body politic needed to recognize the unique potential that a Jewish Palestine would have to cover that vital artery and shield it from injury.[195]

While the Suez Canal served as England's "chief-sea communication with India and Australasia," a Jewish Palestine under the Crown would provide overland links between Egypt and British-occupied Mesopotamia, especially with the construction of a number of new transportation networks underway.[196] Whether by developing a more efficient land bridge from the Eastern Mediterranean to the Persian Gulf or acting as a buffer for the Suez Canal, the need for a fast and reliable route to India remained central to the strategic arguments presented by Zionist leaders during this time. Without a "firm and immediate connection" to that subcontinent, they maintained, the very future of the Raj was at stake. If isolated from Great Britain, colonial India easily could fall under the influence of that power's foremost imperial rival in Asia, Japan.[197] When the military correspondent for *The Times* questioned the significance of the war's Middle Eastern campaign in Palestine, dismissing it as "'Lloyd George's baby,'" the BPC countered by suggesting that perhaps that journalist considered India merely an older baby of Lloyd George.[198]

In addition to the military and strategic arguments presented by the BPC, members also explained how merchants in a new Jewish Palestine would be situated to "blaze the way" for British commercial interests within the Middle East, from that region to India and as far away as China and Japan. They would take advantage of the existing Jewish networks, both within and outside of the British Empire, and make overtures to established Jewish trading houses in port cities such as Hong Kong, Shanghai and Yokohama.[199] While the Kadoorie family was not mentioned by name, the well-known Shanghai-based financier Sir Eleazer Kadoorie, who led the Zionist movement in the Far East and maintained ties with his ancestral home in Baghdad, would have been an especially valuable contact.[200] In addition, enterprising Jewish settlers would study and eventually master the languages of the "Orient," thereby gaining insights into the needs and desires of millions; for the British Empire, a Jewish Palestine would become nothing less than the "key to the riddle of Asia" and the first critical step in the creation of a "great machine of commercial penetration."[201]

According to Zionist arguments, a Jewish Palestine also would benefit England financially by doing what the Arabs, oppressed by Ottoman rule, had been unable to do: turn the region into a thriving, prosperous nation;[202] for the Jew was "a born colonist" who "understands more than any other man upon earth how to utilize all the advantages available," and through his industrious spirit he would, given the opportunity, "open up the treasures of the Palestinian soil" and bring "colossal" wealth to the country.[203] As immigration increased, so too would tax revenues received by His Majesty's government. In the context of this argument and over the course of the First World War period, the BPC issued at least one hundred reports and articles documenting in detail the output and/or growth in productivity of individual Jewish colonies either for a specific period or since settlement. One article explained how, while Jews had been colonizing the land for forty years, they had not yet begun to "colonise the sea," an untapped resource with the potential for yielding considerable returns relative to the investment, especially as new zoological studies were shedding light on ways to improve enterprises such as fishing and sponge harvesting.[204] With a strong commodity-based economy, a Jewish Palestine could provide England with raw materials for manufacture and a growing market for its finished products.

This vision of prosperity depended on the London-based JCT and its subsidiary, the Anglo-Palestinian Company, also known as the "Zionist Bank," with branches in Jaffa, Jerusalem, Haifa, Beirut, Hebron and Safed. According to Sokolow, the JCT and other WZO trusts and funds were modelled on British trading companies, the "peaceful conquests" of which had contributed more to empire building than had the actions of soldiers.[205] In addition, the Anglo-Palestinian Company seems to have had a special relationship with the British government, as Weizmann reported that it was allowed to issue shares during the war, a privilege not granted to similar institutions. He related also that the company had established the "modern machinery" of commerce and finance in that part of the Middle East, replacing the presumably outdated or stagnant "native" system.[206] The bank extended loans to settlers and promoted the import/export trade as part of its mission "to facilitate business transactions by Jews and to promote the spirit of industrial enterprise in Palestine."[207]

As in European discourses during the "Scramble for Africa," Palestine was depicted as "backwards" and "underdeveloped," and therefore in need of colonists, capital and enterprise so that the region might be opened to "progress" and "civilization."[208] Given how the partition of that continent both contributed to the expansion of the British Empire and influenced the development of political Zionism,[209] it is not surprising that those who made the case for the colonizing power of Zionist financial institutions and practices after 1917 relied upon the 1870–1914 period as a frame of reference, employing ideas and examples associated with it. In Sokolow's previously mentioned discussion, he emphasizes the great potential of the JCT, and its balance at the time of £250,000, by explaining that the British East African Company began with the exact same amount of money and now administers 200,000 square miles of territory; similarly, Cecil Rhodes started with £1,000,000 and went on to found Rhodesia.[210] One BPC report contrasted the quintupling of Jewish settlers in Palestine with the modest growth rate of the French *colon* population in Tunisia, describing the Zionist "genius" for colonization as unique in world history, in part because it was based upon the sound fiscal practices and institutions developed by members of the practically minded industrial and commercial middle classes.[211]

France, of course, was not only Britain's foremost imperial rival in the "Scramble for Africa" but also a First World War ally with ties to the Middle East. Still, the BPC and the other Zionist leaders in England at the time opposed any plan, French or otherwise, that did not assume continued British administration of Palestine after the war. The BPC referred repeatedly to the possibilities of partitioning the region or establishing a condominium there not just as undesirable but as the "two great evils." When French propaganda called for the inclusion of Palestine in France's soon-to-be acquired Syrian territories, BPC members warned that Britain could not be silent on the matter, otherwise "judgment may go against us by default."[212] The primary objection that these Zionist leaders had to a French rule in the country had to do with the centralizing tendencies of the Third Republic and its approach to imperialism, or its celebrated *mission civilisatrice*, which measured success not by the evolution of nations along their own individual paths but, rather, by the degree to which colonized peoples approximated French culture and accepted or internalized the political ideas of the mother country.[213] The BPC considered the political institutions of the United States to be more liberal than those of the French, but still "somewhat rigid in type," with nothing even comparable to the "wonderful graduation of the various States in the British Empire."[214] Not surprisingly, the Germans and the Ottomans appeared in this wartime discourse as the least capable of governing Palestine: "Prussianism" was synonymous with the forcing of uniformity on diverse peoples and cultures, and continued Ottoman rule was imagined either as allowing for this oppressive German approach or as playing different races off against one another, Turks, Arabs and Jews, in order to maintain control.[215]

The British Empire, however, was exceptional in that it fostered an appreciation of human diversity and support of individual national development, at least according to the arguments presented by those associated with the BPC. Quoting the South African statesman Jan Smuts, the committee's publication *Palestine* related how the empire and commonwealth did not stand for standardization or even assimilation but, rather, encouraged "a fuller, a richer and more various life among the nations which compose it.'" Because of this approach to imperial rule, multiple cultures, religions and languages coexisted safely and securely under the British flag.[216] Unique in world history, only the English understood how to draw from the most noble imperial ideals of the ancients, the Greek understanding of a colony or daughter state and the Roman concept of *imperium cum libertate*, and apply them to contemporary concerns.[217] Because His Majesty's government understood the importance of striking this delicate balance between maintaining control and allowing for a certain degree of freedom, only it could facilitate the evolution of a "specifically Jewish civilization" in Palestine, a civilization that eventually would become the "heart of the Jewish state."[218]

If Jews in Palestine looked to England as a model, it was not because they hoped to Anglicize, but rather because its people provided a good example of how to create a harmonious or complementary relationship between a flourishing national life, on the one hand, and loyalty to a larger imperial state, on the other. As one EZF flyer explained:

> Zionism contemplates for the Jew, as an element in the Empire of which Palestine forms a part, a recognition of distinct nationality which the foremost people – England most prominently – have shown to be not alone consistent with but essential to the highest conceptions of loyalty and allegiance to the state.[219]

This quotation could be understood as implying that "English" and "Jewish" were two separate, even mutually exclusive, nationalities within the empire, a belief expressed by certain Zionists such as Moses Gaster.

However, the EZF, which had focused on winning over the Jews of England ever since its inception in 1899, took care to address that audience in ways that recognized their unique position and connection to the country. In 1920 the EZF published a "manifesto" or a "call to Anglo-Jewry" in which it explained how the latter had a "double privilege and a double obligation" to support the Zionist cause so that they might "serve the land of our Fathers and the land of our adoption, in one."[220] In that same year a *Zionist Review* article described the move of WZO headquarters from Germany to London, next door to the EZF offices, or the new "nerve-centre of the Zionist world,"[221] in terms that conflated a sense of shared ancestral history with that modern development in England:

> expanding house on Great Russell Street is regarded as the modern heritor of the legendary home of the Patriarch Abraham, which stood at the intersection of cross-roads with ever open doors facing the four points of the compass, or its equivalency of those ancient days, so that all might enter.[222]

As other Zionist materials circulated at that time explained, the whole of the British Empire was a "successful essay" in the concept of "double allegiance," or simultaneous loyalty to both a distinct nation and the imperial state to which it belonged, and just as being a good Australian, Canadian or South African made an individual a better subject of the king, the Jewish nation turned to the British Empire because they understood that "the better Jews they are the better British subjects they will be."[223] Those and other White settler colonies could serve as a model for achieving Zionist goals, particularly with regard to the path towards self-governance. One report from the BPC likened the Jewish settlers in the Middle East to the early colonists of Canada and Australia, explaining that the former, like the latter, could progress through several stages of development under British "tutelage and protection" before gaining autonomy. It imagined the role of His Majesty's government in Palestine as analogous to that of a parent, or perhaps more accurately a midwife, assisting in the birth of a healthy, independent nation. The report went on to describe that government as the only one capable of reconciling the unity of the empire as a whole with the "freedom of its constituent units" and thus the "fullest realization of their nationalist aspirations," which for the Zionists meant the eventual creation of a Jewish state.[224] As Robert Cecil told a crowd at a demonstration at the London Opera House in favour of the Balfour Declaration, while Americans and others might speak of "national self-determination" as a new concept, the British Empire was, in fact, the first organization to teach that principle to the world.[225]

These types of statements would have been appreciated by supporters of British imperialism who sought to counter demands for independence, made by nationalists from South Asia to Africa and the Middle East, with the argument that those in Westminster were far better qualified than local leaders to determine precisely how and when, as well as if, home rule should be granted. Zionists praised the British Empire and presented their movement as an exceptional nationalism which would strengthen that body, as opposed to contributing to its dissolution. In addition, it would harness Jewish "intellectual power" to combat nationalists in Egypt and India and expose anti-English feeling in those countries as a "mere fairy tale."[226] In 1918, the same year that Egyptian nationalists hoped to send a *wafd* or delegation to the Paris Peace Conference in an effort to gain recognition as a sovereign state, the EZF distributed a booklet relating the "indescribable enthusiasm" and "deepest gratitude" for His Majesty's government expressed by a crowd of eight thousand in Alexandria gathered to listen to a reading of the Balfour Declaration.[227]

In addition to its ability to counter nationalist movements that threatened the integrity of the empire, Zionism was presented as a noble cause consistent with British liberal ideals. According to this line of reasoning, Jewish emancipation was defined in collective rather than individual terms. In other words, while Lucien Wolf and the CFC argued for the equal treatment of all religions and races under the law, whether in England or in a British-controlled Palestine, the Zionists maintained that individual liberty, however desirable it might be, was a fundamentally inadequate solution to the "Jewish problem," which required "national liberty."[228] Only the creation of a Jewish Palestine under a British administration which then would develop into an independent state ensured the emancipation of the Jewish people. Siding with small nations struggling in the face of tyranny, they explained, was consistent with British traditions, from the support of Greek independence in the early nineteenth century to the defence of Belgian neutrality in the early twentieth.[229] By coming to the aid of the Jewish people and thus righting one of the great wrongs of humanity, British expansion in the Middle East would appear to the rest of the world not as a vulgar pursuit of wealth but, rather, as animated by a "spiritual force."[230] Securing the moral high ground, then, would carry considerable weight during peace negotiations, as "moral strategy" was as important in the later stages of war as military strategy was during the earlier ones.[231]

The Zionist call for the creation of a Jewish Palestine in order to liberate an oppressed people raises the question as to what would happen to the overwhelming majority of those who already lived there and were not Jewish but Arab and either Muslim or Christian. This concern was raised repeatedly by opponents of the WZO programme, from Wolf and the CFC, to statesmen such as Lord Curzon, to Palestinians themselves.[232] The response given by the BPC, EZF and other Zionist leaders in England at the time tended to be based on the reimagining of that country and of the Middle East more generally. According to their vision, a temporary British administration would oversee the implementation of extensive demographic and economic changes in the region so as to allow for the simultaneous and harmonious development of two distinct and separate nation-states, one Arab and the other Jewish.[233]

The most important demographic shift would be the influx of the hundreds of thousands of people, primarily from Eastern Europe and Russia, necessary to turn Palestine into a Jewish country. As long as the new settlers followed an English model, or at least adopted policies consistent with those of the English regarding toleration of minorities and economic development, the existing non-Jewish Arab population need not experience displacement or other hardship as a result. As Weizmann stated at the Paris peace conference, "Palestine should become as Jewish as England is English." After all, Jews in England knew from their own experience that being a member of minority in that country did not prevent them from thriving and occupying positions of influence.[234] Similarly, even the highest echelons of public office were open to non-English people, with the most obvious examples in this context being that of the prominent statesmen David Lloyd George and Arthur Balfour, who by nationality were Welsh and Scottish, respectively.[235] In addition, once the new Jewish settlers had transformed the wastelands of the country into centres of productivity and showed their Arab neighbours by example how an "Oriental" people could embrace Western technologies and methods without sacrificing their own traditions and ideals, Palestine, like England, would have the economic base necessary to support a large population relative to its size.[236]

Large-scale immigration remained an essential element of the Zionist response to the argument, presented by Wolf and the CFC, that the creation of a Jewish Palestine necessarily would require the imposition of legal disabilities on the existing non-Jewish inhabitants. For as soon as Jews became the new majority in the country it would be possible to have a polity that was at once a Jewish state and a fully functioning democracy, with its Muslim and Christian citizens enjoying equality under the law.[237] This position, however, depended upon strict discriminatory policies at the point of embarkation, with charter companies ensuring that only Jews travelled to Palestine for the purpose of relocation. In fact, when the Colonial Office proposed encouraging Maltese immigration in order to alleviate the unemployment problem on the island, the BPC not only objected but regarded the suggestion as evidence that the Colonial Office was unfit to make decisions that would have an impact on the future of Palestine.[238]

Learning from the Jewish settlers and a suddenly flourishing Palestine, as well as freed from the Ottoman yoke and benefiting from British tutelage, the "new Arabia" or soon-to-be-created Arab state would experience transformational prosperity also.[239] As Mark Sykes told an audience gathered in celebration of the Balfour Declaration at the Hippodrome in Manchester in December 1917, the Mesopotamian canal system would be reconstructed; Syria would become the granary of Europe; and Baghdad, Damascus and Aleppo all would grow to be as large as Manchester.[240] While Zionist leaders remained unsure as to what city would become the capital of a new Arab state or exactly how its boundaries would be drawn after the war, they were, nevertheless, confident that because the Arabs of the Middle East already had a number of "national centres" in the region, in Egypt, Syria, on the Arabian peninsula and in Mesopotamia, they would have "no claims and no ambitions" in Palestine.[241] Implied, although not stated outright, was the assumption that as these cultural and economic hubs began to thrive, they naturally would attract Arabs from Palestine, who then would leave the country of their birth voluntarily. One article imagined the position of the Arab who decided to remain in Jerusalem as similar to that of the Jew who chose to reside in Baghdad: both would be a member of a minority in the city and state in which they lived and have a national home elsewhere, yet both would also be free from discrimination and have equal rights with their fellow citizens.[242] Sykes's description of the goodwill and cooperation between Jews and Arabs that would accompany a revival of Arab civilization in the Middle East was met with cheering and a standing ovation.[243]

It is important to emphasize that, as inspiring as these types of discourses may have been for Zionists in England, Jewish and non-Jewish alike, their vision for a post-war Middle East involved a considerable degree of imaginative and even fantastic thinking. Mark Sykes, in fact, had a history of relying upon "fanciful notions" which had no connection to reality regarding that part of the world.[244] Not only did Palestine and its surrounding areas lack the industrial base and infrastructure of England at that time, but also its people were reeling from the impact of war, the spread of disease and the devastation of famine. The dream of the future Middle East described in the previous paragraphs would take generations to achieve even if the people of the region accepted and supported it, and the vast majority did not. Yet the BPC encouraged British statesmen and others not to become side-tracked by immediate practical issues but, rather, to tap into their "creative imagination," which was essential to true statecraft, and even "grasp the romance" of what it would mean to establish a Jewish Palestine in the course of human history.[245] Consistent with the Orientalist tradition of distracting from concerns of the present by evoking images of the past, the BPC's publication *Palestine* explained that the Semitic empires of the ancient world would come to life again and find a modern counterpart, and that the political splendour of the "Arab genius" would flourish as it had under the great Caliphates of the Middle Ages.[246]

These visions of the future Middle East characterized by peace, prosperity and a harmonious coexistence between Jews and their Arab neighbours belie the far more ethically fraught JNF practice of buying land in Palestine for settlement by Russians and Eastern Europeans, resulting in the displacement of the people who already lived and worked on it. In 1914, when the JNF representative Dr Bodenheimer travelled from Cologne to visit England, he explained how at that time 12,000 Arabs resided in the Jewish colonies of Palestine, but that if the EZF could improve its fundraising efforts, all could soon be replaced by Jewish immigrants.[247] One Zionist pamphlet published in 1918 acknowledged that in the previous ten years there had been an "increasing tendency to replace systematically and sometimes at considerable economic disadvantage Arab labour by Jewish labour." However, rather than propose an alternative course of action, it simply goes on to say that Zionists are not motivated by malice or ill will, it is just that "we want the colonies to be Jewish and to be worked by Jews." In other words, these policies were formulated not because they were "against" the Arabs but, rather, out of a desire to "make the country Jewish."[248] With this goal in mind, the EZF and JNFCE, like their parent bodies the WZO and JNF, avoided including images of Arab workers in its representations of Palestine.[249]

Zionist leaders, however, did not consider JNF policies regarding land and labour as in any way precluding a sense of kinship between Jews and the Muslim and Christian Arabs of the Middle East. For example, when addressing the king of the Hejaz, Nahum Sokolow spoke of "Semitic solidarity" and described the Zionists as "old friends and admirers of Arab civilization."[250] Similar sentiments regarding the importance of Arab and Jewish Semitic cooperation were expressed in a popular EZF pamphlet just pages after that same publication maintained the need to replace Arab workers with Jewish ones.[251] Demonstrating this affinity visually, Chaim Weizmann wore a *keffiyeh*, or traditional Arab head covering, in the widely available photograph of him standing next to Emir Feisal during a visit to the latter's camp near the Gulf of Aqaba. Yet shortly afterwards, Weizmann told T.E. Lawrence that he hoped for a "'a completely Jewish Palestine in fifty years.'"[252] As contradictory as these words and actions may seem, they are, in fact, very much a part of the Zionist colonization process, and not unusual, at least with regard to British imperialism in the Middle East. Just as British officials could identify with the Egyptian man while at the same time working to undermine the existing social and political structure of the country and see no contradiction, so too could Zionist leaders identify with

Arabs as brothers and members of the same "Semitic race" while working to create a Jewish Palestine.[253]

Balfour, San Remo and a new feminist dimension to Zionism in England

When Mark Sykes emerged from the all-male War Cabinet meeting to tell Chaim Weizmann that the Balfour Declaration had been approved, he used the phrase "it's a boy!"[254] to communicate success as well as the idea that a new nation was being born. That same document publicly expressing a British sympathy with Zionist goals inspired Vera Weizmann and two other women, Rebecca Sieff and Romana Goodman, to create a new female organization dedicated to advancing the position of Jewish women and girls at home and abroad based upon their role as mothers of that new nation, both literally and metaphorically.[255] While the three had been active members of the EZF, they felt that their contributions did nothing to foster the belief that the Jewish woman had a distinct and important role to play in the development of a Jewish national home in Palestine.[256] In 1918 they founded the Federation of Women Zionists (FWZ), explaining that "the position which a Jewish Palestine is going to occupy within the British sphere of influence places a special responsibility on Jewish women in this country both in regard to their British citizenship and their Jewish solidarity."[257] Echoing this sentiment, one FWZ conference attendee explained, "I am here as a lover of my people and as an Englishwoman."[258]

One Zionist woman from Manchester, Bertha Claff, expressed her support for the British state visually, as shown in the photograph of her "in fancy dress" for a ball held in Bournemouth (Figure 3.2). Hers is no ordinary ball gown. The bodice is covered with a pattern of Union Jack flags, and the hat depicts that same flag on the front. Written on the skirt, in letters larger than her hands, are the words "Buy British Empire Goods." The word "British" appears on the top of her hat as well. She looks more like a human billboard or walking advertisement than someone ready to enjoy the evening.[259]

Such a display goes well above and beyond the expectations of the loyal Briton, and it should be understood as a kind of theatre in which, as a well-known Zionist, Claff draws attention to the new alliance between the British Empire and that nationalist cause. It is also a particularly feminine form of political activism, for while Claff may not have been able to take part in the War Cabinet negotiations that led to the Balfour Declaration, or even have the same power or status as did her husband and the other male members of her family, she did have the ability to express herself creatively through dress. In addition, her call to buy British goods is reminiscent of the female

192   *An empire of many cultures*

Figure 3.2 "Bertha Claff pictured in fancy dress for a ball in Bournemouth."

abolitionists who went door to door urging housewives to boycott sugar grown in the West Indies: in both cases women understood that even if they lacked official positions of authority in society, their household purchases, nevertheless, were tied to the larger economy and, therefore, could be used to exert political influence, whether to combat slavery in the early nineteenth century or to support the imperial state on which the future of Zionism depended in the early twentieth.[260]

The FWZ also found a way to tap into the often unnoticed economic power of housewives, at least those of the middle classes, by asking supporters to donate their jewellery to the cause. While some jewel fund committee reports admonish members for not sacrificing their most precious pieces, one meeting at Vera Weizmann's house produced £1,500 worth of gems, a substantial amount during that period and in comparison to the £450 collected in monetary donations on that same day.[261] In addition to eliciting contributions for the JNF and other Zionist institutions, FWZ leaders assumed the responsibility for coordinating female Zionist organizations throughout the British Isles and sought to promote a sense of "Jewish national consciousness" amongst women and girls there. The organization disseminated EZF and WZO propaganda and promoted Zionist education, including the study of Hebrew as a living language. Although some female societies chose to associate with the EZF directly, by 1919 the FWZ had affiliated groups based in England (Manchester, Liverpool, London, Bradford, Leeds, Newcastle, Grimsby and Bristol); Ireland (Dublin, Cork and Belfast); Scotland (Glasgow); and Wales (Cardiff and Swansea).[262]

The most distinguishing feature of this new organization, however, was its commitment to the economic and social well-being of Jewish women and children in Palestine.[263] In 1918, when Chaim Weizmann and Israel Sieff served on the Zionist Commission to that country, Vera Weizmann and Rebecca Sieff travelled there as well. While the husbands made contacts with the British military administration, the wives "went deeply into the conditions under which the women and children were living" and "returned [to England] with full and most moving reports of the needs as they saw them."[264] After the war's end, Romana Goodman renewed her relationship with the Jewish Women's League for Cultural Work in Palestine (Verband jüdischer Frauen für Kulturarbeit in Palästina), a Berlin-based organization associated with WZO that helped to provide vocational training and therefore economic independence for women in that country. The Kulturverband, as it also was known, organized lace-making workshops in Jerusalem, Safed and Jaffa and served as the primary supporter of a training farm in Kinneret, near the Sea of Galilee.[265]

The members of the FWZ continued to work in harmony with the EZF, for the leaders of the Manchester Zionist community were a closely knit group, often related by blood, marriage, business association or all three. They celebrated holidays together, and when the FWZ sent a representative to the EZF every few weeks, it was not unusual for her to see her husband at the opposite end of the council table.[266] Certainly the official public or government roles available to the men helped the women to become involved in the cause. However, the influence and connections of the wives were important to their husbands and the movement as well. It was Vera who dissuaded Chaim from leaving England for a position in Berlin and introduced him to C.P. Scott, editor of the *Manchester Guardian*, who put him in touch with the formulators of foreign policy in the British government.[267] In addition, Vera had been involved in social work as a physician, a professional role which provided contacts for Zionist endeavours in England while at the same time making her particularly attuned to the health and welfare needs of Jews in Palestine.[268]

One of the goals of Vera Weizmann and the other leaders of the FWZ was to create a second female Zionist organization, which also would strive to safeguard the interests of Jewish women and children in Palestine, but would do so on an international level. Just as the Balfour Declaration had been a catalyst for the formation of the FWZ, the Supreme Allied Council in San Remo, Italy – during which international recognition of that commitment and of the British Mandate for Palestine were confirmed – helped to inspire the creation of the Women's International Zionist Organization (WIZO) in 1920. San Remo made an "indelible impression" on Rebecca Sieff, who attended meetings there. Afterwards she often referred to that experience and how it helped to bring her to the realization that it was her "bounden although joyful duty, to assume the leadership of the world movement of Zionist women."[269] The previously mentioned link, through Romana Goodman, between the FWZ and the Jewish Women's League for Cultural Work in Palestine, or the Kulturverband, provided the founders of WIZO with the necessary initial contacts and networks to begin to build a new international organization, for in addition to England and Germany the Cultural League also had branches in the Netherlands, Poland, Russia and Palestine.[270] As Michael Berkowitz has explained, the germinal female Zionist activities which had been "fired in a Central European social welfare crucible" and grafted onto the Yishuv in Palestine were subsumed by the Anglocentric WIZO in 1919.[271]

Through both the FWZ and the WIZO, Jewish Zionist women in England mobilized themselves around the mission to transform girls from Russia and Eastern Europe, especially those used to life in the cities and towns, into *Chaluzoth* or female pioneers equipped to settle rural Palestine. In 1921, at the first WIZO conference, that organization resolved to create a girls' school for domestic sciences, and in the following year the FWZ decided to buy land and a hostel for training in the requirements of a "girl pioneer's life."[272] There students learned skills such as cooking, cleaning, vegetable gardening and poultry raising. At the fourth annual FWZ conference, Edith Eder presented a report on work in Palestine and, after expressing gratitude for the British Mandate, explained how the new state must be built upon "fine, well-grown, self-dependent, economically satisfied men and women." She showed several pictures, including one of two *Chaluzoth* cooking; both had been trained at a WIZO-run kitchen in Jaffa and afterwards moved to a "lonely settlement far out in the country." Establishing a female agricultural college was necessary as well, if the new immigrants were going to survive and eventually thrive in the more remote areas where inexpensive land still remained available for purchase.[273]

According to Eder, not only would the Jewish female settlers contribute to making the country productive, but also they would help to civilize it through their attention to cleanliness and hygiene. She showed the audience a picture of "white-veiled, suitably clad" *Chaluzoth* preparing food for Jewish immigrants who had arrived recently in Tel Aviv, explaining that despite having to work in "primitive tents" those female pioneers provided excellent meals "spotlessly served." In addition, through training in "housewifery" they learned how to clean and do laundry, with the latter being especially important in "an undeveloped country" like Palestine where "water is very scarce and appliances primitive in the extreme."[274] Based upon familiar Orientalist and imperialist assumptions, these discourses complemented and added an important dimension to contemporary representations made by the BPC; for while the BPC repeatedly juxtaposed clean and modern Jewish neighbourhoods and other places of settlement with their supposedly dirty and unhygienic surroundings, the FWZ echoed this contrast and attributed it to female labour, thus foregrounding the essential role of Jewish women in the Zionist civilizing mission.

In addition to maintaining a high standard of cleanliness and good order, the *Chaluzoth* were expected to bear children, and in that regard the FWZ and the WIZO provided assistance as well. As Eder explained, "it is our primal duty as women to use our utmost endeavours to see first that healthy babies are born." She then made reference to immigration restrictions to Palestine, implying that population growth, and therefore the eventual realization of the Zionist dream, depended upon the ability of Jewish women already living there to give birth and raise future generations. Leaders in both organizations discussed the need to establish maternity and infant welfare centres in order to reduce infant mortality among settlers. One already-existing institution in Nevé Zedek, a Jewish suburb of Jaffa, served as a successful model for offering pre- and post-natal care.[275]

As practical as FWZ/WIZO projects were, they tended to be conceptualized in lofty, abstract, even spiritual terms and with the understanding of the maternal, the feminine, the family and the nation as all deeply imbricated. Organizers spoke of creating "sacred spaces" and inventing "beautiful" new traditions for "our pioneering womanhood."[276] One FWZ conference speaker was applauded for her statement that "as women" they had an obligation to see that "private family life" formed the foundation for a national home in Palestine.[277] In addition, as mothers maintained Jewish traditions while at the same time implanting a love of national ideals in their children, the standing of Zionism would improve in the eyes of the world.[278] Even Jewish women who did not have children of their own would find their maternal instincts "awakened and fostered" once they began to assume their full responsibilities in the Zionist movement.[279]

The idea that Jewish women had a role to play in that nationalist cause was not an unfamiliar concept and had been a part of the male-dominated culture of political Zionism for years. For example, in Herzl's utopian novel *Altneuland*, published in 1902, both sexes had political equality in a flourishing Zionist society set in future Palestine. Also, Nahum Sokolow sought to appeal to women by explaining that only they could strengthen the people by making the Jewish home a temple and family life like "a dear, antique embroidery ... folksy, pure." Still, these positive discourses that included women in the Zionist vision encouraged them to focus on private, domestic concerns at the expense of involvement in the public sphere. Sokolow's pamphlet ends with "will you come back to your house, O Jewish woman," while the female characters in Herzl's novel choose domestic over civic life.[280] Even feminist members of the WZO, who contributed modern views about the need for female independence, nevertheless worked within the largely patriarchal structure established by the congresses.[281]

Only by creating their own female Zionist groups and networks on the national and international levels, FWZ/WIZO leaders reasoned, could they begin to channel their beliefs about the value of the feminine into the public political arena of nation building in such a way so as to initiate a re-evaluation of Jewish gender roles on a grand scale, thus elevating the position of women and girls in their various home communities as well

Figure 3.3 Seated left to right: Vera and Chaim Weizmann with Arthur Balfour and Nahum Sokolow, Palestine, 1925. Other Zionist leaders standing in the back row.

as in Palestine. As Rebecca Sieff, who was both a feminist and suffragist as well as Zionist, explained, one of the goals of the FWZ was to educate Jewish people, male and female, so that both might realize the "value of women's work" and then the two sexes would be able to labour on an "equal basis."[282] Along the same lines, a contemporary WIZO memorandum stated, "It is especially difficult for Jewish women to overcome their innate sense of inferiority vis-à-vis their men-kind; only in organizations and societies of their own can they display their real capacity, initiative and power of organization."[283] As the British–Zionist alliance solidified, first with Balfour and then with San Remo, the FWZ/WIZO founders came to the realization that the struggle to achieve the Zionist dream provided an opportunity like no other for Jewish women to mobilize and demonstrate their different but equally important role in the nation and larger society, both to themselves and to their male counterparts.

It is hardly surprising, then, that they helped to create a female version of the "new Jewish man." Through the regular WZO congresses emerged a concept of masculinity based upon the idea that, once freed from the confines of the ghettos and crowded urban spaces of Europe and allowed to build a life for himself in his homeland, the Jewish man would transform into a rugged and robust pioneer farmer, purified through his connection to manual labour and the soil. In images produced by the WZO and circulated by the EZF, the Jewish settler and worker is depicted almost always as male; only occasionally does a woman appear in these representations, and when she does it is as his wife, standing "quietly" beside him.[284] FWZ/WIZO leaders, however, contributed a new ideal of Jewish femininity: that of the *Chaluzoth*, carefully selected, "strongly built and vigorous" girls who, through education and training, would become the "future Palestinian peasantry."[285] Like their male counterparts, they too would be revitalized by embracing the spirit of national life and working on the land. They too would have the skills and the strength to "settle" the country and thus become true equals and partners to "the new Jewish man."

The women's training farm at Kinneret, so central to the development of the Jewish female pioneer farmer, both as an ideal and in terms of lived reality, was founded in 1911 by Labour Zionist Hannah Meisel. Meisel had had strong ties with the WZO and continued to be a leader in female agricultural education after the First World War. Her answer to contemporary Zionist discourses about the need to create new masculine "muscle Jews" was not to accept the submissive female as his natural counterpart but, rather, to advance the ideal of the "muscle Jewess." For Meisel, even the celebration of the manly man became an avenue for gender equality. Yet, despite working together on numerous occasions and holding certain similar beliefs about the need for strong and robust *Chaluzoth*, Meisel often felt herself at odds and even in conflict with WIZO leaders whose urban, bourgeois sensibilities and commitment to domesticity kept them from appreciating what she considered to be the true value of agricultural labour, creating independent and self-sufficient female farmers.[286] Worthy of note, although not necessarily surprising, women's involvement in agriculture and land settlement in Palestine and the ways in which those activities might contribute to a refashioning of their roles in the new society and state were ignored, for the most part, by male Zionist leaders, and even when praising the Kinneret school Tolkowsky describes it as a place where "Jewish girls are taught to become good farmers' wives."[287]

One interesting source that sheds light on how WIZO and FWZ members imagined rural Palestine is a collection of wooden books with pictures of the "the holy land." In between the images are pressed flowers indigenous to the different scenes depicted. The physical presence of the dried flowers was meant to create a connection, both tangible and aesthetic, between the viewer and regions in that country that most would never visit. The flora of Palestine differed from that of northern Europe, but through a medium that had been a popular pastime since the Victorian era, especially for middle- and upper-middle-class women, the foreign became familiar. In addition, because flowers had certain feminine and "ladylike" connotations in early twentieth-century English society, these books embodied a link with a distant land understood as both natural and feminine.[288]

The Zionist women who looked through these books may even have imagined the female settlers in Palestine and their children, on whose behalf they worked, to be like the flowers themselves, for the need to provide facilities to ensure the birth of healthy offspring to populate the country was understood by FWZ and WIZO organizers as critical for the "flourishing" or "flowering" of a Jewish Palestine. In fact, while the reader is told that the dried flowers grow wild in the regions depicted on the images, none actually appears in these scenes. It is as though the flowers that are natural and indigenous to the region have disappeared. They, like the Jewish people, at least according to Zionist ideology, had been uprooted but, once returned to their native land, would thrive.

Most of the scenes depict the land as devoid of people and signs of human activity as they are of flowers. When buildings do appear, often they blend seamlessly into the landscape, sometimes with crumbling rocks in the foreground suggesting that even if they are not ancient ruins, they are nevertheless part of an undeveloped, antiquated Palestine. One picture with Mount Hermon in the distance presents a particularly inviting scene to anyone wondering what it might be like to settle in the "empty" lands so often mentioned in Zionist discourses. Here the viewer looks over an expansive valley from the top of another peak. Healthy, lush trees growing naturally show land that is fertile but, with the possible exception of a few rectangular patterns, uncultivated. The countryside is open and welcoming, almost as if it is being discovered by the viewer, a perspective reminiscent of the "monarch-of-all-I-survey" scenes so common in British imperial literary and visual culture.[289] Tellingly, the place names on the images are written in English, Hebrew and Russian, but not Arabic, despite the fact that most of the people who lived in Palestine at the time would have known these regions by their Arabic names.

Conclusion

Anglo-Jewish leaders who rejected political Zionism when it first appeared in London in the late nineteenth century did so, to a great extent, because they valued certain liberal traditions and beliefs and understood them as providing the means for Jewish emancipation both at home and abroad. After the outbreak of the First World War, Lucien Wolf and the CFC began to present arguments based upon those familiar assumptions but reformulated so as to apply specifically to Palestine in the event of that country falling under British control; in other words, the anti-Zionist side of the debate amongst Jews in England took a new imperial turn. This turn was predicated upon the idea that, just as different nations, cultures, ethnicities and religions could coexist harmoniously and on the basis of political equality in England and the British Isles, so too could Jews and their non-Jewish neighbours live together in Palestine, should the imperial reach of His Majesty's government extend into that region. Jews would not need special protection or even to become the majority in that country. Rather, like the "self-made man," celebrated by the English middle class, they could rise through their own efforts and achieve an ascendancy all the more solid and stable for having been earned. This alternative to political Zionism would allow Palestine to become a world centre for Jewish culture without compromising the liberal principles so important to the status of Jews elsewhere, especially in Eastern Europe and Russia, where Wolf hoped that British influence could be used to secure their legal emancipation after the war.

The Zionist side of the debates amongst Jews in England also took a new imperial turn during the First World War as it became increasingly likely that Palestine would be ruled by the British. This turn, initiated in 1917 by a group of Manchester-based, Jewish, Zionist leaders calling themselves the British Palestine Committee, presented that nationalist movement and the British Empire as in need of each other, with the latter as comprised of diverse peoples, nations, cultures and religions and therefore particularly qualified to oversee the political development and harmonious coexistence of Jewish and non-Jewish peoples in the post-war Middle East. According to the new Zionist vision in England at the time, the British government was capable of fostering the simultaneous development of a Jewish civilization in Palestine, to become the foundation of an independent Jewish state, and an Arab civilization based elsewhere in the Middle East, possibly around Damascus or Baghdad, to become the foundation of an independent Arab state. Just as the Welsh, Scottish or Jewish person could live and prosper in England, despite being in the minority and belonging to a nation outside of that country, so too, the Zionists reasoned, could the Arab in a "Jewish Palestine" and the Jew in a "new Arabia" both expect to live free from discrimination or legal disability. In addition, as a Semitic people with ties to the East, European Jews who settled in Palestine would help to bring Western methods, technologies and prosperity to the Arab world, while at the same time strengthening British imperial connections to India and even China. As inspiring as discourses celebrating "Semitic solidarity" and even a future "renaissance of Semitic civilization" under the auspices of the British Empire may have been amongst Zionist Jews in England during the First World War period, it is important to acknowledge that the enormous political, demographic and economic changes necessary to turn Palestine into a country with a Jewish majority never were pursued by the British government, despite the Balfour Declaration, nor did such changes have the support of the people in the region.

Still, it would be difficult to overstate the importance of the Balfour Declaration for Zionist Jews in England. Not only had the EZF been a relatively weak and ineffectual body within the world Zionist movement since its inception in 1899, but even as late as 1916 Chaim Weizmann expressed his frustration with a negotiation process that seemed to be accomplishing nothing, explaining that he was "sometimes driven to despair" as his efforts appeared "almost like an irony, like the attempt of the fool who tried to empty the sea with a bucket."[290] Yet, after the issue of the Balfour Declaration, or the moment in 1917 when Jewish world history and Anglo-Jewish history intersected,[291] Weizmann emerged as a leader of world Zionism, a living symbol of the movement for a generation, and both he and Balfour were added to the pantheon of world Zionist heroes.[292] During that time, from roughly 1917 until 1937, a certain segment within Anglo-Jewry was able to play a pivotal role in WZO politics, and British Jews continued to have influence both in that organization and in Palestine throughout the Mandate period.[293]

The Zionist movement experienced a spike in support in England during the years immediately following the Balfour Declaration. Donations increased exponentially, and when asked to contribute £40,000 in order to send a commission to Palestine, English Jews "rose to the occasion," exceeding that amount and prompting one Zionist leader to proclaim that "no fund launched for Jewish purposes in this country ever met with more instantaneous success."[294] Between Balfour and San Remo, membership in the EZF grew dramatically as well.[295] This new interest, combined with British commitments and international recognition, helped to generate a sense of optimism amongst Zionist Jews in England. As one contemporary report expressed, "The land is even now practically ours … The land is ours if we have the will and energy to make it ours."[296]

Zionist efforts in Palestine very likely would have "died in the cradle" if not for British occupation of the region during the First World War. When Allenby entered Jerusalem in 1917, the Jewish population in the country had already fallen from 85,000 in 1914 to 55,000.[297] In addition, the Ottoman stateman, military commander and governor-general of Greater Syria at the time, Cemal Pasha, had already made plans to eradicate the Zionist movement, as he considered it to be a form of treason.[298] While British policies during the interwar period were not always aligned with or unilaterally supportive of Zionist goals, leading one modern scholar to describe Britain as more like a step-parent than a parent, the mandatory regime nevertheless sanctioned Jewish mass immigration and encouraged the development of autonomous Jewish political and even military institutions,[299] all of which would prove vital to the creation of the State of Israel. On the day that the British Mandate ended, May 14, 1948, a "National Council, representing the Jewish people in Palestine and the Zionist movement of the world" met to declare the independent State of Israel in Tel Aviv, that coastal metropolis which had been imagined as both an outpost of the British Empire as well as the first true Zionist city.[300]

Yet, despite the developments beginning in 1917 in England and Palestine that would forever link the history of the British Empire with that of the world Zionist movement, the majority of English Jews remained either opposed or indifferent to the idea of a Jewish state until the mid-twentieth century. After the initial euphoria during the 1917–21 period, interest began to wane. Some former EZF contributors gravitated towards other causes, such as the trade unions or communism, while others decided that the battle had already been won.[301] Only by the early 1950s did both the majority of English Jews and the institutions representing them ally with Zionism, which by that time meant support of the State of Israel.[302]

This development resulted from a combination of factors, social, demographic and political. As British society became more democratic generally, upwardly mobile middle-class Jews found in Zionism a vehicle through which to challenge the elite power structures that had dominated Anglo-Jewry since the nineteenth century. As the modern scholar David Cesarani has explained, between the wars, and especially by the 1930s, that nationalist ideology which required the democratization of communal institutions served as a "surrogate and shibboleth" for ethnicity, a political basis for a social movement characterized by a power shift from one section of the Jewish middle class to another, from the *haute bourgeoisie* to the *petit bourgeoisie*.[303] In addition, as those from the latter category increasingly left the immigrant enclaves of the cities for suburban neighbourhoods where pressure to erase cultural difference accompanied social integration, Zionism provided a way to articulate a secular, non-apologetic Jewish identity,[304] while at the same time creating a new avenue for Jewish solidarity and sociability.[305] Finally, as the horrors of the Holocaust were exposed after the Second World War, the argument that only a Jewish state could prevent history from repeating itself had powerful emotional appeal.[306]

Given that the people whose words and actions are examined in this chapter lived through the First World War, a conflict that many believed would put an end to German aggression and even war itself, they hardly could have anticipated the profound political, military and social changes that the twentieth century would bring. Those developments, which included the end of the British Mandate over Palestine and the creation of the independent Jewish State of Israel, proved to be far more influential in convincing Anglo-Jewry to identify with Zionism than did the imperial arguments examined in this chapter. Yet, while the historical circumstances, majority opinion and even the specific terms of the debates may have changed, the debates themselves remained a constant. Given the various ways in which the topics of nation, ethnicity, culture, liberalism and imperialism continue to emerge in discussions surrounding Zionism and the State of Israel amongst Jews, not only in England but also in a number of modern, democratic societies, it is worthwhile to consider how these salient issues were represented, understood and made meaningful during the pivotal years when the Zionist movement first intersected with an expanding British imperial state.

Notes

1 For example, see Durba Ghosh, "Another Set of Imperial Turns?" *The American Historical Review*, Vol. 117, No. 3 (June 2012), 772–93.
2 The term "Anglo-Jewry" is used refer to English Jews, but also includes those in the British Isles more generally as is conventional in the field of British Jewish studies. As Todd Endelman explains, the term is "too well established to be dropped" and does not distort the historical reality given that the overwhelming majority of Jewish Britons lived in England during that time." Endelman,

The Jews of Britain, 1656 to 2000 (Berkeley: University of California Press, 2002), 12.

3 David Feldman, *Englishmen and Jews: Social Relations and Political Culture, 1840–1914* (New Haven, CT: Yale University Press, 1994), 2, 23, 46; Michael Clark, *Albion and Jerusalem: The Anglo-Jewish Community in the Post Emancipation Era, 1858–1887* (Oxford: Oxford University Press, 2009), 9, 26–8 and 50; and Geoffrey Alderman, "English Jews or Jews of the English Persuasion? Reflections on the Emancipation of Anglo-Jewry," in *Paths of Emancipation: Jews, States and Citizenship*, edited by Pierre Birnbaum and Ira Katznelson (Princeton: Princeton University Press, 1995), 129–30.

4 These debates are discussed in Feldman's *Englishmen and Jews*, especially in chapter 1, "Jewish Emancipation and Political Argument in Early Victorian England," 28–47.

5 While the BDBJ traces its history to a resolution presented to George III in 1760, that body operated sporadically and on a small scale prior to 1835–36, when it was placed on "permanent footing." Clark, *Albion and Jerusalem*, 109–10, and see pp. 26–49 and 109–69 for further discussion of the BDBJ, emancipation and communal politics.

6 Clark, *Albion and Jerusalem*, quotation at p. 109 and pressure group at p. 123; and Acc/3121/A/010, MBBD, 1864–71, x 250, BDBJ, LMA.

7 William Rubinstein, *A History of the Jews in the English-speaking World: Great Britain* (London: Palgrave Macmillan, 1996), 71, cited in Clark, *Albion and Jerusalem*, 110.

8 Clark, *Albion and Jerusalem*, 113–15. While Chaim Bermant dubbed this group the "cousinhood" because of the ways in which their familial and financial relationships intertwined and likened them to the English gentry, they were not aristocrats. Therefore, David Cesarani's term *haute bourgeoisie* is more accurate. Chaim Bermant, *The Cousinhood: The Anglo-Jewish Gentry* (New York: Macmillan, 1971) and David Cesarani, "The Transformation of Communal Authority in Anglo-Jewry, 1914–1940," in *The Making of Modern Anglo-Jewry*, edited by David Cesarani (Oxford: Basil Blackwell, 1990), 139, fn. 104. Provincial congregations were marginalized, if represented at all, Reform Jews were excluded and dissent was not tolerated. Clark, *Albion and Jerusalem*, 39–43 and Aubrey Newman *The Board of Deputies of British Jews 1760–1985 A Brief Survey* (London: Vallentine Mitchell, 1988), 16.

9 Clark, *Albion and Jerusalem*, 33, 39–40, quotation at p. 39. Feldman, *Englishmen and Jews*, 24, also notes the alliance between the BDBJ and the Chief Rabbi, whose ecclesiastical authority acted as the counterpart to the Board's secular supremacy.

10 Newman, *Board of Deputies*, 9, makes reference to those who questioned the representative nature of the Board even when it was first established.

11 Quotation from Bermant, *The Cousinhood*, 60.

12 Quotation from Clark, *Albion and Jerusalem*, 32. Alderman notes that Jews in the 1850s declared themselves to be "merely a section of nonconformist society" like the Unitarians and Quakers. Alderman, "Reflections on the

Emancipation," 129. Protestant dissenters and Catholics were no longer subject to legal disabilities after 1829.

13 Unlike the political Zionists, whose programme would dominate the debates of the early twentieth century, those Victorians did not regard emancipation as a failure, nor the creation of a sovereign Jewish state as the solution. Endelman, *Jews of Britain*, 186–7.

14 Chovevei (also spelt Hovevei) Zion, or "Lovers of Zion," was founded in Russia in response to the 1881–82 pogroms. With regard to that movement and other religious, spiritual or philanthropic efforts on the part of nineteenth-century English Jews for the benefit of their coreligionists in Palestine, see Stuart Cohen, *English Zionists and British Jews: The Communal Politics of Anglo-Jewry, 1895–1920* (Princeton: Princeton University Press, 1982), 3–21; Feldman, *Englishmen and Jews*, 343–4; Endelman, *Jews of Britain*, 187–8; and Eugene Black, *The Social Politics of Anglo-Jewry, 1880–1920* (Oxford: Basil Blackwell, 1988).

15 Clark, *Albion and Jerusalem*, 226; Endelman, *Jews of Britain*, 79, 164–5; Feldman, *Englishmen and Jews*, 137.

16 Endelman, *Jews of Britain*, 150.

17 Between 1881 and 1914 120,000–150,000 Eastern European Jews settled permanently in Great Britain. Eighty per cent of them lived in London, Manchester and Leeds, with an additional 7 to 8 per cent in Liverpool, Glasgow and Birmingham. Endelman, *Jews of Britain*, 127–9. During that time the Jewish population quintupled. Cohen, *English Zionists*, 18. Clark, *Albion and Jerusalem*, 238, notes the "spectacle of Jewish separatism" as the result of both cultural differences and class disparities between Anglo-Jewry and the new immigrants. On outcast London and degeneration see Endelman, *Jews of Britain*, 156.

18 David Feldman, "Jews and the British Empire c. 1900," *History Workshop Journal*, Vol. 63, No. 1 (Spring 2007), 70–89; Feldman, *Englishmen and Jews*, 127, 310, 329 and 171–4; Clark, *Albion and Jerusalem*, 106–7. A good example from the period is Lucien Wolf's article, "What Is Judaism? A Question of Today," *Fortnightly Review* (Aug. 1884), 239–41.

19 As Endelman, *Jews in Britain*, 158, notes, even the thrift and industry of struggling Jewish immigrants was portrayed as problematic, as those characteristics allowed them to undercut and replace English artisans.

20 Feldman, *Englishmen and Jews*, 78–82, 94–120, 153 and Endelman, *Jews of Britain*, 153–5.

21 Clark, *Albion and Jerusalem*, 147–54, 168, 259. A Foreign Affairs Committee was created by the BDBJ in 1877, and it had a good relationship with the FO, Clark, *Albion and Jerusalem*, 146–7; Feldman, *Englishmen and Jews*, 122–3, quotation at p. 122.

22 Cohen, *English Zionists*, 51; Cesarani, "The Transformation," 115. Also see V.D. Lipman, *A Social History of the Jews in England, 1850–1950* (London, 1954), chapters 3–4; I. Finestein, "The New Community, 1880–1914," in V.D. Lipman, *Three Centuries of Anglo-Jewish History* (London: Heffer, 1961),

107–23; and Black, *Social Politics*, 1–3, 8–70. Bermant *The Cousinhood*, 259–60, notes that the CFC served as an instrument of the cousinhood.
23 Endelman, *Jews of Britain*, 260, explains that Jews did not "fit comfortably" into the categories usually reserved for minorities, and that British officials and others of influence seemed to understand that to be the case and "never demanded that Jews define their group character in formal, abstract terms, explaining how their collective identity intersected with that of the English nation and the British state."
24 For discussion of this perspective, see Clark, *Albion and Jerusalem*, 165, 257–8. At p. 258 he states, "Britain and Anglo-Jewry were symbionts in this sphere, complementary organisms operating in tandem to improve the world."
25 This dynamic relationship between the Jews and the British state, including the contested nation and the ambiguous and unstable nature of emancipation, is an organizing principle and theme of Feldman's *Englishmen and Jews*.
26 *The Complete Diaries of Theodor Herzl*, edited by Raphael Patai (New York: Herzl Press and Thomas Yoseloff, 1960), I, 276–7 and *Speeches, Articles, and Letters of Israel Zangwill*, edited by Maurice Simon (London: Soncino, 1937), 132. Both as cited in Hani Faris, "Israel Zangwill's Challenge to Zionism," *Journal of Palestine Studies*, Vol. 4, No. 3 (1975), 77.
27 In "One Hundred Years of Zionism in England," *European Judaism: A Journal for the New Europe*, Vol. 25, No. 1 (1992), 40–7, David Cesarani explains how Zionism amongst Jews in that country can be understood in terms of four distinct phases. The first is the period of the previously mentioned Chovevei Zion, beginning in the late nineteenth century and lasting up until Herzl's appearance. References at p. 40.
28 Eugene Black relates how Zangwill, "Anglo-Jewry's leading litterateur," helped to open doors for Herzl during his visit in 1895–96. Black, "A Typological Study of English Zionists," *Jewish Social Studies*, Vol. 9, No. 3 (Spring–Summer 2003), 20–55, reference at pp. 24–5.
29 See Michael Stanislawski, *Zionism: A Very Short Introduction* (Oxford: Oxford University Press, 2016), 22–5, quotation at p. 24.
30 Stuart Cohen, "Anglo-Jewry and Zionism: The Initial Confrontation, 1895–1900," *Michael: On the History of the Jews in the Diaspora* (Tel Aviv: Tel Aviv University Press, 1986), 49–74, at p. 50.
31 Bermant uses the word "cool" in *The Cousinhood*, 248; "studied silence" is from Cohen, *English Zionists*, 32. Herzl's efforts to court a European Jewish plutocracy met with a similar response. He received almost no support from wealthy philanthropists, a number of whom regarded his ideas as both impractical and ideologically dangerous. Stanislawski, *Zionism*, 24–5, 28.
32 Claude Montefiore was also a liberal theologian and grandnephew of Sir Moses Montefiore. Cohen, "Anglo-Jewry and Zionism," 71; Paul Goodman, *Zionism in England: English Zionist Federation 1899–1929* (London: English Zionist Federation, 1929), 13. The quotations are from the 1897 meeting and cited in Cohen, *English Zionists*, 47.
33 From the June 1897 issue and quoted in Goodman, *Zionism in England: English Zionist Federation*, 14.

34 Endelman, *Jews of Britain*, 188.
35 Cesarani, "One Hundred Years," 42.
36 See Leon Pinsker's influential *Auto-Emancipation: An Appeal to His People by a Russian Jew*, which appeared in Berlin in 1882, in addition to Herzl's *The Jewish State* published in Vienna in 1896.
37 For analysis of Zionism in the context of late nineteenth- to early twentieth-century emigrant colonization projects see Tara Zahra, "Zionism, Emigration, and East European Colonialism," in *Colonialism and the Jews*, edited by Ethan Katz, Lisa Leff and Maud Mandel (Bloomington: Indiana University Press, 2017), 166–92. As Zahra notes, pp. 168 and 187, Zionism was one of the only of such colonial schemes to "take root" or be realized in practice, even outlasting the states that "incubated" it. Zionism differed from other settler movements, emigrant and otherwise, in that the goal from the very beginning was to create an independent state and it succeeded in doing so. Caroline Elkins and Susan Pederson, *Settler Colonialism in the Twentieth Century* (New York: Routledge, 2005), 2–3. Also see Elizabeth Thompson, "Moving Zionism to Asia: Texts and Tactics of Colonial Settlement 1917–21," in *Colonialism and the Jews*, edited by Ethan Katz, Lisa Leff and Maud Mandel (Bloomington: Indiana University Press, 2017), 320.
38 Cesarani, "One Hundred Years," 40–1.
39 David Cesarani, "The Importance of Being Editor: *The Jewish Chronicle*, 1841–1991," *Jewish Historical Studies*, Vol. 32 (1990–92), 259–78, at p. 265. Zangwill would break from the WZO in 1905 to establish the Jewish Territorial Organization, committed to a Jewish state and land of refuge outside of Palestine. This change would be prompted by a new awareness of the non-Jewish, Arab population in Palestine and their concerns. Faris, "Israel Zangwill's Challenge," 84, 87.
40 Endelman, *Jews of Britain*, 189. The centrality of intercommunal politics and the frustrated aspirations of these early English Zionist leaders is an organizing principle of Cohen's, *English Zionists*.
41 Francis Montefiore was ineffectual, despite his connections. Quotations are from Endelman, *Jews of Britain*, 189.
42 Reproduced in Stanislawski, *Zionism*, 29–30.
43 Feldman, *Englishmen and Jews*, 343–4.
44 These issues are discussed by Stanislawski, who also explains that in addition to the strictly political Zionists, Congress delegates included those who advocated the creation of a secular Hebrew culture for the new state, the religious opponents of that secular approach and, finally, a number of socialist groups and subgroups. Stanislawski, *Zionism*, 30–4.
45 Derek Penslar, "What We Talk about when We Talk about Colonialism: A Response to Joshua Cole and Elizabeth Thompson," in *Colonialism and the Jews*, edited by Ethan Katz, Lisa Leff and Maud Mandel (Bloomington: Indiana University Press, 2017), 327–40, quotation at p. 335.
46 A "Vienna Committee" of WZO had already begun the preliminary work necessary to create the JCT even before establishment of the EZF. Letter from Herzl

to "Mr. Chairman," Vienna, Feb. 28, 1898. Printed in Goodman, *Zionism in England, 1899–1929*, 15. While Herbert Bentwich and other English Zionists had hoped that the JNF administrative headquarters could be in London, along with its registered office, headquarters were located instead in Vienna and then moved to Cologne. "The Jewish National Fund: Its Object" (London, 1908), pamphlet translated from the German and published by the JNF, issued and distributed by the EZF. By 1912, the JCT would have subscribed capital of £260,000, with its Whitechapel Branch holding deposits and current accounts of up to £50,000. 1912, DD1 45151, CZA.

47 Through the JCT individuals could donate to the Palestine Land Development Company, which bought large tracts of land in that country and then parcelled and resold them in order to help "small capitalists" who wanted to live and work on it. New Year's bulletin from the year 5669 (1908–9), "The Palestine Land Development Company," 3–4, A150/16, CZA. The Anglo-Levantine Banking Company would be used by settlers as well, "Zionism," 1912, DD1 45151, CZA.

48 This particular quotation is from a letter from the Jewish National Fund Committee of England, July 21, 1914, KKL1/38, CZA. However, this sentiment and phrase appears in letters, flyers and other EZF and JNF/JNFCE materials in the CZA throughout the early twentieth century.

49 The quotation is reproduced in Barbara Tuchman, *Bible and Sword: England and Palestine from the Bronze Age to Balfour* (New York: Ballantine, 1956), 292. Herzl expressed similar sentiments during a visit to London during the previous year when he commented that, given how the British flag waves over every sea, the Zionist idea, which is essentially "a colonizing plan," should be "easily and quickly grasped in England." Quoted in Eitan Bar-Yosef and Nadia Valman (eds), "Introduction," in *"The Jew" in late Victorian and Edwardian Culture: Between the East End and East Africa* (London: Palgrave Macmillan), 23.

50 Paul Goodman, *Zionism in England, 1899–1849: A Jubilee Record* (London: Zionist Federation, 1949), 2.

51 The emergence of political Zionism in England first caused a split within the Chovevei Zion and then the disbanding of that organization in 1902. While a number of former Chovevei Zion supporters shifted their allegiance to the EZF and the WZO, "no intellectual or functional line can easily be traced from the tame proceedings of the Chovevei Zion Association to the rigorous agitation later promoted by the English Zionist Federation," Cohen, *English Zionists*, 10, 20. Cohen discusses the Chovevei Zion and Jewish Zionist activity during the late nineteenth and early twentieth centuries, making a persuasive argument for the distinctive nature of the EZF. Also see Black, "A Typological Study," 20–55. In addition, EZF supporters regarded Chovevei Zion activities in much the same way as they did other colonization efforts in Palestine, such as those by wealthy Jewish philanthropists like Sir Moses Montefiore, as being "timid" and "romantic" as opposed to practical and political. Goodman, *Zionism, 1899–1929*, 7–9, 14.

52 See Endelman, *Jews of Britain*, 189; Cesarani, "The Transformation," 115; and Clark, *Albion and Jerusalem*, 249.
53 When I use the term Zionism with reference to the twentieth century, I am referring to the political Zionism of the EZF and WZO, or the plan to create a Jewish state, not the spiritual, religious or sentimental Zionism of the Chovevei Zion or similar nineteenth-century approaches.
54 Herzl initially refused the East Africa offer, yet changed his mind in light of a new wave of pogroms against Jews in Russia combined with efforts to limit immigration to England. Feldman, "Jews and the British Empire," 80. For discussion of this issue, see Cohen, "Storm over East Africa and Stress within the English Zionist Federation, 1904–1914," in his *English Zionists*, 79–123; Stanislawski, *Zionism*, 32–4; and Eitan Bar-Yosef and Nadia Valman (eds), *"The Jew" in Late Victorian and Edwardian Culture: Between the East End and East Africa* (London: Palgrave Macmillan, 2009), especially the chapters by David Glover and Meri-Jane Rochelson, 131–60.
55 Feldman, "Jews and the British Empire," 82–5.
56 Tuchman, *Bible and Sword*, 310–16, 324, 334.
57 Cesarani, "One Hundred Years," 40, 42; Endelman, *Jews in Britain*, 189; and Feldman, *Englishmen and Jews*, 345–6. Also see Black, "A Typological Study."
58 Or, as Endelman put it, "die of neglect." *Jews in Britain*, 189.
59 Letter from JNF headquarters to JNFCE, Oct. 28, 1912, and responding letter, Feb. 2, 1913, both in KK1/37; letter dated May 25, 1913, KK1/39. All in CZA.
60 The phrase "its seat" most likely refers to the fact that even though the JNF administrative headquarters were in Cologne, as an English limited liability company, its registered address was in London. Letter to Lionel de Rothschild, London, July 7, 1913, K1/39; letter to JNFCE from headquarters in Cologne with regard to 1916 (with early 1917 documents), KK1/41; also, letter dated Sept. 1911, KKL1/37. All in CZA.
61 Letter from the JNFCE to JNF headquarters in Cologne, Jan. 16, 1912, KK1/37, CZA.
62 Stated by the well-known Zionist leader Dr. Bodenheimer, JNFCE meeting April 9, 1914 KKL1/38, CZA.
63 Todd Endelman explains in his review of Cohen's *English Zionists* that EZF leaders "consistently failed to consider whether the fundamental assumptions of classical Zionism, such as the eternality of antisemitism and the failures of emancipation, were applicable to a liberal state such as England, where conditions were quite dissimilar to those in the continental countries where Zionist ideology was conceived." Here Endelman is responding to and elaborating on Cohen's presentation of the EZF leadership as "'a barren assemblage ... [who] ... made virtually no independent contribution to Zionist theory.'" Todd Endelman, *Jewish Social Studies*, Vol. 45, No. 3/4 (Summer–Autumn, 1983), 339–41, quotations at p. 340. Cohen, *English Zionists*, 158–9.
64 JNFCE correspondence regarding self-taxation, March 1912, KKL1\37, CZA. While self-taxation may have worked better in the Austro-Hungarian Empire

than in England, the Austrian Zionist League took shekelim from and paid dues directly to the EZF. "A Happy and Prosperous New Year to the Jewish Nation," 5669 [1908–9], KKL1. All in CZA.

65 Most of the activities discussed in the EZF papers of the CZA during this early period took place in London or Manchester. The head offices were in London, and from there EZF leaders corresponded with what they referred to as "the provinces," which included Manchester and Liverpool in England; Edinburgh and Glasgow in Scotland; Cardiff and Swansea in Wales; and Dublin and Belfast in Ireland. According to Goodman's *Zionism, 1899–1929*, by the end of 1914 the EZF had fifty affiliated societies, with thirteen in London, thirty-five in "the provinces," and two in the colonies, in Shanghai and Melbourne (p. 30).

66 The EZF sent delegates to the WZO congresses, every year or two years depending on how often they were held. Material from international Zionist congresses during the late nineteenth and early twentieth centuries can be found throughout the EZF collections in the CZA, particularly in the A15/1 file. The EZF corresponded and met with WZO leaders who were based in Vienna, Cologne and Berlin. Zionist organizations outside of the British Isles and Empire mentioned in EZF records include those in Petrograd, Paris, Berlin, Vienna, Copenhagen, Holland, Rome, Venice, Tunis, New York, Buenos Aires and Stockholm.

67 For Zionist culture see Michael Berkowitz, *Zionist Culture and West European Jewry before the First World War* (Chapel Hill: University of North Carolina Press, 1993), specific references at pp. 38, 189.

68 Even after the outbreak of the First World War, the shekel cost no more than one shilling and was believed to be affordable enough for "every Jew and Jewess" in the country to buy one. "The Shekel," Oct. [?1917], DD1 45151; "Shekelim and Congress," 9, in the EZF's 29th annual report, June 1917–June 1928, London, KH4 20412; letter from the EZF to Sokolow, Aug. 13, 1917, Z4/40601; flyer entitled "London Shekel Day," Oct. 19, 1919, DD1 45151; "What Is Zionism? What is the English Zionist Federation?" 3, DD1 45151. All in CZA. The price was later raised to two shillings.

69 EZF newsletter or bulletin beginning "A happy and prosperous year to the Jewish Nation," 5669 [1908], 2, A150/16, CZA.

70 The term "commissioner" was used by the JNF and describes individuals who were appointed to each "Jewish centre" for the purpose of organizing cooperation among various groups with regard to collections. "The Jewish National Fund EZF, London 1908: Its Object," pamphlet translated from the German and published by the JNF. Towns and cities in Great Britain that contributed to the JNFCE repeatedly over the years include Belfast, Birmingham, Blackpool, Brighton, Dublin, Edinburgh, Leeds, Liverpool, London, Maidenhead, Manchester, Newcastle, Newport, Pontypridd, Richmond, Sheffield, Swansea, Tradegar and Worksop. From CZA materials related to the JNFCE 1901–20.

71 The word "honour" is used in a letter from Zangwill to Braby, 1902, A120/678, CZA. "Moral investment" appears repeatedly.

72 Michael Berkowitz comments on the spiritual dimensions of fundraising, with regard to WZO and the JNF, in *Western Jewry and the Zionist Project, 1914-1933* (Cambridge: Cambridge University Press, 2003).
73 Advertisement begins with "An Earnest Appeal ...", included with JNFCE documents in KK1/41, CZA.
74 Donation lists can be found throughout the EZF collections. From time to time Christian donors appear on the lists. For example, "A Christian lady" is mentioned on the "List of Contributions for the Month," Cheshvah, 5669 [1908–9], A150/16, CZA. In the same issue of the newsletter it is noted that "Christian sympathy with our Movement is always welcome" (A150/16–46), CZA.
75 The description of the 1900 event comes from S. Lipton, "Zionist Reminiscences," *The Zionist Review*, May 1920, 9.
76 One Zionist woman from Manchester later recalled how, as children, she and her brother used to collect pennies on Sunday for the cause, repeating those words. Oral interview with Selina Roland, Nov. 5, 1976, tape 205, Manchester Jewish Museum (henceforth MJM). This slogan became a part of WZO culture generally and stems from Schapira's vision that through the fund box all Jews could contribute to the JNF, even those living in poverty.
77 "The Jewish National Fund: Its Object," 9.
78 Letter to the Secretary of the JNFCE, May 22, 1911, KKL1/36, CZA.
79 Document from 1909 KKL1/36; "A Happy and Prosperous New Year to the Jewish Nation" (1908–9), A150/16; and a general letter from the JNFCE regarding fund boxes, KK1/41. All in CZA.
80 The quotation is from Berkowitz, *Western Jewry*, 107.
81 Letter from the EZF to the JNF headquarters in Cologne, May 31, 1910, KKL1/35; and letter from the EZF to Dr. Bodenheimer, JNF headquarters in Cologne, June 2, 1910 KKL1/35, both in CZA.
82 "The Land Fund," KKL1/41; letter to the Secretary of the EZF, Dec. 11, 1911, KK1/37; "The Nahalah Campaign," unclear date, KKL1/42. All in CZA. Stray document, "Nahalah" section, with JNFCE papers, KKL1\42, CZA. While some of these documents can be found among 1918 papers, this fundraising strategy pre-dates the First World War.
83 The quotations are from a letter to Thomas May, Dec. 6, 1911 and EZF letter, Dec. 11, 1911, KKL1\37; JNFCE report, Sept. 1917, KK1/41. All in CZA.
84 "The Jewish National Fund: Its Object," 13, 18.
85 WZO visual culture was important for Jewish Zionists in Germany and the United States as well as Britain. See Berkowitz, *Zionist Culture* and *Western Jewry*. With regard to Great Britain, Berkowitz notes in *Western Jewry*, 105–6, that a "great part of Zionism's visual sensibility" was "tied to the fundraising instruments." With regard to illustrated cards, postcards, stamps and telegraph forms see JNFCE meeting minutes, Feb.–June 1909, KKL1\34; letter regarding Herr Wolffsohn's visit, KK1\35; and letter from EZF, March 1912, KKL1\37. All in CZA. Stamps with images of Theodor Herzl, who came to personify the "Zionist ideal" and became central to pre-war Zionist iconography, and of the Wailing Wall were especially popular, and some were enlarged to be used

as wall decorations. For Herzl as the champion and embodiment of Zionism see Berkowitz, *Zionist Culture*, 99–103. The reference to iconography is in *Western Jewry*, 26.
86 "The Jewish National Fund: Its Object," quotation at p. 3, image of the telegraph at p. 10.
87 With regard to the slide shows from 1908 onwards see: "Propaganda," in EZF report, n.d., 2, KK1/42; Bulletin, KKL1/; letter from JNFCE, Dec. 22, 1911, KKL1/37; JNFCE letter, April 5, 1914, KKL1/38; and Union of Jewish Literary Societies, 1913, KKL1/38. All in CZA.
88 Dr. J. Snowman, "Physical Conditions of Palestine," 41–2, stated that although the Jewish settlers were geographically European, the "Semitic races possess greater powers of acclimatization than Aryan races" and that "among Jews the comparative rarity of intermarriage with the races whose countries they inhabit, makes a great demand on the innate vitality of the Jewish race." The agricultural potential and produce of the country are discussed by Professor Warburg in "The Resources of Palestine." These two lectures were delivered under the auspices of the London Zionist League in 1906 and published in 1907 by the EZF in *The Physical and Political Conditions of Palestine*.
89 Agriculture as a foundation for other developments including education is discussed in "The Jewish National Fund: Its Object" (1908), 5. Berkowitz also makes reference to secular educational institutions as a pre-First World War theme in Zionism in *Western Jewry*, 100.
90 Prior to the First World War, most films and slide shows produced by the WZO were created under the auspices of the JNF. Berkowitz, *Western Jewry*, 106.
91 "Mr. Rosenberg's Cinematograph Films," JNFCE, Sept. 3, 1911.
92 The quotation is from his lecture, "Palestine from the Destruction of the Temple to 1800" given under the auspices of the London Zionist League in 1906 and published in the EZF's pamphlet *The Physical and Political Conditions of Palestine*, 4.
93 For example, the West London Zionist Association organized a fortnightly series of educational lectures on the history and development of Zionism. Letter to Sokolow from the West London Zionist Association, Aug. 1917, Z4\40601, CZA. "Living Hebrew," in "A Happy and Prosperous New Year to the Jewish Nation," for 5669 [1908-9], A150\16, CZA. "The Jewish National Fund: Its Object," printed in that same year, related that in Palestine Hebrew had already become a living language and such a natural part of everyday life that children used it even when playing (p. 24). Endelman, *Jews of Britain*, 146, notes that Zionists taught Hebrew to thousands of students in the British Isles prior to the First World War, particularly in London, Leeds, Glasgow, Liverpool and Manchester.
94 Goodman, *Zionism in England: The English Zionist Federation*, 19–20, 23.
95 The reference to *Ostjuden* and native garb is quoted by Virginia Hein, *The British Followers of Theodor Herzl: English Zionist Leaders, 1896–1904* (New York: Garland, 1987), 142.
96 Bar-Yosef and Valman, "Introduction," in *"The Jew,"* 15.

97 Jacob de Haas, for example, one of the founders of that organization, felt certain that by appealing to Jewish immigrants from Russia and Eastern Europe, the EZF would succeed in undermining the hegemony of the Anglo-Jewish elite, whose institutions or "almost self-elected bodies," he likened to the rotten or pocket boroughs held by English aristocrats prior to franchise reform. Quotation in Hein, *The British Followers*, 50. The fact that the majority of these immigrants remained indifferent or opposed to Zionism did not deter EZF leaders from claiming to represent or have a special affinity with them. Black, "A Typological Study," 46.

98 Goodman, *Zionism, 1899–1929*, 12.

99 "Assyrian King" is from Stanislawski, *Zionism*, 28 and "well-kempt prophet" is from Bermant, *The Cousinhood*, 239.

100 Berkowitz, *Zionist Culture*, 135–7, quotation at p. 137.

101 Letter of appeal for the fund for the assistance of Yemenite Jews, n.d. with 1913 materials and a stray letter from 1913, both in KK1/39, CZA.

102 This project of relocating Yemeni Jews to Palestine had begun in Berlin even before the JNFCE became involved. *Von den Juden des Yemen* (Berlin: Orient-Verlag, 1913) Library of Congress, Washington, DC.

103 Fund for the Assistance of the Yemeni Jews letter of appeal, KK1/39. The committee published appeals in the *Jewish Chronicle* and the *Daily News and Leader*, with the editor of the *Zionist* to write a review of it. Letters from the JNFCE *to Die Hauptbureau des Judischen Nationalfonds*, Cologne, Feb.–April 1913 and letters from S. Lipschitz of the JNFCE, Feb. 1913, KKL1\37; Also, JNFCE reports 1913–1914, KKL1/38. All in CZA.

104 Willingness to work for low wages is noted in Derek Penslar's "Is Zionism a Colonial Movement?" in *Colonialism and the Jews*, edited by Ethan Katz, Lisa Leff and Maud Mandel (Bloomington: Indiana University Press, 2017), 275–300, reference at p. 282.

105 Letter to Professor Chaim Weizmann, Jewish National Fund Committee of Manchester, June 1913, KK1/39, CZA.

106 Document discussing Yemeni homes, no title or date but with letter to Paul Goodman, Dec. 28, 1914, KK1/39, CZA.

107 "Prizes for Yemenite Working Families," n.d. with materials from 1915, KK1/39, CZA.

108 Leon Simon, "Palestine," *The Zionist Review*, Oct. 1918, 94–5.

109 As Berkowitz explains, Congress Zionism was in essence a middle-class movement, appropriately connected to Basel, "a model of bourgeois European normalcy." Berkowitz, *Zionist Culture*, 39. Similarly the majority of English Zionist leaders during this time were neither powerful elites nor part of the great mass of workers, but came instead from the "second or third tier of Anglo-Jewish society." Black, "A Typological Study," 21.

110 Thompson, "Moving Zionism to Asia," 320 and 321, fn. 17.

111 While settlers during the first Aliyah (1881–1904) had relied more heavily on Arab labour than did those of the second Aliyah (1904–14), this change had to do with socialist ideals of avoiding labour relations that resembled

bourgeois oppression, not with a desire to eliminate an Arab presence. Stanislawski, *Zionism*, 37.

112 As Penslar explains, the overwhelmingly Ashkenazi Zionist leadership and intelligentsia adopted the attitude of *mission civilisatrice*, inspired by the Paris-based Alliance Israelite Universelle, and regarded the Arabic-speaking Jews of the Middle East and North Africa as "degenerate yet improvable." Penslar, "Is Zionism a Colonial Movement?" 282.

113 After waiting in London for three months he was finally seen, although not by the Permanent Under-Secretary Sir Arthur Nicolson, with whom he had an appointment. Sokolow then was denied a second meeting with the FO and instructed to send any updates or reports he had in writing via post. Jonathan Schneer, *The Balfour Declaration* (New York: Random House, 2010), 107–10.

114 Endelman, *Jews in Britain*, 190. Despite the internationalist nature of the movement, Zionist Jews tended to support the nations in which they lived during the First World War, maintaining that the victory of their own country and its allies ultimately would advance the Zionist cause. This was true of German, Austrian and Ottoman Zionists as well as of British, Russian and French ones. Berkowitz, *Western Jewry*, 7–8 and Stanislawski, *Zionism*, 39.

115 After October 1914, Weizmann began to meet with and, in the process, influence a number of statesmen who either were or would become involved in British foreign policy decisions, including Lloyd George. "The London Bureau Its Origins and Work," Z4/40252, CZA. Cesarani notes that in 1915 Weizmann and "a small circle of Zionist activists" began to lobby the government. Cesarani, "The Transformation," 120. The quotation in the text is from Robert Lieshout, *Britain and the Arab Middle East: World War I and Its Aftermath* (London and New York: I.B. Tauris, 2016), 198–9.

116 Endelman, *Jews in Britain*, explains that during the First World War the "most prominent opponents of Zionism came from well-to-do families that had been settled in Britain for several generations and were accustomed to setting the community's agenda and representing its interests to the state." Those Anglo-Jewish community leaders had been content to ignore Zionism in Britain as long as it remained "low-key" and "ineffectual," but moved to counter it as it gained influence in Whitehall (191). In effect, the First World War propelled the "Zionist movement from the periphery to the center of communal politics" (186).

117 "III Difficulties of Political Zionism," Acc 3121 E3/67/1, BDBJ, LMA.

118 From "The Palestine Question: Report on a Conference of the Honorary Officers [of the BDBJ] with Delegates of the Zionist Organizations," April 27, 1915, 12, Acc 3121 E3/204/2, BDBJ, LMA. The inserted quotation, "any Christian government in its senses," comes from a letter to James de Rothschild, Aug. 31, 1916, Acc 3121 E3/204/3, BDBJ, LMA. The BDBJ was the institutional stronghold of the anti-Zionist camp in England during the First World War, as Endelman notes in *Jews in Britain*, 192.

119 CFC report, April 22, 1915 and "Mr. H.S.Q Henriques' Views on the Palestine Question," Confidential Memorandum, April 28, 1915, both in Acc 3121 E3/204/2, BDBJ, LMA. H.S.Q Henriques refers to the lawyer, historian and scholar Henry Straus Henriques who later would become president of the BDBJ. In that same month the CFC communicated its support for British imperialism in Palestine: "The Conjoint Committee agree[s] with the Zionists that efforts should be made to bring Palestine under the British Empire as being most favourable to Jewish development in that country." CFC reply to the EZF, enclosed in Wolf to Oliphant, April 28, 1915, The National Archives, Kew, FO/371/2488/51705.

120 Wolf to Weizmann from a conversation between the two recorded in a confidential memorandum by Lucien Wolf, Aug. 17, 1916, Acc 3121 E3/204/3, BDBJ, LMA. Wolf became the FO's "regular contact." Endelman, *Jews in Britain*, 192–3 and Lieshout, *Britain and the Arab Middle East*, 193.

121 Because Wolf was given *carte blanche* with regard to the CFC, the committee bore his "unmistakable stamp" during the war years. Mark Levene, *War, Jews, and the New Europe: The Diplomacy of Lucien Wolf, 1914–19* (London: The Littman Library of Jewish Civilization, 1992), 42–3, including fn. 20, quotation at p. 43. Levene discusses Wolf's diplomatic manoeuvrings in depth, particularly with regard to his concern for Jews in Russia and Eastern Europe and the Paris peace conference in 1919. Under Wolf the CFC had a "close and confidential" relationship with the FO. "Confidential Statement," from the Presidents to the AJA and the BDBJs, Oct. 1915, Acc 3121 B2/9/14, BDBJ, LMA. Also see the CFC report in the letter to Rothschild, March 1, 1915. Foreign Affairs Committee file, Acc 3121 C11/2/6, BDBJ, LMA. Wolf's background differed from that of the Anglo-Jewish elites who led the communal bodies he represented, the BDBJ and AJA. In addition to being a journalist, or professional man, he was the son of a political migrant: his father left Bohemia during the turbulence of 1848. Josef Fraenkel, "Lucien Wolf and Theodor Herzl," *Transactions of the Jewish Historical Society of England*, Vol. 20 (1959–61), 161–88, reference at pp. 162–3. Still, he was born to a "comfortable middle-class liberal family." Chimen Abramsky, "Lucien Wolf's Efforts for the Jewish Communities in Central and Eastern Europe," *Jewish Historical Studies*, Vol. 29 (1982–86), 281.

122 The reference to "British spirit and traditions" is from a document outlining a plan for Palestine from late 1914, Acc 3121 E3/204/1, BDBJ, LMA. "Tooth and nail" is from a letter to James de Rothschild, Aug. 31, 1916, Acc 3121 E3/204/3, BDBJ, LMA.

123 The quotation is from the same typed document outlining a plan for Palestine noted previously and from late 1914, Acc 3121 E3/204/1, BDBJ, LMA.

124 "IV. Compromise on Cultural Judaism." This document follows "III Difficulties of Political Zionism," Acc 3121 E3/67/1, BDBJ, LMA.

125 Letter dated Sept. 16, 1915, Foreign Affairs Committee File, Acc 3121 c11/2/14, BDBJ, LMA. This same statement is also in a CFC memorandum following a "Confidential Statement made to the Council of the AJA and BDBJ by the Presidents," Oct. 1915, Acc 3121 B2/9/14, BDBJ, LMA.

126 Wolf to Zangwill, May 1916, Foreign Affairs Committee Files, Acc 3121 c11/2/8, BDBJ, LMA. Zangwill, it should be noted, had already become critical of the EZF and WZO by this time.
127 From a confidential memorandum written by Wolf regarding a meeting with Weizmann arranged by Rothschild, Aug. 17, 1916, Acc 3121 E3/204/3, BDBJ, LMA. This same sentiment, that the CFC would not object to Zionist efforts to secure national or special rights for Jews in Palestine as long as those goals were not expressed until a later date, can be found in the confidential report regarding negotiation between the CFC and Zionist leaders dated April 27, 1915, Acc 3121/ E3/204/2, BDBJ, LMA.
128 1916 document signed by Wolf in Foreign Affairs Committee Files, Acc 3121 c 11/2/8, BDBJ, LMA.
129 "Statement on the Palestine Question," signed May 17, 1917. The statement itself is longer than the quotation here. CFC Minute Book, Acc/3121/c11A/2 and in Acc/3121 c11/12/53/2, both in BDBJ, LMA. While one passage in this document calls for "reasonable facilities for immigration and colonisation" and "such municipal privileges in the towns and colonies inhabited by them as may be shown to be necessary," and those words were repeated often during negotiations, in part because they served as a place of common ground upon which both the CFC and the Zionists could agree, they should not be interpreted as evidence of the CFC conceding to the creation of legal privileges or disabilities based on a Jewish or religious identity in Palestine, because the CFC used the above phrases even as it vehemently opposed that position, as in the document in question. This statement generated considerable backlash within the BDBJ and AJA, but that reaction had more to do with the high-handedness and presumption on the part of its authors than it did with Zionist sympathies, and it did not alter the fundamental "political constellation" of those bodies. Cohen, *English Zionists*, 243–313; Cesarani, "The Transformation," 115–22; and Endelman, *Jews of Britain*, 193–5. "Political constellation" is from Cesarani, "The Transformation," 122.
130 For discussion of the triumph of the entrepreneurial ideal in English society amongst all classes see Harold Perkin, *The Origins of Modern English Society* (New York: Routledge, 2nd edn, 2002), especially chapters 7 and 8. With regard to the Anglo-Jewish elites, Chaim Bermant describes them as "Smilesian before Smiles and Victorian before Victoria." They were "super-Smilesians," and despite having achieved a plutocracy, nevertheless regarded it as a meritocracy. Bermant, *The Cousinhood*, 425, 427.
131 Wolf often related the importance of maintaining a united Jewish front both to the Zionists and the British government. For example, Wolf explained in an interview with Cecil that the CFC had not expressed their beliefs publicly in order "to preserve the apparent unity of the Jewish community." Meeting with Cecil described in a letter from Wolf to Mr Montefiore, May 8, 1917, Acc 3121 c11/12/54/12, BDBJ, LMA.
132 Discussion of the political significance of the non-Zionist, Jewish schools, colonies and other institutions in Palestine, often connected to the BDBJ, appears

repeatedly. For example, in a meeting between Wolf and Cecil described in a letter from Wolf to Mr Montefiore, May 8, 1917, Acc 3121 c11/12/54/12; in a meeting with Balfour described in confidential memorandum, Jan. 31, 1917, Acc 3121 c11/12/53/2; and in a letter to Zangwill, 10 Nov. 1916, Acc 3121 E3/204/3. All in BDBJ, LMA.

133 In these discussions Board members drew from the thought of Ahad Ha'am, né Asher Ginsberg, whom one board member praised as "the greatest of living Hebrew writers." BDBJ Report on Ahad Ha'am, not dated but among the 1914 materials, Acc 3121 E3/204/1. See also "Statement on the Palestine Question," May 17, 1917, Acc 3121 c/12/53/2; "Conjoint Foreign Committee of the BDBJs and the AJA Statement on the Palestine Question" with 1917 materials, Acc 3121 G2/3. All in BDBJ, LMA. While Ahad Ha'am was, in fact, a Zionist, his emphasis on the need to nurture the cultural and spiritual aspects of Jewish life in Palestine made at least some of his ideas appealing to those who sought an alternative to the WZO programme.

134 With regard to qualifying for citizenship, as the "Statement on the Palestine Question" explained, any nation based on a secular or racial definition of Jewishness would deny the very essence of Jewish life, which was spiritual. Yet establishing a Jewish state defined by religion would be equally problematic, given that Jews did not agree with each other regarding practice or belief and none would support a system of religious tests, as those would interfere with freedom of conscience. "Conjoint Foreign Committee of the BDBJs and the AJA Statement on the Palestine Question," May 17, 1917, Acc 3121 c 12/53/2 and Conjoint Foreign Committee Book, Acc 3121/c11A/2. Both in BDBJ, LMA.

135 "III Nationality Outside Palestine from Statement on the Palestine Question," May 1917, Acc 3121 c11/12/53/2 and letter from Wolf to Rothschild, Aug. 31, 1916, Acc 3121 E3/204/3. Both in BDBJ, LMA.

136 Lucien Wolf, notes on the Zionist Memorandum, Oct. 11, 1916, Acc 3121 E3/204/3, BDBJ, LMA.

137 The speech is among the 1916 materials, Acc 3121 E3/204/3, BDBJ, LMA.

138 For example, the report discussing the ideas of Ahad Ha'am notes that the "Hebrew character" had much in common with the "English character." With late 1914 materials, Acc 3121 E3/204/1, BDBJ, LMA.

139 "Difficulties of Political Zionism," Acc 3121 E3/67/1, BDBJ, LMA. While the author of this document is not given, based on Wolf's role during this time and the way that this particular passage echoes his letter cited previously with regard to the Irish, Poles and Finns, he is mostly likely the author, or at the very least one of the contributors.

140 Letter from the CFC to the South African Jewish Board of Deputies, Jan. 1916. Use of the word "shipwreck" to describe these fears appears frequently in CFC and BDBJ documents throughout the period, for example, in a statement by Lucien Wolf in that same year. Both documents are in the Foreign Affairs Committee Files, Acc 3121 C11/2/8, BDBJ, LMA.

141 Letter to Rothschild, Aug. 1916, Acc 3121 E3/204/3, BDBJ, LMA.

Zionist debates 217

142 Untitled speech, n.d., with 1916 materials, Acc 3121 E3/204/3, BDBJ, LMA.
143 Confidential CFC report on the Palestine Question and negotiations with the Zionists, April 1915, Acc 3121 E3/204/2, BDBJ, LMA.
144 Letter from Wolf, June 1915, Acc 3121 E3/204/2, BDBJ, LMA.
145 Aug. 31, 1916, Acc 3121 E3/204/3, BDBJ, LMA.
146 "Notes on the Zionist Memorandum," Oct. 11, 1916. Acc 3121 E3/204/3, BDBJ, LMA
147 FAC Reports 1917, Acc 3121 c11/2/12 and a speech by the Russian Zionist Yechiel Tchlenov (also spelled Chlenov), April 1915, for CFC members only, Acc 3121 E3/204/2. Both in BDBJ, LMA.
148 This theme runs throughout Levene's *War, Jews, and the New Europe* and is also reflected in the collected papers of Lucien Wolf, RG 348 FA, housed in the archives of the YIVO Institute for Jewish Research, New York.
149 The Russian visitor, not mentioned by name, was referred to as a publicist and a member of the Jewish Committee of Petrograd. Confidential document, July 1915, FAC files, Acc 3121 C/11/2/5/2, BDBJ, LMA.
150 "Confidential Statement" from the Presidents to the AJA and the BDBJ, Oct. 1915, Acc 3121 B2/9/14, BDBJ, LMA.
151 The CFC also had to tread carefully with regard to Jews in Romania, as efforts on their behalf could contribute to anti-Allied feeling in the country. Letter to Dr. Stern from the CFC, July 4, 1916, Foreign Affairs Committee File, Acc 3121 c11/2/9/2, BDBJ, LMA. After late August 1916, when Romania declared war on Austria-Hungary, the CFC was able to "include the Romano-Jewish question among the questions arising out of the war." Meeting of the Joint Foreign Committee, 1916, "Board of Deputies, 1916–1921 Agenda and Reports," Vol. I, Acc 3121 a/3, BDBJ, LMA.
152 Memorandum on meeting with Balfour, Jan. 31, 1917, Acc 3121 C11/12/53/2, BDBJ, LMA.
153 For example, the CFC requested approval for an appeal for donations for the relief of Jewish victims of the war in Russia to make sure that the text did not contain anything that the government might consider objectionable. Letter to Mr Oliphant of the FO, Dec. 5, 1916, Acc 3121 C11/2/10, BDBJ, LMA. The CFC also recorded having sent documents with an overview and chapter on Russia to the FO, letter to Montefiore, Oct. 3, 1916, FAC file, Acc 3121 C11/2/9/2, BDBJ, LMA. Wolf was known to sometimes use government approval as a way of then later implying co-authorship. Levene, *War, Jews, and the New Europe*, 87.
154 Letter to Rothschild describing the meeting, Aug. 13, 1915, Acc 3121 c11/2/14, BDBJ, LMA.
155 Correspondence between Bryce and Wolf, May 1916, FAC Files, Acc 3121 c11/2/8, BDBJ, LMA. Wolf's criticisms of the Russian treatment of Jews remained a sensitive issue and however encouraging FO representatives may have been in person to Wolf, they also treated his advances with caution. As Cecil minuted in March 1916, "if and when we are allowed by our allies to say anything worth saying to the Jews, it should not be left to Mr. Lucien Wolf

to say it." Cecil minute, March 14, 1916, The National Archives, Kew, FO 371/2817/42608.
156 Letter from Joseph Reinach, April, 1917, Acc 3121 C11/12/53/2, BDBJ, LMA. The CFC worked with the Alliance Israelite Universelle, founded in Paris in 1860 to improve the conditions of Jews around the world, especially in North Africa and the Middle East. Wolf reported that his trip to Paris was successful and that he had strengthened the bond between like-minded British and French Jewish communities. "Co-operation with Foreign and Colonial Bodies" and Confidential CFC report, Oct. 1916 in Acc 3121 B2/9/14, BDBJ, LMA.
157 Wolf's meeting with Balfour in a Confidential Memorandum, Jan. 1917, Acc 3121 c11/12/53/2, BDBJ, LMA.
158 Letter to Oliphant, April 21, 1917, Acc 3121 C11/12/53/2, BDBJ, LMA. These bodies repeatedly expressed the idea that only they were the legitimate representatives of Jewish interests. For example, in a letter to the Secretary of State Viscount Grey in 1916, the presidents of the BDBJ and the AJA stated that they trusted that His Majesty's government would not make any final decisions regarding Palestine until "the detailed views have been ascertained" by the CFC. Confidential, No. 2, letter to Right Honourable Viscount Grey signed by David Alexander, Claude Montefiore and Leopold de Rothschild, Oct. 1, 1916, Acc 3121/G2/3, BDBJ, LMA. The letter goes on to state that the CFC represented "all the largest Jewish congregations in the British Empire and many other Anglo-Jewish bodies." However, only rarely did they consult British Jews outside England. They did on occasion enlist their support, as in 1916 when the BDBJ sent a letter to Jewish organizations in Toronto, Canada; Cape Town and Harrismith, South Africa; Bombay, India; Sydney (2), Adelaide, Melbourne (2), Ballarat and Brisbane, Australia; Wellington and Auckland, New Zealand; Hong Kong; Shanghai, China; Kobe and Nagasaki, Japan asking them to contact their local authorities with regard to the condition of Jews in Russia and Romania. Presumably thirteen of the eighteen bodies agreed to do so immediately, since soon after these letters were sent, the BDBJ sent reminder telegraphs to just five of them (in Toronto, Melbourne, Bombay, Auckland and Cape Town), Oct. 1916, Acc 3121 C11/2/9/2, BDBJ, LMA.
159 Untitled speech, n.d. with 1916 materials, Acc 3121 E3/204/3, BDBJ, LMA.
160 Untitled document dated Aug. 1916, Acc 3121 E3/204/3; Confidential Memorandum, Jan. 1917, Acc 3121 c11/12/53/2; and typed document outlining plan for Palestine from late 1914, Acc 3121 E3/204/1. All in BDBJ, LMA.
161 By the end of 1914 both Arthur Balfour and David Lloyd George had begun to meet with Chaim Weizmann, and from 1915 onward he and a small group of Zionists, which included Nahum Sokolow and Lord Lionel Walter Rothschild, began lobbying the government. In addition, Harry Sacher, Israel Sieff and Simon Marks occupied what Schneer calls the "secondary tier" of those involved in the manoeuvres that preceded the Balfour Declaration. Schneer, *The Balfour Declaration*, 117.
162 Margaret MacMillan, *Paris 1919: Six Months that Changed the World* (New York: Random House, 2002), 415.

163 Endelman, *Jews of Britain*, 190–1, quotation at p. 190. Reference to these Orientalist myths is in Black, "A Typological Study," 20. For more on philo-Semitism see W.D. and H.L. Rubenstein, *Philosemitism: Admiration and Support in the English Speaking World for Jews, 1840–1939* (London: St. Martin's Press, 1999). The reference to the German government is from Robert Lieshout, *Britain and the Arab Middle East: World War I and Its Aftermath* (London: I.B. Tauris, 2016), 213, 217, 224. WZO representatives succeeded in portraying their opposition within Anglo-Jewry as an elite group out of touch with the wishes of the Jewish people as a whole. Lieshout, *Britain and the Arab Middle East*, 223; Weizmann and Rothschild made this case to Balfour, 220; Cecil and Milner also became convinced, 217.

164 Endelman notes the "widening diplomatic entanglement" that contributed to this position in *Jews in Britain*, 186. Also see, Barbara Tuchman, "Lord Shaftesbury's Vision: An Anglican Israel," *Bible and Sword*, 152–79. Yaron Perry discusses Christians who contributed to the Zionist movement and at the same time sought to convert the Jews living in Palestine in *British Mission to the Jews in Nineteenth Century Palestine* (London: Frank Cass, 2003).

165 David Lloyd George, *Memoirs of the Peace Conference* (New Haven: Yale University Press, 1939), Vol. II, 720, cited in Tom Segev, *One Palestine Complete: Jews and Arabs under the British Mandate* (New York: Henry Holt, 1999), 36.

166 Mark Sykes coordinated the meetings between Zionist representatives and statesmen from the War Cabinet, War Office and Foreign Office. Tuchman, *Bible and Sword*, 334; "The London Bureau Its Origins and Work," Z4/40252, CZA.

167 Montagu was not a member of the War Cabinet, but was brought into the discussion. When he became Secretary of State for India the appointment was opposed in the *Morning Post*, where he was called a "'political-financial Jew' of un-English mien and doubtful allegiance," Bermant, *The Cousinhood*, 264. His statement to Lloyd George about being forced back into the ghetto is at p. 258. The reference to a blow to Jewish Britons and a people who do not exist is from Montagu's diary and quoted at pp. 262–3.

168 Bermant, *The Cousinhood*, 192.

169 MacMillan, *Paris 1919*, 416; Lieshout, *Britain and the Arab Middle East*, 225.

170 The reference to Balfour needing to exert little effort is in Lieshout, *Britain and the Arab Middle East*, at p. 8. A detailed analysis explaining this deeply flawed bureaucratic–political process in which Montagu and Curzon's reasonable positions and expertise could be swept aside in favour of underdeveloped theories, and in the case of Mark Sykes "fanciful notions" with little or no connection to reality, is presented by Lieshout in *Britain and the Arab Middle East*, 1–10 and 419–423. The reference to Sykes is at p. 422.

171 Z4/40601, CZA; also widely available. The importance of the Balfour Declaration with regard to its role in initiating a new era in Zionist history and in the relationship between that movement and the British government has been well documented. As Berkowitz, *Western Jewry*, 28, relates, the Balfour

Declaration is one "of the greatest watersheds in the history of Zionism, by all accounts." Similarly, Elizabeth Thompson, "Moving Zionism to Asia," 319, notes that with the Balfour Declaration the fortunes of Zionism were reversed overnight, with Zionist Jews celebrating around the world. The Zionist movement as a whole was "utterly elated" by the Balfour Declaration, which seemed to put the nationalist goals first outlined in the Basel Programme within reach. Stanislawski, *Zionism*, 43.

172 "From Protectorate to Autonomous Dominion," BPC report, file Z3/89, CZA. While there is no date on this report, the content reveals that it was written after the beginning of the First World War and before the establishment of Palestine as a British Mandate. The other documents in the Z3/89 file seem to have been created during the war but before the Balfour Declaration. Sieff, Marks and Sacher were brothers-in-law and a part of a closely knit community connected by commercial and familial as well as Zionist interests, which will be discussed in the following section on female Zionist organizations.

173 In the first issue of *Palestine* (Jan. 26, 1917) the BPC included a statement explaining its goals: the committee "has been founded to urge upon the British nation and the British government the importance of including, when the peace settlement comes to be made, Palestine within the British Empire, and of giving every facility and encouragement to the development in Palestine of a Jewish national life" which will be a "source of strength to the British Empire" (p. 6). The offices of the BPC were in Manchester until 1919, when they were moved to Piccadilly, London. The editor, however, remained in Manchester, *Palestine*, Jan. 4, 1919, last page.

174 Albert Hyamson, the British official and "Zionist advisor" who would serve in Mandatory Palestine helped to craft propaganda celebrating the new British–Zionist alliance during this time, including the film *The British Conquering Palestine for the Jews*. Hyamson, "Changing Languages of Empire and the Orient: Britain and the Invention of the Middle East, 1917–18," *Historical Journal*, Vol. 50, No. 3 (2007), 661–4, cited in Thompson, "Moving Zionism to Asia," 320, fn. 326.

175 Berkowitz, *Western Jewry*, 197–8, notes Zionism's protean, national and international nature. On those same pages he describes it as self-consciously hybridized and as a nationalist movement, voluntary association, charitable society, fraternal order (for women and men), youth club, proto-non-profit body and proto-special-interest lobby. Along the same lines the editors of *Colonialism and the Jews*, Ethan Katz, Lisa Leff and Maud Mandel comment that the scholars who contributed to that collected volume found the relationship between colonialism and Zionism to be "a historically moving target." "Introduction: Engaging Colonial History and Jewish History," 17.

176 Looting and violence directed at Jews during the First World War, especially those with German-sounding names, is from Endelman, *Jews in Britain*, 184–5. Tony Kushner notes that the anti-alien feeling in Britain, inseparable from antisemitism, had increased over the 1905–14 period and "intensified to the point of hysteria" during the First World War. Kushner, "The Impact of

British Anti-Semitism, 1918–1945," in *The Making of Modern Anglo-Jewry*, edited by David Cesarani (Oxford: Basil Blackwell, 1990), 198. Also see David Cesarani, "An Embattled Minority: The Jews in Britain during the First World War," in *The politics of Marginality: Race, The Radical Right and Minorities in Twentieth Century Britain* edited by Tony Kushner and Kenneth Lunn (New York: Frank Cass, 1990), 61–81.

177 Ever since the German Kaiser Wilhelm II arranged for Herzl to have an audience with the Ottoman Sultan Abdülhamid II in 1898, WZO supporters had entertained this idea, and that possibility appeared in WZO/EZF propaganda during the pre-First World War period.

178 Letter from JNFCE May 11, 1914, KK1/38; JNFCE letter to *Die Hauptbureau*, Cologne, May 24, 1914, KK1/38; "The National Fund," July 8, 1914 KKL1/38; JNFCE document 1915, K1/40; JNFCE document on report from Scotland Yard, April 25, 1916, KK1/40; JNFCE letter to Keren Kayemeth, The Hague, May 10, 1916, K1/40. All in CZA.

179 "Monthly Bulletin Issued by the English Zionist Federation," May 1915, DD1, 45151, CZA.

180 "Floor to roof" is from "Jews and the Declaration," *Palestine*, Dec. 15, 1917, 184. The Rothschild quotation is from *Great Britain, Palestine and the Jews: Jewry's Celebration of its National Charter* (London: Zionist Organisation, 1918), 42. The Sykes quotation has been reproduced in Tuchman, *Bible and Sword*, 326. That meeting was two months after the Balfour Declaration. Also see "The Great Demonstration," *Palestine*, Dec. 8, 1917 and "The Opera House Demonstration, July 14," *Palestine*, July 27, 1918, 198.

181 "Programme of a Jewish Demonstration at the London Opera House," Dec. 1917. Mention of both anthems appears in, for example, "Programme of a Public Meeting," in 1918 and the "Jewish Demonstration at the Royal Albert Hall," 1920. All documents are in DD1 45151, CZA. These and other types of gatherings brought the Zionist message into quarters "hitherto inaccessible." A report by M. Shire to the EZF, 1918, A\19\285. For a number of mass-meeting programmes, announcements and other materials see folder DD1\45151, CZA. In addition, other references to these meetings and demonstrations can be found in: JNFCE letter, Nov. 29, 1917, KK1/41; JNFCE to KK, The Hague, Nov. 1917; Z4/40574; Z4/40601; EZF letter to Dr. Tchlenov, Nov. 16, 1917, Z4/40601; EZF letter of announcement, Oct. 11, 1918, Z4/40620; and "English Zionist Federation," no date but with 1918 documents, Z4/406/21. All in CZA.

182 EZF materials from the period prior to the Balfour Declaration contain positive references to the Ottomans, noting, for example, that Zionist settlers are loyal subjects of the sultan or that Jews have lived in the Ottoman Empire relatively free of persecution for centuries.

183 For example, the forty-page booklet on "British Projects for the Restoration of the Jews" was published in 1917 and "A Jewish Palestine: the Jewish Case for British Trusteeship" was distributed two years later. Both of these publications are in Z4\40565 of the CZA. Pamphlets and similar materials

would be ordered and printed by the hundreds or thousands. For example, one EZF fund-raising effort required 30,000 pamphlets and 100,000 circulars, in English and Yiddish. "Report given by Mr. Marks, Secretary of the Zionist Organization, London Bureau," n.d. but after Balfour, Z4\40564, CZA.
184 "The Liberation of Galilee: Jewish Rejoicings at Jerusalem," from the Anglo-Jewish Press Agency, Oct. 24, 1918, EZF, Z4/40620, CZA. Along the same lines, in 1918 the BPC published a series of articles in *Palestine* describing the warm reception given to Allenby and his troops by the people of Tel Aviv and Jerusalem in the form of official ceremonies, public demonstrations, private hospitality and "genuine friendship": "Life in Palestine," April 20; "Work and play in the O.E.T," April 27; "Travel in Palestine," July 20; and "General Allenby and Jerusalem Jewry," July 27. In "Jerusalem, Jewry and the War," July 6, the Balfour Declaration is described as having done more to resuscitate the people of that city than any relief committee.
185 Samuel Tolkowsky, "The Jewish Resettlement of Palestine: Address Delivered at the Annual Conference of the English Zionist Federation on February 3rd" (London: English Zionist Federation, 1918), 7.
186 Berkowitz, *Western Jewry*, 109.
187 I.L. Reid, "A Narrative 1914–1919. Remembered and Illustrated by I.L. Reid, No. 12819, Sergeant, 17th – The Leicestershire Regt," 162, LBY 94/2354, Imperial War Museum, London. The idea of an "oceanic interculture" between Great Britain and its colonial territories has been explored by a number of Atlantic world historians, for example, Joseph Roach, *Cities of the Dead: Circum-Atlantic Performance* (New York: Columbia University Press, 1996).
188 Tolkowsky, "The Jewish Resettlement," 7. Tel Aviv originated as the Jewish quarter of Jaffa. Berkowitz, *Western Jewry*, 112.
189 Berkowitz, *Western Jewry*, 112. Also see the illustration "Herzl Street in Tel-Aviv (Jaffa)," in Israel Cohen (ed.), *Zionist Work in Palestine* (London: T.F. Unwin, 1911), 172; Berkowitz, *Zionist Culture*, 150–1; and Yossi Katz, "Ideology and Urban Development: Zionism and the Origins of Tel Aviv, 1906–1914," *Journal of Historical Geography*, Vol. 12, No. 4 (1986): 402–24. Representations of Tel Aviv as clean, suburban, Western space appear repeatedly in Zionist publications during this time as well. For example, "The Beginnings of the Renascence," *Palestine*, July 20, 1918, 103; "Travel in Palestine," July 20, 1918, 186; "A Jewish Renascence," Sept. 7, 1918, 40, all in *Palestine* 1918; and Samuel Tolkowsky, *The Jewish colonisation in Palestine: its history and its prospects* (Zionist Organization London Bureau), 1918, 20.
190 Berkowitz, *Zionist Culture*, 157. Tel Aviv was not declared a city until 1934, or during the Mandate period.
191 Berkowitz, *Western Jewry*, 94 and 107, quotation at p. 107.
192 Simon, "Palestine," 94. The author refers to the Judean colonies, which would include Tel Aviv, given his description and its proximity to Jaffa.
193 Nahum Sokolow, *History of Zionism, 1600–1918* (London: Longmans, Green and Co., 1919), liii.

194 "Palestine and the British Press," April 7, 1917, 86 and "After Paris," November 22, 1919, 116, both in *Palestine*. In the first article the author also states that "Just as the British press sees that Palestine must be British, it sees that to be British it must be Jewish."
195 "From Dan to Beersheba," Nov. 29, 1919, first page. Similarly, "Palestine and Foreign Policy," May 24, 1919, describes the British Empire as hinged on the area of the Suez and a Jewish Palestine as the only secure form that hinge can take. Also see, "Zionism and the Entente," Oct. 17, 1917, 111. All in *Palestine*. The strategic importance of a Jewish Palestine for the British Empire in India also is related in the EZF pamphlet written by Albert Hyamson, "British Projects for the Restoration of the Jews," 1917, in the EZF collections of the CZA but also widely available.
196 "Palestine and the British Press," *Palestine*, April 7, 1917. Report on the BPC, Z3/89, CZA. The BPC's publication ran regular articles on the topic of new roads and railroads being built or planned by the Jewish settlers.
197 "Two Germans on Jewish Palestine," *Palestine*, June 16, 1917, 161–2.
198 "The Military Situation," *Palestine*, April 20, 1918, 82. In "A Separate Peace with Turkey," *Palestine*, June 23, 1917, the author maintains that securing the borders of Egypt and the defence of India were the two most important problems with regard to British foreign policy and that a Jewish Palestine solved both.
199 "British Commerce and a Jewish Palestine," *Palestine*, Dec. 13, 1919, first page.
200 The Hong Kong Heritage Project (HKHP) Archives in Kowloon holds extensive materials on the Kadoorie family and Jewish communities in Hong Kong and Shanghai during the period in question, or the late nineteenth and early twentieth centuries. The following materials are from that collection. Clippings from *The Jewish Chronicle*: E.S. Kadoorie "A Herzl Memorial – A suggestion from Hong Kong," Sept. 2, 1904, 18, in file COO83; "New Life in the East," Nov. 26, 1909, 18, in COO47; stray clipping on the "Opening of the Laura Kadourie School in Baghdad," Jan. 5, 1912, 24 in COO58; booklet by Dennis Leventhal, "The Jewish Community of Hong Kong," published by the Jewish Historical Society of Hong Kong, 1988, in COO108; "A Philanthropic Tradition: the Kadoorie Family," booklet created by the Hong Kong Heritage Project, 2012. Page 6 of that document notes that Sir Eleazer (Elly) Kadoorie was President of the Shanghai Zionist Association from 1915 to 1929 and played an instrumental role in securing the endorsement of the Balfour Declaration by China, Japan and Thailand. The Kadoorie family was a part of a larger community known as the "Baghdadi Jews" who, over the generations, had made their way from Ottoman Mesopotamia first to British India and then to China and, in the process, embraced a British identity and treaty port mentality. Chiara Betta, "From Orientals to Imagined Britons: Baghdadi Jews in Shanghai," *Modern Asian Studies*, Vol. 37, No. 4 (2003), 999–1023, HKHP Archives, file COO256. References to EZF correspondence with Jewish Zionists in the British Empire, including Shanghai, and to the

Shanghai community's fortnightly publication *Israel's Messenger* can be found in "British Empire," n.d. but with 1917 materials Z4\40601; letter to H.J. Morgenstern, Dec. 1918, Z4\40564; "A Happy and Prosperous New Year to the Jewish Nation," KK1\33 and A150\16; correspondence between Mr Marks and Mr Lewis, 1917, Z4\4060. All in CZA.

201 The "riddle of Asia" is from "The Administration of Palestine," July 12, 1919, 170; language study and the "great machine" is from "British Commerce and a Jewish Palestine," Dec. 1919, first page. Other EZF materials that discuss Jewish trading connections and their development both within the Middle East and extending into the Far East include: "The Land-Bridge of Palestine," Jan. 5, 1918, 205; "German Opinion and Palestine," Jan. 19, 1918, 223; "Lord Bryce on Palestine," July 13, 1918, 184; "The Victory and After," Oct. 12, 1918, 74; "The Future of Haifa," April 19, 1919, first page; the speech by Chaim Weizmann, "The Zionists and Palestine," Feb. 14, 1920, 4–5. All in *Palestine*.

202 "Agriculture in Palestine," March 31, 1917, 77–8 and "Palestine and the Peace Conference," Feb. 8, 1919, 3. In addition, the idea that the "regeneration of the East" was too great a task for the Arabs alone is expressed in "Sir Mark Sykes," Feb. 22, 1919, 21. All in *Palestine*.

203 "Two Germans on a Jewish Palestine," June 16, 1917, *Palestine*, 162, 164.

204 "Palestine Waterways," *Palestine*, May 17, 1919, 117.

205 Sokolow, *History of Zionism*, xlvii.

206 "The Jewish Colonial Trust, Ltd. Issue of Shares," Chaim Weizmann, July 4, 1918 and "Some Points about the Jewish Colonial Trust, Ltd.," EZF, 1918. Both in Z4/40620, CZA.

207 "The Jewish National Fund: Its Object," 4. In "Moving Zionism to Asia," Elizabeth Thompson explains that Zionism "aimed to build a separate, autarkic, and superior economy tied to the metropole" (p. 320).

208 These terms can be found repeatedly in EZF materials throughout the period studied.

209 Zionism had developed against the backdrop of the "Scramble for Africa" and had been influenced by it ever since the publication of Herzl's *The Jewish State*. Mark Levene, "Herzl, the Scramble, and a Meeting that Never Happened: Revisiting the Notion of an African Zion," in *"The Jew" in late Victorian and Edwardian Culture: Between the East End and East Africa*, edited by Eitan Bar-Yosef and Nadia Valman (London: Palgrave Macmillan), 201–21, reference to Herzl at p. 22.

210 Sokolow, *History of Zionism*, xlvii.

211 Report of "The British Palestine Committee," Z3/89, CZA.

212 BPC report "From Protectorate to Autonomous Dominion," n.d. but written between Jan. 1917 and April 1920, file Z3/89, CZA.

213 "Palestine and the Peace Conference," *Palestine*, Feb. 8, 1919, 2.

214 "French Propaganda," March 22, 1919, 51: "Palestine and the Peace Conference," Feb 8, 1919, 2; and quotation from "America and Palestine," Dec. 28, 1918, 164. All in *Palestine*.

215 "Jews and Palestine," June 9, 1917, 155; "Djemal Pasha and Zionism," Aug. 11, 1917, 24; "The Young Turks and the new Russia," June 21, 1919, 150. All in *Palestine*. Sokolow, *History of Zionism*, 77.
216 "The Revision of War Aims," June 30, 1917, 179. A similar quote by Smuts appears in "An Essential War Aim," Aug. 4, 1917, 11. Both in *Palestine*.
217 Herbert Sidebotham, *England and Palestine: Essays towards the Restoration of the Jewish State* (London: Constable and Co., 1918), 184–5. Sidebotham was a journalist for the *Manchester Guardian*, member of the BPC and frequent contributor to *Palestine*.
218 The quotation is from Harry Sacher's pamphlet, "A Jewish Palestine: The Jewish Case for British Trusteeship" (London: Zionist Organization, 1919). It is discussed in "A Jewish Palestine," *Palestine*, March 8, 1919, 36–40. Similar ideas appear elsewhere in Zionist publications during this period. For example, the idea that the freedom of internal development distinguishes the British Empire from all empires of the past ("Palestine and the Defence of Egypt," *Palestine*, May 12, 1917, 124) or that the Englishman is exceptional in his appreciation of variety with regard to attitudes of cultures ("Jews and Palestine," *Palestine*, June 9, 1917, 155).
219 "Zionism," a flyer, undated, but with 1919 materials, DD1 45151, CZA.
220 "A Call to Anglo-Jewry: Manifesto by the English Zionist Federation," *The Zionist Review*, June 1920, first page. As mentioned previously in the discussion of the CFC's position, certain Zionists, most notably Gaster, repeatedly maintained that Jews were Jewish, not English, by nationality. This, however, need not interfere with their rights and duties as British citizens or loyalty to the Crown. Gaster, "Judaism – a National Religion," in *Zionism and the Jewish Future by Various Writers*, edited by Harry Sacher (London: John Murray, 1916), 93–4.
221 Since 1905 the WZO headquarters had been located in Cologne and Berlin. After 1920 it was moved to 77 Great Russell Street, London, where it operated next door to the head offices of the EZF at No. 75 of the same street. Stephen Wendehorst, "Zionism in Britain and Germany: A Comparison," in *Two Nations: British and German Jews in Comparative Perspective*, edited by M. Brenner, R. Liedtke and D. Rechter (Tubingen: Mohr Siebeck, 1999), 201.
222 "Wanted a Zionist Salon," *Zionist Review*, May 1920, 7.
223 "French Propaganda," March 22, 1919, 51 and "England and Palestine," Jan. 26, 1917, 2. Both in *Palestine*.
224 "From Protectorate to Autonomous Dominion," BPC report, no date but written between Jan. 1917 and April 1920, file Z3/89, CZA. The EZF corresponded and shared materials with Zionist leaders in Montreal, Canada; Auckland, New Zealand; Sydney and Melbourne, Australia. "British Empire," n.d. but with 1917 materials Z4\40601; letter to H.J. Morgenstern, Dec. 1918, Z4\40564; "A Happy and Prosperous New Year to the Jewish Nation," KK1\33 and A150\16; correspondence between Mr Marks and Mr Lewis, 1917, Z4\4060. All in CZA.
225 Quoted in Sokolow, *History of Zionism*, 102.

226 The reference to "intellectual power" and "fairy tale" is from "Zionism and the Entente," *Palestine*, April 20, 1918, 85.

227 Over twenty organizations participated in this mass meeting, and a telegram was sent to 10 Downing Street. Under section "Demonstration in Egypt," in *Great Britain, Palestine, and the Jews: Jewry's Celebration of its National Charter*, 55–6 (1918). In the EZF collections of the CZA but also widely available.

228 The term "national liberty" is repeated in Zionist materials and appears, for example, in Sokolow (quoting Gaster), *History of Zionism*, 62. "A Russian Revolution," *Palestine*, March 24, 1917, 71, explains how political equality of all citizens under the new regime in no way diminished the Zionist movement in Russia, as the rights of the individual and the rights of a people are not one and the same, and the "restoration of the Jewish nation" remained every bit as much of a necessity. "Labour, the Pope, and Palestine," *Palestine*, Aug. 18, 1917, relates that the Labour Party understands that the "Jewish problem" is not limited to liberating "the oppressed individual Jew" but also includes liberating the "oppressed Jewish nationality."

229 "Zionists and the Entente," *Palestine*, Oct. 17, 1917, 112. The reference does not mention specifically the defence of Belgian neutrality but, rather, implies it by referring to Britain's entry into the First World War in order to defend the rights of small nations.

230 For demonstrating "spiritual force" as opposed to the vulgar pursuit of wealth, "Immediate Work in Palestine," *Palestine*, Jan. 19, 1918, 222. Also "The Palestine Committee," *Palestine*, March 16, 1918, first page. The "The Settlement of Syria," *Palestine*, Nov. 1, 1919, 92, comments that while liberal-minded people are sometimes cold to Zionism, they shouldn't be, for restoring the Jews to Palestine is a great liberal ideal in that it involves "righting the oldest of national wrongs."

231 "Stockholm: Its Significance," *Palestine*, Aug. 11, 1917, 20.

232 For opposition to Zionism in the form of Palestinian identity see Rashid Khalidi, *Palestinian Identity: The Construction of Modern National Consciousness* (New York: Columbia University Press, 1997). The objections of Wolf, the CFC and Curzon are discussed previously in this chapter.

233 Occasionally the Armenians were included in this discussion: during a demonstration supporting the Balfour Declaration, participants spoke of how British statesmen would preside over cordial relations between Arabs, Jews and Armenians, each of whom would have their own nation in the Middle East, "The Great Demonstration," Dec. 8, 1917; that a Jewish Palestine, Arabia, and Armenia together would serve to protect British India, "Damascus and Baku by a Student of the War," Aug. 24, 1918, 18; and the idea that Jews, Arabs and Armenians are all oppressed peoples in need of their own independent state, "The Commission," May 17, 1919, 120. All in *Palestine*.

234 Quoted in "Zionist Policy," *Palestine*, Jan. 31, 1920, 195. Also cited in MacMillan, *Paris 1919*, 418.

235 This argument is put forth in "Jews and Arabs II," *Zionist Review*, Jan. 1920, 139–41.

236 "Jews and Arabs," *Palestine*, March 24, 1917, 69. As Weizmann explained in the previously mentioned speech, Jewish immigrants would not "go into the country like Junkers," a reference to the expansionist and militaristic Prussian aristocracy, but instead move to deserted or unoccupied areas. "Zionist Policy," *Palestine*, Jan. 31, 1920, 195. Along the same lines, Jewish expansion into Palestine had brought progress to the country overall and therefore benefited the Arab inhabitants "morally, intellectually, and materially." "The non-Jews of Palestine," *Zionist Review*, Dec. 1917, 124. Herzl too had presented the idea that a modern and progressive Jewish state would be beneficial to the Arab population of Palestine, liberating it from Ottoman feudalism. Stanislawski, *Zionism*, 26.

237 Sokolow quoted both Weizmann and Rothschild explaining, in response to the CFC's letter to *The Times*, that there would be no need for Jews to have special privileges at the expense of other races and nations in Palestine. Sokolow, *History of Zionism*, 63.

238 "Palestine and the Colonial Office," *Palestine*, Feb 1, 1919, 201–3.

239 Just as the Jews of the Middle Ages had "brought the torch of culture" to the West, so the Zionists would bring Western civilization to the East. Sokolow, *History of Zionism*, xlvi. "A 'Clearing-House of Ideas,'" *Palestine*, March 1, 1917, 48. Jewish Palestine as an example is from "The Jews and the Arabs," *Palestine*, March 17, 1917, 63.

240 *Great Britain, Palestine and the Jews*, 40.

241 "Jew and Arab," *Palestine*, March 24, 1917, 68 and "Jews and Palestine," *Palestine*, June 9, 1917, 157. Friendly relations were imagined between a new Jewish Palestine with its capital in Jerusalem and a new Arab state with its capital perhaps in Damascus or Baghdad in "Baghdad and Jerusalem," July 28, 1917, 7 and "The Victory and After," Oct. 12, 1918, 74. Both in *Palestine*.

242 "Baghdad and Jerusalem," *Palestine*, July 28, 1917, 7.

243 Related in *Great Britain, Palestine and the Jews*, 40.

244 Lieshout, *Britain and the Arab Middle East*, 422–3, quotation at p. 423.

245 The reference to "creative imagination" is from "The Anniversary of the British Declaration," Nov. 30, 1918, 133 and the reference to "romance" is from "Palestine and the Colonial Office," Feb 1, 1919, 203. Both in *Palestine*.

246 H. Sidebotham; the reference to the Arab Caliphates is from *Palestine*, April 13, 1918, 78, and the Semitic empires of the ancient world is from his *England and Palestine*, 238.

247 JNFCE report, April 1914, KKL1/38, CZA. By 1918, the JNFCE had established a separate "pioneer fund" in addition to the land fund for the purpose of putting Jewish pioneers or settlers in newly acquired territories. As committee members explained, it would put "Jewish national labour on Jewish national soil." JNFCE report, April 1918, KKL1/42, CZA. Four years later the EZF established a Palestine Committee for the purpose of advising Jews considering settling in Palestine and those interested in investing "money in ways that assist the colonisation of that country by Jews." EZF pamphlet "What is Zionism?" 3–4, n.d. but with 1922 documents, DD1\45151, CZA.

248 The Zionist Organisation, *Great Britain, Palestine and the Jews: Jewry's Celebration of Its National Charter* (London, 1918), 72.
249 With regard to WZO, Berkowitz notes that "one is hard pressed to find a picture of an Arab laborer", *Zionist Culture*, 149. The same is true with regard to the EZF materials that I have examined during this period, both in England and in Israel.
250 Document beginning "Mr. Sokolow sent ...," Oct. 1918, Z4/40620, CZA. Sokolow was a naturalized British citizen.
251 Zionist Organisation, *Great Britain, Palestine and the Jews*, 51.
252 Report by Lawrence and quoted in Neil Faulkner, *Lawrence of Arabia's War: The Arabs, The British and the Remaking of the Middle East in WWI* (New Haven, CT: Yale University Press, 2016), 402. Weizmann was the head of the Zionist Commission to Palestine. That commission sought, with the help of what it referred to as the "civilised" British state, to enlarge the colonies in Palestine and increase the number of Jewish settlers within them. EZF bulletin No. 1, "The Zionist Commission in Palestine" June 1918 and "The Zionist Preparation Fund: Aims and Objects of the Palestine Commission Explained," n.d. with 1918 materials, both in Z4/40621, CZA. It also sought to "lay the foundations and to commence the superstructure of a Jewish Palestine." "The Palestine Commission," *Palestine*, March 16, 1918, 42. Also see, *The Zionist Commission in Palestine. Aims and Objects Explained* (London: Zionist Organisation, 1918).
253 "Semitic race" is mentioned in, for example, "The Kinship of Jews and Arabs," *Palestine*, April 28, 1917, 110.
254 This incident is related in MacMillan, *Paris 1919*, 416 and in Eugene Rogan, *The Fall of the Ottomans: The Great War in the Middle East* (New York: Basic Books, 2015), 349.
255 As a result of the Balfour Declaration they went from being "passive" contributors to the cause, with little appreciation for its political aspects, to understanding the Zionist movement as of "utmost significance to every Jewess as well as every Jew." "The Women's Part: History of the WIZO," 1926LMA/4175/02/01/017.
256 Rebecca Sieff, "WIZO The Beginnings," in the booklet entitled "WIZO: Ten Years of WIZO Endeavor and Achievement," 12, X041/075 LMA/4175/02/01/006. "Report by Mrs. Goodman" (1921), LMA 4175/02/01/017. The secondary or supportive role played by women in the EZF, despite constitutional equality, reflected that of the WZO more generally in that while female members of WZO had voting rights (Penslar, "Is Zionism a Colonial Movement?," 288), Zionism in Europe was self-consciously and predominantly male centred (Berkowitz, *Western Jewry*, 177).
257 "Federation of Women Zionists in the United Kingdom," Dec. 1918, X041/074 LMA/4175. Sieff served as President, Weizmann as Vice President and Goodman as Treasurer. This organization is referred to in contemporary documents as both the "Federation of Women Zionists in the United Kingdom" and "The Federation of Women Zionists of Great Britain and Ireland." In this study, it is referred to as simply the Federation of Women Zionists.

258 Report of the Conference of the FWZ, Jan. 1919, words spoken by Mrs Model, first page, X041/074/LMA/4175, LMA.
259 The photograph was taken just after the end of the First World War and is housed in PD 30 10/79, MJM.
260 For more on the history of female anti-slavery activism see Clare Midgley, *Women Against Slavery, the British Campaigns, 1780–1870* (Routledge: London and New York, 1992).
261 Report on the Jewell Committee meeting, X041/073 LMA/4175/01, LMA.
262 "Women's Societies Affiliated to the F.W.Z.," with 1919 materials. Glasgow and Liverpool had a "Young Girls Zionist League" and a "Young Ladies Zionist Society" in addition to women's Zionist organizations. X041/074/LMA/4175/1/3/3–4, 1/1/5. Goodman, *Zionism, 1899–1949*, 47, notes that by 1929 the FWZ had thirty-seven affiliated bodies. Most likely there were more, given that Goodman only reported the existence of twelve societies in 1919, fewer than the FWZ records show.
263 From the organization's constitution as outlined at the conference of Jan. 12, 1919.
264 Rosalie Gassman-Sherr, *The Story of the Federation of Women Zionists of Great Britain and Ireland, 1918–1968* (FWZ and Deaner Printers, 1968), 18.
265 That organization combined the culture and networks of central European female feminist and social service organizations with the goals of Zionism. Gassman-Sherr, *Story of the Federation*, 14–15; "FWZ of the UK Second Annual Conference," 1920. LMA/4175/2/1/7; and Berkowitz, *Western Jewry*, 179–1.
266 Gassman-Sherr, *Story of the Federation*, 7–12. Simon Marks and Israel Sieff brought the growing resources of the department store Marks and Spencer into Weizmann's camp in 1913. Black "A Typological Study," 30 and "The Zionist Federation Celebrates 100 Years of Zionism," Bill Williams Collection, Centre for Jewish Studies, University of Manchester.
267 Gassman-Sherr, *Story of the Federation*, 7.
268 Berkowitz, *Western Jewry*, 183.
269 The quotation is from Gassman-Sherr, *Story of the Federation*, 17. Gassman-Sherr notes that with the establishment of WIZO, the FWZ became a branch of its brainchild. WIZO would give support to thousands of women and children and mobilize Jewish women in over fifty countries over the course of the following decades. *Story of the Federation*, 19, 21. For more on the work and impact of Rebecca Sieff and WIZO, both before and after the creation of the State of Israel, see Beth Hatefutsoth, *Speaking for Women: Rebecca Sieff and the WIZO Movement* (Tel Aviv: The Nahum Goldmann Museum of the Jewish Diaspora, 1990), Bill Williams Collection.
270 Gassman-Sherr, *Story of the Federation*, 17 and "The History of WIZO," no author, written in the 1930s, LMA/4175/02/01/017.
271 Berkowitz, *Western Jewry*, 180–1. Berkowitz also notes that the Jewish women's organization the Jüdischer Frauenbund, created in Germany in 1904, provided a model for female Zionists in terms of networking activities and combining political, feminist and social welfare concerns. *Western Jewry*, 179.

272 "The History of WIZO," no author, written in the 1930s, LMA/4175/02/01/017.
273 Report of work in Palestine given by Edith Eder at the fourth annual conference of the FWZ, July 23, 1922, LMA/4175/02/01/017. This report also appears in *Addresses Delivered on the Occasion of the Fourth Annual Conference of the Federation of Women Zionists by Mrs. Paul [Romana] Goodman, Dr. Vera Weizmann, and Mrs. Edith Eder* (London: WIZO, 1922). Quotations and picture at pp. 13–14. *Chaluzoth* is also spelled, or transliterated, as *Haluzoth*. For scholarship on the struggle of Jewish women to define themselves as pioneer-labourers as well as wives and mothers in Mandate Palestine, see Deborah Bernstein, *Pioneers and Homemakers: Jewish Women in pre-State Israel* (Albany, NY: SUNY Press, 1992).
274 Bernstein, *Pioneers and Homemakers*, quotations at pp. 13–14.
275 Report of work in Palestine given by Edith Eder at the fourth annual conference of the FWZ, July 23, 1922, LMA/4175/02/01/017, 17–18, quotation at p. 18.
276 "Sacred spaces" is from FWZ, July 1920, X041/074/LMA/4175 and inventing beautiful traditions is from Eder report of work in Palestine, 16.
277 International Conference convened by the FWZ, July 1920, X041/074/LMA/4175.
278 Implied in Mrs Model's Report of the Conference of the FWZ, Jan. 1919, X041/074/LMA/4175. Also, Berkowitz, *Western Jewry*, 182 and 193, explains that WIZO work and representations of it played an important role in asserting the importance of social conscience in Zionism.
279 Memo from WIZO to the Central Council of the Zionist Organisation, 8, X041/074/LMA/4175.
280 Both are cited in Paula Hyman, *Gender and Assimilation in Modern Jewish History: The Roles and Representations of Women* (Seattle: University of Washington Press, 1995), 143–4, 146, quotations at pp. 149–50. Sokolow's pamphlet, "Idishe froy", was published by the EZF in 1917 in Yiddish.
281 Berkowitz, *Western Jewry*, 185.
282 The FWZ of the United Kingdom report, second conference, 4175/02/01/017, LMA. Rebecca Sieff focused on improving working conditions for women in England, including ensuring equal opportunities to pursue a career in the trades and professions and guaranteeing equal pay for equal work. Both she and Romana Goodman were suffragists. Goodman, whose activities always had been "somewhat coloured by a feminist outlook," dedicated herself to that cause with "great ardour." Reference to Sieff in Gassman-Sherr, *Story of the Federation*, 8 and Goodman in Sieff's "WIZO The Beginnings," in "WIZO Ten Years of Endeavor and Achievement," 0X041/075/LMA/4175/02/01/006–0012, LMA.
283 Memo of the Women's International Zionist Organization to the central council of the Zionist Organisation, 8, XO41/074 LMA/4175, no date. This document seems to have been from 1920 or 1921, based on its content and location in the archives. The original is underlined for emphasis.

284 Berkowitz, *Zionist Culture*, purification through soil, 37; reference to Nordau on space, 107; "quietly," 142; and chapter 4, "Zionist Heroes and New Men," 99–118.
285 Report of work in Palestine given by Mrs Eder at the fourth annual conference of the FWZ, July 23, 1922, LMA/4175/02/01/017.
286 Gerald M. Berg "Zionism's Gender: Hannah Meisel and the Founding of the Agricultural Schools for Young Women," *Israel Studies*, Vol. 6, No. 3 (Fall 2001), 135–65. Reference to "muscle Jews" and "muscle Jewesses" at pp. 143–4; new interest in agricultural settlement, p. 145; gender equality though manliness, p. 148; and discussion of conflicts between Meisel and WIZO, pp. 154–6. See also, Margalit Shilo, "The Women's Farm at Kinneret, 1911–17: A Solution to the Problem of the Working Women in the Second Aliyah," *Jerusalem Cathedra* (1981), 246–83.
287 Samuel Tolkowsky, *The Jewish Colonisation in Palestine: Its History and Its Prospects* (London: Zionist Organisation, 1918), 19.
288 These wooden books are kept in a separate box, but with the other contemporary FWZ/WIZO materials, 4175/3/3/4, LMA.
289 While WIZO did not grant me permission to reproduce this image, it is available in the LMA: Hermon, wooden book 1, LMA/4175/3/3/4. "Monarch-of-all-I survey" in the imperial context is discussed by Mary Louise Pratt, *Imperial Eyes: Travel Writing and Transculturation* (New York: Routledge, 1992), 197.
290 Weizmann to Dorothy de Rothschild, 12 Nov. 1916, quoted in Lieshout, *Britain and Arab Middle East*, 198.
291 Cesarani, *The Making of Modern Anglo-Jewry*, 1.
292 Stanislawski, *Zionism*, 44; Berkowitz, *Western Jewry*, 26, 32.
293 The pivotal role of Anglo-Jewry is related by Cesarani in "One Hundred Years." The reference to Mandatory Palestine is from Endelman, *Jews in Britain*, 219.
294 "Report given by Mr. Marks, Secretary of the Zionist Organization, London Bureau at the Special Conference of the English Zionist Federation of November 3rd," 1918, Z4\40564, CZA. Also, Black notes that contributions to the organization increased from just over £500 in 1916 to just over £120,000 in 1918, although he suspects some inflation in the numbers. Black, "A Typological Study," 35. While the City of London had always been a critical financial centre for the Zionist movement, by 1918 it had become a "clearing house" for funds from throughout the world, including China, Europe, Russia and the United States, necessitating the hire of advisors trained in English business and commercial methods. Mr Marks' report, n.d. with 1918 documents and after Balfour, Z4\40564 and "English Zionist Federation Report of the Palestine Committee," n.d. with 1919 documents, Z4\40574, both in CZA. In addition, by 1918 "every branch" of Zionist work conducted from the new Zionist Bureau in Piccadilly, London, received "generous assistance" from the British government. "The London Bureau Its Origins and Work," Z4/40252, CZA.
295 It grew from 4,000 to 30,000 members, although Black, "A Typological Study," 35, notes the possibility that these numbers could be inflated. Goodman, *Zionism, 1899–1929*, 42, relates that while the EZF had twenty-three London

constituents and thirty-eight in the provinces in 1917, by 1921 the membership had expanded to about 234 affiliated bodies and a membership of 30,000.

296 "The Zionist Preparation Fund: Aims and objects of the Palestine Commission Explained," with 1918 documents, Z4/40621. Reference is made to the Allied recognition in this document.

297 This decrease was the result of policies to expel Russian and other Jews who had immigrated to that region but refused Ottoman citizenship, the deportation of Zionist leaders, and the decline in population more generally due to famine and disease. Thompson, "Moving Zionism to Asia," 318.

298 Roberto Mazza, "'We Will Treat You Like the Armenians': Djemal Pasha, Zionism and the Evacuation of Jaffa, April 1917," in *Syria in WWI*, edited by M. Talha Cicek (New York: Routledge, 2016), 87–106. Mazza makes a convincing argument that while Djemal/Cemal Pasha was anti-Zionist, he was not antisemitic as has been claimed. Palestinian opposition to Zionism was believed to be a contributing factor to his position as well. For the development of Palestinian opposition to Zionism see Neville Mandel, *The Arabs and Zionism before WWI* (Berkeley: University of California Press, 1976) and, more recently, Khalidi, *Palestinian Identity*.

299 Penslar, "Is Zionism a Colonial Movement?" quotation and reference at p. 279. Here Penslar footnotes Segev, *One Palestine Complete* and the essays in part 2 of Nachum Gross's collected works, *Lo'al ha-ruah levadah: 'iyunim ba-historiyah ha-kalkalit shel eretz-yisra'el ba-'et ha-hadashah* (Jerusalem: Magnes and Yad Ben-Zvi, 1999). Thompson, "Moving Zionism to Asia," 321, notes that by 1922 the Zionists had expanded their areas of settlement, creating a "separate and superior society" linked directly to the metropole.

300 The original document, in Hebrew, remains in Tel Aviv. However, both that text and the English translation are widely available.

301 Endelman, *Jews of Britain*, 216; Cesarani, "One Hundred Years," 42–3; Cohen, *English Zionists*, 282.

302 Newman, *The Board of Deputies of British Jews*, 28; Endelman, *Jews of Britain*, 195; Black, "A Typological Study," 23.

303 The terms "surrogate and shibboleth" are from Cesarani, "The Transformation," 140. Cesarani uses *haute and petite bourgeoisie* to describe this class conflict in "One Hundred Years," 42. After 1919, the BDBJ itself became more democratic, admitting female deputies and deputies representing secular societies and organizations. Newman, *The Board of Deputies of British Jews*, 22. See also Cesarani's, "A Funny Thing Happened on the Way to the Suburbs: Social Change in Anglo-Jewry between the Wars, 1914–1945," *Jewish Culture and History*, Vol. 1, No. 1 (1998), 5–26.

304 Endelman, *Jews in Britain*, 217. For more on social antisemitism see pp. 196–200.

305 Berkowitz, *Western Jewry*, 196.

306 Jewish communities not only in England but throughout the world shifted towards supporting Zionism, with anti-Zionists among them finding themselves in the minority as opposed to the majority. Stanislawski, *Zionism*, 54–5.

Conclusion: some comparisons, some reflections

Networks, trajectories and intersections

The previous chapters have shown how, as British expansion into the Middle East reached its apogee during the First World War, the movements examined, Bahá'í, the Woking Muslim Mission and Zionist, all intersected with that imperial state in ways that would have profound consequences for the future development of each.[1] It is worthwhile, then, to consider and compare briefly the trajectories of those movements and the networks that sustained them as they crossed commonly accepted boundaries between East and West and metropole and periphery, beginning with the Bahá'ís. During the latter part of the nineteenth century, the Bahá'ís had extensive networks in the Middle East, and to a lesser degree in Central and South Asia, yet only rarely did they encounter British people or territories, and when they did, contact was made in the peripheries, not the metropole of empire, in Egypt under the "veiled protectorate" and various urban centres in British India and Burma. By the early years of the twentieth century, however, the London artist Ethel Jenner Rosenberg began to visit the Bahá'í leader, 'Abdu'l-Bahá, in Ottoman Acre. Soon Bahá'í communities developed in the Greater London and Manchester areas, and by the time he visited Great Britain in 1911, and again in 1912–13, 'Abdu'l-Bahá had enough followers in England to host him and arrange numerous interviews and speaking engagements. One admirer who assisted him in London, Wellesley Tudor Pole, later served as an intelligence officer during the First World War and provided the critical connection between the vulnerable Bahá'í community in Palestine and the British army in 1918. As a result of this new link, 'Abdu'l-Bahá became a valued and trusted advisor to the British during the Mandate period, a role which then enabled him to establish the Bahá'í World Centre in Haifa, laying the foundation for the development of a new world religion.

Like the Bahá'í networks of the late nineteenth and early twentieth centuries, those associated with political Zionism during that same period originated and began to develop outside of the British Empire before extending into the metropole via English people who embraced the cause. Interestingly, Jewish Zionist and Bahá'í farmers, both of whom were living in exile and had fled persecution – in the case of the former in Russia and Eastern Europe and in the case of the latter in Iran – settled not far from one another in the Jordan Valley. In 1899, the same year that Ethel Jenner Rosenberg became the first English Bahá'í living in England, eleven British Jews attended the WZO Congress in Basel and then established their own branch of that body in London, the EZF. In both cases, London and Manchester became important centres of community activity and organization, and supporters of both movements worked to spread their new-found beliefs in England and elsewhere in the British Isles. At the same time, they maintained connections with others of like mind abroad, in Europe and the Middle East. Finally, as troops advanced into Ottoman Palestine in 1917–18, thereby extending the British imperial reach into a part of the Middle East of central importance both to the Zionists and the Bahá'ís of the world, the metropole-based advocates of each cause became linch-pins within their respective movements, using their contacts at Whitehall to secure much-needed support in the region.

Despite these similarities, the WZO members and the Bahá'ís were connected neither practically nor ideologically. They remained two distinct and separate movements comprised of different people who rarely, if ever, interacted with one another. In terms of their beliefs and goals, the two hardly could have been more incompatible, for while political Zionism was a nationalist movement, Bahá'u'lláh and 'Abdu'l-Bahá taught that national boundaries were dangerous illusions, pitting human beings against one another and acting as barriers to the realization of the unity of humankind. Therefore, the tendency of both Bahá'í and Zionist networks to develop in comparable ways and sometimes along seemingly parallel trajectories in England and the Middle East should be understood not as indicative of an alliance or affinity between the two but, rather, as a reflection of larger imperial and global processes, economic and political, as well as of the importance of Palestine to each movement.

Bahá'í and WMM leaders both expressed their misgivings about the creation of a Jewish state in Palestine, while at the same time welcoming Jewish people into their respective universalist movements. Likewise, even though individuals from Jewish backgrounds could become Bahá'ís or Muslims, those who lived in England and mobilized themselves publicly around the Zionist debates during the early twentieth century showed no interest in doing either. 'Abdu'l-Bahá spoke of that nationalist movement with diplomacy and caution, stating that the "world of humanity owes to the Jews a homestead of their own," while also warning those "responsible for kindling the flame in this new hearth" to "see to it that the heat warms and does not scorch both friends and neighbours alike."[2] WMM members tended to be more critical of Zionism, but during the war years expressed opposition to it as individuals and through other organizations, not as a body.

The Bahá'ís and the WMM originated in the nineteenth century and within Perso-Islamic cultural traditions.[3] Both renounced militancy, welcomed people from all backgrounds and regarded all of the major world religions, including Buddhism and Hinduism, as coming from the same God and therefore expressing spiritual truth. Yet, despite having remarkable similarities, the two movements came into being and developed separately. The early Bahá'í leaders were born in Tehran in north-central Iran, were exiled to the Ottoman Empire and then spent decades imprisoned in Acre on the Mediterranean coast. Their followers had to rely upon personal relationships, travel by foot and the hand-carrying of letters to keep in contact with them and with one another. In contrast, the first Muslim missionaries to arrive in Woking, England came from the Lahore area in the Punjab region of British India; they were English educated, well connected and prepared to use the cultural, technological and political apparatus of that empire to serve their mission. Despite the occasional crossing of paths, the Bahá'ís and supporters of the WMM had little or no contact with or understanding of each other, and there is no evidence of cross-conversion between the two.[4]

The Bahá'í leader, 'Abdu'l-Bahá, happened to be visiting England at the same time that the WMM was making its debut in that country. In January 1913, just as Kamal-ud-Din was launching an organization to spread his faith in the Occident, sixty-eight-year-old 'Abdu'l-Bahá', who had spent most of his life as a prisoner of conscience in Acre, was taking his second and final tour of the West in order to share the teachings of his father, Bahá'u'lláh, a name which means "the glory of God" in Arabic. Despite having only a vague understanding of each other and the movement that the other led, the two men met at an event celebrating the opening of the Shah Jahan mosque, where the new Muslim mission was based. There, in the small town of Woking, not far from London, 'Abdu'l-Bahá received hospitality and even delivered an address to the crowd on the threshold of that building. The leaders of the two movements were drawn together in part because of their shared Islamic heritage and because each held broad and inclusive views with regard to religion, which explains their presence at a mosque and tolerance of each other. Yet the fact that they met at that particular mosque in Woking can be explained only by the pull of the Greater London area as a metropolitan and imperial centre.[5]

Unlike the networks of the Bahá'ís and Zionists, which first came into being outside of the British Empire and became interlaced with those of that state only as its authority expanded into Palestine, WMM networks emerged in the context of the Raj. Still, it was not until after the outbreak of the First World War that the new relationship between that mission and the British state developed, which helped the fledgling organization to weather a turbulent and difficult period and, in the process, establish itself upon a firm foundation in the Greater London area. This wartime link between state and mission began in late 1914–15, when the imam of the Shah Jahan mosque at the time, Sadr-ud-Din, started meeting with representatives from the India and War Offices in order to ensure that the remains of British Muslim soldiers who had died as a result of fighting in France would be transported to Woking to receive proper funeral and burial services according to Islamic rites. As the WMM became increasingly established over the course of the war, its founders were able to create new networks that extended more deeply into English society, while at the same time maintaining previous ones with their supporters in India. After the war, mission leaders would go on to extend missionary activities, publications and networks into Europe.

Considering the metropole–periphery dynamic in relation to the networks of each of the movements examined in this study as they wove in and out of the British Empire and between East and West complicates the common assumption that, in the context of imperialism, ideas, practices and cultural models developed in the metropole and then emanated in various, usually diminishing, degrees from the central to the more peripheral regions and then from there onto the outskirts or borderlands. Bahá'í and Zionist beliefs travelled from outside of the empire to the metropole, and later informed action in Palestine as British borders expanded to include it, while, conversely, the message of the WMM developed in the peripheries of colonial India, was disseminated in the Greater London area and spread to Europe beyond the realm of His Majesty's government. In each case the metropole was not the place of origin for the core or canonical ideologies of the movements in question but, rather, and significantly, served as the international nexus where people from different, and often otherwise unconnected, parts of the world were able to meet, and therefore where equally diverse ideas could make their way from one area of the periphery to another, from periphery to outside the empire and vice versa.[6]

Also unexpected or not commonly found in studies involving the British Empire and movements and networks within it are connections to Europe, especially Germany. After all, that country was far from being a periphery but was, rather, a formidable imperial power in its own right, locked in a bitter struggle with its British rival during the First World War. Yet all three of the movements in question had contacts and interests in Europe before and/or after the war, and Germany had particular significance for

Baháʼís, members of the EZF and founders of the WMM, even though each movement also had soldiers fighting on the side of the Allies. In addition to the creation of the Berlin Muslim Mission, based on the Woking model, after the war, members of the EZF relied upon like-minded organizations in both Berlin and Cologne, while the Stuttgart area surpassed London, Manchester and Paris as an early twentieth-century Baháʼí hub.[7] Any real examination or analysis of the continental branches of these movements falls outside the scope of this study. However, their very existence reminds us that, in addition to its role as the metropole of a vast global empire, England and major cities within it were not unconnected to Europe, and in a number of respects could be considered a part of it. Therefore it is not surprising that a Europe-wide movement like Zionism would find sympathetic supporters in England, or that those who embraced a religious, philosophical system seeking to unite the peoples of the East with those of the West, as in the case of the Baháʼís and the Woking Muslim missionaries, would endeavour to spread their beliefs on both sides of sea and channel.

Perhaps less surprising, although also worthy of note, is the importance of Haifa for all three movements and for the British Empire. By 1911, the year that EZF lecturers began to travel around the British Isles showing film images of Haifa and talking to audiences about its importance with regard to their nationalist movement, ʻAbduʼl-Bahá had already begun to establish the Baháʼí spiritual and administrative centre on the slopes of Mount Carmel, overlooking the port town, and was preparing his own trip to Great Britain. Within ten years the British government would begin efforts to turn Haifa into a centre of industry and a major Mediterranean port, measures which Jewish Zionist leaders in England and ʻAbduʼl-Bahá in Palestine both saw as having great positive potential. Interestingly, Baháʼís, Ahmadiyya Muslims from India and Jewish Zionists would all live in close proximity to one another on Mount Carmel in the city of Haifa by the 1920s.[8]

As with Germany, the developments on Mount Carmel in the 1920s go beyond the bounds of this study. Yet, like the book as a whole, those examples speak to the complex ways that people and movements, already characterized by a hybridity between Occident and Orient both culturally and practically, could intersect with an equally hybridized empire during a period when the British state had reached the height of its involvement in the Middle East; for as His Majesty's government attempted to counter the Ottoman sultan's call to jihad during the First World War, both by conquest in that region and by gaining legitimacy from Muslim authorities, its centuries-old process of eastward expansion into Islamic lands continued. British interests and influence in those parts of the world had begun gradually in the late sixteenth and early seventeenth centuries, with the first trade agreements and diplomatic missions, and by the early twentieth century Britain's imperial networks had extended into Persian or Iranian, Ottoman and former Mughal territories, imposing themselves upon, becoming interwoven with or disrupting and then reconfiguring pre-existing networks.[9] The fact that Bahá'í, WMM and Zionist networks all interlaced with those of at least one of the aforementioned Islamic empires and English society before becoming involved with those of officialdom reflects the hybridized nature of both the movements in question and the British imperial system more generally, which included Eastern peoples, beliefs and traditions, even as its dominant discourses reinforced Western or Anglo-centric assumptions.[10]

Some final thoughts

While the leaders of each of these movements, Bahá'í, WMM and Zionist, may have found it necessary to form relationships with representatives of the British government during the First World War period, none could be considered a victim of that state. Rather, all were intelligent, rational people who both found and created meaning in that larger imperial culture, making their intersections with it possible and allowing them to realize goals that were independent of and therefore capable of outlasting the empire itself. The Bahá'ís sought to spread the teachings of Bahá'u'lláh, which they succeeded in doing, becoming, over the course of the twentieth century, a major, independent religion with millions of followers around the world. The founders of the WMM strove to invigorate Islam and bring it to the people of the Occident. By maintaining their base in the Greater London area during the First World War, the WMM emerged from that conflict able to continue its work in Great Britain and contribute to the development of the first ever Europe-wide Muslim networks, thereby helping to initiate what would become a new era in Western–Muslim relations. Finally, the Zionist dream of creating a sovereign Jewish state was realized the day following the end of the British Mandate over Palestine, May 14, 1948, with the declaration of the independent State of Israel and its international recognition soon afterwards. Yet, interestingly and significantly, while the historical circumstances and actors may have changed, modern, twenty-first-century debates about Israel revolve around many of the very same issues as did those of the Zionist and anti-Zionist Jews in England during the early twentieth century: the relationship between nation and ethnicity; liberal values, imperialism and antisemitism.

One of the most important aspects of British imperial culture that became meaningful for the Bahá'í, Muslim and Jewish leaders discussed in this book was its diversity. For both the Bahá'ís and members of the WMM, the fact that the empire could bring together people from a variety of different backgrounds helped to illustrate the human capacity for transcending commonly accepted divisions such as those based on, for example, race, nation or religion. As an original theorist of globalization, 'Abdu'l-Bahá understood that empire as reflecting the interconnectedness of the modern world that already existed in reality, but still needed to be forged as an identity.[11] For Kamal-ud-Din the diversity of believers drawn to the imperial metropole, and as a result to events in Woking, provided a microcosm of the *ummah* and a demonstration of the unifying power of Islam.

Jews in England who mobilized themselves on both sides of the Zionist debate also valued the diversity in the British Empire because they saw it as evidence that Jews either already had or could make a place for themselves within it. According to the anti-Zionist position, Jewish people were one of a number of assimilative ethnicities in England and Great Britain more generally. Those among them who were religious could practise their faith as freely as could nonconformist Christians and others outside the Anglican Church. In addition, Jews would not need to become the majority in a British-controlled Palestine so as to create a global cultural centre there. As long as the region was governed according to liberal political and economic principles, they could achieve a kind of ascendancy through hard work and merit, as many already had done in England. Their efforts would contribute to the strength of the country as a whole, while at the same time allowing them to develop Jewish institutions and places of historical interest. Individual Jews, then, from all over the world, would be able to travel to what would become a flourishing centre of Jewish culture and return to their homes profoundly enriched by the experience.

On the Zionist side of the debate, the different peoples and nations within the British imperial system demonstrated that empire's ability to foster the development and eventual independence of a Jewish state in Palestine. Just as Canadians and Australians could participate in institutions of self-governance without compromising their allegiance to the Crown, so too could Jews in Palestine work towards the establishment of an independent Jewish state while remaining loyal British subjects. Criticisms that Zionism threatened the well-being of the non-Jewish Arabs who already lived there were countered with the proposal that under British auspices a new economic infrastructure could be developed capable of supporting both the existing population in Palestine and the influx of immigrants necessary to create a Jewish majority. The minority – primarily Christian and Muslim Arab – would then be able to live and prosper in a Jewish state just as those belonging to nations outside of England, such as the Jews or the Scots, did in that country. In addition, as the British most likely would gain administrative control over a large part of the post-war Middle East, that government could begin to build the foundation for an independent Arab state as well and, under British tutelage, the two nations could grow and flourish side by side in a spirit of Semitic solidarity, even ushering in a renaissance of Semitic civilization. It is important to note that while those discourses may have been inspiring to advocates of the Zionist cause in England, such a plan was not considered feasible by those with expertise and experience and in the region, nor did it have the support of the majority of the people who lived there.

As with diversity, liberalism – or at least certain aspects of it – had real meaning and value to the people in this study, Bahá'ís, Muslims and Jews. Religious freedom and tolerance remained important to all. The Bahá'ís respected democratic ideals to the extent that individual members became activists in the women's suffrage movement. 'Abdu'l-Bahá introduced that topic into conversations with British officials when they came to visit him in Palestine, and he encouraged the creation of feminist networks across the East–West divide. Leaders of the WMM, and especially those whose ideas appeared in that body's organ, the *Islamic Review*, focused on their constitutional rights as British subjects, maintaining their right to travel anywhere in the empire and teach their faith; to produce a Muslim press and print culture; and to criticize their government and its policies without having their loyalty questioned.

Jews in England on both sides of the Zionist debates understood their position as in line with British liberal values and traditions. The anti-Zionists, as represented by Lucien Wolf and the CFC, championed the principle of individual equality before the law regardless of race or religion as the key to Jewish emancipation both at home and abroad, for if Jews received any advantages or preferences in a British-controlled Palestine, they argued, even in terms of deciding who would emigrate to that country, those policies then would be used by antisemites to justify discrimination against Jews elsewhere, whether in England, Eastern Europe or Russia. Those in England on the Zionist side of the debate also expressed concern for Jews in Eastern Europe and Russia, but tended to understand human rights in collective rather than individual terms, presenting the argument that protecting small nations was a British liberal tradition and citing support for Greek independence in the early nineteenth century and commitment to Belgian neutrality in the early twentieth as evidence of it.

One interesting observation with regard to this project as a whole is that when I first embarked upon it I did not imagine that the First World War, or any other war for that matter, would assume a prominent place in the study. After all, my original intention was to explore the histories of three religious minorities in England – Bahá'ís, Muslims and Jews – and their ties to the Middle East. Likewise, while the historical characters who emerged from my archival research may have hoped to shape the world and its future, all presented ways of doing so that did not involve military conquest or armed conflict. Yet, despite a general disinclination towards violence, none could avoid the impact of the First World War, and the histories of each movement discussed, Bahá'í, WMM and Zionist, all were influenced by it in significant, even pivotal ways.

It is especially sobering to reflect upon the impact of war on the two universalist religious movements in the study, the Bahá'ís and the WMM, for while both rejected militant jihad and hoped to unite humankind in a spirit of love and fellowship, neither could avoid the conflict around them. The WMM established itself in England in 1913 with the intention of countering negative stereotypes that Westerners had about Islam, including the belief that it was the religion of the sword. However, with the outbreak of the First World War the following year, they soon discovered that continuing their work in England hinged upon their ability to provide religious services to Muslim soldiers and thus support the war effort. In addition, they began to incorporate Islamic teachings about war and discussion of Muhammad as the ideal soldier and general into their discourses in order to remain relevant to new and potential converts. 'Abdu'l-Bahá spoke of the need to end the arms race and establish lasting peace during his tours of the West in 1911 and again in 1912–13, yet after the outbreak of the First World War he and his community in Palestine found themselves in real danger and most likely wouldn't have survived had it not been for the occupation of Haifa by British forces in 1918. It seems that the ability to avoid war and its impact is, in and of itself, a form of privilege, one which none of the historical actors in this study was able to enjoy.

Notes

1 The war itself was simultaneously an apogee in the development and extension of the British global imperial system as well as the beginning of its decline, as is the case for European imperial systems more generally. Andrew Jarboe and Richard Fogarty (eds), *Empires in World War I: Shifting Frontiers and Imperial Dynamics in a Global Conflict* (London and New York: I.B. Tauris, 2014). This point is both reflected in the essays and noted by Fogarty in the Introduction, 8–9.
2 Wellesley Tudor Pole, *Writing on the Ground* (London: Neville Spearman, 1968), 158–9.
3 The Perso-Islamic context of the origins of the WMM is discussed in chapter 2 of Ron Geaves, *Islam and Britain: Muslim Mission in an Age of Empire* (London: Bloomsbury Academic, 2018), 15–30.

4 In addition to their meeting in Woking, described in the following paragraph, 'Abdu'l-Bahá and Kamal-ud-Din also met at the Conference of Religions in Paris in 1913. Both reference to that meeting and to the absence of evidence regarding cross-conversion is from L.C.G. Abdo, "Religion and Relevance: The Bahá'ís in Britain 1899–1930," PhD thesis, SOAS, University of London, 2003, 25 or section 1.9 "Religious Liberalism – Islam."

5 'Abdu'l-Bahá's visit to the Shah Jahan mosque is well documented and can be found in Bahá'í, WMM and Woking archives and publications.

6 Often applicable is the idea that colonial or imperial processes did not begin in the metropole and then expand outwards but, rather, that the categories of metropole and periphery were themselves created through these new global encounters. Nicholas B. Dirks, "Introduction: Colonialism and Culture," in *Colonialism and Culture*, edited by Nicholas B. Dirks (Ann Arbor: University of Michigan Press, 1992), 6.

7 Robert Stockman notes that in 1913 there were more Bahá'ís in Germany than in England and France combined. Stockman, "The Bahá'í Faith in England and Germany, 1900–1913," *World Order*, Vol. 27, No. 3 (Spring 1996), 38. Germany continued to be an important centre for Bahá'ís after the war as well, as documented in that community's archival materials and *SoW*.

8 The relationship between the WMM and the Ahmadiyya movement in India is explained in the beginning of chapter 3. For more on the Ahmadiyya Muslims in Haifa see Emanuela Del Re, "Approaching Conflict the Ahmadiyya Way: The Alternative Way to Conflict Resolution of the Ahmadiyya Community in Haifa/Israel," *Contemporary Islam*, Vol. 8, No. 2 (2014), 115–31. The importance of Haifa for Jewish Zionists and of Mount Carmel specifically as a place of Jewish settlement in the early twentieth century is related in Michael Berkowitz, *Western Jewry and the Zionist Project, 1914–1933* (Cambridge: Cambridge University Press, 2003), 110.

9 As Alan Lester has explained, in most cases "the webs structured by British colonial interests were either layered on top of pre-colonial networks, adding new levels of complexity, or those pre-colonial networks were fundamentally disrupted and restructured as a result of British interventions." Lester, "Imperial Circuits and Networks: Geographies of the British Empire," *History Compass*, Vol. 4, No. 1 (2006), 124–41, at p. 134. Along the same lines, Eric Wolf has stated, "Everywhere in this world of 1400, populations existed in interconnections ... If there were any isolated societies these were but temporary phenomena." Wolf, *Europe and the People without History* (Berkeley: University of California Press, 1982), 71. These ideas are as applicable to the study of British imperialism in the Eastern as well as the Western hemisphere.

10 This system brought together people with a variety of backgrounds and beliefs and from different continents, not unlike the Atlantic networks with which the British Empire also intertwined. The study of Atlantic world systems has been explored by a number of scholars in recent decades, such as David Armitage and Michael Braddick (eds), *The British Atlantic World, 1500–1800* (New York: Palgrave Macmillan, 2002); Paul Gilroy *The Black Atlantic: Modernity*

and Double Consciousness (Cambridge, MA: Harvard University Press, 1993); and D.W. Meinig, *The Shaping of America: A Geographical Perspective on 500 Years of History*, Vol. 1: *Atlantic America, 1492–1800* (New Haven, CT and London: Yale University Press, 1986).

11 This general understanding of 'Abdu'l-Bahá and the Bahá'í teachings are discussed throughout chapter 1 of this book. However, this specific description of 'Abdu'l-Bahá was first presented by Juan Cole in "Globalization and Religion in the thought of Abdu'l-Bahá," in *Bahá'í and Globalisation*, edited by Margit Warburg, Annika Hvithamar and Morten Warmind (Denmark: Aarhus University Press, 2005), 58 and 68.

Index

Abbas Effendi 25–28
'Abdu'l-Bahá 68–71, 233, 234, 239, 241
   in Egypt 50–51
   in Great Britain 21–22, 37–50,
      53–58, 66–67, 98, 235
   in Palestine 1, 7–8, 10, 12–13, 21, 25–28,
      30–36, 41, 58–66, 237, 240
   knighting ceremony 61
Abbas Ali Baig 107, 117
Abdo, L.C.G. 75, 86, 242
   see also Osborn, Lil
'Abduh, Muhammad 27
abolition 9
   abolitionist 38, 105, 192
   see also slavery
Abrahamic 28, 101
   see also Bahá'í; Christian; Jew; Muslim
Abramsky, Chimen 214
Abu-Sinan 58, 83, 86
Acre 16, 24, 26–36, 39, 45, 48, 49, 58,
      64–66, 235
   see also Palestine
Adler, Herman 153
Adler, Nathan 149
Adrianople 23
   see also Edirne
Afaqi, Sabir 79
Africa 54, 98, 99, 105, 106, 110, 153, 180,
      187
   East 156, 166, 184
   North 26
   "Scramble for Africa" 184
   South 62, 123, 185, 186
   sub-Saharan 30
   West 66, 112
   see also Egypt
al-Afghani, Jamal al-Din 110
Al-Arish 156, 166, 178

Aleppo 189
   see also Middle East
Afnan/s 26, 27, 51
agriculture 63
   Zionist initiatives 160, 161, 198
   see also farm; land; settlers
Ahad Ha'am 216
   see also Ginsberg, Asher
Ahmadiyya 93–97, 237
Ahmadi 95–99
   see also Islam
Al-Azhar university 25
   see also Cairo
alcohol 108, 124
Alderman, Geoffrey 203
Alexandria 50, 180, 187
   see also Egypt
Aliyah 166
   see also immigration
Allenby (General), Edmund 7, 8,
      59–63, 67, 177, 179, 180, 201
Alliance Israelite Universelle 151
alterity 12, 16, 102, 109, 150, 163, 180
   see also identification; Occidentalism;
      Orientalism; the Other
Amanat, Abbas 72, 79
Ameer Ali, Syed 110, 126
America/n 25, 30, 31, 35, 55, 180, 186,
Amin, Qasim 41
ancient 28, 42, 60, 107, 125, 163, 185, 186,
      189, 198
Ancient Israel 108, 158, 159, 161, 162, 178
Antiquity 181, 162
Anderson, Benedict 19
Anglican 38, 101, 149, 239
   see also Church of England
Anglicize 150, 185
   see also assimilation

Index

Anglo-Jew/ish/ry 14, 15, 17, 147–152, 156, 166, 167, 170, 186, 199–202
Anglo-Jewish Association (AJA) 5, 151
   see also Conjoint Foreign Committee
Anglo-Ottoman Society 110
Anglo-Palestine Company 155
Ansari, Humayun 73, 131, 132, 134–136, 138–140, 142, 143, 145, 146
antisemitism/antisemitic 3, 101, 150, 152, 155, 156, 177, 238
Arabia 98
   Arabian Desert 125
   Arabian Peninsula 107, 122, 127, 189
   new Arabia 189, 200
Arabs/Arabic 13, 14, 16, 24, 50, 52, 64, 65, 98, 100, 112, 116, 118, 121, 126, 127, 163–166, 173, 177, 180, 183, 185, 187–191, 199, 235, 239
Arab civilization 189, 190, 200
Arab culture 43, 164, 166
Arab state 14, 189, 200, 240
Arab Revolt 125–127
aristocratic/aristocracy 46, 50, 94, 100, 169
Armenia/ans 226, 232
Armitage, David 242
arms race 48, 52, 70 124, 241
Arnold, Matthew 56
art/ist 34, 38, 46, 170, 233
Ascendancy 5, 94, 95
   Jewish Ascendancy 166–170, 199, 239
Ashcraft, Richard 19
Ashkenazi 164
Asia 99, 105, 179, 182, 183, 233
   Central 26
   East 30
   South 25, 26, 49, 51, 52, 59, 66, 89, 110, 127, 180, 187
   South-east 25
   South-west 27
   see also Burma; India
   see also Jew
Asquith, Herbert 40, 122
assimilate/assimilation 3, 152, 170–171, 175, 185
assimilative ethnicity 3, 5, 14, 170, 172, 175, 239
   see also Anglicize
Austrian 152, 175, 176
   see also Vienna
Austro-Hungarian 153, 157
Aziz, Zahid 134, 141, 146

Báb, the 23, 26, 27
   see also Sayyid 'Ali Muhammad
Bábi 12, 23, 26, 28, 42, 98
babies 124, 195
Baghdad 189, 200, 227
   Bahá'ís in 23, 28
   Jews in 183, 223
Bahá'í
   communities 26, 39, 51, 233
   leader 7, 12, 28, 68, 233, 235
   persecution 8, 24, 26, 33, 35, 39, 50, 65, 69
   sympathizers 22, 58, 59
   teachings 29, 30–33, 36–38, 42, 44, 49, 52, 57, 62, 66, 71, 234, 238
Bahá'í News 35
Bahá'í World Centre 1, 10, 64, 233
   see also Haifa
Bahá'u'lláh 9, 12, 13, 21, 23, 32, 40, 43, 46, 48, 49, 62, 64–66, 69, 235
   exile in Acre 24–27
   at Bahji 27–28
   followers of 26, 31, 34, 51
   see also Mirza Husayn 'Ali Nuri 23
Bahji 27, 28, 55, 62
Bahiyyih Khánum 32, 34
Baku 26
Balfour (Lord), Arthur 7, 59, 60, 118, 156, 166, 174, 176–179, 188, 191, 196, 197, 200, 201
Balfour Declaration 2, 7, 128, 163, 172, 176, 179, 186, 187, 189, 191, 194, 200
Balkans 52, 105, 109, 130
Balyuzi, Hasan 72–74
bank/banker/banking 149, 150, 155, 170, 183, 184
Baring (Lord), Evelyn, Earl of Cromer 118, 156
Barney, Laura Clifford 31, 33, 45, 76
   see also Dreyfus-Barney 81, 82, 84
Bar-Yosef, Eitan 207, 208, 211, 224
Basel Program 154–155
Basra 127, 145
   see also Iraq
Bath 30, 46
Bausani, Alessandro 74
Bedouin 125, 167
Beirut 27, 183
Ben-Bassat, Yuval 73
Bentwich, Herbert 154, 207
Berg, Gerald M. 231

Berkowitz, Michael 194, 209–213, 219–222, 228–232, 242
Berlin Muslim Mission 92, 130, 237
Bermant, Chaim 203, 205, 212, 215, 219
Besant, Annie 38
Betta, Chiara 224
Bhabha, Homi 12, 20
Bible 39, 101, 102, 108, 122
  biblical 44, 176, 177
  Gospel 122
  Old Testament 107
Birmingham 151
  see also metropole
Birnbaum, Pierre 203
Black, Eugene 204, 205
Blomfields 41, 46, 63
Blomfield, Eleonore 40, 41
Blomfield (Lady), Sara Louisa 33, 34, 38, 40, 41, 44–47, 59, 67
  Parveen Khanum 41
Blomfield, Mary 40, 41, 46, 63
Board of Deputies of British Jews (BDBJ) 149, 151, 152, 167, 169–174
Bodenheimer, Dr. 190
Bohdanowicz, Arslan 139, 146
Bolles, May 31, 75
  see also Maxwell, May
Bombay 26, 51
  see also India
border 1, 4, 10, 23, 24, 51, 95, 112, 147, 162, 223, 236
borderland, 4, 5, 236
boundaries 2, 4, 10, 16, 22, 40, 41, 52, 66, 98, 174, 175, 189, 233, 234
boycott 192
Braddick, Michael 242
Breakwell, Thomas 75
Briand (Prime Minister), Aristide 174
Brighton 117
  see also Kitchener Indian Hospital
Bristol
  Bahá'ís in 48, 56, 59
  Zionists in 193
British culture 40, 70, 130
British East African Company 184
British East Africa Protectorate 156
British government 1, 8, 10, 11, 15, 52, 65, 67, 71, 90–92, 95, 114–116, 118, 127, 151, 156, 167, 169, 174–176, 179, 183, 193, 200, 237, 238
  see also Foreign Office; War Office; Whitehall

British Muslim Societies 98
British Palestine Committee (BPC) 6, 7, 13, 14, 148, 178, 182–189, 195, 199
Browne, Edward Granville 27, 28
Bryce (Lord Viscount), James 174
Buddhism 33, 102, 235
  Buddha 28, 101
Bulgaria 150
Burma 25, 26, 32, 233
  see also Mandalay; Raj
Byfleet 42

Cabrera, Miguel 18, 19
Cairo 12, 25, 50, 51, 59, 62, 64, 68
Caliph 92, 123–124
Caliphate 6, 114, 128, 190
Cambridge 27
Campbell (Reverend), Reginald 38
Cannadine, David 80
Cardiff 159, 193
  see also Wales
Caspian Sea 26
Catholic 28, 101, 108, 148, 150
  see also Christianity
Cecil (Lord), Robert 174, 186
  see also Foreign Secretary
Cemal/Djemal Pasha 8, 59, 201
Central Islamic Society 98, 110, 127, 128
Central Powers 4, 58, 92, 113, 115, 174, 176
  see also Bulgaria; First World War; Ottoman Empire
Cesarani, David 201, 203–206, 208, 213, 215, 221, 231–232
Chamberlain, Joseph 156
charter companies 167, 188
Cheyne, Thomas 44
children 27, 29, 30, 47, 123, 159, 193, 194, 195, 198
Chovevei Zion 149, 150, 152, 153, 155
Christ 48, 95, 108
Christianity 32–33, 36, 38, 55, 93, 95, 101–107, 121
Christian missionary 55, 91, 95, 96, 102–109, 128
Church of England 107, 108, 148, 150
  see also Anglican
Church of Scotland 39
citizen/citizenship 42, 61, 170, 175, 188–191
civilization 11, 14, 16, 29, 39, 42, 55, 64, 69, 70, 118, 121, 126, 174, 180, 182, 184, 185, 189, 190, 200, 240

civilized 54, 107, 166
Claff, Bertha 191–192
Clark, Michael 203–205
class 2, 29, 34, 48, 100, 159
   middle class 5, 47, 51, 66, 100, 149,
      150–154, 159, 164–165, 181, 184,
      192, 198, 199, 201–202
   privilege 46, 59
   working class 54, 153
Clayer, Nathalie 146
Cohen, Stuart 204–208, 215, 222, 232
Cole, Juan 53, 54, 73,74, 79, 243
collective rights 15, 148, 153, 157, 240
   national rights 15, 157, 240
colonial 51, 54, 95, 169, 175, 180, 182,
   236
   territories 55, 107
   postcolonial 3, 4, 147
Colonial Office (CO) 188
colony/colonies 95, 118, 149, 153, 156, 160,
   163–166, 181, 183–186, 190
commerce 63, 178, 182–184
communism 201
   socialism 100, 153
Conjoint Foreign Committee (CFC) 5, 14,
   147, 151, 167–175, 187–188, 199,
   240
constitutional/ism 10, 24, 27, 110, 111, 129,
   175, 240
conversion/converts 25, 42, 235, 241
   to Islam 89–91, 95–108, 111, 113, 114,
      116, 119, 120, 123, 128, 130
Cooper, Frederick 139
Cowen, Joseph 154
creativity 3–9, 13, 22, 37, 46, 66, 128, 157,
   165, 189, 191
Cromer (Lord) *see* Baring (Lord), Evelyn
cultural nationalism 170
Curzon (Lord), George, Viceroy of India
   118, 177, 187
Cyprus
   Bahá'ís in 28, 68

Damascus 63, 189, 200
   see also Arabia; Middle East
Dangerfield, George 78
Davidoff, Leonore 81
de Haas, Jacob 154, 212
Del Re, Emanuela 242
degeneration/degenerate 150, 166
Delhi 26
   see also India

democracy/democratic 3, 9, 12, 15, 16, 22,
   24, 25, 49, 53, 62, 69, 100, 157, 160,
   167, 174, 188, 201, 202
Derby (Lord) 151
   see also Foreign Secretary
diaspora
   Iranian (Bahá'í) 25, 26
   Jew of the 170
Dirks, Nicholas 242
Disraeli, Benjamin 150
discourse 11, 54, 70, 107, 109, 184, 195
   dominant 8, 22, 149, 238
   imperialist 13, 15, 63, 128, 166, 181, 185
   Islamic 91, 96, 102, 104, 115, 118, 121,
      126, 127, 241
   Orientalist 12, 15, 105, 106, 162
   Zionist 14, 160, 180, 189, 196–200, 240
diversity 1–4, 10, 14, 16, 17, 90, 91, 98, 99,
   114, 130, 147, 171, 185, 239, 240
donation 158, 159, 164, 192, 200
Dreyfus, Hippolyte 31

economy 48, 52, 169, 183, 192
Eder, Edith 194–195, 230–231
Edinburgh 39, 42, 56, 159
   see also Scotland
Edirne 23
   see also Adrianople
education 99
   Bahá'í 22, 29, 42
   educator 3, 42
   female 29, 42, 197
   Western 51, 63, 94
   Zionist 161, 193, 197
Edwardian 43, 66
Egypt 22, 59, 64, 69, 177, 182, 187, 233
   Bahá'ís in 25, 49–53, 65, 68, 70, 71
   veiled protectorate 25, 50, 234
   see also Alexandria; Cairo; Sinai
Egyptian Expeditionary Forces (EEF) 6–7,
   64, 127, 177, 178
Eid celebrations 99, 100, 117, 119
   Eid al-Adha 98, 101
   Eid al-Fitr 98, 106, 119
El-Arish 6
   see also Egypt
Elkins, Caroline 206
emigrant colonization 153
Endelman, Todd 18, 202, 204–208, 211,
   213–215, 219, 220, 231, 232
English culture 67, 171, 176
English language 96, 47

English Zionist Federation (EZF) 5, 7, 13–17, 147–148, 152–167, 176–181, 185–187, 191–201, 237
Enlightenment 40, 70, 111
Esperanto 112
Esslemont, John 55
ethnicity 2, 4, 5, 10, 16–17, 53, 100, 147, 150–151, 171, 199, 202, 238, 239
  ethnic strife 15
  multi-ethnic 153
  see also assimilative ethnicity
Europe 6, 9, 24, 40, 52, 62, 113, 121, 123, 166, 179, 236
  Central 155
  Eastern 15, 149, 162, 172, 173–174, 188, 197, 199, 234 240
  Western 92, 172
Ewence, Hannah 145

Faizi, A.Q. 73
Faris, Hani 205, 206
farm 193, 197
farmer 154, 160, 170, 197, 198, 234
  see also agriculture
Faulkner, Neil 18, 228
Federation of Women Zionists (FWZ) 7, 191–198
Feener, Michael 133
Feisal, Emir 190
Feldman, David 203–206, 208
feminism 39, 41
  feminist 7, 36, 37, 40–42, 63, 67, 118, 191, 196, 197, 240
First World War (WWI) 1, 4, 9, 11, 14, 16, 17, 233, 236, 238–241
  effects on Bahá'ís 8, 22, 29, 40, 50–52, 58–65, 67, 68, 70
  effects on Jews 147, 163, 166, 167, 172, 174, 178, 180, 183, 184, 187, 199–202
  effects on Muslims 5, 6, 13, 92, 93, 97, 109, 113–126, 128–130, 236, 237
flower 165, 198
flower day 179
  see also garden
Fraenkel, Josef 214
Fraser, Isabel 38, 71, 77–79, 81–83
Friedmann, Yohanan 133
Foreign Office (FO) 5, 7, 59, 109, 126, 127, 151, 166, 177
Foreign Secretary 7, 151, 166, 174, 176, 177

  see also Balfour (Lord), Arthur; Cecil (Lord), Robert; Derby (Lord)
Fogarty, Richard 142, 241
funds
  WMM 125
  WZO 124, 183
fundraising 156, 157, 158, 159, 160, 190
Fussell, Paul 85

Galilee 58
  Sea of 27, 193
Gandhi, Rajmohan 84
garden
  Bahá'í 37, 38, 43, 44, 64
  Jewish 165, 194
Garlington, William 73
Gassman-Sherr, Rosalie 229, 230
Gaster, Moses 154, 161, 170, 171, 185
  see also Zionism
Gaza 6, 7, 14, 127, 177–178
  see also Allenby, Edmund; Ottoman Empire; Palestine
Geaves, Ron 20, 131–134, 141, 145, 146, 241
Geertz, Clifford 9, 19
Gelvin, James 133, 140
gender
  Bahá'í 36, 43, 67
  Islamic discourse 104
  Jewish 196, 197
  see also Muscle Jew/ess
generation 9, 11, 14, 43, 91, 93, 108, 110, 149, 152, 160, 170, 172, 189, 195, 200
George V (King) 41, 61, 118
Germain, Eric 146
Gerwarth, Robert 18
Getsinger, Louisa (Lua) 75, 86
ghetto 162, 172, 177, 197
Ghosh, Durba 202
Gilham, Jamie 131–135, 138–142, 145, 146
Ginio, Eyal 73
Ginsberg, Asher 216
  see also Ahad Ha'am
Goodman, Paul 162, 205, 207, 209–212, 231
Goodman, Romana 191–194, 228–230
Grady, Tim 145
Grey (Sir), Edward 122
Green, Nile 19, 132, 133, 137
Greenberg, Leopold 154

Index

Haifa 2, 237
  Bahá'í community 1, 7–9, 16, 22, 36, 41, 44, 50–51, 58–67, 233, 241
  Zionist importance 161, 180, 183
  see also Bahá'í world
Hall, Edward Theodore 35, 43, 57, 58, 70, 76, 80, 85
  "*Villers Plush*" 57
Halliday, Fred 131
Hardinge (Lord), Charles, Viceroy of India 118
Harrison, Brian 78
Hassall, Graham 73
Hasted, Rachel 141–142
Hatcher, William 74–75
Hatefutsoth, Beth 229
Hatikvah 159, 179
Headley (Lord) 99, 100, 105, 108, 116
  see also Saifur-Rahman Sheikh Rahmatullah Farooq
Hearst, Phoebe Apperson 31
Hebrew 158, 159, 161–163, 170, 173, 181, 193, 199
  see also Ivrit B'Ivrit
Hebron 183
  see also Middle East
Hein, Virginia 211–212
Hellaby, Madeline 81
Herrick, Elizabeth 38, 40, 46, 47
Herzl, Theodor 151–163, 181, 196
  Altneuland 181, 196
  The Jewish State 152
  see also World Zionist Organization (WZO)
Hindu 101–102, 104, 127
  Arya Samaj 51, 95
  Brahmo Samaj 51, 95
  see also India
Hinduism 101, 235
Hijaz/Hejaz 5, 126, 129, 190
  see also Arabia
Hofman, David 85
Hollinger, Richard 75
Holocaust 202
Hong Kong 183
Hourani, Albert 88
housewives 192, 195
Howkins, Alun 81
humanitarian 21, 37, 67, 70, 163, 174, 176
hygiene 180, 195
  clean 47, 103, 181, 194, 195
  cleanliness 180, 195
Hyman, Paula 230

ideal/s 42, 53, 98, 104, 108, 162, 170, 185, 240
  Islamic 6, 122, 125, 126, 129, 241
  Jewish 152, 158, 188, 195, 197
  liberal 3, 9, 10, 12, 15, 16, 17, 22, 51, 62, 69, 71, 90, 96, 111, 113, 129, 148, 149, 157, 187
  social 47, 48, 54
ideology 14, 56, 57, 67, 121, 125, 153, 158, 179, 198, 202
  imperial intersectional 10, 11, 13, 17, 22, 62, 69, 70, 90, 93, 101, 113, 115, 129, 130
  nationalist 153, 202
  Orientalist 15, 70, 163
identification 13, 16, 49, 69, 71, 102, 163
  see also alterity; Occidentalism; Orientalism
identity 15, 239
  Bahá'í 54
  Islamic 93, 98
  Jewish 149, 171, 202
imperial turn 2, 5–7, 13–17, 147, 158, 166, 175, 178, 199
imperialism 3, 11, 16, 105, 128, 147, 167, 180, 184, 186, 190, 202, 236, 238
India 4, 5, 11, 17, 25, 53, 116, 128, 182, 183, 187, 236, 237
  Bahá'ís in 25, 26, 32, 50, 51, 63, 70
  British 10, 21, 51, 93, 102, 181, 233
  Muslims in 90–107, 109–112, 114, 117–120, 123, 126, 129–130
  see also Raj; Viceroy of India
industry 5, 13, 63, 170, 237
Ioannesyan, Youli 75
Iran 62
  Bahá'ís in 8, 12, 21–28, 32, 35, 36, 41, 50, 57–60, 62, 65, 69–70
Iraq 27, 114
Ireland 56, 57, 160, 171, 193
  Belfast 57
  Dublin 159, 160
  Ulster 171
Islam 13, 16, 17, 55, 63, 66, 90–98, 100–102, 108, 111, 115, 121–123, 126, 130, 236, 239
  Islamic civilizations 118, 126
  Islamic heritage 11, 235
  Islamic teachings 11, 112, 116, 123, 124, 241
  Islamic world 12, 43, 67
  Islamic writings 11, 90, 125

Islamic Review 16, 90, 120, 240
Israel 3, 176, 201, 202
Istanbul 12, 162
Ivrit B'Ivrit 162
  see also Hebrew

Jaffa 180, 181, 183, 193, 195
Jarboe, Andrew 141, 142, 241
Jawad, Haifaa 139
Jerusalem 63, 189, 201
  Bahá'ís 60, 62
  Jews 158, 161, 183, 193
Jesus 23, 95, 101, 105, 107, 108, 113, 122
  see also Christ
Jew 16, 148, 152, 158, 159, 170, 171, 175, 183, 189, 200
Jewish Colonial Trust 155, 158, 183, 184
Jewish emancipation 148, 149, 172, 174, 187, 199, 240
Jewish National Fund (JNF) 155–161, 163–165, 176, 179, 181, 190, 192
Jewish State 152, 185
Jewish Women's League for Cultural Work in Palestine (*Verband jüdischer Frauen für Kulturarbeit in Palästina*) 193, 194
Jihad 4, 92, 110, 113, 129, 237, 241
Johnson, Rob 86
Johnston, Hank 19
Jordan 7
  Valley 27, 60, 234
Judaism 32, 101–102, 163, 175
justice 29, 42, 43, 49, 53, 63, 116, 122, 174
  injustice 48, 62, 63, 70, 104, 116, 129, 173, 175
  social 22, 69

Kabir, Nahid Afrose 131
Kadoorie (Sir), Eleazer 183, 223
  see also Shanghai
Kamal-ud-Din 109–112, 128–131, 134–141
  missionary work 89–91, 97–100, 101, 103 105, 113
  origins in India 93–96
  thoughts on First World War 115, 122, 123, 126, 127
Karbala 42
Katz, Ethan 20, 206, 212, 220
Katz, Yossi 222
Katznelson, Ira 203
Keane, John 19

keffiyeh 190
  see also Arab
Khan, Adil Hussain 20, 132
Kheirella, Ibrahim 75
Kidwai 127
Kipling, Rudyard 105
Kitáb-i-Aqdas 24, 49
  see also Bahá'í
Kitchener (Lord), Horatio Herbert 123
Kitchener Indian Hospital 117
Klandermans, Bert 19
Konbaung dynasty 25
Krishna 28, 101
  see also Hinduism
Kushner, Tony 220, 221

Lahore 89, 93–95, 97, 100, 102, 103, 112, 115, 118, 235
  see also India; Kamal-ud-Din
Lambert-Hurley, Siobhan 131
Lamingtons 46, 50, 59
land/s 4, 27, 43, 57, 65, 70, 94, 148, 153, 156, 169, 182
  Bahá'í initiative 27, 60
  borderland 4–5, 236
  Eastern 12, 16, 70
  Holy 65, 126, 176, 198
  Islamic/Muslim 30, 104, 109, 110, 237
  ownership 148
  Zionist initiative 155, 159–161, 164, 181, 183, 186, 190, 194, 197–199, 201
  see also settlers
language 2, 25, 28, 29, 46, 47, 96, 103, 109, 112, 116, 147, 150, 158, 161, 162, 164, 170, 181, 183, 185, 193
Lawrence, T.E. 190
League of Nations 124
lectures
  Bahá'í 45, 51
  Muslim 101, 107, 111, 122
  Zionist 160–161, 237
Lee, Anthony 75
Leff, Lisa 20, 206, 212, 220
legal disabilities 5, 15, 148, 153, 172, 173, 188, 200
Lester, Alan 242
Levene, Mark 214, 217, 224
Levine, Philippa 80
Liberalism 3, 5, 10, 51, 53, 66, 69, 71, 148, 149, 157, 169, 175, 202, 240
  see also Enlightenment
Lieshout, Robert 18, 213, 214, 219, 227, 231

Lipman, V.D. 204
Liverpool 38, 39, 47, 56, 89, 97, 134, 151, 193
Lloyd George, David 118, 166, 176–177, 182, 188
London
  City of 150, 155, 158, 164
  East End 104, 153, 154, 162, 170
  Greater 1–2, 11, 90, 126–129, 233–238
  Hyde Park 90, 158
  Westminster 38, 42, 48, 53, 187
  see also metropole
London Muslim Mission 97
Lunn, Kenneth 221

Macaulay (Lord), Thomas Babington 102, 172
Maharaja Ranjit Singh 94
Manchester 2, 233, 234
  Bahá'ís in 35, 39, 44, 47, 50, 57, 66
  Jews in 6, 151, 156, 159, 164, 176, 179, 189, 191, 193, 199, 209, 237
  see also metropole
Manchester Group 6, 7, 178
  see also Marks, Simon; Sacher, Harry; Sieff, Israel; Zionism
Manchester Guardian 193
Mandalay 25
  see also Burma; Raj
Mandel, Maud 20, 206, 212, 220
Mandel, Neville 232
Manela, Erez 18
Marks, Simon 178, 218, 220, 229, 231
Martin, Douglas 74, 75, 77
maternity 195
Maude, Roderic and Derwent 86, 87
Maxwell, May 75
  see also Bolles, May
Mazza, Roberto 232
McClintock, Anne 81
Mecca 6, 12, 125, 126
  facing 117, 118
Medina 12
Meinig, D.W. 243
Meisel, Hannah 197, 231
Melucci, Alberto 19
meritocracy 170
Mesopotamia 27, 114, 182, 189
  see also Iraq; Middle East
metropole 2–3, 16, 22, 36, 89, 99, 100, 107, 113, 114, 120, 125, 128, 129, 233, 234, 236, 237

imperial 21, 28, 31, 49, 66, 102, 112, 239
Western 91, 93
Middle East 66, 89, 105, 233–234, 241
  Bahá'ís in 24, 25, 27, 32, 60–69
  British involvement in 4, 5, 9, 15, 16, 44, 92, 93, 106, 110, 114, 115, 147, 177, 183–183, 187–188, 237
  Jewish relationship with the 149, 153, 163
  WMM's relationship with the 125–128, 179
  Zionist plans for 14, 164–167, 184, 186, 189–190, 200
Midgley, Clare 229
Midhat Pasha 27, 74
missionary 10, 102, 106, 127
  Muslim 11, 17, 89–93, 95, 111–112, 114, 118, 128–130, 132, 137, 236
  Christian 55, 95, 103–104, 109
migration 164
  emigration, Jewish 168
  immigration, Jewish 5, 150, 166, 183, 188, 195, 201
  see also Aliyah
Miller, William 74
Mirza Abu'l-Fadl Gulpaygani 25
Mirza Ahmad Sohrab 59, 63, 64, 70, 79, 82–88
Mirza Ghulam Ahmad 12, 93, 94, 97, 132, 134, 135, 136, 137
  see also Ahmadiyya
Mirza Muhammad-'Ali 65, 67, 68
mission civilisatrice 184, 213
Mitchell, Timothy 82
Momen, Moojan 20, 74
Montagu, Edwin 177, 219
Montefiore, Claude 153, 205, 218
Montefiore, Francis 154, 206
Montefiore, (Sir) Moses 149, 154, 205, 207
Morten, Marjorie 76
Moscow 26
  see also Russia
Moses 23, 39, 101, 113
mother/s 179, 185
  Bahá'í views 32, 42–43, 47, 52
  Muslim views 124
  Jewish views 191, 195
Mount Carmel 36, 64, 237, 242
Mount Hermon 198
Mughal 11, 94, 95, 118, 127, 238

Muhammad (Prophet) 11, 23, 97, 98, 102, 103, 107–110, 116, 122–124, 129, 241
multiculturalism 1–5
Munirih Khanum 32
Muscle Jew/ess 197, 231
Myanmar 25
   see also Burma

Naidu, Sarojini 118, 143
Nash, Geoffrey 73, 132, 146
nationalism 15, 62, 148
   Bahá'í opposition to 51–52, 70
   Jewish debates on 162, 167, 170–171, 175, 182, 187
   see also Zionism
Nayriz 23
Nazareth 27
network 2, 233–236, 238, 242
   Bahá'í 22, 24–27, 31–34, 39, 44, 49, 51, 53, 56, 65–71
   feminist 240
   Jewish 163, 183, 194, 196, 229
   Muslim 94, 95, 100, 120, 135, 146
   transportation 182
Neve Zedek 195
Newman, Aubrey 203, 232
nonconformist 21, 38, 90, 122, 239

Occidentalism 105
Omissi, David 141
Orientalism 11, 12, 16, 125, 126, 163
Osborn, Lil 75
   see also Abdo, L.C.G.
the Other 15
   see also alterity
Ottoman Empire 4, 8, 24, 27, 28, 36, 58, 62, 63, 65, 69, 92, 110, 113, 115, 126, 155, 166, 173, 175, 179, 235
Ottoman Sultan 4, 150, 237
Oxford 30, 44, 50, 56, 160
Özcan, Azmi 139

Palestine 4–8, 127–129, 148–149, 152, 154, 158, 234, 237, 239–241
   Bahá'ís in 21–22, 26, 31–32, 36, 51, 55, 58–71, 233
   Jewish colonization 149, 153–155, 160–165, 167–175, 177, 178, 181–182, 184–185, 188–202, 236
   Mandate of 7, 64, 194, 200, 201, 202, 220, 230, 233, 238

Ottoman 4, 66, 155, 163, 234
   Jewish 6, 182, 183, 187–189, 191
Palestine 6, 178, 185, 189
Pankhurst, Christabel 40, 78
Pankhurst, Emmeline 40, 78
Pan-Islam 6, 91, 110
Paris 237
   Bahá'ís in 31, 33, 41, 52
   Jews in 152, 174
Paris Peace Conference 92, 187, 188
Parkinson, John Yehya en-Nesr 103, 123
Parsees 51
   see also India; Zoroastrianism
Patai, Raphael 205
patriotism 52, 54, 119, 154, 174–175, 178
peace
   Bahá'í concept of 24, 29, 52–55, 57, 58 62, 81, 241
   Jewish concept of 169, 183, 190
   Muslim concept of 11, 115, 121, 123–126, 130
   negotiations 93, 167, 170, 172, 176, 187
Pederson, Susan 206
Penslar, Derek 206, 212, 213, 228, 232
Perkin, Harold 215
Perry, Yaron 219
persecution 109, 234
   of Bahá'ís 24, 26, 33, 35, 39, 50, 65, 69
   of Jews 15, 156, 173–175
Persian 46, 69
Perso-Islamic 11, 127, 235
Petach Tikva 163–165
Pickthall, Marmaduke 73, 114, 121, 124, 127, 140, 145
   see also converts
pilgrimage 31, 33, 35, 45 49, 55, 64
pilgrim/s 24–27, 32, 35, 36, 45, 50, 58, 70
Pinsker, Leon 206
pioneer
   Bahá'í 3, 71
   Jewish 160, 194, 195, 197, 227, 230
Platt, Gerald 19
Pocock, J.G.A. 19
pogrom 173, 175
Pole, Wellesley Tudor 64, 68, 86–88
   liaison of 'Abdu'l-Bahá 54, 59, 60, 68
polytheism 107
population 65, 90, 95, 123, 181, 182, 184, 195
   Arab 173, 188, 206, 227
   civilian 116, 123, 124

Index

English 171
Jewish 157, 169, 210
native 166, 171, 173, 177, 180, 188, 239
postcolonial 3, 4, 147
poverty 10
  Bahá'í view of 29, 47, 48
  Jewish struggles with 150, 156, 210
Powell, Avril 113
Prasad, Y.D. 145
Pratt, Mary Louise 231
press 174
  anti-Muslim sentiment 5, 121, 126, 129
  Bahá'ís in the 46, 69
  Jews in the 153, 173
  Muslims in the 90, 97, 103, 109–112, 119, 120, 240
Prime Minister 110, 122, 166, 174, 176
  see also Briand, Aristide; Lloyd George, David
print
  Afnan printing press 26
  culture 10, 22, 69, 111–113, 129
  Jewish 160, 173
  Muslim 103, 111–113, 240
privilege 23, 34, 43, 89, 94, 99, 118, 149, 169 173, 183, 186
  class 46, 59
  legal 167, 215
progress/ive 11, 41, 51, 63, 70
  Bahá'í 29, 39, 42, 48, 49, 69
  force 9, 53, 161, 175
  Jewish 151, 161, 165, 168, 172, 175, 181, 184, 227
  thinkers 2, 3, 25, 27
propaganda 104, 184
  in the First World War 93, 116, 127
  Zionist 160–163, 193
Protestant 132, 137
  dissenting 101, 148, 204
Punjab, the 12, 99, 103, 133, 134, 235
  history of 94, 118, 128
  Muslims in 93, 95
public sphere
  Bahá'ís in the 37, 59
  Jews in the 165, 196

Qadian 96, 97, 144
  Ahmadiyya split 97, 133, 134
  see also Ahmadiyya; India
Qajar 21, 23, 77
  see also Iran
Quaker 108, 149

Quilliam, William Henry 89, 97, 99, 128, 133, 134, 135, 145
Qur'an
  understanding 23
  Bahá'í usage 27
  WMM usage 11, 102, 103, 108, 122, 127, 130, 143
Qurratu'l-'Ayn, Tahirih 42

Rabbani, Ahang 82, 83, 86
race 2–4, 211, 227, 228, 239–240
  Bahá'í teaching on 29–32, 54
  human 42, 48, 52, 53, 71
  Jewish concept 147, 150, 179, 185, 187, 191
  Muslim concept 98, 100, 109, 121
  whiteness 3
racism 10, 54, 62, 70
Raj 25, 96, 113, 182
  Bahá'í 51
  Muslims 89, 94, 97, 110
  see also India; Viceroy of India
Ramadan 124
Ramleh 50, 82–83
Reinach, Joseph 174, 218
Rhodes, Cecil 184
Rhodesia 184
Ridgway, Sarah Ann 47, 81
Roach, Joseph 222
Robinson, Francis 20, 136
Robinson-Dunn, Diane 20, 88, 131, 137
Rogan, Eugene 18, 86, 140, 228
Root, Martha 79
Rosenberg, Ethel Jenner 30–51, 66–67, 233–234
Rothschild, James de 167, 172–173, 177, 179, 213–216, 217, 219, 227
Rothschild, Lionel de 148–149, 208, 218
Rover, Constance 88
Rubinstein, William 203
Ruhe, David 72, 73, 74, 77, 88
Russia
  Empire 26, 153, 176
  Jews in 15, 161, 173–174, 188, 194, 199, 208, 212, 214, 217, 218, 231, 234
Ryad, Umar 146

Sacher, Harry 178, 218, 220, 225
Sadr-ud-Din 106, 111–112, 132, 137, 142, 143, 236
  missionary activity 91–92, 97, 130
  on the First World War 116–118

Saeed, Sadia 133
Said, Edward 20
Saifur-Rahman Sheikh Rahmatullah Farooq 100
Samarqand 26
Samuel (Sir), Herbert 60, 61, 88
San Remo 7, 194, 197, 201
   Conference 7, 17
   Supreme Allied Council 194
Sanyal 133
Sayyid 'Ali Muhammad 22
   see also the Báb
Schapira, Hermann 159, 210
Schneer, Jonathan 213, 218
Scotland 55
   Bahá'ís 39, 56–57
   Zionism 193
Scott, C.P. 193
Second Temple 161
   Solomon's Temple 127
Secretary of State 218
   for the colonies 87, 156
   for India 132, 142, 177, 219
   for War 123
Seddon, Mohammad Siddique 131
self-made man 5, 47, 169, 199
Segev, Tom 219, 232
Semitic
   civilization 14, 189, 200, 240
   Renaissance 14, 200
settlers
   female 7, 194, 195, 198
   Jewish 5, 15, 153, 155, 160–162, 164, 166, 168–170, 175, 176, 181–184, 186, 188, 197
   white 156, 186
Sevea, Iqbal 133
Sevea, Terenjit 133
Shah Jahan mosque 89, 93, 97–99, 103, 105, 116, 117, 119–120, 122, 125–126, 130, 134, 136, 139, 235, 236, 242
Shahjehan, Begum of Bhopal 130
Shanghai
   Jews in 183
Sharif Hussein 5, 127
   see also Mecca
Shauar, Soli 73
Shearmur, Jeremy 134–136, 139
shekel/im 209
   day 179
   system 158
Shia 8, 21–24, 32, 35, 63, 64, 98

Shilo, Margalit 231
Shiraz 23, 26, 27
   see also Afnan; the Báb; Iran
Shoghi Effendi 20, 30, 45, 71–72, 77, 87
   succession controversy 65, 67, 76
Sieff, Israel 178, 193, 218, 220, 229
Sieff, Rebecca 191, 193, 194, 197, 228, 229, 230
Sikh 11, 12, 51, 94, 95, 132, 136
   see also Punjab
Simon, Leon 212, 222
Simon, Maurice 205
Sinai 5, 6, 156, 178
   see also Egypt
Singh, Gajendra 132, 141
slavery 9, 105, 192
   see also abolition
Smiles, Samuel 169, 215
Smith, Peter 20, 72–76, 79, 83, 88
Smith, Phillip 74, 75, 76
Smuts, Jan 185, 225
socialist/s 48, 206, 212
   Muslim 100, 101
   Zionist 153
Sokolow, Nahum 166, 172, 182, 183, 184, 190, 196, 209, 211, 213, 218, 222, 224, 225, 226, 227, 228, 230
soldier 38, 52, 62, 64, 92, 100, 122, 124, 141–143, 183, 237
   Black 60, 70
   British 11, 25, 57, 70, 179
   Indian 117–119, 126, 236
   Muslim 6, 17, 93, 113, 115–120, 123, 125, 126, 129, 236, 241
solidarity 16, 19, 240
Somme 57
   see also First World War
South Africa 62, 123, 216, 218
   see also Africa
South America 153
   see also America
Sprague, Sydney 25, 73
Stanislawski, Michael 205, 206, 208, 212, 213, 220, 227, 231, 232
Star of the West 35, 51, 76
Staunton, Colonel 60, 61
Stead, William Thomas 53, 84
Stockman, Robert 72, 86, 88, 242
Stoler, Ann Laura 138
Storrs, (General) Ronald 60, 61
Strachan, Hew 18

Subh-i Azal, Azalis – Mirza Yahya Nuri 28, 45, 68, 74
subject 24
  British 46, 110, 111, 129, 151, 186, 239, 240
  colonized 16
  Indian 10
  Muslim 10, 11, 110, 116, 129, 240
  Jewish 151, 178, 186, 239
Sublime Porte 23
  see also Ottoman Empire
suffrage 88
  Bahá'í support for women's 39–41, 46, 47, 49, 63, 69, 77–79, 82, 240
Sufi/Sufism 20, 96, 99, 132, 133, 134, 135, 145
Sulayman Khan-i-Tunukabuni 26
Sultan Abdu'l-Hamid 221
  see also Ottoman Sultan
Sultan Jahan, Begum of Bhopal 130, 131
Sultan Mehmed V 92, 113
  see also Ottoman Sultan
Sunni 24, 32, 35, 97, 98, 99, 123
  see also Islam
Swansea 160, 193
  see also Wales
Sykes, Mark 177, 179, 189, 191, 219, 221, 224
Syria 42, 51, 59, 83, 184, 189
  Greater 8, 201

Taussig, Michael 18
teacher 101
  Bahá'í 25, 26, 83
  see also education
technology 13
  Bahá'í opinions on 56, 70
  Muslim opinions on 103, 112, 121
  Zionist opinions on 161
Tehran 23, 58, 235
  see also Iran
Theosophy/Theosophical 34, 38, 51, 66, 102
Thompson, E.P. 54, 84
Thompson, Elisabeth 206, 212, 220, 224, 232
Thornburgh-Cropper, Mary 30, 31, 36, 37, 39, 43, 76, 77
Thorne, Susan 137, 142
Tiberius 161
Tidrick, Kathryn 84
The Times 18, 87, 138, 140, 142, 182, 227

Tolkowsky, Samuel 180, 181, 198, 222, 231
Townshend, George 85
trade union 172, 201
Treasury, British 155
Tripoli 52, 83, 105
Troll, Christian 135
Tuchman, Barbara 207, 208, 219
Turbiyyn, Ahmad 82
Turk/Turkish 23, 25, 74, 109, 116, 127, 138, 140, 185, 223
Turkistan 26, 27, 72
  Ashkhabad 26

Ulrichsen, Kristian 18
Ummah 6, 99, 110, 116, 126, 129, 239
Union Jack flag 117, 191
Unitarian 149
United Kingdom 36, 158
  see also Scotland; Wales
United States 32, 35, 41, 174, 176, 185
Urdu 112, 116

Valman, Nadia 207, 208, 211, 224
Vambery, Arminius 56, 85
Van der Veer, Peter 85
veil 46
  see also Islam
Versailles 180
  see also First World War
Viceroy of India 118, 177
  see also Curzon (Lord), George, Hardinge (Lord), Charles; Raj
Victoria (Queen) 9, 24, 26, 49, 96, 150
Vienna 46, 152, 153, 162

Wales 56
  Zionism 160, 193
  see also Cardiff; Swansea
war 202, 240, 241
  Bábi 23
  Bahá'ís on 40, 52, 57–59, 61
  Boer 150
  Franco-Prussian 151
  Muslims on 11, 111, 113–130
  see also First World War
War Cabinet 7, 177, 191, 219
War Office 7, 44, 219, 236
Warburg, Margit 74, 211, 243
wealth 34, 94, 103, 157, 183, 187
  Bahá'í teachings on 29
  Jewish discrimination based on 150, 154

Weinberg, Robert 71, 75, 76, 77, 80, 81, 82
Weizmann, Chaim 7, 156, 167, 169, 173, 175, 176, 178, 183, 188, 190, 191, 193, 196, 200, 212–215, 218, 219, 224, 227, 228, 229
Weizmann, Vera 191, 192, 193, 194, 196, 230, 231
Welch, Alice Mobarikah 100, 119, 144
Welch, William 82, 88
Western Front 6, 57, 93, 116
see also First World War
Whig 148, 172
Whiggish 149
Whitehall 5, 118, 166, 213, 234
Whitehead, O.Z. 75, 76
Whyte (Mrs.), Alexander 39, 59
Wilberforce, Basil 38, 77
Woking 16, 90, 92, 97, 103, 105, 113, 130, 235–237
community 100–101, 118, 120–122
mosque 101, 107, 116, 117, 119
The Woking Herald 101, 136, 141, 142
Woking Muslim Mission (WMM) 1, 11, 89, 119
Wolf, Eric 242
Wolf, Lucien 5, 14, 15, 167–176, 187, 188, 199, 240
Women's International Zionist Organization 7, 194, 230
Women's Social and Political Union 40
Wood, Gordon 19
World War One *see* First World War

World Zionist Organization (WZO) 5, 6, 148, 154–177, 170, 173, 176–177, 183, 196, 200, 234
congress/es 156, 158, 160, 197, 209, 234
culture 148, 158–160
leaders 181, 186
programme 167, 170, 187
propaganda 193, 197

yard 165, 181
Yemen, the 163–166, 181
see also Middle East
Yiddish 163
Yishuv 150, 194
Yoseloff, Thomas 205
Young Ottomans 24
Young Turks 36, 73, 225

Zahra, Tara 20, 206
Zangwill, Israel 152, 154
Zanjan 23
see also Middle East
Zionism 15, 17, 147, 150–158, 161–162, 167, 174–175, 178, 185, 187, 195, 196, 199–202, 233–235, 237, 239
anti-Zionism 5, 14, 15, 17, 147, 156, 199, 238, 239
political 148, 152, 154, 155, 161, 184, 196, 199, 234
Zionist Commission to Palestine 193
Zoroaster 23, 101
Zoroastrianism 32
Zurcher, Erik-Jan 18

EU authorised representative for GPSR:
Easy Access System Europe, Mustamäe tee 50,
10621 Tallinn, Estonia
gpsr.requests@easproject.com

www.ingramcontent.com/pod-product-compliance
Lightning Source LLC
Chambersburg PA
CBHW051607230426
43668CB00013B/2008